DEATH &
DISSYMMETRY

הרי/הנג־לצ־235

CHICAGO STUDIES IN THE HISTORY OF JUDAISM

Jacob Neusner,
William Scott Green, and
Calvin Goldscheider,
Editors

DEATH &
DISSYMMETRY
The Politics of Coherence
in the Book of Judges

MIEKE BAL

THE UNIVERSITY OF CHICAGO PRESS
Chicago and London

Mieke Bal is professor of comparative literature and Susan B. Anthony Professor of Women's Studies at the University of Rochester. Her books include *Lethal Love: Literary Feminist Interpretations of Biblical Love Stories* and *Murder and Difference: Gender, Genre and Scholarship on Sisera's Death.*

The University of Chicago Press, Chicago 60637
The University of Chicago Press, Ltd., London
© 1988 by The University of Chicago
All rights reserved. Published 1988
Printed in the United States of America

97 96 95 94 93 92 91 90 89 88   5 4 3 2 1

Library of Congress Cataloging-in-Publication Data
Bal, Mieke, 1946–
    Death and dissymmetry: The politics of coherence in the
Book of Judges / Mieke Bal.
        p.   cm.—(Chicago studies in the history of Judaism)
    Bibliography: p. 285
    Includes index.
    ISBN 0–226–03554–9. ISBN 0–226–03555–7 (pbk.)
    1. Bible. O.T. Judges—Criticism, interpretation, etc.
    2. Women—Crimes against—Biblical teaching.
    3. Murder—Biblical teaching.   4. Feminism—Religious
aspects.   I. Title.   II. Series.
BS1305.2.B34   1988
222'.3206'088042—dc19   88–15508
                                                                        CIP

For NANNA VERHOEFF

CONTENTS

ACKNOWLEDGMENTS

This book was written during my year at the Harvard Divinity School as a fellow in the Women's Studies in Religion Program. The biblical scholars who took a genuine interest in my work were two visiting scholars, who became more than fellow travelers through the year. Whenever I needed it, Patrick D. Miller was willing, even eager, to go over the Hebrew and let me take advantage of his thorough knowledge of the language and the texts. Both he and J. Gerald Janzen asked me questions and challenged my most daring hypotheses without ever rejecting them a priori. I owe them confidence in the project and its outcome, apart from detailed help. Constance Buchanan, the director of the program, was always willing to read my drafts from the perspective of the nonliterary feminist that I am so eager to reach with this study. My co-fellows in the program, Jody Billinkoff, Amy Lang, Mercy Oduyoye, and Mary Segers, were helpful supporters and created the interdisciplinary environment that I needed. My friend Fokkelien Van Dijk taught me Hebrew and gave me inspiration and critical feedback. My friend Ria Lemaire, who took over so many of my duties in Utrecht during my absence, and who, by the example of her own impressive work on ancient texts and her always eager interest in my project, has been a major source of inspiration for me, deserves special gratitude. So does Ernst van Alphen, who has discussed, challenged, and supported every bit of it.

From Cambridge, via a last semester at Utrecht, I definitively moved to the United States, to Rochester, where I was given opportunities to try out parts of this book. In the final stage, suggestions for improvement came from my new colleague at the University of Rochester, William Scott Green, who took his role as series editor extremely seriously, from the stage of wooing the manuscript to that of weighing its details. First Peggy and Robert Ellsberg, and later Jane Carter provided very valuable help in correcting my English. Finally, since this book focuses on the position of the daughter and the response of the mother to what happens to her, to whom can I dedicate it but to my daughter Nanna, who cheerfully shared this year with me—my privilege, her exile—and inspired more of the book than she can realize.

INTRODUCTION

Men love death. In everything they make, they hollow out
a central place for death, let its rancid smell contaminate
every dimension of whatever still survives. Men especially love
murder. In art they celebrate it, in life they commit it. They
embrace murder as if life without it would be devoid of passion,
meaning, and action, as if murder were solace, stilling their sobs
as they mourn the emptiness and alienation of their lives.
Andrea Dworkin

The Book of Judges is about death. It is one of those numerous monuments of antiquity that celebrate death and that we celebrate, because
of their respectable old age, without realizing that we celebrate death
in the same move. It is, however, in the way we celebrate it, read and
misread it, that we can become aware of our own attitude toward
death. In Judges there is death in all forms, each violent. The book is
full of murder: public and private murder, war and individual murder.
It openly celebrates murder. And murder, in this text, is related to
gender. Men kill women, and women kill men. And men kill men.
The man-man murders are, with only one exception,[1] collective murders: wars. The woman-man murders are derived from that primary political kind of murder: women kill heroes and military leaders. The
man-woman murders are different. Men, mighty men, kill innocent
young daughters. This fundamental dissymmetry is the thread that will
lead us through the labyrinth of the confused, unclear, enigmatic Book
of Judges.

In the canonical order, Judges is the seventh book of the Hebrew
Bible; it follows, with the Book of Joshua, the five central books of the
Pentateuch and precedes the Books of Samuel and Kings. It is consid-
ered one of the historical books, and as such it recounts the wars
fought to establish the Israelites in Canaan (e.g., Childs 1986; Smith
1971). In the Jewish tradition, it is considered a prophetic book. In the
Western culture at large, it is best known as the book of heroes like
Ehud, Deborah, Gideon, and Samson. The heroes, leaders of the

1

people, are known as "judges," a title that has less juridical than political content. The judges were local leaders who in times of war became
military heroes. Although dating the biblical books is extremely difficult, its composition is generally supposed to have taken place between
the ninth and the seventh centuries B.C. (Boling 1975, 11), several centuries after the events are assumed to have taken place. The book consists of a sequence of stories related to the conquest of Canaan, which
alternate in a typical, cyclical order. From a general statement on the
deserved oppression the unfaithful people has to suffer, the text moves
to a perspective on the merciful deity who will once more help the
people by raising up a deliverer. The next episode, then, is the particular story of the feats of such a deliverer, usually a combination of a
battle and a trick to defeat the enemy leader. Hence, there is a systematic alternation between collective stories of the people as a whole and
individual stories of particular heroes, battles, or tricks.

The present study is very little concerned with this image of the
book. Inherent to my project is to tease out of the book what has hith-
erto been underexamined. In order to change the perspective, the established priorities are reversed. What is seen to be central will be
marginalized, and what has been treated as marginal will become
central.

This study is about women's lives and deaths. It is about the complex and fascinating relations between text and social reality. And it is
about method. The development of a feminist method of interpretation of ancient texts as sources for our understanding of the history of
gender-ideology and as connected to present-day culture is the underlying purpose of this voyage through the Book of Judges. Disturbing
because of its violence, fascinating because of its focus on women's
lives, useful because of its textual character of both historical and literary narrative, the Book of Judges provides more resources of a feminist
hermeneutics than I had ever hoped to find.

This book is the conclusion of a six-year-long project, started in
1980, and the third in a series of three studies on biblical narrative. In
the first, *Lethal Love: Feminist Literary Readings of Biblical Love Stories,* I
have approached the texts, a collection of famous love stories about
wicked and/or tricky women, from the perspective of a critical narrative theory.[2] The enterprise was one of confrontation: a confrontation between the ancient texts, the modern rewritings of them, and
extant narrative theory. All three were engaged in the exchange, truly
engaged: all three were criticized by way of the confrontation and by
the contact with the other discourses. Although the starting point was
anchored in literary theory, the method developed was offered as a tool

for biblical and literary scholars alike. In the second volume, *Murder and Difference: Gender, Genre and Scholarship on Sisera's Death*, the perspective was reversed. The two versions of the murder of Sisera, in Judges 4 and 5, were confronted with various disciplines that constitute the field of biblical scholarship. The approach there was semiotic. Academic disciplines were considered as *codes*, as implicit rules on the basis of which scholars attribute meanings to texts. The recurrent question was: do the disciplines close off or open up meaning? Special focus on the difference between the two versions, different in genre and in gender, allowed me to develop a plea for interdisciplinary interpretation as the most fruitful approach.

Starting from biblical scholarship, the literary analysis became part of the semiotic method I argued. While the first book addressed literary scholars in the first place, hoping to interest biblical scholars in that discipline, the second addressed the biblical scholars primarily, hoping to show literary scholars and others that their interests were concerned as well. In this third book, the concluding volume of the trilogy, the primary audience consists of all who have a serious interest in the history of gender-relations, in the lives of women, and in the methodological problems involved in interdisciplinary historical research based on textual sources. Although the audience addressed is more general, the book is primarily a women's studies endeavor. The three volumes are autonomous, although interrelations are numerous. I will point out those relations in the notes, and I apologize beforehand for what may seem like self-indulgent self-references, but it is necessary to do so to avoid repetition.

The task that I address in this study is too enormous for me, and I can only hope to accomplish elements of it. Avoiding the realistic fallacy that challenges any textual aspect that does not fit a preconceived image of "reality"—a "logic" of realistic representation, mostly derived from nineteenth-century Western realism—I will try to think the relations between text and reality differently. Rather than seeing the text as a transparent, immaterial medium, a window through which we can get a glimpse of reality,[3] I see it as a figuration of the reality that brought it forth and to which it responded. And rather than seeing the text as literary in the esthetic sense, as a fiction that has no connection to reality,[4] I will try to show how the literary and linguistic choices made in the text represent a reality that they both hide and display.

Throughout this study, I build up my argument in the margins of biblical scholarship, exploiting what that field has to offer while refusing to take any of its premises for granted. My relationship to the field is thoroughly dialectic. I am keenly aware that it is always problematic to use the results of a given field of research, while at the same time contesting them. Yet, such is also the only possible way to participate in a field from a radically alien perspective; to conquer it on feminism's own terms and to contribute something new to the field itself, on *its* own terms. I sometimes use the results against the assumptions on which they are based, and invariably practice upon them a "hermeneutics of suspicion" (Schüssler Fiorenza 1982). It should be clear from the outset that it is not by free choice but as an acknowledgment of its inevitability that I seem from time to time to step into the role of the Philistine: the "other," the alien who cannot but be iconoclastic by virtue of her otherness, and that in my turn I sometimes seem to present the "legitimate insiders," those who were there when feminism came in, as Philistines.

Two major claims of biblical scholarship are challenged in my project. Current biblical scholarship assumes that the Book of Judges is composed of a collection of various elements from different sources. This hypothesis is as undeniable as the detailed results based on it are more often than not unverifiable. The endeavor and major theses, not the sometimes valuable results of "separation of sources," the attempt to reconstruct the origin of the book, among the most frequently practiced type of analysis for ancient texts in general, have been criticized in *Murder and Difference*. I will not repeat the argument here. As much as I can, I will ignore that debate here. Although I do accept the heterogeneous origin of the book, I will deal with the text as a whole, composed out of many sources, yet at one time—the time of the final redaction—conceived of as one text. One practical consequence of that position is the unconditioned adherence to the standard text, based on the Masoretic Text (MT), even where this text is frequently challenged by scholars. As I will argue on specific occasions, this rigidity is not based on some unavowable fundamentalism, but on the conviction that amendments, even well-grounded, have been too often motivated by unargued and unarguable biases. Sticking to the MT is one way to deconstruct those efforts at imposing on a text which has been culturally privileged, the tendencies of a different culture.

Another approach, which indifferently accepts the basic hypothesis of source analysis, views the book as coherent in the historical and theological sense. Thus Boling has said that "the Book of Judges is an ancient exploration of the people's claim to have been ruled by Yahweh in a period that was, for them, one of revolutionary social change" (1975, 5). Because of its place in the series of *historical books*, Judges is primarily considered as historiography. This does not mean that scholars naively believe it to be factually true. The different conceptions of historiography itself that underly it are fully acknowledged. I mean to suggest that, in spite of that acknowledgment, the approaches to the book inevitably start from the idea of history, and in this particular context, history *as* theology, as the fundamental *coherence* of the book.

One single example suffices here: in spite of the acknowledged impossibility to establish a chronology of the events narrated in Judges, not a single commentary[5] refrains from attempting to do so, or at least bringing up the problem of chronology. The very notion of chronology presupposes that Judges recounts events that really happened, and the events that compose the chronology are about wars and politics. The stories of women in Judges are not so much domestic—indeed, most of them are political or interwoven with political events—but tend to elude insertion in the chronology. That chronology, and in particular, military-political chronology, is one way of practicing historiography, by no means the only or even the most obviously relevant one, is by now a well-known fact. Yet, the efforts to restore a chronology, efforts which go hand in hand with a repression of the women's stories, predominate Judges' scholarship. There seems to be a major interest in keeping to this line for reading of the book. It is the interest underlying the reading with the historical coherence that I will try to explain.

My major aim is not to deconstruct what I will call the political coherence, the obsession with military and political chronology as a guideline to the book, although that deconstruction will be part of the enterprise. I will primarily focus on what is left out, repressed, by such readings, and show thereby *why* the strong attachment to the political coherence responds to a need so deeply rooted in the interaction between the book and its modern, committed readers. I want to explain why the political coherence is a tool—or should I say weapon?—in the politics of the critics: a politics of coherence.

This study will establish a *countercoherence*. This countercoherence, which is a deconstruction in its own right but also more than that, will enforce awareness of a reality that is also represented in the book: the reality of gender-bound violence. Moreover, I will argue that the impression of extreme violence that the book makes is due less to the political struggle that seems to be at stake—the conquest—than to a social revolution that concerns the institution of marriage, hence, the relations between men and women, sexuality, procreation, and kinship. That social revolution during which the property over women shifts from her father, the "natural" owner, to the husband, the arbitrarily chosen, "cultural" owner, is represented with more acuteness than the political chaos. Indeed, the political chaos may even be the consequence of the social revolution which I will describe, rather than its cause. This reversal implies another reversal: I will focus on the stories in which the political violence of the battles yields to the violence in the lives of individuals. In these stories the main characters are nameless young women. The namelessness of these women is one of the strategies to achieve their oblivion, but as the victims of sexual violence they have been inscribed in the book as indestructible traces.

The narrative figuration not only of these characters and their horrible fate but also of the causes of their murders will be the primary object of the analyses. I hope to show how we can see ancient narratives, not as sources for knowledge that lie outside them, but as the materialization of a social reality that they do not simply and passively reflect, but of which they are a part and to which they respond. My hypothesis will be that the murders of young women in the book are caused by uncertainty about fatherhood—indeed, by the transition between an ancient and not very stable structure of kinship in which the daughter remains in her father's house and, consequently, where her children belong to her father, a structure variably indicated as uxorilocal, matrilineal, or duolocal and which I call, for reasons to be specified later, *patrilocal*, and the virilocal, patrilineal one.

Since criticism of current assumptions is part of my enterprise, it is necessary to say a few words on the status of my own interpretations, even if I will discuss it more fully in the conclusion. On the one hand, I consider with most contemporary literary theorists that interpretation is in the first place a reader's response, necessarily based on the reader's personal input, assumptions, and biases. I will demonstrate this on several occasions when discussing the interpretations of others, and while I take my own feminist assumptions as an explicit starting point, I will gladly leave it to my readers to point out my own unacknowledged biases whose influence I can neither see nor deny. Yet, I do not think that my interpretations are arbitrary, useless or fictitious, and my defense is not only that they have at least equal rights. I will try to protect them from these charges in three manners.

First, I will check my interpretations by the use of a method, that of narrative theory. Since the texts are narrative, such a method provides some measure of adequacy, although, of course, no guarantee. All it can do is allow the reader to follow the steps taken, which is promising some measure of intersubjectivity. But, secondly, methods being based on contemporary academic divisions of disciplines, they also tend to cut off the analyses where the material proves more recalcitrant to those divisions. To be more concrete: although our texts are narrative, they oftentimes hit the limits, on one side of philology

or linguistic criticism, on the other of anthropology and history or social criticism. It is a major accomplishment of women's studies to have
shown the need of interdisciplinarity in order to counter the arbitrary
or biased limits of scholarship when confronted with "real life." The
danger of eclecticism inherent in such disciplinary openness is in turn
checked by a third protection the sustained focus on the issue of gender. However damaging unacknowledged biases may be, as soon as
they are brought to awareness they can help structure the argument.
The limitations of my feminist perspective are clear and lead to the
willing neglect of commonplace issues. Since I do not aim at a comprehensive understanding of all aspects of Judges, only of the repressed
and neglected ones, such one-sidedness is no less acceptable than that
of all current scholarship on the book. By its very limitations, my perspective is powerful in its obsession with hardly perceptible details.
The reversal I will try to enforce between detail and main line, in
keeping with Naomi Schor's argument (1984), does more than just
bring neglected elements back; it allows us to glimpse a possible
alternative main line that changes the entire status of the book as
document.

The reversals will often surprise the reader, and I expect they will
be more acceptable for those who are used to the hermeneutics of the
repressed advocated by psychoanalytic interpretation. Openness to unexpected associations is indispensible in a case such as ours, where not
only the final redaction of the book, but more substantially, layers of
centuries of exegesis have joined efforts to cover up what was no more
felt as relevant. I count, as a fourth protection, on the force of quan-
tity: the great number of details that point in the same direction, the
great number, also, of details that remain incomprehensible without
the alternative coherence I will propose, will hopefully carry the persuasion of more reluctant readers. Once the argument is completed,
the concluding chapter will again discuss the issues of method as it in-
teracts with the analyses carried out.

CHAPTER ONE

THE COHERENCE OF POLITICS AND THE POLITICS OF COHERENCE

> The judges, too, each when he was called, all men whose hearts were never disloyal, who never turned their backs on the Lord—may their memory be blessed! May their bones flower again from the tomb, and may the names of those illustrious men live again in their sons.
>
> *Ecclesiasticus* 46:11–12 (introductory quote in Boling 1975)

Why do we, with Ben Sira the author of the quoted celebrational phrase, think of the judges as heroes? This introduction outlines both the motivations for the usual readings of the book and the method for a different reading. An intertextual reading gives Ben Sira's celebration of the illustrious men of the Book of Judges at least a triple meaning. As quoted by Boling (1975), it represents a double reading of the Book of Judges, first by the ancient writer, then by the modern commentator who quotes it as an introduction to his commentary on the book. As a beginning for my own chapter, it comments, first, on Judges, second, on the reading of Judges by the author of Ecclesiasticus, and third, on Boling's reading of the quotation as a reading of the book.

Ben Sira celebrates the judges as loyal to their god and brave in military action, thus pointing at the two major themes of the book according to the tradition: the establishment of the Israelites in their monotheistic religion and in the promised land. They deserve a blessed memory. Boling's book amply demonstrates that he agrees, in spite of his occasional criticism of the judges' behavior. The memory is represented in three forms: flowering bones, names, and sons. The three are rhetorically related: "flowering bones" is a metaphor for the perpetuation—the memory—of the name through the son. As for tombs, flowering or not, I want to reverse the perspective. I am interested in the tombs, not of the judges but of the judges' daughters, the young girls who are killed. As for names, those girls died nameless. And for sons, there were almost none. The only judge who had sons had many, seventy-one to be precise, and lost all of them but one. The others had none. The lack of sons is the tragedy and major impulse of the judges. Ben Sira denies the facts of the book, and Boling, like so many others, simply repeats that denial. The view is false, not only because names and sons were the judges' problems rather than their assets for glorious memory, but also because such a view represses the side effects of the false view *as* a denial of the more negative view: the appeal to the names of the judges as a burial of the namelessness of their victims. Boling reads Judges through Ecclesiasticus and through the numerous readings that are interposed between the text and today's readers.

In this study the judges will not be celebrated, the ideology of the book will not be repeated, and the faithfulness of the men toward their god will be analyzed and related to their loyalty and disloyalty to their other relatives rather than uncritically assumed. It is not easy to read the book without the burden of later readings obscuring it. We can, however, propose a counterreading, one that uses previous readings polemically, analyzes their fallacies, and takes their insistent falsifications and distortions of the text as a starting point.

Two Views of the Book of Judges

In the current editions of the Hebrew Bible, the Book of Judges consists of twenty-one chapters. The stories told are alternately war reports, statements on the people's transgressions in terms of religion and in terms of exogamic marriage, and stories of individuals—the events surrounding the so-called judges. Some of these stories concentrate on one particular event, mostly military or related to the military, some are "biographies," relating several episodes of the life of one judge. The first chapter, which presents the story of Othniel's ascension to the position of judge, the third, which tells how Ehud tricked King Eglon in order to kill him, the fourth, in which the victory over Sisera attains its climax in Yael's murder of him, are examples of the first type. Jephthah's career from the expulsed son via the sacrifice of his daughter to his subsequent victories and Samson's life story, which begins with his genesis and ends with his death, are examples of the second type. Some stories hover between these two genres, like Gideon's story, which recounts more than one episode but does not give a full account of his life, and Micah's story in chapters 17 and 18, where the storyline is almost incomprehensible. In the final sequence of three chapters, the story circulates around one man, but this man is neither judge nor hero. I will argue later that this sequence revolves around a woman rather than a man; but in this first round, I simply stick to the traditional interpretations. What does our culture do to these stories?

The Book of Judges circulates in modern culture as a subject of both "popular" and "scholarly" post-texts.[1] The two views of the book are more related than the proponents of the second would like and it is arguable that they support each other. Both rest on the principle of coherence,[2] thus supporting a mode of reading on which the present study will focus. This coherence, which readers desire much more than texts exhibit, is projected onto individual stories in popular readings and onto the book as a whole in scholarly readings.

The first view, the "popular" one, takes the stories out of context, selects some of them, and represses others. The selected stories circulate as *ideo-stories*. By that term, I mean a specific but as yet unrecognized literary genre. An ideo-story is a narrative whose structure lends itself to be the receptacle of different ideologies. Its representational makeup promotes concreteness and visualization. Its characters are strongly opposed so that dichotomies can be established. And its fabula is open enough to allow for any ideological position to be projected onto it. Ideo-stories, then, are not closed but extremely open;[3] however, they seem to be closed, and this appearance of closure encourages the illusion of stability of meaning.

The most obvious ideo-story used in modern popular culture is that of Samson and Delilah. In a recent issue of the *National Examiner*, a typical tabloid paper, this story is, for example, rewritten in an article entitled "Devilish Ladies Who Everybody Loves to Hate,"[4] including such subtitles as "Lustful," "Terrible," and "Immoral." The heroines of the article are Lilith, Jezebel, Delilah, and . . . Sappho. A subtitle on the latter is, "Her only suitor was a bisexual." It is easy to poke fun at such journals and stay away from them. But the point is to realize what use is made of ancient texts in modern culture. What mechanisms allow writers to juxtapose these four figures and conclude that Delilah was a liar (which she was emphatically not),[5] that Sappho seduced and destroyed men, and by implication that all lesbians do? The combination of the four figures is a function of the principle of coherent reading. Whatever material we put together, it has to be related. Both within and between the four stories, contradictions and problems are repressed. The discrete contexts of the stories are denied by heaping them together. This centripetal tendency works also in scholarly endeavors.

In the scholarly view, the tendency to impose coherence moves in the opposite direction, though, as I will try to show, with basically the same results. The stories are not, here, taken out of context, but drowned in their context. The book is taken as a whole, its topic is determined, and the individual stories are subordinated to it. This is how Boling stands in contradiction to his own endeavor. As a philologist, he goes over the details of the text, and as a textual critic he traces them back to their different sources. Yet he quotes the celebration of the illustrious men of Judges as the opening of his book. In spite of his critical discussion of the quotation (1975, 3–5), it works to prepare us for the denial of the men's disloyalty to their women and to their god, of their obstinate tendency to "go astray." And this act of quoting prepares us to subordinate the stories of women to the overall project of the establishment of the people in the land and in the religion. This subordination is imposed on us by way of the opening quote.

How History Constructs Itself

Often in this study, my starting point will be notes in biblical commentaries on Judges. The biblical commentary is a strange literary genre which I chose to work from for a generic reason. The five commentaries that I will use in this study have two aspects in common.[6] They are philological, hence, they are open to discontinuities of the text and to the possibility of "corruption" via the process of copying from the various sources the stories come from. One would expect this openness to protect the commentators from naive impositions of coherence. We will see that it fails to work that way. Secondly, they all assume that the book is, in the first place, a historiographical work. Although no contemporary scholars assume that historiography was in biblical times as "factual" as it tries to be today,[7] the commentators do start from the premise that they know what the book "is about" and that the topic is some variant of the "real life" history—be it a prophetic, theological history—of the Israelites. But what, then, is history? Again, the five commentaries agree on that premise.

The conflict, or contradiction, can be illustrated with the treatment of chronology. Despite the acknowledged difficulty, impossibility even, of establishing a chronology for the book, Boling starts with a chronological chart, and the other commentaries all start with at least a discussion of the "problem of chronology." Chronological development is so much a part of their view of history that it seems unthinkable to ignore the question and to assume, for example, that the traditions collected in the book deal with a *type* of event, a type of figure—the "judge"—whose occurrences could be juxtaposed in some configuration other than chronological.[8] The chronological indications are acknowledged as few and as either fictional or later additions; nevertheless, the attempt at chronology seems irresistible. Why? I think that the chronological problem serves the purpose of establishing a coherence that may be totally alien to the book,[9] but which allows the next step to be taken: the definition, of course implicit, of history as primarily military and political history.

The eagerness to narrow history down to a narrative of war and political leadership is at least partly due to a number of "centrisms." Within those centrisms, which include ethnocentrism, androcentrism, and theocentrism, but also more subtle forms, the stories of murder are, for various reasons, disturbing.

For the reader who focuses on religion, they seem hard to accept, even within the divine plan that the book alleges as their defense. They challenge the modern view of the religion to which most commentators are committed, be it Jewish or Christian. But they also challenge the disciplinary boundaries that we have inherited from the recent past. "History" in the narrow sense of the narration of military, economic, and political change prevents scholars from seeing other issues and continuous structures. Among the biases that obscure a comprehensive understanding of the past is the tendency, close to ethnocentrism, to take the present as the starting point and norm. And, of course, androcentrism, the tendency to start from the central place of men in history and to consider the participation of women in history as an abnormality.[10]

With this set of presuppositions, the obvious gesture is to subordinate the stories about women to the major historiographical project, which is nationalistic and religious, and in relation to which the murder stories are just the unpleasant but unavoidable fulfillment of the divine plan. If my hypothesis is correct, then the conception of what history is, hence, what the topic of the book is supposed to be, comes out of concerns that have no intrinsic relation to historical reality.

Feminist historians have been troubled by the question of just what history is. Women are blatantly absent from history, many claim, because of the restrictive view of history as sociopolitical *change* (Thompson 1980). Women are more involved in continuity, while men bring about change. Although this is an interesting point and leads us to interdisciplinary collaboration between history and anthropology (Pomata 1983),[11] it does, in a sense, beg the question. For what kind of changes are considered truly "historical"?

The answers vary, but are no more than rephrasings of the same hypothesis in different dichotomies: because women are predominantly private figures and men public figures; because women are related to

nature and men to culture; because women are caring and men are ag-
gressive, notably in the public sphere, hence, men cause the wars that
make history; because, in brief, women are dominated, men dominate.
None of these consistently binary, essentialist, and universalistic answers addresses the question of what history is. They adopt the presupposition that we know what it is, that women do play a minor role in
it, and that it is what it has always been thought to be.

If we take the Book of Judges as historiography, we have a problem immediately. None of the above answers fits. Women do act in the
public sphere. The three women who kill men do so in the interest of
their group. Delilah is, we should remember, an exact parallel to Yael:
both kill the hero of the enemy, except that Delilah's group is a different one, the Canaanites, called alternately "foreign" or "original inhabitants." They do bring about major political changes by their acts.
The figure of Deborah, a juridical, political, religious, and military
leader, does not exactly fit any of the dichotomies. She does not stay
home to take care,[12] rather she takes care of the people by leading the
attack on the enemy. Furthermore, there is no trace of a more "natural" relation to nature for women than for men. The character who has
the most intimate relation to nature is Samson, who flees into it, magically creates springs, and hides in caves.

On the other hand, the men who kill women kill in the private
sphere. They kill daughters, young women, virgins, for no or hardly
any political reason. The men who get killed meet their fate, in two
cases out of three, after going willingly into a private home and engag-
ing in a private relationship. In those two cases they were not the aggressors, they were attacked. In Samson's life, only the very last event,
his death, is clearly public. At least two of the heroes do not have a
political position but work hard to achieve one, either by violence
(Abimelech) or by shrewd negotiation (Jephthah). Their political,
public status is not a fact but an issue. The war against the Benjaminites at the end of the book has been caused by a private crime.
The war against Sisera is religious rather than political and is instigated
by a woman. In short, the commonplaces about history and women's
absence from it are seriously challenged by this historical book. Two
gestures are to be expected here: either the book is forced into the conventional concept of history or it is denied historical status. Both gestures have been made. I opt for a third one: to use this "anomaly" to
challenge our view of "history."

Yet, I will not ignore the claims about why it "is the case" that
women are absent or unimportant in history; not because I believe it,

but because the very dichotomies that are alleged to *cause* that situation are, in fact, *issues* within the historiographic text. That is, Judges is about precisely the production, the construction, of these ideas of history. A thorough analysis of this ancient text affects therefore the enterprise of women's history as a whole.

Whatever view of history one adopts, the result will always be that certain topics stand out as the figure against the ground. If one chooses to consider only wars, the international wars at that, to be history, as quite a few biblical scholars tend to do,[13] then the Book of Judges would be divided into three parts. The first two chapters, wherein the theological and political theme of "going astray" is presented, will be considered an introduction. Chapter 3 will be the first of a series of stories that form the bulk of the book. Each of these core-stories relates some individual hero to a major war against the outside enemies. This series goes on until Samson, clearly a legendary hero, creates a problem. This is solved by attributing the anomaly to a later insertion. The last five chapters, all "private" stories set against an internal war, would be considered the epilogue. Indeed, this is how all five commentators see the composition of the book. Other scholars are unhappy with the hypothesis of separation of sources and a clumsy redactor[14] and try to justify the composition otherwise, and some of these efforts are quite interesting (e.g., Polzin 1980; Gooding 1982). The basic tripartite division into introduction, bulk, and epilogue is, however, never seriously challenged, even though it is clearly modeled on a rhetorical prescription alien to biblical culture.

In a book that has twenty-one chapters, isolation of the introduction is less disturbing than the elimination of three chapters as allegedly alien material and the elimination of five chapters as an epilogue. The result of the excision is that only ten chapters remain as "authentic" material. The Samson traditions are, indeed, so clearly folkloric that they doubtless do come from different sources; but then, are the other stories less folkloric? In other words, the excision is based on the assumption of coherence of the remaining sections. This coherence, moreover, supports an ideological stance: to what extent is the decision to consider the saga as alien also inspired by the Canaanite perspective clearly visible in it? As soon as we reverse the perspective, Delilah becomes another Yael, a patriotic heroine. In chapters 17 and 18, a story of the religious "going astray" of Micah, who steals silver from his mother and later forges idols with it, a story situated between private and public, seems extremely relevant as a sequel to the sexual transgressions of Samson. Although some connection is acknowledged, mainly through the figure of Delilah as conflated with Micah's mother, the story is not integrated into the bulk of the book. And the final three chapters create an irreducible problem.

Chapter 19 presents the story of a young woman who is exposed by her husband to gang-rape. She is tortured, raped, and murdered, and her husband cuts her into twelve pieces. Why is this story here, and why do we know it so little? Even professionals in biblical scholarship often hardly know it. This woman is nameless. The crime is avenged in an intertribal war against the guilty tribe, the tribe of Benjamin. Guilty of what? Of sexual violence against a woman? No, of violation of the husband's property. This is the husband's answer, adopted by many critics. Just as Boling subscribes to the celebration of Jephthah, who in his sacrifice of his daughter murdered her,[15] so also do commentators subscribe to the text-internal first reading of the event of Judges 19, which leads to the obliteration of sexual violence. Writing this story out of the bulk of the book, and out of the status of major history of the period of the judges, partakes in the imposition of a political-military view of history.

Another motive that is implicit in this and other similar interpretations is the connection between maleness and nationalism, and between maleness and a variant of individualism. If Micah has to be eliminated, it is also because he is not a hero; he does not fit the ideal scheme that defines the "bulk" of the book, the combination between national war and individual heroism. That is also why the first two chapters of the book do not really count either. The story of the gang-rape and murder do not affect a hero; the husband is nameless and is a civilian and an ordinary man, not a warrior and a leader. Finally, the elimination of the last two chapters is also related both to the lack of an individual hero and the chapters' concern with an internal war, which would give the lie to the argument that the book is devoted to the settlement of the Israelites among the foreign tribes of Canaan. This is how history constructs itself, and the tool is thematization.

The Construction of a Different History

These then are some of the fallacies that underlie the attempt to construct political struggle as the object of the historiography of Judges. Stripped of the chronological fallacy, the political, military, and religious theme of going astray stands out as one of the many themes the book "is about." This theme is the other side of the attempt of the Israelites to establish their specificity through monotheism, endogamy, and the conquest of the land. But the book is also about lineage, fatherhood, and the lives of young girls. It is about virginity, mothers, and violence. It is also about sex, obedience, and death. And, finally, it is about power and its dissymmetrical distribution, the conflicts and competition it generates, its consequences for those who have it and for those who lack it. These themes are related, but must be assessed in their plurality and differences.

If there are many different issues involved, it is precisely because the book is historiographic. Analyzed carefully, it yields information on so many different aspects of the life of the people it is concerned with that we might even appeal to it as a model of full-fledged historiography. But this is possible only on the condition that we let the differences and the confusions, the chaos and the lack of linear development, the interrelations between private and public concerns, fully come to the fore. Hystoriography changes genre, then: rather than inscribing coherence—a coherence built out of male preoccupations—it inscribes the chaotic "fullness of life" that we have learned to eliminate from historiography.

A first step is not to assume any part of the book to be of minor importance, nor to consider any of its details irrelevant. Taking for granted the variety of sources, we will start with other questions, namely, why is the book composed as it is, of these materials, and how do the different stories speak to each other? It would be fallacious, however, to pretend that any form of "completeness" in interpretation can be achieved. I am as much subject to the centripetal tendency, the impulse to coherent reading, as anybody else. The next act of awareness, then, will be the determination of which coherence will replace the one I have just rejected as reductive and contradictory. This is how the idea of reading with a "countercoherence" comes into sight. A countercoherence relates the "official" reading to what it leaves out; it relates the texts to the needs of the reader; it relates everything that is denied importance to the motivations for such denials. The countercoherence will start precisely where repression is the most flagrant. Since men are said to lead the game, I will start with the women; since conquest is said to be the issue, I will start with loss; since strength is said to be the major asset of the characters, I will start with the victims.

The countercoherence starts where the traditional readings try to exclude or reduce the impact of women on the history of the people. I will not start from the premise that there is a coherence of the "private realm" to be established to counter the coherence of politics. It is the interpretation of politics that must be changed, not its distribution among the sexes. Rather than the coherence of politics, it is the politics of coherence that has to be countered: the tendency to use a self-evident, commonsense coherence for purposes of active repression. While refusing the assumption that the major issue of the book as history is political, I also reject the assumption that the place of women in that history can only be found in the margins left by political coherence.

Neither the content nor the object of the book is the sum total of history; its text—as texture, as linguistic, literary representation—is part of it as well. The method that I will present shortly is meant to allow reflection on the relation between narrative as a mode of discourse and the social reality it represents. Narrative itself, as a form, a project, and the fixation of a voice, is a means of expression of a culture that is establishing its own history. The narrative analysis should offer insight into the functioning of narrative for social and political purposes—not in a naively realistic sense, but in a deeper, more culturally anchored way. Part of what I will try to demonstrate, therefore, is the relation between narrative devices and the politics of coherence. Representation will be discussed as a meaningful act of cultural expression as well as an instrument of political and social oppression. The method I propose will account for these relations.

I will go about this project in the following way. In the remainder of this introductory chapter, I will construct a first outline of the male and female characters who are related to murder. I will focus on the two sets of individual murders, woman-man murders on the one hand, man-woman murders on the other. A first comparison between those two sets reveals a basic dissymmetry of power. I call it a dissymmetry because, more than an absence of symmetry—asymmetry—the issue is a fundamental struggle to enforce and strengthen dissymmetrical (unequal) power relations. At the end of that first outline, I will present a method of analysis that is meant to bridge the gap between the textual structures and the social reality they represent.

In chapter two, the focus will be on the female victims. I will start from the most famous one, Jephthah's daughter, and try to argue for an intrinsic relation between her fate and the idea of her virginity. Confronting her with the other women who relate to virginity will bring to the fore a doubleness of the view of virginity, a double language. The female side of that doubleness will be enhanced, since the opposite view has dominated and obscured it. As this chapter will at the same time be a demonstration of method, I will painstakingly step by step analyze fragments of the text, the commentaries about it, and modern thinking on the issue of virginity. As a sample of that thinking

I have chosen Freud's essay on virginity. I hope to show how the perspective of women's studies is able to use scholarship in a way radically different from its traditional use. I will use the essay by exploiting its vulnerability to critique while also exploiting its potential to increase insight.

Freud's text, as well as any other scholarly text I will use, should not be seen as a "source" or authority. I use those texts as *subtexts*, as texts that can shed some light on the ancient text, mediated by my reading of both, in that their discourse resembles the discourse of Judges. The result will not be a master-discourse in which the ancient text is the object and the scholarly text a tool. A dialogue between three discourses, which mutually illuminates and criticizes each other, would be a more appropriate image.

Chapter three continues this line, using the insight that confusion lies at the basis of the idea of virginity, even in our modern times. The many female characters who in some sense fit the category thus broken open will enrich the potential of the concept to produce different images of women. The characters that we know as "Samson's mother," as "concubine," and as "whore" all turn out to share concerns and, especially, to share the hostility and possessiveness of men over them, yet they escape these men, which leads to the attempt to separate them into varied and oppositional categories.

Chapters two and three lead to the conclusion that virgins, being caught in contradiction and temporal suspension, are so disturbing to the male view that their sacrifice becomes almost unavoidable. Chapter four, then, analyzes sacrifice in Judges. From a prior analysis of "proper" sacrifice, a series will be established which leads from Gideon's sacrifice, via Manoah's, Jephthah's, and Samson's rivals' to what I will argue to be the antisacrifice in chapter 19. Sacrifice relates the political coherence to the countercoherence: it is a socially sanctioned and politically exploited means of overcoming irresolvable "private" problems. On the one hand, Girard's massive theory of sacrifice as founding violence[16] and on the other hand Jay's gender-specific, rigorously social theory of sacrifice as a compensation for the lack of lineage inherent in patrilineal systems[17] are the two subtexts with which, in this chapter, Judges is brought into dialogue. This is also a place where the book will be seen, not as evidence, but as a representation and an acting out of the essentialist fallacy that connects women with nature, men with culture, and thus writing fatherhood as a problem.

In the fifth chapter, the use of language in this violent conflict will be discussed. The subtext, here, is speech-act theory. Language is not in Judges the fascinating game of seduction that Felman (1980) pictures in her book on speech-act theory. It is the instrument of murder. Thus, our concern is the use of language as weapon. Jephthah will be the dubious hero of this part of the discussion. As a master of killing speech-acts, he will exemplify the attempts to use language as a means to insure the power that fatherhood should, but fails to, attribute to the "heroes of might." It is not a coincidence that in this book filled with insecure and problematic fathers, both language and the penis are used as deadly weapons.

The sixth chapter will be devoted to the construction of an 'architectural' composition of the book. Where murder takes place in the house, at the exit of the house or at its threshold, space seems to be a relevant structural representation. The idea of the house, moreover, relates the spatial domain to the historical, thus undermining the dichotomy. The same word—house—denotes both a place and lineage. And lineage, as we will see throughout this study, is the founding problem in the book, and one that cannot be placed in, indeed challenges any opposition between, private and public. The connection between space and time is hard to perceive because it has an uncanny aspect. What makes it uncanny is precisely the place of the father at the crossroad between chronology and space.[18]

Chapter seven, finally, introduces the characters of the female murderers. They come at the end, to fill in a fundamental gap that the Book of Judges displays. The women who kill do not kill only for political purposes; they also kill 'for' the other stories. They introduce anger, an anger that, again, cannot be referred to as either political or private. Hence, they will be seen as figures that help construct the book as a representation of the life of the people, in all its aspects, in all its chaos, in all its disturbing problems. In that chapter, a hypothesis will be formulated that accounts for the impression of excessive violence that the book cannot fail to convey as soon as we defamiliarize ourselves from the coherence of the conquest. But that impression comes from a direction quite different from the "devilish ladies we all love to hate."

The Coherence of Dissymmetry

In order to counter the repressive and oppressive bearing of the endlessly repeated political coherence, I propose to establish a counter-coherence. Its purpose is not to "prove" that this is how the book should be read. The purpose of my endeavor is to show that such a counter-coherence is a possible, and in many ways a preferable, way of reading.

It is possible to the extent that the texts do not resist it. It is preferable, in the first place, because it does not simply repeat the ideological slogans superimposed on the narrative material, and in the second place, because it gives new insights into the social background of the book; indeed, it turns the background into a foreground. Hence, the counter-coherence provides the book with a motivation; it explains its own possible impact on the composition of the book. Moreover, it solves quite a few problems that the traditional coherent reading has not solved. And finally, it does justice to the impact on the lives of women of those social institutions and revolutions out of which the book emerges. Thus, it helps thinking through the relations between text and (historical) context in a quite different, seldom explored manner.

The following sections offer a first sketch of the countercoherence drawn from a brief examination of male and female characters. Once the direction of the countercoherence is indicated, a few remarks on method will be proposed. These have no orthodox instrumentalist status. The method proposed, a narratological model of analysis, is used throughout this book as a heuristic tool that reveals problems rather than solves them. The bulk of the tentative answers that will be offered in the course of this study come ultimately from other disciplines, mainly anthropology, history, and textual criticism or philology. The methodological project should be seen as an attempt to explore the limits of what disciplinary work can and cannot perform.

Heroes of Might and Women of Death

The story of Jephthah begins with a description of his ancestry and ends with the establishment of a mourning ritual: "And it was a task in Israel that the daughters of Israel went yearly to sing the daughter of Jephthah the Gileadite four days in a year" (11:39–40). The story of the rape and murder of the nameless concubine in chapter 19 begins by describing her marriage to a Levite and also ends in a horrifying manner that is fully understandable only if we take it as a ritual, too: "And when he was come into his house, he took the knife and seized his 'concubine' and divided her, limb after limb, into twelve pieces, and sent her throughout all the borders of Israel" (19:29). The former ritual brings forth memorialization, the latter slaughter, war, and more abduction and rape. The victim of the first murder accepts her death; the second victim never speaks. Between these two stories of the murders of young women, a third one almost passes unnoticed, bringing the series to the magically complete three.[19] Her story begins by introducing her husband and ends with a violent murder by a group as in chapter 19 and with her burning as in chapter 11: "And the Philistines came up and burnt her and her father with fire" (15:6). These three female characters will represent the basis of the countercoherence, as against the "official" coherence of biblical commentaries. Their death is my beginning. The mode of their death will be measured against their lives, their stories, and their positions as subjects. Those positions will be analyzed in relation to power and compared to other modes of violent death in the book. These characters will be taken as paradigmatic of female characters in Judges, and the other characters will be placed in relation to them. Given their fate, their namelessness, and their subordination, both in their lives and in the texts, to the men who control them, such a privilege seems appropriate as a counterstrategy.[20]

Who is Jephthah? The murderer of his daughter is introduced as a *gibbor hayil.* I translate this expression as "a hero of might." Several different translations for it circulate (see McKane 1958). It will be a key term in this study. The adjective *hayil* indicates faculty or power, wealth, skill, excellence, bravery. The substantive *gibbor* refers to "the young vigorous man apt for all that is virile" (Koehler and Baumgartner 1958, 168)[21] or "strong, valiant man" (Brown, Drivers, and Briggs 1962, 150). This definition is marvelously explicit on the nuances of the concept and its maleness. I cannot see why the qualifier "young" is justified. Boling (1975, 196) translates the two words together as "knight," the Jewish Publication Society (hereafter JPS; in Cohen 1980, 250) as "mighty man of valour," and Soggin (1981, 203) as "mighty warrior." Martin has "a great warrior" (1975, 136), and Gray (1986, 314) "a mighty warrior." I reject "knight" as anachronistic. It refers to a feudal system wherein nobility and lineage counted as much as personal performance. I find it especially inappropriate in the case of a man whose lineage is questionable.[22] "Valour" is not an obvious choice either; the merit of Jephthah's behavior is doubtful, in spite of Ecclesiasticus 46:11–12 and other eulogies of him. Moreover, his actual actions point to shrewdness, rather than to valour. And his hasty vow, inspired by insecurity, is not a sign of great bravery.

I consider "warrior" too limited a translation of *gibbor.* Although the book is never without wars of sorts, except in the "breaks" that mark the ends of the stories, the importance of the many situations wherein the *gibborim* are confronted with nonmilitary action makes a more general translation more plausible. Moreover, the term implies some sort of leadership beyond that of the simple "warrior." I choose the concept of *hero* as the translation that is the most appropriate in the context of Judges for the following reasons. The term has a place both in epic literature and in literary theory (Hamon 1977). It is common enough to be acceptable, yet specific enough to establish a particular class of male characters. The adjective is the modifier that sheds some light on the nature of heroism. The translation "might" combines power and, possibly, personal ability, efficiency, or skill. I will argue that it is Jephthah's primary existential goal to deserve that modifier, and thus to compensate the loss of status in history as the son of a "harlot." He stands for the idea of heroism that underlies the book.[23]

The Levite of chapter 19 is nameless. He is not a *gibbor*. He has no power. He only has the power to take a concubine. This power, however limited, is power over life and death: it saves his own life and condemns the woman. With that power, he is able to seize her, and to bring her out to be tortured and raped (19:25). In the course of the story, he becomes more and more powerful. If, in the beginning, the woman was able to leave him (19:2), the man successfully wins her back from her father. From that moment on, he can afford to not consult her about the safest place to spend the night, to throw her out to the rapists, to take her up and fling her onto the donkey, and finally to cut her into pieces. The episode that follows, the intertribal war against the Benjaminites that undermines the political coherence, is instigated if not led by this man. He becomes, *a postiori*, almost a *gibbor*. The woman's power decreases, the man's power increases.

Samson's bride, burnt to death in 15:6, is a complex case, somehow standing in between the two others. Her groom is one of the clearest examples of a *gibbor* that the book has to offer, and the concept, in his case, refers to physical power rather than to wit. She is killed, however, by the Philistines, but they murder her in response to an act of Samson. She is not taken away from her father by the man but, since the father kept her, he dies, too. As in chapter 19, the missing power of the man who owns her is countered by the plurality of the men who act upon her. In all three cases, the victim is powerless against the "might" of men.

This powerlessness of the victims is the first element of the countercoherence. It is not a mindless subordination. All three young women show, at some point of their stories, some autonomy of action. It is not a lack of initiative or capacity that condemns them, but the "might" of the men, the *gibborim*, who are socially entitled to exercise power over them.[24] The powerlessness of their situation is reflected on the literary level by their namelessness. In the following section, I will compare the status of the three women and their killers with three seemingly symmetrical cases: three women who kill a man.

Lethal Ladies

The best-known story of the Book of Judges is doubtless the story of Samson, and the episode best known of that story is the "betrayal"[25] of the hero by Delilah. Her conspiracy with the Philistine chiefs eventually costs Samson his life. Symmetrical to the death of the hero's first wife, Samson's death is not brought about by Delilah's hands proper. She leaves it to the Philistines to capture and mutilate him and to the hero to kill himself. It is her action, however, that makes the subsequent events possible.[26]

This story is very popular in modern culture. It has been depicted in painting, film, lyric, and popsongs, in which it invariably represents the same theme: the betrayal of a man in love by the woman whom he loves. It is the exemplary life of an ideo-story; it has been taken out of its context in the Book of Judges wherein it does not stand alone in its genre, and more specifically out of the story of Samson, where it is counterbalanced by the prior murder of the first woman Samson loved. And the textual details that have been considered problematic, the internal "inconsistencies" of the story, have been explained away, repressed, or simply removed. In the same spirit of censorship, the text has been completed by additional information, which makes it even better suited for the purpose of illustrating an "eternal" truth: women are treacherous, especially in love. The additions are mainly motivations for behavior that the modern reader cannot easily understand.[27]

The second best-known murder story is the murder of Sisera by Yael, narrated and sung in chapters 4 and 5. Here, too, a woman takes a man into her house, probably lures him into love, and kills him (Zakovitch 1981; Bruns 1954). The differences, however, are also striking. The victim is the enemy of the people. Hence, he is not qualified to be a *gibbor*, although he would qualify if the story were read from a Canaanite perspective. Were the perspective reversed, Sisera's status as the head of the extremely dangerous and superior Canaanite army would certainly make the term *gibbor* applicable to him. More importantly, such a reversal of perspective would make Yael the heroine into a mere murderess. Commentaries show that the difference is less crucial than the similarities. Yael is constantly blamed for her act, or at least for the way she did it: breaking the sacred law of hospitality.[28]

Between these two murders, a third woman kills a man. Again, the man is powerful, a *gibbor,* and like Jephthah, he is of questionable lineage. The woman who kills him is nameless. She does not lure him into her house or bed, and there is no love at stake. Or is there? The scene is brief: [29]

> And a tower of strength [was] within the city, and fled to the place all the men and the women and all the lords of the city and shut themselves in, and they went to the roof of the tower.
> And went Abimelech to the tower and fought against it, and went close to the gate of the tower to burn it with fire.
> And cast a woman an upper millstone upon the head of Abimelech and broke his skull.
> And he called quickly unto the young man his armour-bearer and said to him: draw your sword and kill me, that they say not: a woman slew him—and pierced him his young man, and he died. (9:51–54)

The *gibbor,* here, is very similar to Jephthah. He is the son of a concubine. His revenge against his "illegitimate"[30] status is drastic: he kills his seventy brothers. His name, Abimelech, means "my father is king." It betrays his preoccupation. He usurps the power that lineage denies him and becomes "king" in the name of the father. It is this usurper who approaches the tower of Shechem too closely. The woman who stands on the tower throws a millstone upon his head. His reaction shows that his status of *gibbor* is at stake.

Abimelech's order to his armour-bearer echoes the prediction of Deborah in 4:8, that Sisera will fall by the hand of a woman—a denial of honor to the Israelite leader Barak, the failed *gibbor.* The opposition between the honor of the *gibbor* and the shame brought by the hand of a woman is conventional in much epic literature and has, in this case, a more specific social background.[31]

The status of the victims of these three lethal women is in all cases that of a leader, a "head." If they are *gibborim,* that concept becomes more negative. Although these men have might, they are not all equally heroic. Notably, Abimelech's status as usurper of his brothers' power, as slayer of the entire family of his father, and as a man who is supported solely by the dubious brothers of his mother stresses the quality of "power" that characterizes the *gibbor,* while removing the accompanying idea of merit. Sisera is an enemy of the people, while Samson's merit is seriously compromised by his repeated transgression of the Nazirite law, and his tendency to fall in love with the "wrong" (i.e., enemy and foreign) women. Sisera abandons his army in distress and abdicates the token of his power, his chariot. Samson not only kills for personal motives alone, he also goes "astray" with the daughters of the Philistines. These women kill all three in the interest of their people.

Gender, Sex, and Dissymmetry

We can now briefly compare the three stories of murder of women and the three stories of murder of men by women. The following differences are striking at first sight. In the first three cases, the women were utterly powerless. They were submitted to a man or to several men. The men had power over their bodies, their sexuality, their lives. The men can give the women away or keep them for themselves. The female killers kill the men in different circumstances. The men are themselves powerful. They are heroes involved in military leadership. Killing such men is extremely dangerous and requires wit.

The second difference is in the kind of power exercised over the victim. The women are killed, but the concubine is also raped and tortured. Samson's bride is given away to somebody else before she is killed. Hence, while the women only do the socially useful killing, the male power varies. The killing of these young women fulfills no military function and is accompanied by other forms of violence against women. Since their murders are not militarily useful, we will have to address the question whether they were socially useful for other reasons. This question will be addressed in chapters 3 and 4.

A third difference concerns the relation between power and sexuality. The three female killers live as independent women;[32] the female victims are somebody's property. The stories of Yael and Delilah are often considered stories of sex. In Delilah's case it is told that Samson loves her and spends the night with her. He sleeps on her knees, and is caught in her "inner chamber." It is through his sexual relationship with Delilah that Samson comes into her power and ends up losing his own. In the case of Yael, many features in the text suggest this theme as well (see Zakovitch 1981). Although some of the features interpreted as sexual by Zakovitch are more obviously related to mothering, there is enough to support a sexual reading.[33] Like Delilah, Yael invites her victim into her own home. It is this act that provides the most convincing evidence for Yael's independence. The woman-with-the-millstone is not related to any particular man. She is not sexually involved with Abimelech, but the *image* of her standing on the tower and of the man approaching the tower too closely suggests a sexual isotopy on a different, metaphorical level.[34]

Modern readers tend to stress the sexual aspects of the stories of Delilah and Yael. The ideological use of the stories depends on it. Thus the underlying claim is that the women's identity can be simply derived from their sexuality, or rather, from that of the men. It is only through sex that the women gain access to the men at all. And since, in this perspective, the identity of men depends heavily on their control over women as sexual beings, this reversal of power is what threatens them most. This is the strongest motivation of the survival of these stories as ideostories.

The three victims have a different status in relation to sex. They all depend on men. Even if Jephthah's daughter takes some initiative to turn her fate into something more positive, she can only do so within the limits of fatherly power. Samson's bride was the object of the hero's desire. She was given to him, but before the marriage could take place, she was given away to another man. She still lives in her father's house. Hence, she is dependent on two men. Samson's desire for her, as well as her father's possession of her, ultimately causes her death. The concubine is the explicit victim of sexual aggression. She is, first, taken away from her father, then given away, then raped, tortured, and cut into pieces.

The daughter of Jephthah "had not known man" (11:39). She seems an exception to the sexual aspect of the murders, for she is neither raped nor in any other way involved in a sexual plot. But the explicit reference to her virginity does betray a preoccupation with sex, and with her sexual ripeness.[35] In the case of the murderesses, the sexual aspect of the stories is expressed in seduction. For the female victims, it is related to power(lessness). Between seduction and power there are connections, but also radical differences.[36] Those differences lie in the position of the victim. The radical difference is in the participation, or lack of it, of the object of desire in the success of the action upon her. The object of seduction submits more or less willingly to the seducer. Hence, she or he is a subject, however secondary. The exercise of power leaves the object no choice, hence, no opportunity for subjectivity, no subject-position. This difference produces a basic dissymmetry between the two sets of stories and the positions of killers and victims therein.

The treatment of the sexual motif in subsequent readings of the book is significant. It is underscored in the cases of the murderesses; it tends to be marginalized or to disappear in the cases of the victims. Jephthah's sacrifice is mostly considered a tragic dilemma and, although the father is not always excused, he is mostly pitied. The significance of his daughter's murder is undermined by her virginity, interpreted as betokening the futility of her life. But the most striking marginalization of the victim's sexuality is the treatment of the murder of the concubine.

The story is very little known to begin with, for no reason other than suppression. Secondly, it is invariably dealt with as a "study in hospitality." It is true that hospitality is at stake, but this is true for the entire book. The dangers incurred by travelers, due to the disorganization of the land and the cohabitation of several peoples, are doubtless important considerations within the editorial framework that repeatedly regrets that "in those days there was no king in Israel, every man did what was right in his own eyes" (21:25), and the subsequent war against the Benjaminites shows that the story of the concubine has served, to some extent, an etiological function.[37] But all this does not remove the scandal of the repression of the sexual brutality and the participation of the husband in it. The outrageous horror of such a story cannot be explained away by any logical argument or narrowly historical consideration, let alone by the imposition, through editorial comment, of the proper coherence to read from. A satisfactory interpretation of this story should not only interpret the text, its details and its structure, and its relation to the sequel, but also, its horror as such, as well as the repression of it. Moreover, there is no reason why the theme of hospitality should be disentangled from the rape-motif, the particular form of violence that is called to represent chaos in general. The embedding of the event within issues of national and religious importance makes the story even more shocking in its sexual aspect.

It is precisely in the "labor" for this repression[38] that the political coherence and the countercoherence shift places. The "official" coherence of war and theology allows a hierarchy of interests to be established at the cost of a clear view of the relations between the different domains of the life of the people. If the chaos in the land is expressed through the absence of a king and the selfishness of the men's behavior, then the contempt for the women's lives and bodies and the desire to take absolute power of them, as exemplified in this story in particular, may very well be the cause rather than the consequence of this chaos. The countercoherence would then be entangled with the political coherence, and that is, I presume, the danger against which the political coherence has been protected. The dissymmetry in power-position between the characters in the two sets of murder stories will be considered in this study as the figuration of the chaos.

Other Female Characters

The double opposition between male and female on the one hand, and between victim and killer on the other, brings a basic dissymmetry to the fore. This configuration needs to integrate now the positions of other female characters. The first woman appearing in Judges is Achsah. This daughter of Caleb appears in 1:12, where her father promises her to the victor of Kiriat-sepher, "the city of writing, or of books" (Slotki 1980, 89).[39] The victor is Caleb's younger brother Othniel, who is to become the exemplary judge. The gift is significant: the man who qualifies as a *gibbor* deserves the possession of the chief's daughter. Although she is the object of a deal between men, Achsah does show remarkably independent features. At the moment she is given away, she goes to her father to claim better lands.

The next occurrence of female characters proper is in chapter 4, where the main character is the prophetess and judge, Deborah. But before she appears, we have met the sentence expressing what "going astray" in the book means: "And they forsook Yahweh and served Baal and the Ashtaroth. And the nose of Yahweh burnt against Israel" (2:13–14);[40] and, "And they took their daughters for them for women and their daughters they gave to their sons and they served their gods" (3:6). The latter quotation shows the relation between the two aspects of "going astray." Yahwistic monotheism and endogamy are the two sides of the same law: faithfulness to the "self" and separation from the "other." The relation between intermarriage and idolatry cannot but be based on a similarity, in the rhetoric of morality, between religious and sexual life, between relationships to deities and to women.[41] The similarity is established, in this verse, through the juxtaposition of the two elements. Often the one—monotheism, faithfulness to "self"—comes to stand as the metaphorical expression of the other—endogamy, separation from the "other." The well-known expression, "the people went whoring after other gods," is the clearest instance of this relation, which has a profoundly interesting background.

The women who are here 'taken' and 'given' cannot be considered full characters in the narratological sense. They do not act, they do not have the slightest subject-position, and they are not individualized. Denying character-status to women who have no power to act would be coming close to a noncritical paraphrase of the text, since it is precisely part of the ideological makeup of the latter.

Deborah appears at the beginning of chapters 4 and 5. The latter is the older of the two texts. The reversal of the chronological order is

a consistent gesture within the editorial policy that cannot be explained away by cognitive logic. The argument that the narrative had
to be told first in order for the song to be understandable is only acceptable within the ideology that dictated the reversal in the first place.
Deborah, according to the song, introduces herself as "Deborah, a
mother in Israel." In chapter 4, the narrator introduces her, and she is
described as "woman prophetess a woman of torches, she was judging
Israel at that time" (4:4). The second description can be considered as
an explicit explanation of the first which, by the time that chapter 4
was composed, was no longer understood. The use of familial metaphors for social roles is systematic. The Israelites are referred to as
"sons of Israel," and in 11:40 the young women are described as "the
daughters of Israel."

" members "

Deborah as well as Yael, who appears in 4:17, have their place in
the category of active main characters and will not detain us here. The
next secondary character to appear is Sisera's mother, who is evoked in
the last strophe of the song, sitting at her barred window and anxiously
waiting for her son to return. The evocation is obviously contrasted
with the event just sung, in order to give the lie to the optimistic expectations of the enemy women. These Canaanite women refer to potential captive "girls" (uteruses) as part of the attempt of the women to
reassure themselves by giving expression to the fate of captive women
in the rude language that suits *gibborim* rather than fellow women.
Thanks to the joint efforts of Deborah and Yael, the fate evoked does
not befall Israelite women in this story. Hence, the girls are hypothetical, not actual, characters. But later in the book, the very same
fate will befall the "girls" of the devastated city of Jabesh-gilead, as
well as the virgins of Shiloh. The verb of which the "uteruses" are the
object in the hypothetical quote in the song is "to divide" rather than
"to give." The latter verb indicates that the woman is handed over
from one owner to the other, in mutual agreement between the two
men, while the former indicates the act of stealing or taking women
considered available for public use. Their protectors and owners having
been eliminated, either by murder, as in Jabesh-gilead, or because they
were absent, as in Shiloh, these women assume the status of public
property. The extreme consequence of this idea will be carried out literally in chapter 19.

After the woman-with-the-millstone who kills Abimelech in
9:53, Jephthah's daughter in chapter 11, and the casual mention of the
mothers of unsatisfactory status in chapters 8 and 11, the companions
of the sacrificed virgin break the daughter's solitude. They also break

her ahistorical position, providing her with the remembrance only accessible to men of the proper lineage. Their position will be discussed
further in chapter 3. Samson's mother clearly belongs to the group of
motherly figures, that is, strong and, hence, dangerous women. It is
often noted that she is stronger in faith than her husband. But she also
adds to the message of the "messenger of Yahweh" a phrase that will
ultimately condemn Samson: "until the day of his death" (13:7).

Another nameless woman in the Samson story is the bride's
younger sister. She is proposed as a stand-in for her elder sister when
Samson, after his failed marriage, comes back to visit the woman he
believes to be his wife. The gift of the younger sister is rejected, and
she may well have been among the later victims of the sacrifice of the
bride. The "harlot" of Gazah, Samson's antagonist in the brief episode
between the first marriage and the relationship with Delilah, is among
the women characters whose reputation is one of treachery. But the
subject of betrayal is not specified in the text.

Delilah will be discussed at some length in chapter 7. The money
at stake in the dispute between Micah and his mother in chapter 17
constitutes the alleged link (Slotki 1980, 286) between the two characters of Delilah and this mother. This metonymic link between the
two stories is an argument against the chronological bias of the political coherence. The commentators who, according to Slotki, assume
this metonymic logic, also claim that Micah is the Levite of the following story. The power of this mother appears in the fear her curse inspires in her son: he restores the stolen money to her because of it.

The victim of chapter 19 is the last individual female character in
the book. After her, a group of women are mentioned as victims of the
slaughter of Jabesh-gilead: the group of women who have "lain by man"
are killed, while the four hundred "virgins who have not known man
by lying with him" are brought out to serve as uteruses to the tribe of
Benjamin.

The secondary female characters are easy to accommodate within
the tentative structure of countercoherence, the coherence of dissymmetry. They are either mothers, strong and powerful, be they legitimate wives or concubines and harlots, or they are the objects of
acts by the men who possess or take possession of them. Given away
in the best of cases, they are stolen, raped, or killed in the worst. Exceptions to this rule are Sisera's powerless mother and the friends of
Jephthah's daughter.[42] Both exceptions are limit-cases. Sisera's mother
may be depicted as dependent, sitting behind the bars of her window,
waiting in vain for her son; but she does take power—an imaginary

power over the Israelite women—by identifying with the warriors. She identifies with the *gibbor* whose death, by Yael's hand, she is still unaware of.

The friends of Jephthah's daughter identify with the victim without becoming powerless. In line with the sacrificed daughter herself, they act to overcome the finality of her premature death by making her immemorial. By this act of commemoration, a crucial form of power, the friends become the limit-case of the type of the daughter-victim. They manage to give her life; hence, they become, in a sense, mothers themselves. In the case of Sisera's mother, identification confers false, illusory, and alienated power, while at the same time it devaluates the character's status as a mother; in the friends' case, it helps to overcome the absolute powerlessness of the position with which they identify.

The Language of Power

The principle of coherence that will guide my reading of the book is the dissymmetry of power: power over the body, over life, over language. The nuances of this hypothesis of coherence will have to be filled in in specific ways in order for my study to have something new to bring to our understanding of the book's social meaning. Moreover, we will have to work out the relations between the social reality underlying this coherence and the representation of that reality in the biblical text. Naive realism will have to be avoided, as will the opposite fallacy, the esthetic-literary approach that focuses on chiastic structures, ring compositions, and the like, as if any connection to reality had to be carefully eschewed.[43] In the remainder of this chapter, I will briefly present the method of narratology that will be the heuristic starting point of the analysis in this study. Needless to say, this method is not all-encompassing.[44] It does, however, allow us to establish connections between textual features and social meanings, and that is more than most methods of either historical or literary schools do. Moreover, the narrative mode of discourse is so closely related to the historiographical project that it cannot be considered just a literary mode; it serves a social, ideological purpose.[45]

In the preceding section, I have mentioned the absolute lack of subject-position that characterized the women given and taken in marriage (2:13–14; 3:6). I will now use that case for all its obviousness as an example of method. The women are mentioned only casually. The silencing of their voices (how do they think about the marriages?) signifies them as ideologically silenced. On the level of discourse, these women are not subjects: they do not speak. On the second level of the narrative, the level of vision or focalization, they are not subjects either. Their vision is not given, not considered, and not responded to. There is, however, a third level on which subject-positions are distributed in narrative: the level of the fabula,[46] of what happens, of the events. On that level, the women do not act either; they are not subjects but objects of action, typically given away or taken. Within the fabula as a series of events, however, the event of which they are the objects, does have consequences. It is an important event that not only figures the difficulty of the Israelites' project to establish their otherness, but narratologically speaking, it triggers the following episode: Yahweh's anger—subjugation as punishment and subsequent war. This event is indeed crucial for the individual stories to happen at all. It is, even, the event through which the political and the individual coherences shift places. Hence if it is true that the women have no subject-position at all, their relevance as elements in the story has to be assessed. Their marriages replace the untenable chronology on which most commentators try to base the book's composition.

This level of relevance helps us see narrative as a genre function in the dynamics of ideology. The powerlessness of the women promotes the development of the narrative. Their lives, as part of the countercoherence, are crucial for the political coherence to establish itself. Moreover, the awareness of this functional position often triggers the fallacy known as "blaming the victim." It can easily lead to a displacement of responsibility. Therefore, it is crucial to be attentive, both to the lack of subject-position and to the narrative role these women do play after all. Without prior assumptions about the condition of women in the biblical period that produced the book, the textual figurations of subject-positions open to women or closed off from them give some insight into what sort of lives, what sort of contributions to society, were, not so much "real," but "thinkable" for women.

The tension between position and role that we notice here can be reformulated as follows. A character can be without position of subjectivity,[47] while still, as an element in the dynamic of narrative, being the figuration of a role. This can happen at the three levels of speech, vision, and action. As a result, the analysis will be much more refined than a sheer assessment of subject-positions can be. This entails consequences for the critical project of this book.

The position I will take here toward the gender-value and content of the book cannot be determined on the basis of the very dichotomy which I will try to overcome. The position of most feminist biblical scholars is based on a hierarchy of speakers. Trible (1978; 1984), in spite of her critique of male behavior toward female charac-

ters, maintains a positive view of the Bible based on an attempt to ex-
onorate Yahweh from the scandal caused by male characters. Even if all
narrative agents treat women horribly, the voice of the deity is often
invoked to save the ideological tenor of the overall text. Narrative theory does not accommodate such a view. It places the divine character
on the same level, *as a character* that is, as the other characters. It is
precisely this methodological rigor that allows a narratological analysis
to become truly critical. It also allows the analysis to become historical, in contrast with analyses based on the realistic fallacy that cannot
allow for historical analysis unless factual truth can be proven. If truth
there is, it lies in the structures of positions and roles, the distribution
of power they display.

In contrast to Trible's position, other feminist biblical scholars
claim that the overall ideology is basically patriarchal and sexist (e.g.,
Fuchs 1985 and 1988). The latter claim seems historically more plausible than the former, but I find it slightly simplistic, too, and, paradoxically, noncritical. In both cases, though not to the same extent,
respect or anger toward the culture and the religion in which the Hebrew Bible has been incorporated directs the interpretation. My opposition against both "reformist" and "radical" interpretations can be
argued as follows. Both positions are based on a dichotomy, as if only
two possibilities, "good" versus "bad" situations for women, existed.
The result of such an endeavor cannot but be anachronistic and will be
of little help for a better understanding of the nuances and subtleties of
gender-relations.[48] Moreover, the methodological basis of both positions is a nonproblematic realism that is equally anachronistic and
noncritical toward the historiographic project of the book itself as a
male enterprise.[49] Those studies tend to take the text at its word, to
take the characters as real and the events that happen to them as historical, without taking the structure of the text *as narrative* at its word,
with its specific strategies of representation.

In my perspective, it is not so much the overall ideology that will
come to the fore, but rather the gaps, breaks, inconsistencies, and
problems that any ideology necessarily entails. Those features, which I
call *textual problems* will be taken seriously as clues. Enhancing these
problems rather than explaining them away or ignoring them, I will try
to grasp the politics of coherence, both in the book and in the modern
readings that are metonymical extensions of it. This approach allows
me to see the problems which modern readers encounter in the book
and to explain those problems as gender-related.

I will start from the question of the subject, the whodunnit or,
rather, the who-does-what question. For each level of the narrative,

the subject will be examined: on the level of speech and narration itself, the speakers and narrators; on the level of vision, the subject of
focalization; on the level of the fabula, the agents of the actions which
form the episodes. In order to elaborate this basic model further, three
groups of questions can be derived from the basic question of the subject. These categories will in turn be related to *positions* of subjectivity,
to *roles* in the narrative, and to the success and the distribution of *actions* in these three domains.

Positions. The term "position" refers to the question "who does
what?" It helps to delimit subjects and the models in which their
subject-positions are described. Positions can be discerned on the three
levels of narrative discourse.

Speech implies speakers. Access to the spoken word within the
world of the fabula is a first conspicuous place where power is distributed;
hence the question "who speaks?" The absolute silence of the 'concubine' contrasts with the laborious conversations between her father
and her husband, her husband and the host, the host and the rapists. It
contrasts also with the limited yet crucial speech that Jephthah's daughter is allowed to utter. The status of the speaker in relation to the narration as a whole leads to the question whether we hear the voice
attributed to an explicit speaker or to some implicit authority. At what
points do speakers alternate with the anonymous narrator? Furthermore, the linguistic model of speech determines the nature of the
speech-act. Which models have been chosen and by which speaker:
the monologic *versus* the dialogic model, the constative *versus* the
overtly performative model, or, in the case of the latter, the differences
between, for example, request and demand, between imperative and
interrogative. All these differences can determine the outcome of the
fabula through the distribution of power which they entail.

Let me quote one example here: the evolution of speech-acts
performed by the concubine's owner in chapter 19. This evolution
proceeds from "speaking to her heart" (19:3), as the ideal model of
dialogue, to monologue, when he later speaks about her, to speechless
violence when he throws her out to the rapists. The evolution of this
sad abuse of language reaches its climax when language becomes out of
order. The symbolic act at the end of the story speaks of the speechless-
ness of violence and the setting aside of language as a means of main-
taining cultural order.

In the domain of vision the identity of the subjects of vision or
focalizers [50] entails the question of responsibility for behavior based on
somebody's point of view. Samson responds to the woman's "whin-
ing" by giving in, both at his wedding and with Delilah. Is the view

presented by her ("you do not love me") the one he adopts himself? The meaning of the verb "to see" thematizes the meaning of the focalization: in its epistemological tenor, it relates visual perception to understanding. It is in that double sense that it is used in 16:18: "and when Delilah saw." This specifically biblical epistemology contrasts correct seeing with error of vision. It has a strong impact on the meaning of stories. In the example of Samson it leads to an interpretation of the (self-)betrayal of the hero that differs considerably from the traditional one.[51]

The identity of diegetic agents is to be confronted, in the analysis, with their position in the fabula. Hence, the initial question "who acts?" has to be followed up by specifications. Do each of the characters act in their turn, or are some characters only acted upon? Are characters named or nameless; is their action physical or only mental; is it integrated within the network of the overall fabula, or does it seem isolated? The position of Jephthah's daughter and that of the concubine need comparison. Although the former does ultimately assume the power to undo her fate as the unfulfilled obliviated virgin, her action does not influence the fabula. The next episode does not follow up on hers, and Jephthah goes on with his conquest of power as if nothing had happened. The position of the concubine as the absolute object denies her any access to power, except at the very beginning of the story. Her falling down on the threshold, however, does entail the next sequence of the fabula. It signifies the violation of property, the issue that her husband takes to be at stake in the event. Moreover, it shifts the countercoherence back onto the political coherence, demonstrating their inextricability.

Narrative roles do not coincide with subjective positions. As we have seen, characters who are denied subject-positions can still fulfill roles in the fabula. This tension between positions and roles enhances the dissymmetry of power in that it displaces responsibility. Hence the question: which character is central in the episode or the fabula as a whole?

Is the grammatical subject of the sentence the causal subject of the action? This question concerns the level of speech. The most obvious case of a displacement between the two is Jephthah's blaming of his daughter-victim in 11:35. Speech turns the daughter into the grammatical subject, an efficient way to repress the identity of the subject responsible for the event, in other words, the *causal* subject.

The central position of female focalizers in the Samson story points to a role that severely limits the range of action of the *gibbor*. Special attention to the expression "behold" will show the role of the beholder to be narratively functional. The spatial point of view to which a focalizer has access distinguishes the almighty view of Yahweh from the limited view of the main characters and from the even more reduced view of the powerless figures. Sometimes the female characters have access to more information than the *gibborim*. Yael responding to Sisera's "order" in 4:19 shows that she understands his words better, that she takes his language more seriously, than he does. She rightly interprets the expression "none" as the answer to the question "is there a man here?" and carries this prediction of Sisera's death out, while he expressed it without understanding.

The position of the subject of the fabula is further specified by the comparison of other involvements in action by the same character. Is the character playing a mono-active role, or is it, in its turn, the object of other characters' action? The relation between the character and the program of the narrative, the teleology of the fabula in which it functions, further illuminates the extent to which the action entails narrative power. The nameless women, taken and given away, do play a role in the narrative of the political coherence, but are denied a role in the popular afterlife of the book. In the countercoherence proposed here, however, they recover their role as part of the category of female objects that will be assumed to inspire the actions of the murderesses.

A third level of analysis inquires into the evaluative reactions of later readers in comparison with the text. This is the level of *action* itself, in speech, in vision and in fabula activity. The results of position- and role-analysis are confronted to the efficiency of the actions: the question of relative success. Success of narrative action should not be measured against the political coherence of the book. It is a relative evaluation of the distribution of the power to carry out intentions.

On the level of speech, the adequate use of linguistic models by speakers will be evaluated. If a character gives an order, the social rules of speech require that she or he be in a position to do so; otherwise, the order is futile and the response cannot be termed obedience or disobedience, since the category of obedience presupposes authority. Sisera's order to Yael will be the typical example of such an inadequate use of a linguistic model (4:19). Sisera is not in a position to give an order. Hence, his speech-act can be qualified as inadequate. Its failure will be analyzed as a combination of misfire and abuse.

Vision can be evaluated as adequate or inadequate in relation to the intention of the viewer or to the object of vision. The categories of spying, of secrecy, of lying can be characterized in this framework. Again, Sisera turns out to be a failing narrative agent when he evaluates Yael's tent as a safe place because her tribe lives in (recent) peace with his employer (4:17). Adequate vision can be measured against "truth" of the fabula. Jephthah's prevision of what he will see coming out of his house is obviously wrong, not so much because the tradition of women meeting the victor could have given him a clue but, narratively, because it clashes with the subsequent vision, where he sees someone that he had not seen in his prevision.

Narrative action is to be evaluated in relation to the intention of the agent, to the intention of the power that controls the agent's destiny, and to the efficiency of the overall narrative program. If we consider that Samson desires to be handed over to the Philistines, his action of self-betrayal is adequate in relation to his (unconscious) intention. In relation to the intention of Yahweh, who wanted him to begin to deliver the people from the hand of the Philistines, it is adequate, too. The narrative program on the level of self-determinacy and of deliverance both need this action. The question that remains unanswered, then, is why Delilah is needed as a narrative agent to bring about the action, hence, what Samson's status as a hero comes to.

A second set of questions on this level of analysis concerns the distribution of action among the characters. The order in which subjects do or do not have access to speech, to vision, or to diegetic activity is relevant here. It does not suffice, for example, to argue that Jephthah's daughter does have some power, since she does take the position of speaker and of diegetic agent. The bearing of her actions is further determined and, as a matter of fact, circumscribed by the order in which the speech of her father precedes her. The absolute nature of his speech-act precludes her possible range of action. It is this aspect that must be analyzed in order to overcome the dichotomy referred to earlier: it helps us to grasp both the limits within which women have access to action and the choices they can make to extend those limits.

In the following chapters, questions of the type presented here will inform my analyses, with the purpose of the study being a subtle, nondichotomistic perspective of the Book of Judges as an example of the inscription of gender-relations in ancient texts and their aftermath. Given this, a model such as the one I have outlined is useful. It will serve to substantiate the countercoherence that, I will argue, underlies the gap between the two modern views of the book outlined above. Its relevance lies in its inherent power to underscore power; its adequacy, in its relation to the narrative structures and their semiotic status; its workability, in the direct relation between terms and heuristic questions. In order to avoid the tedium of systematic analysis, I will reduce to a minimum the explicit reference to the categories I have just outlined. Readers are referred to Appendix 1, for quick reference to the questions involved in a particular analysis. This appendix is meant to make the method teachable, the procedures accessible, and the analyses verifiable, without encumbering the text with unnecessary terms and charts.

The usefulness of the model lies also, however, in its ability to indicate its own limits. Although, initially, the questions of the subject underlie all analyses, sooner or later the limits of the discipline's efficiency will be reached. The analysis of the book that I intend to carry out cannot but be interdisciplinary in its scope and method. The two opposing boundaries that the narratological analysis will hit are philology on the textual side and anthropology and history on the social side. The question of the subject will be asked, for example, when the status of Jephthah's daughter as a virgin is discussed. The different expressions used by different subjects of speech will then point to a difference in vision. At such a moment, philology needs to be introduced in order to make sure that the interpretation is based on an acceptable analysis of the Hebrew word[52] for virginity. On the other hand, any reflection on virginity has to look into the anthropological background which can be assumed to have produced the text as it stands. It is in these encounters between disciplines that the connection between the narrative structure and the social reality in which it is embedded can best be assessed. The next chapter will demonstrate this point.

CHAPTER TWO

VIRGINITY AND ENTANGLEMENT

> There is no greater moment for a virgin than the one when she
> stops being a virgin, and every sensation of her blood when she
> tries to fight, every sigh she chokes back enhances the value of
> the sacrifice she has to make at that moment.
> Hebbel

One of the central figures in this study, Jephthah's daughter, is said to
"have known no man" (11:40). In the afterlife of the story, she has
become the nameless virgin, precursor of Mary. Virginity, formulated
as a negation, is the feature that characterizes this victim. In this chapter, virginity will be explored as a construct, a danger, and a misunderstanding; as a negation, suspension, and transition; as a gift, a ritual,
and a taboo. The character that embodies the problematic concept of
virginity will be described in her twofold first appearance: the first
mention of her in the narrative, and her first meeting with her father
after the battle.

There are other virgins in the book. They will be introduced,
too: the bride in Samson's unfulfilled marriage; the virgin offered as a
ransom, together with the Levite's concubine, in chapter 19 and her
intertextual mates, the daughters of Lot; the virgins of Jabesh-gilead
and the virgins of Shiloh; and the faithful companions of Jephthah's
daughter, as well as Achsah, the exceptional character of chapter 1.
Some of these women are explicitly referred to as *bethulah*, others are
described with the negation applied to our central case, and some are
simply represented as premarital brides, fiancées, or, to use the very
appropriate old-fashioned term, promised. The network of virgins that
constitutes a line of coherence in the book so far seems to fit pretty
well. This will not remain so when we take a closer look at the meanings and implications of virginity itself.

Of the leading publications on virginity, Freud's essay "The Taboo of Virginity" (1957) is the most illuminating. This is not so because it gives an objective, theoretical, hence, generalizable account of what virginity is. Quite to the contrary, the essay is hardly concerned with virginity at all. That is, however, precisely the reason why it is so significant. Its failure to account for virginity as a phenomenon displays the concept's rootedness in the construction of femininity by male focalization. Two confusions lie at the basis of Freud's essay. First, in spite of the overall male focalization, the perspective of the essay is alternately male and female, sometimes both at the same time, an entanglement of views that the author seems unaware of. The same confusion will be shown to be meaningfully signified in the Book of Judges, especially in chapter 11:31 and 34–40. Second, the essay shifts to and fro between virgin and phallic woman, between innocent young girls and avenging mature women. This will be seen as a crucial confusion that supports the fictional status of virginity and its male background. It will also account for the status of elderly women in the book.

The status of virgins in Judges is narratively related to death, rape, and abduction. The danger that is apparently implied by a woman's identification as virgin calls for explanation. I will argue that the concept of virginity itself is a misunderstanding and that Jephthah's "error" epitomizes it; hence, rather than making a particular mistake, the hero will be seen as partaking in the misunderstanding that encapsulates virginity in general and of which the daughter is a "natural" victim, rather than an accidental one. In order to understand the concept of virginity, I will discuss it in its full negativity. The negative formulation it receives is due to the temporally impossible suspension it entails. This suspension can only be understood as a transition between one state, or stage, and another, a transition that receives the excessively patriarchal flavor of the inacceptability of female autonomy. Existing between positions of daughter and wife, the young, nubile woman belongs to nobody. In context, this means that she is nobody, hence, the negative formulation that describes her. The solution to the problem this state of transition produces for the owners of the women is the act of the gift. Virgins are to be given away, in order to bring their disturbingly ambiguous state to an end as quickly as possible. Jephthah's daughter is no exception in that respect. Within the patriarchal framework of the book, the only way to counter the taboo of virginity is to replace or follow up the ritual entailed by the taboo with yet another ritual.

Bath-Jephthah and Jephthah: The Daughter's Gift

So far, I have referred to the victim of the only fully explicit human sacrifice in the Bible as Jephthah's daughter. It is difficult to think of her otherwise; the text denies her a name. Arguably, it is because of her very namelessness that this character has become, in later rewritings of the story, the secondary character, qualified only as a virgin, a victim, obedient and submissive, even "wise" in her submissiveness.[1] To name this nameless character is to violate the biblical text. Not to name her is to violate her with the text, endorsing the text's ideological position. I feel it is not only acceptable, but necessary, to take some critical distance from the alienating anonymity of the character without, however, losing sight of the structure of subjectivity that it signifies. Therefore, I will give this woman a name, but a name which stresses her dependence and her state. In order to make her speakable, I will call her what she most basically is: Jephthah's daughter, Bath-Jephthah, or, briefer, *Bath*. Bath-Jephthah *versus* Jephthah: the inequality, the dependence, and yet the acknowledgment of this woman as a full character resounds in this name. This much for my initial speech-act. Let us turn to Jephthah's.

Bath's beginning underscores her namelessness and displays a discrepancy in the narrative status assigned to her. Not only is she anonymous, but more than that, her identity is unknown and conditionally described. This is characteristic of virginity. If firstness, freshness, and virtuality are features of virginity, the phrase used by her father in his vow expresses more than he understands: *the first one* to meet him after his victory will be given away. But this firstness is modified by the formulation in Hebrew, where it is expressed in relation to the house of the father, and to separation from it and/or him.

> And Jephthah vowed a vow unto Yahweh and said: If you will indeed/ fully deliver the sons of Ammon into my hand, then the goer-out who/ that will go out of the doors of my house to meet me in my returning in peace from the sons of Ammon will be to Yahweh and I will offer as a burnt offering. (11:30–31)

As a speech-act, the vow is a combination of trade and promise. The as yet unknown being who will meet the hero under specific conditions will be given away. The deal concerns a military victory that Jephthah feels unable to accomplish himself. He needs Yahweh's support. That support was granted to him already by the bestowal of the spirit; the point of the vow, therefore, is to perform this particular, ritual speech-act.[2] We have met this speech-act before: in chapter 1, verse 12. Just as Othniel, there, deserves the chief's daughter as a bride, just so, Yahweh, the real victor, deserves Jephthah's daughter. The speech-act is comparable in both cases and so is the situation: a difficult military situation—a confrontation that the chief feels unable to go through by himself. The vow ends with a difference: the daughter will not be given away as a bride but as a burnt offering. Object of promise, of trade, of gift, and of offering by fire, Bath's position is already delineated before she is even mentioned. It is within this framework that she will be allowed to act.

If Bath appears in the story as an absolute object, Jephthah himself is not a full subject. After several failed attempts to secure the victory through negotiation, he is visited by "the spirit of Yahweh" that produces a *gibbor*. The formulaic phrase consecrates his heroic status and foreshadows his success. The precise nature of the spirit is not, however, what is understood within the Platonic-Christian tradition as the opposite of the body. This spirit assigns might, not understanding. It sustains action, not insight. The place of the spirit on the level of action, rather than focalization, is the source of the tragedy to come. If Jephthah had been gifted with the insight to match his shrewdness—if the spirit had just enhanced the most characteristic feature of the hero—he would have trusted in Yahweh and his vow would have been unnecessary.

The dubious help provided by the spirit of Yahweh is displayed in other cases as well. On the one hand, we have Gideon, who needs triple evidence before he dares to undertake his assignment (6:37–40); on the other hand, we have Samson, who relies too heavily on his faith, trusting to be saved by Yahweh from the hand of the Philistines, even after he himself has broken the pact (16:20). Samson, indeed, shows the true nature of the spirit which is, ironically, bodily. It allows him to slaughter, not to understand. Might, but blindness too, befalls the *gibbor*.

Jephthah's vow, then, is superfluous, due only to a lack of understanding on the part of the mighty man. This beginning mortgages the vow itself, its content, and its realization. It is Jephthah's status as a failing focalizer, as a character who speaks too much and sees too little, who is unable to match speech and action through the mediation of insight, that determines the fate of Bath. Jephthah fails to understand that he should refrain from speaking; the spirit being only physical, he should have acted upon it. Not satisfied to be an agent of deeds, he wants to know, and, not knowing, he replaces insight with a speech that acts. The nature of the speech-act matches his deeds. If his actions will be killing, his words, consistent with them, kill, too. This symmetry is, so to speak, driven home to him, and at Bath's expense.

The content of Jephthah's vow raises many questions. Some commentators have painstakingly argued that the architecture of the houses in the ancient Middle East allows for the suggestion that Jephthah could have expected an animal to be the first being coming out of his house (Boling 1975, 208). This is a typical strand of argumentation that betrays its apologetic character by the sheer effort to prove the hero's innocence, thus ignoring the text. This never really works; Boling's drawing itself shows the pointedness, in the vow, of the specification "the doors" of the house. Those who assume it could have been some animal are instructed by this drawing that differentiates the gate at the front of the inner court from the doors of the house itself. The futility of the question is even more obvious when we take the verb "to meet me" into consideration. Animals, unclean or clean, can hardly be expected to come and meet the hero.[3]

The dramatic irony of the episode draws upon the traditional situation in which both this particular story and its companion pieces in the cultural tradition were known. In that respect, the ritual in which young women came out of the house to meet the victor seems more likely to be alluded to in the vow. If we use the well-known realistic-psychological argument, we may say that this ritual was well enough known for Jephthah to possibly have been aware of the risk he was taking; but obviously, his unawareness is precisely the point. The "normal" procedure of celebration after victory included the participation of his daughter as the dancing and singing maiden to celebrate the victor. But the just expressed insecurity implies that he did *not* consider himself the victor. His appeal to Yahweh in fact cut off the possibility of himself being welcomed as a victor. This contradictory expectation can be seen as a motivation for his "error." His preoccupation with his status as *gibbor* and the glimmering awareness that he did not deserve it conflict and create the impasse.

It is pointless to speculate about Jephthah's thoughts, since we know him only as a character. In the line of the narrative, the conflation of firstness, virginity, and sacrifice is more significant than the possibilities of awareness in the case of a character whose very unawareness stands out as a primary trait. Before turning to the meaning of the daughter in Jephthah's biography and to Freud's essay as it illuminates it, we will now take a closer look at the concept of virginity as it is expressed in the text itself. This analysis does not put Bath and Jephthah in opposition, but Bath and the narrator.

Negation and Denial of Womanhood

In the narrator's discourse, the episode of the daughter's sacrifice closes with the words: "And she had not known man." The narrator does not use the word *bethulah*, traditionally translated as "virgin"; he uses the negative formula. We will consider if the two expressions are synonyms. Second, the relevance of the phrase as the closure of the account of the tragedy and as a transition to the ensuing ritual must be examined. Third, the meaning and value of the idea it expresses, in its negativity, has to be interpreted. Finally, the use of the phrase on other occasions should be examined since its use may be helpful in the determination of its meaning and function in the Bath episode. As this analysis is the first example of my method attempting to integrate narrative structure, philological detail, and social history, I will elaborate all its steps, hoping for the reader's patience.

The expression "virgin" or "virginity" that is usually seen as synonymous to "she had not known man" is used by Bath herself: she speaks. The passage is crucial to our understanding of the character's subjectivity and of the ideology of the text; it has to be quoted in full. First, the JPS translation: "And she said to her father: let this thing be allowed to me: let me alone two months, that I may depart and wander upon the mountains, and bewail my virginity" (11:37). All five commentators render *bethulah* as the direct object of the verb "to bewail."

A first doubt is cast upon the total synonymy between the two expressions by their frequent juxtapositions in the same sentence. Thus, in 21:12, the wife-hunters "found among the inhabitants of Jabesh-gilead four hundred young girls, 'virgins' that had not known man by lying with him." We have here the most explicit definition in the Bible of virginity and one in which apparent redundance seems to support the casual translations of one of its components by the whole concept. But then, we may wonder why it needs to be added that the virgins have not known man, and, specifically, by lying with him, if the noun *bethulah* signifies such a state alone. Of course, there are other solutions to this problem. BDB suggests to read the combination as "a naʿarah who is a betulah" (p. 143). As for the final clause, it is claimed to be a repetition from 21:11. Such suggestions are neither verifiable nor falsifiable, and my sole objection against them is that they are not challenging enough. I prefer to take the text at its letter, for no other than heuristic reasons, and see what can be done on that basis.

In other cases, it is either the one or the other expression that is used. In 19:24, for example, the old host proposes to the rapists: "Behold, my daughter the 'virgin' and his 'concubine'; I will bring them

out, and humble you them, and do with them what is good unto you."
Why would it be that the plunderers of Jabesh-gilead make such a
point of the young women's state of virginity, using the negative phrase,
while the host, here, only uses "virgin" and juxtaposes it to "concubine"? If virginity in the negative sense were at stake, the juxtaposition of the two women would hardly be commendable. For then,
virginity as a special attraction would make the concubine less than
acceptable as a trade for her owner's safety. Lot, for example, offers his
daughters in these terms: "they have not known man"; they are not
referred to by *bethulah* (Genesis 19:8). The difference in use, then,
suggests that what is offered in Gibeah is two women who are for some
reason suitable for the use that is required, rape that is. The aspect of
the daughter that allows her father to juxtapose her to the 'concubine'
is nubility, rather than virginity; she is available, rather than unused.

The second indication against the traditional translation and the
synonymy between the two expressions is the syntactical structure of
the sentence. As has been argued by Keukens (1982), the verb "to bewail" can also have a direct object. In such a case, the object would
carry the accusative particle *et*.[4] This is not the case. The verb "to bewail" (*bachah*) is used with the particle *et* in comparable cases in Genesis 37:35, Leviticus 10:6, and Deuteronomy 21:13. It refers, there, to
verbal expressions of complaint. For the intransitive use of the verb as
we have it here, the meaning "to lament," in some absolute sense, is
appropriate. The preposition *'al* may add an extra element. Again, my
purpose is not to decide a philological question but to take advantage
of its indecidability.

The preposition *'al* is one of the most elusive of all Hebrew pre-
positions. K&B list at least twenty-eight meanings for it, one of which
is the frequent confusion with *'el*, another preposition, for which the
dictionary gives twelve meanings. Our context here is helpful in that
it has another instance of *'al*. In the same speech to her father, Bath
uses the expression *'al-heharim* when she asks permission to go "to the
mountains." This repetition of the preposition before a three-syllable
noun suggests that there could even be a broken parallelism here
(Kugel 1981; Berlin 1985; Alter 1985). With the spatial referent, the
preposition refers to *direction*. In many other cases, it implies *confrontation*. If we combine these two features, we could wonder if the direction "to the mountains" involves also a confrontation with the
mountains, just as it does when the preposition is used in a military
context, where it comes to mean "against." The case that preoccupies
us here is strange in that it combines two opposed directions: "to go
down onto the mountains." But if we take the connotation of con-

frontation, this is not so strange. Our phrase could be modeled upon this first spatial one and translated into the temporal sphere as complementary to the spatial: to go "down" (emotionally) "toward the mountains" in order to be confronted with the solitude in the wilderness (the site of negative, "down" feelings, because threatening) and to lament "toward," in confrontation with, some temporal, parallel state, equally perceived as threatening. A comparable case is Judges 14:16–17, where Samson's bride weeps "before him" as it is usually rendered. Here, too, there is a confrontation: the woman needs information that Samson refuses to yield and tears are used as weapons—the case is both gender-related and close to the military.

Keukens (1982) argues that *bethulah* expresses the nubile state of a grown-up girl. It is a temporal indication of a phase of life: "Das Wort macht keine Angabe über die Unberhürtheit des Mädchen" [The word gives no clue about the untouched state of the girl]. The fact that virginity in the negative sense is clearly an important value for the Israelites, a value that determines the marriageability of a girl, is not necessarily relevant *for the girl* here.

If we take it that *bethulah* can refer to a life-phase, we can establish a series of nouns that also indicate a life-phase of the young woman. On the one side, then, there is the noun *na'arah*, young girl, which we have encountered in Judges 21:12. It seemed there very close to *bethulah*. My hypothesis is that the noun can refer to a phase of near-ripeness just preceding *bethulah;* in some contexts, it is perceived as its synonym, but its (subtle) difference from *bethulah* would be that the young girl it referred to was still in her father's power. Indeed, the wife-stealing scene in 21:12 is a violation of this property. On the other side, there is the *'almah*, the nubile, mostly already married woman, *before her first pregnancy*. Between "virgin" and "wife," the *'almah* is the already-given woman.[5] Her status is special in that she can still be repudiated; she has not yet proven to be worthy of her new state. As such, it is not a particularly enviable phase. Between the one, still possessed and protected by her father, and the other, already possessed by the husband, the *bethulah* is confronted with the passage from the one to the other. The transition from *na'arah* to *bethulah* and then to *'almah*, this whole transition so subtly subdivided by the language between the young woman as property of the father and property of the husband, is a phase of insecurity and danger. The young woman who fails to produce children will be the object of contempt, possibly of rejection. No wonder, then, that the transition is feared, rather than looked forward to. No preposition would be more fitting to express this directionality-in-confrontation than *'al.*

In this view, the state of *bethulah* is first and foremost that of a potential object of gift, a subject of insecurity. How will the girl be given, and to whom? How will her next phase, yet unknown to her, end?

If Bath had been given to a human victor, her fate would have been marriage. The phrase that she uses: "to lament in confrontation with my nubility," can be imagined as referring to a situation like Achsah's. After the victory, the father gives his daughter to the hero, and the daughter undergoes a transition. It is to this transition that an implicit allusion can be read in Achsah's story. When, after the victory, she is about to go to her husband, she comes to her father with her request. Where does she come from at that moment? It has been assumed that she came from some safe place where she had been hidden during the dangers of the battle (Slotki 1980, 159). This interpretation is totally fictional, since no evidence whatsoever supports it. Its underlying assumption is that nubile women need special protection, while, as other stories amply show, the women in general were not removed or provided special protection during a war. If anything, such an interpretation shows the critic's sensitivity to the issue of the young woman's status. In light of Bath's story, and the other similarities between the two stories, each dealing with the gift of a nubile girl, it seems more likely, or at least not impossible to me, that she came from a place "in the mountains," that is, from a phase of transition that prepared her for marriage.

Arnold van Gennep's concept (1960) of the rites of passage imposes itself here. The mountains are the wilderness that represents the transition from one life-phase to the next as from one world to the next. It represents the solitude the initiate has to undergo. This is expressed in Bath's request when she asks to be left alone for two months. The very request is part of the ritual: it is the girl's manner of accepting her gift, her goodbye to her father from whom she parts at the moment of her speech-act. In other words, her words are the accompanying ritual speech-act of the vow which gave her away.

The solitude is requested and delimited, in space and in time. Bath herself specifies the conditions of the ritual; it is her conception of what is her "normal" next phase. Moreover, Bath wishes to bring her friends. Usually, rites of passage are inflicted upon the entire age-group of the community. The friends may be assumed to be her age, to share her state. Both the friends and Bath will be *given away*, given to a man. The ripeness of the young women is going to be distributed by their fathers. They themselves have power only over the ritual that prepares them.

It is often noticed that Bath accepts her father's vow, indeed, encourages him to fulfill it. What critics call her "wisdom" (Boling 1975, 207) may be seen in a different light now. The praise to Bath is couched by J. J. Lias in contradictory terms: "No language is sufficient to do justice to the nobleness of this devoted woman. There are no lamentations, no reproach . . ." (Slotki 1980, 258). Language's impotence is unwittingly invoked, and rightly so, by the critic who then displays it himself. For lamenting is, precisely, what Bath chooses to use her last months for. Submission is interpreted as wisdom or as devotion to the cause of the nation. The submission cannot be denied. It can be read as slightly cynical if we realize that protest would be futile. Being narratively circumscribed as the absolute object, Bath can only act within, not against that position. Knowing that her father owns her, and owes the victor his daughter, she will, in any case, have to go through the transition that awaits all *bethuloth*. She cannot protest; neither can Achsah, nor Bath's friends. But she can lament, and that is what she intends to do, in spite of Boling's and many others' admiration for her refraining from it.

The question that arises at this point is that of the status of the discourse uttered by this character. Her speech is embedded in narratorial discourse. Would the narrator, who does use the other expression, let his character walk away with her language that he could then only obediently quote? Of course, this ancient text is not a modern psychological novel. I view this differentiation of expressions in relation to the oral background of these texts. Just as the formulation of Jephthah's vow is structured according to the standard principles of ritual vows, just so, Bath's discourse is modeled on the kind of language applicable to young women in transition. The discourse fragments were part of the culturally available formulas that narrators had at their disposal. It is not even certain that the composer of this text understood the full extent of the meaning of this "female" language, or that he worried about understanding it.

The phrase, like many others, can be compared to those wandering rocks, glacial tilts that traveled with the ice toward a new and alien world where they were put to a use foreign to their origin. They were used to form tombs, for example. Out of their original context, understood only within the new context, yet indestructable—such wandering rocks are like female ritual language as we have it here.

If the concept of *bethulah*, then, is related to the future of the subject, the idea expressed as "she had not known man" refers to the past. We may now be convinced that the two expressions interpreted as virginity are not synonymous. The concluding phrase of the narrator's account of Bath's fate is usually interpreted as referring to the unfulfilled life of Bath. Having known no man, then, means that she had not produced children. The interpretation is, again, supporting and even overdoing the patriarchal tenor of the text, in that it is based on the narrator's expression alone, ignoring Bath's own view. This conclusion leaves us with the next problem: why the negative phrase, and why this particular distribution among male and female speakers?

The negative expression is, I have suggested, related to the value of the girl as a possible wife. The Benjaminites, in chapter 21, have to be provided with wives, and those women have to be "pure" of prior possession. Needless to say, this value is embedded in the relations between men. The most common interpretation of this value is derived from the defiling effect of sexual intercourse (Douglas 1966; Wenham 1983). There seems to be more at stake here, as I will argue shortly. The use of the expression as the concluding one in Bath's life-story can be considered as the appropriate response of the narrator to the value of the gift. The girl just sacrificed was marriageable, and doubly so: physically nubile—her status as a subject—and morally pure—her value as an object. If Bath herself seemed only concerned with her future, the end of her childhood, and the next phase of her life, the male narrator is more interested in the extent of the sacrifice and in its specific value. His statement makes the gift the one appropriate in the case of a victory accomplished by delegation—by Yahweh, not by the *gibbor*. It places Bath in the same category as Achsah.

Conflating the two expressions in one idea of virginity, as it is seen today, is an act of repression and destruction of the wandering rock that is a leftover of other traditions, adopted without being understood, to be subsequently erased. We may see the difference between the two conceptions grow, indeed, grow out of hand, in the further analyses of this study. But more important is the imperceptability of its expression. The analysis of Freud's essay will show to what extent this is part of the problem of "virginity" itself as a cultural concept. In the next section, I will propose an excursus on this classical text of our culture, which will then, in the subsequent sections, be brought in confrontation with the biblical story of virginity. Thus I hope to show, first, that the concept of virginity is an inherently contradictory, confused projection of male concerns, and, second, that modernity is in no way superior, more advanced, or more rational than the ancient culture it proudly adopts as its predecessor, but just as equally and proudly considers as "less advanced" or as, to use Freud's own terms, "primitive." Rather than as a scholarly master discourse, Freud's text will be seen as a companion piece of Judges, and Freud as a partner of Jephthah. The result of the analyses of this chapter as a whole is hoped to be a clearer understanding of both.

Freud Entangled

The difficulty which Freud experienced in defining feminity, as has often been argued, is due to his confusion of male and female perspectives. The basic confusion is between castration anxiety and penis envy (Jacobus 1986). The result of confusion is entanglement and discursive impotence. Not only does Freud lose sight of virginity; he cannot refrain from leaping over and over again to its opposite, the object of Freud's dread, whom I will designate the post-virginal woman. The Book of Judges displays a similar identification between these two opposite categories of womanhood.

The taboo of virginity refers to the attempt of "primitive man" to avoid deflowering his own wife. A second theme, announced in the beginning of the essay, is the behavior opposed to taboo, yet acknowledged as similar, namely, the high value placed on virginity in "civilized" ideology. Central, then, is what these two behaviors have in common: defloration, as a male act, or as a female experience, or both. Danger becomes the next theme. Then he goes on to the discussion of frigidity. Penis envy, the traditional explanation of everything female, is the final and decisive subject discussed. The assumed relation between penis envy and virginity remains unexplored.

The rhetoric of the essay is interesting. It is set in a properly scientific, objective tone, far more scholarly than Judges' historiographic discourse claims to be.

> The demand that a girl shall not bring to her marriage with a particular man any memory of sexual relations with another is, indeed, nothing other than the logical continuation of the right to exclusive possession of a woman, which forms the essence of monogamy, the extension of this monopoly over the past. (Freud 1957, 193)

The scientific vocabulary ("logical") is symptomatic for the conflation of scientific discourse and personal commitment, just as in sacred historiography. What is logical here is already "justifying" in the next sentence. The juridical terms "right" and "monopoly" are notable, but what is perhaps most striking is the cognitive word "memory" with its complement "past," which substantiates it. It reminds us of the biblical description of virginity from the male perspective: to have known no man.

We are used to interpreting the biblical expression "to know" (*yada^c*) as a simple, if euphemistic, synonym for sexual intercourse. When read against Freud's description of the motivation for the valuation of virginity, "to know" does not mean sex, but sex means "to know." The importance of sex is the knowledge which comes as a result. The loss of innocence is the loss of ignorance, as the story of the paradise of Eden and its loss has taught us.[6] The fact that knowledge rather than, for example, defilement is at stake is consistent with the concern about "right" and "monopoly." This meaning of sex as knowledge is, in the valuation of virginity, extended to the past. Thereby, knowledge becomes memory.

I do not think that the Hebrew expression for sexual intercourse is a euphemism, an expression that softens the crudeness of its content. I think that it is a specification that sharpens the content. The expression conveys the threat involved in sexual intercourse with someone other than the exclusive possessor; such experience provides the knowledge that turns the woman who experiences it into an *other*, an autonomous subject. It is that subjectivity which comes with sexual experience that, apparently, threatens the exclusivity of the possession. But the extension of the monopoly over the past results in the conflation of the husband with the father. This is a major concern in the Book of Judges.

In the paragraph following the first one just quoted, Freud explains the value of this ignorance of the newly wed woman. It produces bondage, a bondage that "guarantees that possession of her shall continue undisturbed." The word "bondage" points to Freud's bad conscience. Not only is bondage the result of longlasting repression ("held in check") of desire in the young woman; it is subsequently explained as an "unusually high degree of dependence and lack of self-reliance," qualities that are exceptional ("unusual"), hence, rhetorically hardly appropriate for generalization. They are, however, generalizable if one acknowledges the systematic oppression of women, or if, as Freud does, one writes about women as a class. They are also negative, pointing at a state of neurosis. The consequence of this is that *every* woman is both exceptional and sick.

The problem raised *re* bondage is seemingly solved by a shift from the feminine to the masculine form.[7] The "bondage in the woman" is explained as neurotic and excessive in the masculine, unmarked form. When the critical phase of expression of the negative side of bondage is passed, the author can shift back to the feminine problem of virginity. "Some measure of sexual bondage is indeed, indispensible to the maintenance of civilized marriage and to holding at bay the polygamous tendencies which threaten it." Theory takes most bluntly the side of the man whose interest in the ignorance, the absence of memory, of his wife receives yet another motivation: knowledge, indeed, would threaten his monopoly. Apparently, there is something to know out there that would drive his wife away from him. The basic insecurity expressed in this ideologeme (Jameson 1981),[8] wherein "to know" comes to mean "to know better," is at work in Judges, most clearly in the Samson story. It turns out to be crucial for the understanding of virginity. That Freud shares this ideologeme is suggested by the strange oblivion regarding the difference between monogamy in the present, where the "right to exclusive possession" does not include previous and future relationships, and its absolute, now obsolete form that requires virginity. I contend that Freud hits exactly the core concern of Judges. The automatic collocation[9] of the issue of the "threat" of polygamy and of virginity shows to what extent Freud himself adopts the ideologeme that extends monogamy from present to past.

The link between overcoming resistance and sexual bondage makes Freud identify the value of virginity with its male version, that of overcoming impotence. The identification facilitates the subsequent step of equating virginity and frigidity that will be the leading theme in the major section of his essay. Before that shift occurs, however, Freud makes the transition from valuation to taboo of virginity, which, in his view, parallels the distinction between "primitive" and "civilized" man. He relativizes that distinction only slightly by noting that "for them [civilized man], too, defloration is a significant act." The use of the noun "act" instead of "happening" or "experience" stresses the subject involved; hence, it points to a male perspective. This shift entails another one: not only is the projected female perspective of resistance and bondage replaced by the male perspective of the partner of the deflowered virgin; the shift from feelings to action, implying a change of narrative level, entails a radically different issue. Unlike the value of virginity with its promise of attachment and monopoly, the taboo concerns the act itself.[10] It is this shift that brings forth the idea of hostility. Already, in introducing the topic, Freud betrays, by the very choice of the noun "act," where the source of all his confusion lies: an unconscious feeling of guilt.[11] What the "primitive" man carefully avoids, while the "civilized" man claims it to be his right, is the act which hurts the woman. The rites of defloration-avoidance do not affect the young woman. She will be deflowered anyway, made available, become an ʿalmah, whoever performs the act. The difference counts only for the man: does he, or does he not, accomplish the "act"? That is the question.

Two aspects remain undiscussed here. First, the stand-in of the groom, in societies where defloration is performed by someone other than the groom, is some member of the community. Hence it is noticeable that the man, in his dread, does not stand alone. Unlike "civilized" man, "primitive" man receives collective support. Hence, the taboo is socially consecrated; so too must be its motivations. Second, and related to this, we may wonder why the "act" is often performed either by an older woman or by other, older men. In the latter case, a mock-coitus follows the perforation of the hymen. As Freud notices, splitting the "act" into two parts is significant. If the man dreads defloration because he knows it will hurt the woman, there is no reason for the mock-coitus. It seems helpful to distinguish these two aspects, as Freud proposes but fails to do. Among several peoples, defloration is performed by the father of the bride (Freud 1957, 195); in other tribes it is done by professional deflowerers.

Among "civilized men" today, the father of the bride is still the one who gives away his daughter as part of the marriage ceremony.[12] We have seen how frequently this occurs in Judges. The relation between this prerogative of the father, which Freud later supports with allusions to the *ius primae noctae* of medieval suzerains, and the social support for the avoidance-rite, as exemplified by the professionalization of the "act," points to a collective concern, a sharing of the dread and, more importantly, a justification of it. Thus, it becomes more and more plausible that texts with a collective importance like the Bible deal with these concerns.

The crux of the essay is the circular argument from the woman's feeling via the male act to the male feeling that inspires his guilt, its projection onto the woman, and thus, ultimately, her hostility. From lasting bondage, defloration leads to lasting hostility; from a value, virginity becomes a danger. From a danger to the woman who is subjected to it, it becomes a danger to the man, subjected to the subjection of the woman who, from an innocent and ignorant virgin, becomes overnight a deadly, phallic woman. By the time we reach the second half of the essay, the prototype of the virgin has been named Judith.[13] This character of the apocryphal biblical book is frequently compared with Delilah and Yael, the two named lethal women of Judges. This is how we will return, via the detour of Freud's entanglements, to Bath, who no longer stands alone, but finds unexpected company.

Once the act is put in the center, and once the man who dreads accomplishing it stands in for the man who claims his right to do so,

Freud sets out to inquire why it is that this dread of virgins is so strong and so general. There is no more attempt, from here on, to understand the virgin herself, until the next reversal takes place in the last section. A first reason, the taboo of blood, is evoked but rejected. When Freud remarks that menstruation is often seen as the possession of the young girl by an ancestral spirit, we cannot but think of the spirit of Yahweh, the indispensible yet insufficient gift to the *gibbor*. After rejecting this explanation, the second suggestion will be worked out more fully. When the fear of something "new and unexpected, something not understood or uncanny,"[14] comes up, Freud relapses into his confusions. First, the experience of defloration can hardly be more "new" for the man than for the woman; the fact that it is *her* defloration that is at stake, while most societies do not require virginity of men, suggests the opposite. Second, while the equation of "new" and "unexpected" may not be obvious, that of "not understood" and "uncanny" is telling. Again, the cognitive dimension is crucial and relates exclusively to the male perspective. The woman who undergoes defloration may not understand what happens to her, but she does not find herself uncanny.

Freud's statement that "the dangers which the anxious man believes to be threatening him never appear more vivid in his expectation than on the threshold of a dangerous situation" underscores the fact that the dangers are never absent—only more acutely present at the defloration scene. The statement surpasses the problem of newness and declares not only defloration, but sex in general, to be dangerous. Defloration is, then, only the beginning of a dangerous situation that will continue afterwards, albeit to a lesser degree. Instead of pursuing the line of his own thought, Freud starts a new paragraph, quotes the name of a colleague, and renders the latter's idea—which amounts exactly to my conclusion drawn from Freud's own statement—as correct, but still not his own. The idea, indeed, is difficult to acknowledge. It holds that sexual intercourse in general is taboo.

"One might almost say," Freud continues ambiguously, either rendering Crawley's or his own conclusion, "that women are altogether taboo" (Freud 1957, 198). Indeed, one might. Judges seems to do so. Women are taboo, hence, they have to be killed; women are taboo because they kill. But this is skipping several stages.

The next step renders more explicit man's dread of women. This "generalized dread of women" (p. 198) may be based on the fact of sexual difference, says Freud, for difference, being mysterious, is "strange and *therefore* apparently hostile" (p. 198; my emphasis). What in this sentence is still only apparent becomes "justified" two sentences later, where Freud offers this central observation: "[. . .] *realization* of the influence which the woman gains over him through sexual intercourse, the *consideration* she thereby forces from him, may *justify* the extent of his fear" [my emphasis]. The clear-cut misogyny that is provided with a justification in this statement is motivated by the existence of the woman as subject. The fact that she becomes entitled to consideration, in other words, that she has to be taken into account, to be listened to, that she is a full subject, *justifies* fear. Freud does not seem to realize that, far from explaining the phenomenon under consideration, he only describes it, legitimates it, and partakes of it. No wonder that it is at this point that he invokes his theory of the castration complex in support of this view.

Speaking in the objectifying third person, Freud states:

> Psychoanalysis believes that it has discovered a large part of what underlies the narcissistic rejection of women by men, which is so much mixed up with despising them, in drawing attention to the castration complex and its influence on the opinion in which women are held. (p. 199)

But scared by the slip that once again rendered the problem one of men rather than of women, the author draws back since "these latter considerations have let us range far beyond our subject." The word "narcissistic" in the last quotation serves as the semantic shifter. It is a narcissistic injury indeed to acknowledge the narcissistic injury that comes with the castration complex; Freud is caught in his own theory, and by his very incapacity to apply it rigorously, he gives evidence of its validity. A new, false start is needed, one that leads to female hostility, to female narcissism, to female defensiveness (p. 201) as a motivation for female behavior which justifies the male taboo. Freud cites cases where "the woman gives unconcealed expression of her hostility towards the man by abusing him, raising her hand against him or actually striking him" (p. 201). The almost biblical language ("raising her hand against him") still avoids the question of the source of this hostility. Freud simply repeats the concept of narcissism, this time, of course, female. Penis envy, supposedly a female attribute but in fact a male projection, is the surprising origin of the male taboo of virginity. It all leads back to the man; his better penis causes it, hence, it is only fair that it falls back on him.

But penis envy refers to the little girl rather than to the virgin. It also refers to the father. We have met the father, in the tribes where he took the "act" on himself. Is Jephthah one of those? The father being the first love-object of the little girl, he is the real lover. "The husband is almost always so to speak only a substitute, never the right man; it is another man—in typical cases the father—who has the first claim to a woman's love, the husband at most takes second place" (p. 203). Again, at the crucial turn of the argument, slips abound. The father is here conflated with the daughter: he does not receive the love, but has only a claim to it. He is the desiring subject of this scenario. But more interestingly, the father is conflated with the husband. In the "primitive" tribes, it was the father who stood in for the husband, precisely because he had no stake in the defloration. Or had he? The real interested party, here, being the father, it should be the husband who would accomplish the defloration in order to save the love for the father. We begin to wonder, now, whether the story told is the father's or the husband's fantasy.

The following step will not answer this question but deepen it, while leading us back to Jephthah. The neat association with "Tobias-nights" rests on a reversal again. Freud sees it as "an acknowledgment of the privilege of the patriarch" (p. 204).[15] The young woman is no longer supposed to be fixated on her old love for her father; it is now explicitly the father who claims his rights. The conflict is one between father and young man over the daughter/bride. The Tobias story, although including a father figure, does not in the least put the father in competition with the son over the woman; the story dramatizes the son's glory over the father, whom he castrates/blinds and, after overcoming his fear of virginity, manages to cure.

The father, however, does not remain the surrogate husband; he is replaced in his turn. This seems consistent with the assumption that he is the one who loves, claims rights, and, hence, has reasons to fear: "It agrees with our expectations, therefore, when we find the images of gods included among the *father-surrogates* entrusted with defloration" (p. 204; my emphasis). Between God and the husband his daughter "has not known," Jephthah looks very much like the father who, in this Freudian fantasy, is caught between the two positions. He has to give his almost nubile daughter away, but to whom, and who will be responsible for what happens? And where lie his claims, his desires?

What is virginity? Freud does not tell us. Constantly confusing the issues involved, he remains—the word is appropriate—impotent. He is caught in, entangled with, the inextricable web of value and taboo, of male dread and female pain, confusing the little girl and the mature woman whom he then calls immature by a synecdoche. He confuses the little boy and his castration anxiety with the woman who threatens him in his fantasy. Sex becomes hostility in general; resentment for specific injury is equated with aggression. The real and the

imaginary belong to the same order, as do the material and the psy-
chic. Both past and present are mixed up, as are memories of the one
and fear for the other. Above all, the virgin is confused with the post-
virginal woman. "To know man" thus becomes the equivalent of "a
man has known her"; hence the male dread. If virginity cannot be defined because of all these confusions, perhaps it is because, in this view,
virginity itself *is* the confusion.

The image we get from this essay is one of an unbearable confrontation. According to its author, the taboo of virginity—this complex of confusions, aggressions, entanglements, and projections—is a
universal phenomenon. I don't believe it is, but the case of Freud's own
discourse shows that it is deeply rooted in our culture. The hypothesis
that the culture of Judges, different as it is from our own, struggles with
these same problems, may illuminate the issues at stake in the murders
of young, nubile girls at the moment of their gift. Defloration entails a
whole series of changes in the woman's life. Her subjectivity is systematically denied; her love is claimed by two men who compete for her,
over her; the moment of givenness is the beginning of a state where
her subjectivity will be constantly undermined by male fear. If a girl
knew what awaited her at her coming of age, in the fantasies and fears
of the men she will have to deal with, she would have every reason to
take two months, to go into the mountains, and to lament.

Love at First Sight

With the Freudian entanglements in mind, Jephthah's encounter with
his already vowed-away daughter becomes revealing. First presented as
an object of speech, Bath is now the object of focalization (11:34).
Again, the commentators point out where the problems lie. The JPS
(Slotki 1980, 257) translates: "And Jephthah came to Mizpah unto his
house, and behold, his daughter came out to meet him with timbrels
and with dances; and she was his only child; beside her he had neither
son nor daughter." Soggin (1981) adds an element that deserves attention: "she was his only child, *much loved.*" The modifier also appears in
Slotki's commentary, where this meaning of the word *yeḥidah* is de-
fended by analogy to the case of Isaac. We will take a closer look at the
quasi-sacrifice of Isaac, radically different as it is from Bath's case, in
the next chapter. The analogy with Isaac is motivated for Slotki by the
existence of Ishmael, the son Abraham already had with Sarah's slave,
Hagar. Since Abraham already had a son, Slotki argues, Isaac cannot
be the only son. Therefore, the word *yaḥid* in Genesis 22:2 cannot mean "only" but must denote "a favorite child" (Slotki 1980,

257). Modern logic is called to obscure an ideologically disturbing message. It is Yahweh who, in Genesis 22:2, uses the word; in the eyes of the twentieth-century scholar, the bypassing of the older child is unfair; hence, he is not willing to ascribe it to the deity. The story of Abraham's sons, however, makes the preference for Isaac an obvious issue and does not allow us to deny that Yahweh is participating in the rejection of the son who, like Jephthah, has no solid legal ancestry.[16] Isaac is called the only child with a clear purpose: to convey that Ishmael does not count.

The philological twist is even more questionable because in Genesis 22:2 the phrase "the one you love" is added to the modifier yahid. The two expressions may very well have an explanatory relation: the son is loved *because* he is the only son. As we know, Abraham had been promised numerous descendants, although he remained childless until a very advanced age. The only son, then, is the only means to realize the promise. The "love" referred to seems, then, closely related to the interest of the history of the patriarch. Indeed, Abraham's status as patriarch, his very being in other words, depends on this son. The son is part of himself. The modern idealization of love is hardly appropriate to express this motivation, although male love may be shaped by it. Being the only son guarantees Isaac the protection the father owes to himself. This is how forms of male love shape male identity through the father's domination.

In Judges 11:34, the modifier yehidah does not receive such a complement. The daughter is bound to the father by interests other than patrilineal descent: namely, by possession. As a daughter, she cannot provide her father with sons. Or can she? As the verse stands, the modifier "only" without its complement receives an altogether different meaning. Where it held protection for Isaac, it holds exposure for Bath. She is not simply "only"; she is alone. She is the only child, the only one to come out of the doors of the house, the only one to confront the father. No one protects her—no God, no mother, no father. She seeks relief within the constraints of the solitude assigned to her: "leave me alone" will be her reply in the next verse.

The verse quoted above (11:34) poses a second problem to the translators, this one not of the subject's definition but rather of its sheer delimitation. What they all translate as "beside *her* he had neither son nor daughter" is literally "from *him*" or "besides *him*." Slotki (1980) gives interpretations by rabbis who argue that Jephthah had adopted other children but that Bath was the only one "from him" (Kimchi) or even, that he was completely childless: "from himself" he had no child; the girl was his stepdaughter (Malbim). Soggin, with his usual casualness, states: "MT has 'apart from him' but this has to be corrected to *sebirin*" (1981, 214). Boling presents the same conjecture, with the addition of an argument, however slight: "represents a contamination from the preceding *lo*, 'to him'" (1975, 208).

In the light of so much certainty about what the text *should* mean rather than what it *could* mean, it seems tempting to explore the possibilities of interpreting the text as it stands, not because the text is always right,[17] but because the motivations for assuming errors are often all but scholarly. Without denying the possibility of error, I wish to explore the hypothesis that the unexpected masculine pronoun is either used deliberately or represents an error of a less innocent kind: a slip.

First, the preposition *min* denotes separation. Separated from him, the narrator writes regretfully, he had no child: no other child or—if we take the separation in the temporal sense, as the one to come—no child left. There is regret over the separation the father has to endure when he gives his daughter away. Reversing the temporal aspect, the separation is experienced as alienation of the self. In the sense of "beside," the illogical confusion between self and object that the phrase would entail, no longer sounds impossible after our reading of Freud's essay. The slip betrays the identification, the self-centeredness, the confusion that the next verse is to express with explicitness and pathos.

The identification represents the daughter as so much part of the father that he ceases to exist apart from her: her departure severs him from himself. The slip expresses an issue similar to, *and* different from, "the one you love" in Genesis 22:2. The contamination now is not linguistic but ideological. It becomes a figure that wonderfully expresses what is at stake in this encounter. As a *mise en abyme*, it shows us what Freud did not manage to say on the rational, scholarly level, but what he somehow touched upon on the discursive level: the core of virginity. The absolute property of the father, the virgin daughter does not only belong to him, as a metonymical extension of him; she is part of him, as a synecdochical integration, which causes her loss to be the loss of himself. His wholeness rather than hers is threatened with loss. As soon as the preposition *min* means not only spatial but also temporal separation, the temporal aspect introduced in the concept of separation reminds us of the meaning of Bath's request: let me lament in confrontation with my nubility. It is the separation to come that constitutes the *narrative of virginity*, of which Bath's story is the most dramatic representation.

A second feature of the verse that deserves some attention is its visual aspect, implied in the vow itself. The first one to *meet* Jephthah must be the first he sees. Has this optic dimension a more specific meaning? Is meeting, perhaps, deadly because it involves seeing? Seidenberg (1966) suggests as much on the basis of another temporal reversal. "Sacrificing the first you see," as the title of his paper rephrases the story, becomes "sacrificing the first you *saw.*" The sacrifice of the daughter ultimately represents for him the renunciation of the mother.[18] The replacement of the mother by the daughter presupposed by this reversal is in its turn based on the replacement of the daughter by the mother, performed by Freud in order to turn the virgin into the phallic mother. Freudian discourse allows for all these reversals, which it legitimizes by the term *overdetermination.* Judges 11:34, however, stresses a more pointed confusion. *Behold,* the oft-used narrative demonstrative that introduces a shift, or an extension, of focalization, is introduced here at a very specific moment of the narrative. From the moment of its utterance on, the question of whom the vow will concern has lingered, "looking forward" to the meeting of Jephthah and his victim, of vow and fulfillment, of present and future. The visual image now emerging fills in this anxious expectation. The clause *vehinne bitho* forms one rythmical unit. Parallel with "behold, his daughter," I would therefore read: behold his-daughter! Identifying with the position of the focalizer Jephthah, who has so much interest in the content of his view, the reader holds her breath. What is *seen* is none other than *bitho,* his-daughter. Father and daughter expressed in one word, the one that, according to Boling, triggers the contamination we have just discussed.

Enhanced by the suspense of her slow introduction, and by this pointed word that inserts the visual aspect of the scene, Bath is the object of vision rather than the subject of the action that follows. Thus read, the following part of the sentence becomes less verbal and more descriptive. "Behold, his-daughter! She comes out to meet him with timbrels and dances." The scene we witness consists of a hero and a virgin brought together for a celebration. The scene repeats the promise of the gift of Achsah and represents a rehearsal of the dancing maidens of Shiloh. What is more, the host at Gibeah will also say, "behold my-daughter." What we see may be less a victory ritual than a wedding. And as the contamination of "him" and "her" has already revealed, it is the wedding that destroys the father. He "knows" that the dance celebrates not him but the real victor, to whom the daughter is due, the real *gibbor,* to whom she is to be given because she will soon be *bethulah,* nubile, and torn away from him. The ultimate displacement in this scene is the threat of the replacement of the father by the still abstract husband. It is a replacement that becomes unavoidable with the approach of *bethulah*, unless a way is found to avoid it. That avoidance is, at least, what Jephthah is trying to bring about.

The text pursues this line in the further enhancement of the visual aspect, the *view* of the daughter: "And it came to pass, when he saw her . . ." The meeting, her coming out of the doors of the house, was a spectacle rather than an act, its account, a description rather than a narration.[19] The crucial event of the entire vow-and-fulfillment episode, the moment of decision, is inscribed in this verb: when-he-saw-her. It is here that his awareness of the consequence of the victory, of his appeal to an ally more competent and more heroic than himself, of his giving away of the status of *gibbor*, is brought about. No wonder the view makes Jephthah "rend his clothes," the ritual gesture of mourning.[20] This symbolic gesture serves as a shifter between the two isotopies of the victory ritual and the wedding. Jephthah is not the first biblical hero to rend his clothes both for death and for non-death, for losing a child to death or to sexuality, to maturity, or to autonomy. Jacob had the same reaction upon *viewing* what could just as well have been the evidence of defloration, but which he took for proof of Joseph's death.[21] Jephthah's speech develops the confusion we have seen already: "Alas, my daughter, *you* have caused me to kneel, and *you* have become the cause of my undoing. For *I* have opened my mouth unto Yahweh . . ." (11:35). At first sight, the reversal here is a simple case of "blaming the victim." The attitude displayed is rightly criticized by many. In the light of the above it becomes consistent that Jephthah blame his daughter, not, of course, for celebrating his victory but for being prepared to marry the real victor, for being ready to leave him, in other words: for reaching *bethulah*. The meeting between father and daughter becomes a confrontation in time: the confrontation with the transition, with the impossibility of postponing the gift of the daughter that will destroy the identity of the father.[22] It is this confrontation that is then played out in the ritual, which is thus provided with a negative emotional load also for the father: *down* to the mountains.

It will indeed destroy the father's identity, as is shown by so many interpretations which see in the lament of the daughter the expression of regret of childlessness. Such an interpretation is, again, based on a conflation of father and daughter. It is a way of taking Jephthah's side. If, indeed, a woman's life receives meaning only through motherhood, it is because it is thus that she provides offspring to the father.[23] Within such a system, the daughter can only bring offspring to her father to carry on his memory if, like Tamar in Genesis 38, she becomes his bride: such is the consequence of a contradictory system which we will

soon come to understand. But this possibility is what Jephthah sacrifices. His memory will die out, not Bath's, if we are only ready to let it
happen so. In the next section we will see how she keeps her own
memory potentially alive; here, we are concerned with the separation
that causes Jephthah's grief.

The expression "*you* have caused me to kneel," interpreted as
"thou hast brought me very low" (JPS in Slotki 1980, 258) or as "you
have dealt me a deadly blow" (Soggin 1981, 213), rings an intertextual
bell. The JPS translation ignores it, smoothing the expression out as
metaphorical and cliched; Soggin renders only one, be it the most obviously relevant one, of its intertextual aspects. The Song of Deborah
uses the same root in the celebration of Sisera's destruction, and the
specific bodily aspects of the expression as it is used there reveal a concern with sexuality, powerlessness, and death. There, the expression
shifted the isotopies of sexuality, birth, and death onto one another.
Here, the deadliness may very well have a sexual overtone as well. The
loss of power implied in the root emphasizes that Bath's coming *bethulah* makes her father lose his grip, his possession over her. The link
between the accented pronoun and the causal verb-form does blame
Bath for something, but it is too strongly expressed to be sufficiently
explained as blaming the victim, especially since the following sentence stresses the father's own subject-position.

How can Jephthah possibly blame Bath for taking his power from
him, while he acknowledges having done that which has caused his
loss of power? It is only at this point that I am willing to introduce the
idea, overhastily proposed by Seidenberg (1966), that castration anxiety is involved. The noun "mouth" allows for a symbolic figure to
emerge. The standard expression for the mode of killing in a military
context is "the mouth of the sword" (e.g., 1:8). Jephthah the *gibbor*
has killed thousands of enemies with the mouth of the sword. Killing is
his speciality; it is part of his life, of himself. As Seidenberg appropriately has it: the soldier is *wed* to the sword (1966, 60)—wed to the
mouth of the sword, that is. The Hebrew expression makes the metaphor more pointed than it can be in English, where the expression runs
"the edge of the sword."

But the sword is not only a soldier's wife. It/she is also the instrument of castration. Not the sword itself, perhaps, but its cutting edge:
its mouth. Opening his mouth, Jephthah has brought about death. But
he sees himself as the victim. The reversal between himself and his
daughter/bride reflects the feeling of utter powerlessness revealed by
the expression "you have caused me to kneel." The separation "from

him" receives a new and quite concrete meaning: once castrated, Jephthah will, of course, have neither son nor daughter.

The reader who is still skeptical about this slightly fanciful figuration of castration is referred to the episode where Jephthah acts it out himself. Having learned, in the sacrifice of his daughter, how cutting words can be, the mouth of the sword is replaced by the mouth itself in a subsequent battle wherein Jephthah is still striving for the status of *gibbor*. In the famous *shibboleth* episode (12:6) Jephthah, far from refraining from verbal violence, employs it extensively.

But if Jephthah is both a failed killer, since he replaces himself by Yahweh, and a verbal killer, a killer "by the mouth" instead of "by the mouth of the sword," he comes to resemble those killers in the book who also kill by the mouth. Both Yael and Delilah destroy the men who choose to come too close to them by tricking them into uttering fatal words. They are generally considered seductresses, using, that is, the other "mouth" at their disposal. The mouth of the sword and the mouth of the female body come to resemble each other, in strategy and in effect.

In the final analysis, then, Jephthah becomes the Freudian virgin: the phallic mother. This can hardly surprise us, as Freud's essay and Judges 11 compete in confusion, identification, and conflation. Does Jephthah become what he fears most, desires most, and fails to understand? The reader who is still unwilling to see the castration-figure in the textual carpet will have to await chapter 5, where the deadly word will be more thoroughly discussed.

Bath's Survival

It is now time to see how the separation "from him" takes place. We have seen how the expression "to lament in confrontation with my nubility" radically changes the meaning of her request and its subsequent realization, focusing as it does on the future rather than on the past, on her subject-status rather than on her value as an object, on the female life-cycle rather than on male possession. The importance of the new translation is confirmed by the repetition, in verse 38, of the ambiguous preposition. Indeed, as if to enhance its goal-orientedness, the narrator now juxtaposes the spatial and the temporal use: "And she departed, she and her companions, and lamented in confrontation with her nubility in confrontation with the mountains" (*'al-bethuleyah 'al-heharim*). The mountains and the wilderness spatially symbolize time. The last sentence of the chapter, in narrating the end of Bath's story, exemplifies the point of the narrative, indeed, the motivation of the book. The passage is translated by the JPS (Slotki 1980) as follows (I italicize the words that will be discussed): "And it *was a custom* in Israel, that the *daughters* of Israel went yearly to *lament the daughter* of Jephthah the Gileadite four days in a year." The noun *ḥoq*, here "custom," allows for two groups of translations: (1) rule, law, prescription, and (2) duty, task. The difference between the two groups is in the involvement of the subject of action. The difference across the two groups is the degree of coercion exercised to obtain obedience. Thus, Joseph in Egypt, running the food supplies as well as Pharaoh's finances, establishes the rule? law? that one-fifth of every gain should be paid to Pharoah (Genesis 47:26). Between rule and law, there is the relative autonomy of the subject. If the subject accepts the rule as good for the public welfare, then we speak of a rule; if the subject is not consulted but the rule simply enforced, we have a law. In the second group of translations, the subject is supposed to act herself, not just to give, pay, or refrain from action. The duty, again, is enforced, while the task may include the subject's willing collaboration.

Bath's friends, her companions who go with her into the mountains, can be seen as the first generation of "daughters of Israel" who take it upon themselves to perform the task described in the concluding verse. Members of Bath's peer-group, they conceive of the "custom" as a task. The translation "task" enhances their subjective activity, while "custom" represents them in a more passive role. The noun "daughters" in combination with Israel is obviously referring to a social role. Similarly, the "sons of Israel" who do the fighting in the book are not the actual sons of Jacob; they are the collective subjects of the wars and the "going astray."[24] These social roles are part of the same category of metaphors as "father" and "mother," used sometimes by implication (the "sons of Israel" being the sons, the descendants of father Jacob-Israel), sometimes explicitly (Deborah calling herself a mother in Israel in the song). Being a "daughter of Israel," then, means having a specific place in society, a place in relation to the other categories, especially to the father. Bath's friends, near-nubile girls like herself, property of their own fathers, *accompany* ("companions") her, both in the spatial-evenemential sense (they go with her) and in the emotional-empathetic sense (they feel with, for her). The other, subsequent daughters of Israel extend this group further in time. Translating *ḥoq* as custom, then, is taking it in a rather flat, passive sense. What is left out is the *motivation* of the subjects performing the task.

What does the ritual consist of, and how does it make sense in relation to Bath's fate? The JPS translation "to lament" is one of those suspect near-unanimous ones; Boling has "to mourn." Soggin, translating the verb as "to commemorate," is the differing one that raises suspicion. And indeed, the verb in question, *tanah*, is not the one used earlier in the chapter for "to lament." It is the one that Deborah uses in 5:11 to celebrate Yahweh's righteous actions. There, the translation "to sing," used transitively as "to recount for celebration," is obvious. The commentators rightly assume that the occasion in the concluding verse of 11 is hardly appropriate for a cheerful celebration, although it is equally true that the wedding-isotopy in the encounter scene would make the ironic reversal of Bath's initial celebration activities plausible enough. But we do not want to use the tricky, all-too-slippery concept of irony prematurely.

The verb has as its central feature the speech-act that is also at stake in Deborah's song: to recount in order not to forget. The book, like the whole enterprise of historiography, is undertaken in order to "remember" by language, to fixate the history of the people in its beginnings, for deeply patriarchal motivations. *Tanah* is the oral counterpart of this endeavor. Memorialization, a form of afterlife, replaces the life that she has been denied. If interpreted in this manner, the verb *tanah* becomes of central importance both in this particular story and in the countercoherence of the book as a whole. It comes to stand for the female counterculture so little of which has been preserved, but whose crucial elements can be recovered.

We reach here yet another dimension of Freud's concern with memory. The verb "to remember," *zachar* in Hebrew, is also present in the modifier "male," which is, in Hebrew, *zachar*. Attempts to relate this word to a form meaning "penis" do not preclude at least homonomy. The concern with memory is either the original motivation for the word or part of its actual semantic content. With this word for maleness, the possibility of memorialization, of history, has become, not only a male necessity, but also a male prerogative, whether or not located in the penis. Where children receive the name of the father in order to establish the father's memory, the "virgins" of Mizpah and the daughters of Israel provide the anonymous daughter, all prepared for oblivion, as the only alternative form of survival within the limits of what is left over of the father's power. If writing history has become a male property, oral history can still be a female prerogative. That is the content of the "task" as of the Song of Deborah: to perform oral history, the history, in this case, of Bath-Jephthah. If the sons of Israel make history by fighting wars and going astray, the daughters of Israel recount the price that such a history requires. What has happened must not be forgotten.

The interpretation sketched above is further supported by the use of the particle/preposition *le*. The "neutral" translation "to lament the daughter" leaves aside the twice repeated *le* that introduces the infinitive of the verb and the object of the action the verb depicts. The rules of grammar do not forbid us to enhance the preposition. Thus the first *le*, "to," becomes "in order to," "with the purpose of"; the second, "for," "on behalf of." The daughters went yearly [to the mountains] in order to pay their tribute to Bath, in order to sing, and by singing, to verbally commemorate on behalf of the daughter. The difference between the traditional translation, which leaves everything as flat and as "neutral" as possible, and mine, which enhances the interests of the daughter, produces the space between what the text may allow and what modernity has done to it—between the wandering rocks and the tombs built with them: "And it was a custom in Israel / and it became a task for Israel / that the daughters of Israel went yearly to lament / in order to recount / the daughter of Jephthah the Gileadite / on behalf of Bath-Jephthah the Gileadite / four days in a year" (11:40). The philological problem of the "except for him" that philology changes into "except for her" is yet deepened by this final phrase of the story. The slip comes true: Jephthah eliminated himself from the survival by commemoration that befalls his daughter. The daughter separated from him will be the only beneficiary of the oral history. Born from a "harlot," killing the virgin-daughter, Jephthah can only return to war and try again to become a *gibbor*, replacing by personal might and heroism the place in history he cannot achieve through the father-line. That is, indeed, what the second half of the Jephthah story is about—the half of the story where no daughter is present.

The critic who suggests that Bath's anonymity is deserved as a punishment because she too readily submitted to her father's desire instead of protecting herself, as was her duty (Seidenberg 1966, 55–56), misses this dimension. The daughter cannot but submit; within the limit assigned to her, however, she exploits the possibility left open to her. Using oral history as a cultural means of memorialization, she makes her fellow virgins feel that solidarity between daughters is a task, an urgent one, that alone can save them from total oblivion. Although she can only be remembered as what she never was allowed to overcome, as Bath-Jephthah, it is she and not the man who does have a proper name who is remembered. She is remembered as she was, in submission to the power of her father, a power over life and death, exclusive possession, which he decided to exercise until death did them part.

CHAPTER THREE
VIRGINITY SCATTERED

Ist es möglich, dass alle diese Menschen eine Vergangenheit, die
nie gewesen ist, ganz genau kennen? Ist es möglich, dass alle
Wirklichkeiten nichts sind für sie; dass ihr Leben abläuft, mit
nichts verknupft, wie eine Uhr in einem leeren Zimmer? Ja, es
ist möglich.
> Rainer Maria Rilke

The Book of Judges is full of virgins. Collective virginity is at stake in
the bride-stealing scenes at the end of the book, as in the formulaic
transitional narratives already quoted in the previous chapter: the
mini-narratives of the "sons" taking and giving "daughters," exchang-
ing virgins with other, pagan tribes. Each of these groups of women
shares some features with Bath. The women who are exchanged with
alien tribes are given away like Bath; the abducted women are selected
for their "virginal purity" or are confronted by the male aggressors
while the women are peacefully dancing and celebrating.

The male view of virginity predominates in the first of the two
stealing scenes that close the book. It may not be a coincidence that
the very scene that spells out this conception of virginity, the bride-
stealing, is described within the isotopy of war and violence. It is one
of the instances where the political coherence meets the countercoherence, and as a consequence, violence increases:

> Go and smite the inhabitants of Jabesh-gilead with the mouth of the
> sword, with the women and the little ones. And this is the thing that
> you shall do: you shall utterly destroy every male/memory, and every
> woman who has known man lying with a male/memory. And they found
> among the inhabitants of Jabesh-gilead four hundred young girls, nubile
> women who had not known man by lying with a male/memory, and they
> brought them to the camp of Shiloh which is in the land of Canaan.
> (21:10–12)[1]

69

The insistent use of *zachar* stresses the interest of the relation between the war and the reproduction of the "sons of Benjamin" for whose sake this scene is staged. We cannot but remember Freud's opening slip: the demand that a girl shall not bring to her marriage with a particular man any *memory* of sexual relations with another is taken here at face value.

Even in a case like this one, where the issue at stake is primarily reproduction of a tribe threatened with extinction, there can be no question of using married women, although they may be more fertile. Nor can the *ʿalmah*, the young, recently married but not yet pregnant woman, apparently do the job. Both the rival males as well as the memory of them has to be "utterly destroyed." So great is, in this male (*zachar*) view, the importance of the history of the people, as distinct from any other people, that the marriageable women have to be "pure" of memory, perpetuating only the sons of Benjamin.

It needs little imagination to realize the consequences this attitude entailed for the marriageable women in question. Witnesses of the murder of all their relatives, including the "little ones," their little brothers and their young, prenubile *naʿarah* sisters, these terrified girls, stripped of their identity, are subsequently captured by the murderers and "brought" to the camp where they will be forced to "know man by lying with a male/memory." Bath's wish for a transition between childhood and such a fate seems only too justified; her fate of being given to death rather than taken by a husband seems almost enviable, if we compare it to that of these four hundred young girls, sister-virgins.

Abduction in war is followed up by abduction in peace. This second "selection" scene enhances the moment of virginity when the girl is handed over from father to husband. Qualified often enough as a "merry ending" of the book,[2] this scene shows murder being replaced by festivity. But the role of the male remains the same. The young, nubile daughters dance, and dancing girls are marriageable; they are to be given away or taken by the warriors. As in the confrontation between Bath and her father, the visual aspect of the scene is stressed, this time twice: "Go and lie in wait in the vineyards, and *see*, and *behold*, if the daughters of Shiloh come out to dance in the dances, then come out of the vineyards and catch every man his woman of the daughters of Shiloh" (21:20–21). Not only do we recall the encounter between Jephthah and his daughter/bride/victim, whose spectacle as dancer entailed the desperate realization of her nubility, but this "merry" scene also extends the scopophilic relation between marriageability, availability, and seeing to the more familiar modern-day relation between voyeurism and rape.[3] Voyeurism, dramatized in the explicit order to the still-unprovided-for sons of Benjamin that they hide and look, is emblematic of the dissymmetry of power.

The sequence of actions, and the accompanying positions, deserves analysis. *First* the men hide and watch. *Then* the girls come out and dance. See and behold: catch. The order to capture the women comes as the consequence of the girls' dancing, rather than of the men's watching without being seen. The girls, like all victims of rape, seem to provoke their abduction. They dance, they are to be watched, and: behold. The memory of the military slogan *veni, vidi, vici* imposes itself nicely.

These two abduction scenes, the violent one and the "peaceful" one, resemble Bath's fate in yet another aspect. They, too, are the consequence of a hastily performed speech-act. They occur because the other tribes had vowed "unto Yahweh" that they wouldn't give their daughters to Benjamin's sons because the "outrage at Gibeah" deserved such punishment. The mouth of the men has again been fatal for the women. The victim of Gibeah is "avenged" by the extension of the category of virgin victims.

Going astray: this was the transgression which, in the formulaic expression used in chapter one, made the nose of Yahweh catch fire. The exchange of women between Israel and the foreign tribes, and the religious counterpart of that transgression—"going after foreign gods"—is the basic wrong that produces, with its consequences and the attempts to repair the damage, the cyclical narrative in Judges. Now, at the end of the book, this transgression is narratively substantiated. The two abduction scenes are the answer to the problem created by the men's inappropriate speech and action. Deadly agents of action, the sons of Israel committed the outrage that entailed this intertribal war. Deadly agents of speech, they performed the over-hasty speech-act that threatens now to exterminate their brothers. The final scene represents the sons of Benjamin as master focalizers, as mastering, that is. The formulaic phrase of the beginning here receives its full narrative unfolding. Focalization, from "seeing" as "seeing the truth," has degenerated. The eye leads to abuse when it becomes the instrument of power, when it is conceived of as the *I*, the center of interest and power; when it becomes the site of exclusive male power, excluding the women whose lives are its object.[4]

Jephthah, the son of a "harlot" and the father of a marriageable daughter who cannot marry, embodies the limits of legitimacy. The sole virgin daughter who is allowed to counteract the fate of the virgins is also the only one to develop into a full narrative subject. She speaks when she verbalizes her request, she focalizes when viewing her state, and she acts out her ultimate potential. In other words: her limited position is fully exploited on the basis of her role and her activities. She occupies the exact middle of the book. Her ascension to narrative subjectivity enables her to organize her place in history. Yet her role is dissolved into an anonymous plurality. This scattering is further pursued and will now be countered by paradoxical yet meaningful identifications.

Paradoxes of Virginity

Our search for the "proper" meaning of the concept of virginity has led to the conclusion that it does not have a "proper" meaning, a center that would always be present. There is a male (property) and a female (proper transition) concept of virginity, and between them, as in the relation of power between the sexes, there can only be dissymmetry. The female view, oriented toward the future and toward integrating the nubile life stage within the whole life cycle, is buried in the plurality of features contained in the male view. The root *proper* is the only proper meaning the concept then retains, while it contains the confusions this word elicits in its turn (Derrida 1972, 107–12, 244). In the remainder of this study, the play on *proper* will guide us through the meanders of the father-husband-daughter relations which I claim as central to Judges. The virgin has no proper name, existing as she does only in the name of the father. She is his exclusive property. But property means both "feature" and "ownership." Ownership is metonymically related to feature: the virgin daughter's first and only feature is to be her father's daughter, her father's property. Here lies the justification of my choice for the "proper" name Bath, the only one that seemed proper, where the name subject has as her only property to be her father's property. But then, again, metonymically, the daughter is bound to the father as an ontological property: she is part of him, his synecdoche. Severed from him, she is no longer a virgin daughter, he is no longer a father. This leads to the last, and in today's culture the first, property of virginity: property as integrity, bodily wholeness, purity, cleanliness.

But again, there is no way to define this feature for the virgin herself, as distinct from the owner. Freud has shown us to what extent the defilement of sexuality has to be seen as symbolic. The memory of the other man is what makes the postvirginal woman unmarriageable. In the equally symbolic context of Levitical law, defilement is related to the loss of body liquid, of blood, for example, which represents a beginning of death.[5] Hence, it is the loss of semen, the male body liquid, that defiles the virgin at least as much as the one-time loss of blood at defloration, as indeed Leviticus 15:16–18 explicitly states. It is from this defilement that the virgin must be protected; if we take it that Judges partakes of these views, it is from this that she has to be purified, apparently, in sacrifice, by fire.

The view of virginity as "proper-ty" suggests that we take a brief look at a few other young women who will be the heroines of the next chapter: the first woman in Samson's nubile life, preceded by the anonymous mother who partakes of some of the features of virginity as well; the virgin daughter of the host of Gibeah, fellow-gift with the concubine; and the concubine herself, whose story will hold yet another surprise. Of these four women, one is an elderly woman and a married mother; another one is married off twice, once without consumation of the marriage, the second time, probably, "properly" married.[6] The third one is only mentioned, while the fourth, a concubine, is, at first sight—the first sight being our contemporary concept of concubinage—the proper opposite of a virgin: a defiled woman, without clear, proper status, held in low esteem, at least by modern critics. Yet all four share features with Bath and with the paradoxical concept of virginity.

Nonvirginal Virgins, Virginal Spouses

Throughout the Bible, the child of a woman long barren is a special gift of Yahweh, one destined to accomplish a divine purpose. Often it is stressed that it is the deity who "closes the womb" of the woman; the husband is powerless and acknowledges this (e.g, Genesis 18:12; 30:2; I Samuel 1:8). Within the countercoherence that I am sketching, the opposition between the powerful deity and the powerless men resembles the one between the father-owner and the husband whom the daughter is denied. Replacing the word "power" by its latinate synonym[7] turns powerless husbands into impotent men, and the powerful deity into the potent father. There are passages where this joke becomes slightly more serious. In the case of Abram/Abraham, the formulation of Sarah's doubt holds an explicit sexual meaning that is as often considered as dismissed but that questions Abraham's potency quite clearly: "After I am waxen old, shall I have pleasure, my lord being old, too?" (Genesis 18:12).[8] That it has to be the foreign guest, the messenger, who fertilizes[9] the woman further supports this interpretation. The story of Samson's conception holds details that relate the mother to virginity as presented throughout the book.

First, she is nameless. As a virgin, she has been handed over from father to husband but, not yet pregnant, she belongs to the category of *almah;* she is not yet a "proper" wife, a mother that is. Hardly is her barrenness[10] mentioned before the messenger of Yahweh appears—to her alone, it should be noted. The absence of the husband here may well signify his absence *as* husband. The pregnancy promised is bound to a condition. In fact, the divine father comes to take his daughter back, for the condition stated with the promise is a condition of purity. Symbolic defilement has to be avoided through strict rules about food and drink. Only a pure mother can bring forth a son upon whom the spirit of Yahweh shall come, so that he will be able to begin saving Israel out of the hand of the Philistines, the unclean, the uncircumcised. The vow of purity is the second feature of "property" assigned to this woman.

That the encounter between the woman and the messenger has a sexual aspect—if only symbolic, of course—is signified most subtly by her *knowledge.* Not only does she know that the messenger is divine, that he is from the father ("very terrible"); more importantly, in Freud's terms, she "brings to her marriage with a particular man memory of" the encounter. The woman's superiority of knowledge over her husband is demonstrated at several points in the chapter. Her knowledge, moreover, is fatal, in the double sense of the word. It predicts Samson's fate, and produces it, thus producing his death. Indeed, on her own initiative, the woman extends the Nazirite vow, thus requiring purity from Samson, not, according to the normal way, for a certain period of time merely, but "until the day of his death." From here on (13:8) Manoah, the husband, enters into a competition with the father, a competition, of course, that he can only lose.

When he asks the messenger to come tell him what has to be done, the messenger again appears only to the woman. He comes when she is outside the husband's house in the open field, alone: "and Manoah, her husband, was not with her." The woman's attempt to include her husband ("and the woman made haste and ran and told her husband . . .") is in vain: the messenger only wants to deal with the woman. The husband's question, "What shall be the rule for the child?" is referred back to the woman: "Of all I said to the woman let her beware." Purity is, indeed, a matter for "virgins," that is, for women in transition—*na'arah, bethulah,* or *'almah*—a matter between father and daughter. The husband may witness, but not participate in the pact between them. Like Abraham in Genesis 18, Manoah next proposes a meal. But Abraham was entitled to do so, since the messengers appeared to him. Sharing a meal is one way of consecrating a bond between father and son-in-law, while excluding the daughter.

Here again the messenger refuses the husband's plea for inclusion. Instead, he proposes that Manoah offer a burnt-offering to Yahweh. Reversing the situation of Jephthah and Bath, the messenger disappears in the smoke of the sacrifice. And again, the husband is impotent, does not *know* his wife('s knowledge). Seeing that the messenger came from the father, he is scared to death. His panic recalls Jephthah's terror. Again it is the woman who knows better, who sees the "logic" of the event that once more opposes the father and the to-be or not-to-be husband.

Calling Samson's mother a "virgin" in the male view, the property of the father and the proper, pure woman, is less of a paradox than it would seem if we remember that the status of the newly married woman who has not yet conceived is but one category removed from the nubile *bethulah*. It is also a quite acceptable idea if we recall the importance, in Freud's essay, of *fright* in the male relation to the virgin. This fright was, as we have seen, merely due to the fact that virginity is the man's own creation. Thus Judith, the childless widow who became the exemplary virgin, bears closer resemblance to Samson's mother than it may appear at first sight—or first fright. Both contribute to the delivery of Israel, kill a hero, do not conceive with their husbands—remaining the *almah* who embodies the transition between virgin and wife. Judith kills through seduction, which is, for Felman (1980), the speech-act par excellence. Samson's mother also kills through a speech-act, since she alters the messenger's speech, transforming it into a prediction; hence, from this perspective, she kills the hero who is not yet born. Judith has already killed her husband, who died before "defiling" her. If Judith beheads the *gibbor* Holophernes, this woman "beheads" the *gibbor* Samson verbally, extending the vow that rests upon his head to his death.[11]

The triangle between father, daughter, and husband dramatized in the prehistory of Samson, the exemplary *gibbor* of the book, is most surprisingly rendered in Rembrandt's painting called *Manoah's Offering*[12] (see fig. 3.1). In the preparatory drawing[13] called *Angel Announcing the Birth of Samson to Manoah* (see fig. 3.2), the husband is completely prostrated. Though kneeling, the woman figures a straight line, as does the messenger flying up. In the background, the little gate, right in the middle, can be taken to represent the womb whose entrance the messenger heads to, while the husband turns his back to it. The painting is different. The little gate has disappeared, while Manoah's attitude has changed, bringing him into a more central position. Both man and woman have their eyes closed, but the contrast in attitudes is telling. While the man closes his eyes in fright, his head facing toward the

Figure 3.1. Rembrandt, *Manoah's Offering.* Reproduced by permission of Staatliche Kunstsammlungen, Dresden.

woman, she, in turn, closes her eyes in intense communication with the deity, the father of her child. She is, at this very moment, conceiving. Manoah almost loses his balance; he is ready to fall down. If he did fall, it would be "between the feet" of the woman (like Sisera, in chapter 5).[14]

It is hoped that the reader who may entertain doubts about the virginal aspects of Samson's mother[15] will be less skeptical in the case of Samson's bride. Once more, the man's vision of the woman he desires condemns her to death. The sequence of events between the first sight and the ultimate death of the woman is often ignored or minimalized; Rembrandt again will be seen to emphasize it. The hero's desire is illegitimate; the woman he wants is of a foreign tribe. Going astray, then, he will be paid back in proper currency. The transgression sets in motion the inexorable series of metonymically motivated transgressions that figure Samson's life story. On the way to "take" the nubile girl whom he wants because he *saw* her, Samson commits the

Figure 3.2. Rembrandt, *Angel Announcing the Birth of Samson to Manoah*, preparatory drawing. Reproduced by permission of Statens Konstmuseer, Nationalmuseum, Stockholm, Sweden.

first transgression of the food law he is subject to: he eats honey from the body of the lion he has himself killed in his first great performance.[16] The event represents the rehearsal of both features that characterize this *gibbor*: physical strength (the spirit of Yahweh) and transgression joined in the manner of his death. Defiled by this first transgression, the mixture of both poles of the domain of the "raw" (Lévi-Strauss 1964), the utmost purity (honey) and the utmost defilement (the cadaver), Samson goes on his way—astray—to become the counterpart of Jephthah. The latter was unable, as a father, to give up his daughter to a husband; as a groom, Samson is unable to "take" the woman from the father. Between father and husband, both daughters have to die.

The ritual aspect of the seven-day wedding feast celebrated by the young men is the symmetrical counterpart of Bath's two months' rite of passage. First, it is crucial that this feast take place *before* the marriage is consummated—an event which, in fact, never happens; second, it is important that the groom's guests be his fellows: unmarried men. This is the meaning of the narratorial comment in 14:10: "for so the young men used to do." The competition Samson initiates is a competition over sexual competence and serves to decide whether or not the groom is, indeed, the most ready of the young men.[17] This test Samson cannot pass. Before he has even tried to consummate his marriage, the virgin "brings memory," is no virgin any more, and the young companions turn out to be more mature than Samson. They have "defiled" his bride—they can answer the riddle that reveals the knowledge of Samson's identity:

> What is sweeter than honey?
> What is stronger than a lion?

Samson immediately replies, using verse and metaphorical language as they have:

> If you had not plowed with my heifer
> you had not found out my riddle (14:18).

In their reply to the unsettlingly illogical riddle—"Out of the eater came forth food / and out of the strong came forth sweetness" (14:14)—the companions display their capacity to domesticate the riddle, making it commonplace; hence, they are able to deal with the stake of the riddle: the bride. She is the strong one of the riddle, who, like the lion, needs to be broken open (deflowered, or killed) in order for her belly to "bring forth" sweetness.

It is from this deadly dilemma, inherent to her position as bride, that I will derive a proper name for this woman. I will call her *kallah*, which means bride, but which is also a near-homonym of *kalah*, which means total destruction, consumption, or annihilation—including by oblivion.

The consequence of Samson's impotence is predictable: Kallah is taken back by her father. When the hero later shows up again, claiming what he assumes to be now his property, he is taught the lesson that he had not yet understood: she has been given to one of the more mature companions. The father who thus exercises his property rights over the virgin—her father would not suffer him to *come in* unto her (15:1)—offers Samson his younger daughter. This offensive way of signifying his place as a young man is unacceptable to the proud *gibbor*. He will avenge the father's refusal to give his daughter up to the hero who claimed her. In a very elaborate manner Samson starts a long-burning fire that will ultimately lead to the death, in a sacrificial fire, of both the bride, her virgin sister, and the overpossessive father.

This virgin/bride both resembles Bath and differs from her. Like Bath, Kallah is taken back by her father,[18] and she, too, will subsequently be burnt to death. She stands alone between the men who make deals over her. Unlike Bath, however, she is threatened at the wedding by her fellow tribesmen, who vow to burn her to death if she maintains solidarity with her groom. This aspect of the scene, which assigns proper subjectivity only to the men, is represented most astonishingly in Rembrandt's painting *Samson's Wedding Feast*[19] (fig. 3.3). It has been noticed (Clark 1978, 74; Schwartz 1985, 179) that the composition of this painting is in imitation of Leonardo's *Last Supper*, which Rembrandt had admired and copied from a reproduction circulating in Amsterdam. The "pale isolation in the middle of the table" (Clark 1978, 74) of the figure of the bride is the most convincing indication of the intertextual reference. Its meaning has passed unnoticed, however. Intertextuality here serves a reversal of values. The bride, far removed from the wicked woman she is supposed to be, is turned into Christ, about to be sacrificed, in her isolated position between the men.

On the left side of the painting, a group of men around Samson are intensely involved in the riddle. They turn away from the woman. The other figures also ignore her. The only figure that turns toward her, also a woman, is powerless: in the grip of a sexually aroused man, she can only close her eyes and bend her head. Her hand attempts to loosen the grip of the man who holds her. It contrasts ironically with the central figure's two folded hands which, in protecting her womb, signify at once the virginity and the isolation of the bride. All the figures, but the bride and her powerless counterpart, are involved in some evil business: competing, with all the means (mean means) at their disposal, for the possession of the lonely figure in the middle.

The story of Kallah is properly a virgin story: the struggle over her as property, the test of the property of her behavior, the proper tribal relations she entertains when giving in to the fellows, the proper position as, ultimately, the father's property, not even to be parted from him in death, and the proper, purifying death that befalls her.

Figure 3.3. Rembrandt, *Samson's Wedding Feast*. Reproduced by permission of Staatliche Kunstsammlungen, Dresden.

This nubile woman pays heavily for the improper behavior of the men around her, as well as for the two improprieties attached to her. She belongs to the impure tribe, the "uncircumcised Philistines," and she has been given to another man, thus "bringing memory" to her marriage. Being both the exemplary and the failed virgin, she demonstrates the paradoxes of virginity itself.

Between Virgin and Wife: Caught Between Men

We are now arriving at the most paradoxical case of my series of virgins: the concubine of chapter 19. I will first present her description through the view of the commentators who, with minor differences, all agree upon the meaning of the beginning of the story. I will propose an alternative reading that has fundamental consequences for the view of virginity throughout the book, while also affecting our view of the book's social and religious background. After a somewhat cursory presentation of the other paradoxical virgins, I will give a careful analysis of this crucial figure and her relations with men that will retrospectively radicalize the previous sections.

Here again we hit the limits of philology where the status of a woman is at stake. The JPS translation (Slotki 1980), conforming to the traditional interpretations of the end of verse 19:1, "took to him a concubine out of Beth-lehem in Judah," receives the following correction in Slotki's footnote (p. 297): "Better: 'he took to him a woman as concubine.'" Boling and Soggin slightly change this translation. Boling (1975, 271) has "He took to himself a concubine, a woman from Beth-lehem in Judah" and stresses in a footnote (p. 273) the geographical reversal of the preceding Levite story. Soggin (1981) finds the indication that the man is a Levite irrelevant, and, always ready to take the text in his own hands, proposes to delete it. He translates the noun *pilegesh* also as "concubine," but adds in a footnote (p. 284) a reference to another footnote which affirms (p. 159) that "*pilegesh* is in fact a legitimate wife, but of second rank."

It is problematic, however, to retain a noun, "concubine," with a meaning that is contradictory to its common usage, whereby concubine is normally defined by the fact that she is *not* legally married but lives with a man in either—depending on one's ideology—"free love" or "sin."

The JPS translates the second verse: "And his concubine played the harlot against him and went away from him unto her father's house to Beth-lehem in Judah, and was there the space of four months." Slotki comments on the complement of the verb: "*against him.* lit. 'upon him,' an unparalleled preposition with the verb *played the harlot.* Kimchi explains as: while still with him" (p. 297). Boling has "She became angry with him and ran away to her father's house" (p. 273) and comments: "She became a prostitute, i.e., was unfaithful, 'against him.' But it is strange that the woman would become a prostitute and then run home. Moreover the verb *znh* is not elsewhere construed with *ꟾ* in this sense." After going over some possible emendations, he concludes by reiterating the strangeness: "As Israelite law did not allow for divorce by the wife, she became an adulteress by walking out on him. This is the reverse of Samson's predicament in 15:1–3." It is interesting that the critic notices the symmetry with Samson's failed marriage without drawing the conclusion that there may be, here too, an unconsummated or otherwise problematic marriage. I will also keep in mind the critic's suggestion that the unclear act, of which she is a subject, does not necessarily entail actual adultery; "walking out on him" in itself would count as a breach of marriage. Since wives had no right to initiate a divorce, any attempt to end a marriage would turn her into an adulteress, which has come to be considered equal to a prostitute. The steps taken trace a recognizable ideologeme.

Soggin, with his usual certainty, translates and comments as follows:

> But the concubine quarreled with him and left him, to return to her father's house [. . .] In no way can this be *zanah* 1 [in the first sense], "practice prostitution," in the sense of "betraying him." [. . .] The responsibility for the matrimonial crisis [sic] must have lain with the husband, at least in view of his later behavior; however, the cause cannot have been very serious, if the wife and the father-in-law are so glad to be reconciled. (1981, 283)

This rather long fragment shows the *kind* of logic appealed to by this biblical scholar, a kind of logic representative of its genre. Whenever Soggin employs expressions that strongly denote certainty ("in no way can this be *zanah* 1"), we can be sure that no argument will be adduced and that the case is dubious. The rhetoric of certainty is not justified by, but *replaces,* argumentation. The anachronistic tone of the picture of the "matrimonial crisis," however moving it may seem, rings false. The hidden argument for the refusal to understand *zanah* 1 in the sense of "practice prostitution" cannot but lie in this anachronism; once we have pictured a scene of husband and wife involved in some trifle quarrel, prostitution *must* be (= Soggin wishes it to be) out of the question. Why? Simply because if the wife acted as a prostitute, then the later, equally dubious translation of "to speak to her heart" as an expression of kindness cannot, at least in Soggin's own moral view, be justified. The husband, whose honor this critic is determined to save, would be debased were he kind to a whore, while he is elevated by his kindness toward an angry wife. It is Christianity, not ancient Judaism, that speaks here.

The rhetoric of philology allows the critics to signal problems without solving them in the light of the story as a whole. Thus they can afford to sacrifice the coherence of the story to their own moral coherence. The influence of this rhetoric is devastating. Phyllis Trible's feminist interpretations suffer from it. In contrast to the other critics, she does have a coherent view of the story. In the section "Desertion"—a somewhat predisposing title—in which this beginning of the story is discussed, Trible stresses that there is a crucial difference in status between the Levite and the woman:

[He] has an honored place in society that sets him above many other males; a concubine has an inferior status that places her beneath other females. Legally and socially, she is not the equivalent of a wife but is virtually a slave, secured by a man for his own purposes. (1984, 66)

The basis of these assertions consists of two sources: the *Interpreter's Dictionary of the Bible*, which expresses much less univocal certainty than Trible suggests, and the unsubstantiated statement by Soggin quoted above. We encounter here a major factor in the paralyzing impotence of much biblical criticism: the repetition of predecessors' thinly supported views without questioning the ideology that underlies them.

The fact that such a lowly woman acts autonomously, that she takes initiative as a full subject, surprises Trible, a surprise which "accounts for the confusion about her conduct." She refers to the difference between the Hebrew MT manuscript, which Slotki and the JPS follow, and the Greek and Old Latin that Boling and Soggin prefer.[20] Approaching the crucial question of the narrative subject, Trible continues: "At issue is the identity of the offended party. Was she unfaithful to him or did he cause her anger?" (pp. 66–67). Trible makes explicit what the other critics leave implicit: that the translation of the verb determines the woman's position as a subject. The locus of this openness is exactly the one where the subjectivity of the female character, whose fate is the most disturbing of the whole book, is at stake.

But leaving the question open at this particular point is also leaving the sources of this openness implicit. This is, however, where we should try to find "a breach toward latency" (Delay 1973–74) that can help us understand the text and its social implications. The problem does not lie with the Hebrew text at all. It lies with the commentators themselves. The first problem is created by their own moral view of what is "possible" (i.e., good) and "impossible" (i.e., bad). This "problem" is then the starting point and the end/goal of the interpretation and of the emendations and separations that help formulate it.[21]

These problems, however, are all based on the assumption that the reason for the woman's departure is a quarrel[22] between the two main characters. Rather than adopting this modern atmosphere as the setting of the story, I will take a closer look at the problematic roots, the noun describing the woman's status, as well as the verb expressing the action, which indicates her subject-position and the role that is derived from it. First, there is the noun that is unanimously translated as "concubine," *pilegesh*. This noun follows, instead of preceding, the

noun *'ishah*, woman. Hence, Boling distorts the text when he translates: "He took to himself a concubine, a woman from Bethlehem."
His reversal is understandable indeed; once we assume the translation
has to be "concubine," then the textual order "he took to himself a
woman, a concubine from Bethlehem" does not seem to make much
sense. Since concubine refers, in the modern view, to the status of the
woman *within* the marriage, she cannot have been a 'concubine' before
the marriage; hence, as a woman from Bethlehem, she was not yet a
'concubine.' But maybe the order of the text indicates that this is a
wrong track. Slotki's footnote follows the same track when it has,
"better: he took to him a woman as concubine." This is a slighter distortion since it respects the order of the words, but at the cost of introducing a preposition *le*, meaning "for," which is absent here. In
1:12–13, for example, it is used when Achsah is promised and given
to the *gibbor* Othniel, "for a woman," traditionally translated as "for
wife," "as a wife." Keeping the exact meaning of the noun open, yet
respecting the order of the words, I translate the clause literally as: "He
took to him a woman, a 'concubine' from Bethlehem." Koehler and
Baumgartner (1958, 761) give as the first meaning of *pilegesh*: "wife, in
the older kind of marriage in which the wife stays in her father's
house." Only as a secondary meaning do they give "concubine, secondary wife." For this second meaning, the sources are quite confused.
In fact, if we were to study all the cases where the noun occurs, there
would be a surprising number where this "older marriage" is a more
likely rendering than the concept of "secondary wife." Moreover, the
status of secondary wives is often indicated by the word "slave" or
"maidservant," not *pilegesh*.

The kind of marriage to which Koehler and Baumgartner refer
is known under different names. One common name is "nomad(ic)
marriage," another one "*beena* marriage." It was often practiced by
nomads. The rationale for it was that the younger man, who was in
charge of herding the flocks, had no stable dwelling, while the older
father of the woman would usually have the wealth and the security of
a real house. Such a marriage is also called duolocal, because the husband lives in two different places—both with his own clan and tent,
and in the house of his wife, whom he visits at irregular intervals. Anthropological terminology does not escape the sort of rhetoric we are
discussing. Both terms—nomadic and duolocal—focus on the husband's situation, not on the locus of the marital union itself. A third
and a fourth term, *uxorilocal* and *matrilineal*, displace the issue in another way. The first does focus on residence but ignores the importance
of the father's position which, as Judges shows, is much more genera-

tive of conflict than the woman's. The second focuses on descendance rather than residence. Although the two issues are obviously related, I hope to show in this study that in Judges the emphasis on *land,* initiated as early as in Achsah's story in chapter 1, is an indication that cannot be neglected. We cannot forget that the Israelites as represented in the book were involved in establishing themselves as a separate people (descendance) in the very conquest of the land (residence).

In order to disentangle some of the confusions attached to the current terminology, I will propose to call this *patrilocal marriage,* thus stressing that it is the power of the father, over and against that of the husband, which characterizes this type of marriage and that the place where this power is rooted, the *house,* is the shifter where residence and descendance meet. The term patrilocal, if used at all, is traditionally synonymous with virilocal marriage, thus conflating husband and father again. If it is at first sight confusing to direct an extant term toward a different use, the advantages of the term in the present use are too important to give up.

Morgenstern, who as early as 1929 and 1931 proposed that this type of marriage was quite frequent in the biblical period and who in fact gives an amazing number of cases where it is clearly at stake, calls it *beena* marriage or matriarchy. The term matriarchy is deceptive, too; it suggests much more power for the *mother* than is actually real. The term "matrilineal," deceptive for its focus on the woman and on descendance rather than residence, is also inappropriate since, as I will argue, the lineage is established through the mother's father—an unstable system which Judges precisely presents as problematic. Both terms, matriarchy and matriliny, displace the issue at stake in the book and overemphasize the mother. Especially in the Book of Judges, the absence of the mother in the victim stories is remarkable. The almost total repression of the position of the mother, which I take to be an important characteristic of the book, precludes the use of a term that implies her importance.

Judges is difficult to date; it is commonly assumed that it goes back to extremely old sources, even if the written version is not so old. This is a first, though not very strongly arguable reason to keep open the possibility of this older type of marriage. The second reason is the story of Kallah, a text-internal reason that is. We have seen, there, how the father seemed to have the right to keep his daughter away from Samson, who after all had married her. No mother is mentioned in the entire story. Samson's visit presupposes that he is indeed her legal husband, and the father does not challenge that belief. He only tries to justify the way he has disposed of his daughter, *in spite of her marriage to Samson.* The assumption that he gave her away because the marriage was not real is contradicted by the father's respecting Samson's rights. This case shows how fundamentally different this patrilocal marriage is from the type of marriage we are more used to and which I will call *virilocal* marriage. Virilocal marriage, which is not to be confused with the structure of the modern nuclear family, is opposed to patrilocal marriage by its residence pattern in the first place. While the patrilocal husband moves into the clan of his wife, without any position of power, the virilocal husband takes his wife to his own clan. The shift between the two systems involves a radical change in power positions between the two men, father and husband.

In Kallah's story, the opposition between patrilocal and virilocal marriage is the conflict that generates the narrative line. A third indication that patrilocal marriage may be at stake is in the order of the introductory words in 19:1. The Levite took a woman, who was such a "nomad-wife," that is, who came from such a tradition. He married a woman who, according to the institution valid in Bethlehem, remained in her father's house. Short visits were the concrete form of married life. In order to reduce anachronism and the fallacy of taking the present as the norm, which I call *parontocentrism*,[23] we need to be aware of the insufficiency of our language to account for the past, anchored as it is in a specific ideology of gender-relations. There is no reason, for example, to assume that patrilocal marriage lasted for life, especially in periods of transition; nor that it was monogamous. A fourth indication that this way of life was at stake can be found in the narrative structure. The story is based on traveling and on the respective positions of father and "husband." In the case of a partilocal, nomadic marriage, this is the "natural" setting for such a story.

The second problematic root is in the verb *zanah.* Even Trible assumes without further questioning that it means "playing the harlot." If such were the case, then the preposition would still create a problem, unique as it is in combination with this verb. The "naturalness" of the translation "to play the harlot against him," assumed to mean "to be unfaithful in offense of him," is an amusing demonstration of the interference of ideology in philology. For it is only within the ideology that considers a woman the full property of a man, and her autonomous sexual behavior an insult to him, that such a translation imposes itself. The combination of verb and preposition may be unique because the story has older elements, dating from times when the combination of *zanah* and *ʿal* was not impossible. We have already been able to play with this particular preposition with surprising results. Let us do it again.

In Bath's story, 'al was assumed to express a goal-oriented relation in time or space, with an element of confrontation. If we adopt this same view here, two interpretations are possible, which I contend are both involved, the ambiguity being partly responsible for the preservation of the story. One possible translation would be: "toward him." Without even having a clear idea of what zanah means, the preposition does suggest, then, that whatever this woman did, it involved, not the leaving of her husband, but the leaving of her father to go toward her husband, and/or the other way around. In other words, she came to visit the man who had acquired her under the stipulations of patrilocal nomad-marriage, and hence, ought to visit her, rather than the other way around. The confrontation involved can be interpreted as directed either toward the husband or toward the father, "him" being unspecified.[24]

What, then, is the act expressed in zanah, of which this woman is the subject? Again, Koehler and Baumgartner start their extensive treatment of the root zanah with the archaic meaning, which they do not, unfortunately, provide with a specific source: zanah "means originally that the husband does not live in his wife's tribe" (1958, 261). The diachronic analysis of the root shows a development from this ancient beginning, to "unfaithfulness" in general, sexual unfaithfulness, and ultimately, "occasionally professional" prostitution. The root does also take male subjects, while male prostitution is nowhere referred to in modern translations of the Bible. The verb may refer to some act related to this type of marriage and to the idea of unfaithfulness,[25] an act that entails the preceding and/or subsequent departure of the woman. Later occurrences of the verb are invariably translated in a negative fashion. They all refer, or are assumed to refer, to sexual unfaithfulness and prostitution. This may very well indicate a linguistic development that parallels an ideological one, which is in turn related to an ethnographic one. But there are doubtless cases where the root does not necessarily have this particular, negative, and sexual, meaning.

If, on the one hand, the woman in Judges 19:2 acts according to the customs of her society, and if, on the other, the word has become so negatively related to unfaithfulness, we must look at one particular use that occurs very frequently. The verb is assumed to be a metaphor whenever it expresses Israel's unfaithfulness toward Yahweh. As we have seen, this unfaithfulness is a major issue of the book. We have also seen the tensions between fatherhood and the need to give the virgin daughter away. Jephthah the father gave his daughter to Yahweh rather than to a man of the next generation. This reflects a tension that, however psychoanalytically informed it may also be, is more concretely anchored in the transition between two institutions of marriage, namely the transition from patrilocal to virilocal marriage.

This interpretation has far-reaching consequences that are not without their impact on Judaic and Judeo-Christian theology. It is my contention that the root *zanah* when used with Israel as its subject is in no way radically different from its other uses. *The father, not the husband, is the offended party.* This is much more consistent with the image of Yahweh as father-god. It does shed a new and, for some, perhaps disturbing light on the metaphor and on the act of "going astray." In our story, too, the young woman, who is supposed to live with her father after her marriage, is unfaithful to him—to the father and to the institution alike—when she visits her husband. This man, who lives himself in the virilocal tradition, considers her return to her father an unfaithfulness against himself. Hence the basic ambiguity of the verse: each party can read it its own way. It seems plausible that a form of unfaithfulness affecting the institution of sexual relations becomes conflated semantically with the later meaning being projected upon the older one. Parontocentrism contributes to the slightly condescending view of the past that inspires negative translations of concepts that are neutral or positive in context. The unfaithfulness—to the father, to the old institution—for the sake of marriage, hence for sex, becomes sexual unfaithfulness. Habituated as we are today to consider virilocal marriage as the only "natural," "normal," hence "moral" one, we have a hard time avoiding the displacement of the offense from the father to the husband.

Considering Kallah, our other case where patrilocal marriage is at stake, we see that while Bath-Jephthah was still so much in the father's power that her only way of separating from him was, first, the rite of passage, then, the sacrificial death/marriage to the father's father, Kallah is half given up by the father. He "gave" her first to Samson, then took her back, then gave her to the other man, but all within the institution of patrilocal marriage which reflects a more archaic, extreme form of patriarchy.[26] The story as we are now looking at it represents a third case of this struggle of the father against his "successor"—the virilocal husband—the man who takes over the daughter. And again, the woman will die from the competition.

The three stories, which are at the center of the present study, together represent the struggle on both a symbolic-psychological and on an anthropological level. In the latter sense, they represent the transition from one form of patriarchy to the next and the different forms of marriage that are the expressions of those forms of patriarchal power. The transition goes in the direction of growing power for the "son," the next-to-oldest generation of men. Symbolically, and this level may be seen as unconsciously informing the development of social institutions, the struggle between father and husband is a competition, *the* competition, between established power and the subject trying, on coming of age, to participate in, gain access to, or overthrow that power. It is a struggle *between men.*[27]

If it is true, and such is my contention, that *zanah* refers to the unfaithfulness of the daughter toward the father-owner, acted out when, willingly or not,[28] she leaves him to live temporarily with another man, then the "metaphor" representing the religious attitude of the people, that other form of "going astray," makes much more sense. It is God the Father who feels abandoned by the nubile daughter who is signified by the expression. The daughter/Israel, leaving her "natural" and unique father, the one who, as her creator, claims her faithful devotion or, in Freud's terms, her exclusive possession, goes away "after other gods," after any god, who seduces her with material goods, with golden images, but who did nothing to bring her into existence. The arbitrariness of the new relationship, the one that is not based on *existential contiguity*, the gratuitousness of the daughter's new engagement, is what strikes the father as unfair. This issue, the dichotomy between "natural" relationships based on creation/generation, or in other words the contiguity between father and daughter, and the arbitrariness of any other relationship, will turn out to be a crucial problem in the book.

Thus Yahweh does not escape the confusion of subject-positions that infects all thinking about virginity. The three stories of the unfortunate virgin daughters whom their fathers cannot give up, the violence of the bride-stealing scenes where the men, unable to be given wives, go out to catch them, and the setting on fire of Yahweh's nose— all of this becomes more and more coherent when seen as traces of an older, more drastic[29] form of patriarchy than the one the stories seem to promote.

The woman who is so utterly victimized in chapter 19, and who therefore alone deserves to be the second heroine of this study, can no longer be referred to as "the concubine." Like Bath, she comes to the story nameless. How can we name her, allow her subjectivity, while still doing justice to her as a figuration of (the lack of) subjectivity? The term that describes her in the text, *pilegesh*, means something like "patrilocal wife": a wife living in the house of the father, a wife who remains a daughter. Playing on the word "house," the motif that becomes so crucial in her story, on the word "daughter" as well as on her place of origin—Bethlehem, "the house of bread"—this woman, who is defined by the location of her married life, will be given the name *Beth*, which is a form of the word *house*. It relates her by near-homophony to her fellow virgin daughter Bath, sacrificed like herself and like herself submitted to the power of the father; here as there the father is critical, in the sense of decisive, when the threshold of the house is transgressed.

So far, I have not yet accounted for Beth's status as a virgin daughter. Technically speaking, within the common, male view of virginity as bodily integrity, she cannot be a virgin. She has been "taken" by the Levite, and she went out of her father's house, in patrilocal unfaithfulness, to visit him. The reason for including her in Bath's group is because the ensuing struggle proves that the issue of property, concerning her, is not settled. At the same time, however, what I call struggle here is not an explicit and harsh fight. It is more of a competition, acted out in all courtesy, symbolically, that is. Significantly, on the narrative level of the story as a whole, and on the anthropological level of the transition from one type of sexual organization to the next, the competition not only takes place *in* the father's house; it is also *about* the father's house. It is his hospitality, his capacity to provide, his indispensibility as the source of the daily bread, which is at stake in the competition. If he lives in Bethlehem, house of bread, and if the story is structured around the tension between inside and outside the house, it is because the theme of this particular competition had to be enhanced.

When he follows Beth to her father's house, the Levite is referred to, exceptional as the expression is, as "her man." Her man arose and went after her to speak to her heart (the preposition *'al* again) to bring her back. After her initiative in turning the patrilocal marriage into a virilocal one, the man immediately understands that this change will entail an increase in his power. He sets out to retrieve Beth, not, as even Trible wrongly assumes, to "speak kindly to her," to resolve the matrimonial crisis, but to persuade her, rationally. The heart was the site of reason, not, as we as post-Romantics think, of feeling. In order to display his wealth and thus substantiate his claim, he brings along his servants and asses. The meaning of these details is double: they symbolize not only the husband's wealth, but also the idea of traveling. And travel there is going to be, again on two levels; literally they will be traveling to the new dwelling and symbolically this man opposes his dwelling to the father's house as an alternative way of living.

The father of the daughter receives him well. No wonder. Coming to visit the daughter, the man now behaves according to the rules of the patrilocal institution. The verse is quite outspoken about the issue. Beth brings the man into the father's house, and "when the father of the girl *saw* him . . . he rejoiced to meet him." This time, the virgin daughter does not come out of the house; instead, she brings the man inside. The man is submitting to the law of the father. Is Beth married? In the father's eyes, she is; the Levite, however, is not content with this form of marriage, which makes him dependent upon the father-in-law.

The next seven verses are devoted to the attempts of Beth's father to retain the man—hence, to keep his daughter—and, on the man's part, to the slow passage from acceptance to rejection of this hospitality. The many days of this process should not be seen as an exact number of days but, as is usual in the Bible, as a representation of "a long time." The sequence makes no mention of Beth. Clearly, her presence is at stake, but her participation is not. While her role is the thematic issue of the scene, her subject-position is ignored. This dissymmetry is the figuration of the story of Beth: the woman caught between systems, between men. In this house of bread, staying (institutionally) and eating are one and the same thing. As for the generous reception, it is hardly likely that the Levite, a man who lives in a tent, would have been able to acquire, as a secondary woman, a slave, the daughter of the owner of the house of bread.

The final decision to leave the patrilocal house is taken, strangely, toward the end of the day. The realistic reader is inclined to wonder why, after so many days, the Levite could not have stayed one more night, in order to be able to make the dangerous trip through a foreign land in a single day. As subsequent events show, it would have been much wiser, either to make the decision earlier, or to wait one more night. That is precisely why it happens this way. The husband's inability is being represented. Narrative differs from "real life"; it has a different logic by which it can represent aspects of "real life" that would remain unseen in a realistic reading of the text. Beth has to be from Bethlehem to show that patrilocal marriage is at stake; similarly, the Levite has to make this unwise decision so that the symbolization of the competition can unfold. The lateness of the hour is expressed rather ambiguously as "the day has weakened." The speaker here, the father, warns the Levite in these words. The weakening of the day then comes to symbolize the weakening of the system, but this phrase is again ambiguous and can be read by each party to refer to the other's: competition leaves both parties weak. Danger, in the form of social unrest and aggression, is the unavoidable temporary consequence of revolutionary change. Within the isotopy of the Freudian confusion, the threat from the father, his warning about danger, will be a stain on the daughter. She will have to pay for it dearly.

The next and last scene that will detain us here is the act of giving Beth up under the pressure of the threat of homosexual rape. The weakened Levite is further weakened and expels Beth. He performs this gesture of renunciation when he can no longer sustain the struggle. It is also the moment when Beth is not herself qualified as a virgin, but is juxtaposed to one. The scene follows upon the hospitality of an old man, father of a virgin daughter, who takes the group of travelers into his house. As a fellow Ephraimite, he protects the Levite against the threat of xenophobic aggression.

Social disorder is often represented as homosexual rape. Combining two forms of transgression, homosexual rape is, in this context, disrespect of two forms of property. The first is the property that a "nubile," rapeable being is defined as being, namely, possessed by some owner. The second is the "proper" relations of sexuality belonging to a social group. The "sons of Belial"—the negative description places the narrator clearly in one camp—who besiege the house explicitly demand the Levite, the guest, to be brought out for rape. The man who did not accept the rules of the patrilocal society, the man who broke the rules of "proper" sexual property, now has no business being safely inside the house of another father. Since the risks of autonomy are what he wanted, they are there to show him how deeply disturbing his desire is to the social order.

The father, his host, protects the man, as Beth's father did by insisting that he stay in the house. Both in Genesis 19 and in this story, the father protects his male guest through the offer of the two virgin daughters. However, the "sacred law of hospitality" is not sufficient to account for this dissymmetry in either case. In Genesis, it is true that the guests are divine messengers and the daughters Lot's own. And perhaps in Genesis giving priority to the property of the other over one's own makes Lot seem commendable—that is, if we ignore the nature of the gift and the subsequent fate of the daughters. But in the case of the host at Gibeah, not even this holds true: offering Beth, he disposes of somebody else's property. She belongs to the guest, hence, he should protect her as well. Or doesn't she? Does this father simply not acknowledge the virilocal marriage, so that he still considers Beth the property of her father? The gift of her would, then, both protect his guest and strip him of his otherness, turn him into a "proper" man submitted to the father. Beth, the stain of the "other" marriage, would be eliminated.

The daughter and the patrilocal wife are both offered as nubile, that is as rapeable, stuff. The sons of Belial are explicitly invited to humiliate these daughters. But the men do not listen to him. They press the guest further. The story of Lot had stopped where the story of Beth enters its most horrible phase. Since the Levite is the man who tried to change the social order, he has to account for it; he has to show that he is up to his claims. He fails the test, utterly. With his last bit of power, enough to condemn his newly acquired wife to the most execrable of fates, he seizes her and throws her out, back into the old system. This gesture is his final renunciation of what he had tried in vain to accomplish, and it is this humiliation of him, not the fate of Beth, that the events of the next chapter will set out to avenge. He fails as the successor of the father, just as the fathers themselves failed to protect their daughters. They clung to their daughters, but they did not save them from exposure.

Seen in the light of social reform and the chaos ensuing from it, the daughter's fate receives ritual meaning. Victimized between two rival groups, she is quite literally sacrificed. Subjectivity is denied her; she becomes merely a role. It is the multiple meanings of the concept of virginity and the contradictions, confusions, and conflations it entails that qualify the virgin daughter for the role of sacrificial victim. It is my contention that there is, indeed, an intrinsic bond between the idea of virginity, the competition between fathers and next-generation men, and the extreme violence that takes the form of ritual sacrifice. It is to the idea of sacrifice itself that we shall now turn.

CHAPTER FOUR

VIOLENCE AND THE SACRED: CONTRIBUTION TO THE ETHNOGRAPHY OF FATHERHOOD[1]

Les raisons qui poussent les hommes à exterminer certains de
leurs enfants sont certainement mauvaises; elles ne sauraient être
futiles.
    René Girard

We will now explore the hypothesis that the violent deaths of Bath,
Beth, and Kallah can be read as ritual sacrifices. A comparison between
those deaths and the two "proper" sacrifices in the book, Gideon's in
chapter 6 and Manoah's in chapter 13, imposes itself. Two major theories of sacrifice will be invoked as illuminating subtexts whose otherness allows for sight of the differences between both the theories and
the sacrifices; as in previous cases, the theoretical texts will be as vulnerable, in the process, as the biblical texts are. They will be read and
help reading, not used as evidence for historical truth.

Bath's death is explicitly called a sacrifice; hence, it stands between the two "proper" and the "improper" sacrifices. In order to argue
the deep, indeed, ritualistically relevant similarity between the cases,
the sacrificial ritual itself will be decomposed[2] and its motivations
analyzed.

From the perspective of method, that is, the interdisciplinarity
inherent to women's studies, it is noticeable that in this chapter, literary analysis shifts from one of its limits, philology which we hit in the
previous chapters, to the other limit, anthropology. This is not to say
that the chapter offers an anthropological analysis of ancient Israelite
society; rather, it offers a literary analysis that draws on anthropological theory in order to further its pursuit of the understanding of gender-
related issues as motivations for the representations we read in Judges.
In other words, the issues are real, not the images and figurations they
lead to.

In order to show how anthropological theory can help us understand how and why sacrifice as represented in these stories went awry, we have to lay the groundwork in a rather technical analysis. We will see how a systematic comparison between features of the 'proper' and of the 'improper' sacrifices produces a network of relations that mutually illuminate the five acts as acts of sacrifice:[3] the two proper sacrifices and the three murders.

Among the many theories of sacrifice in anthropological literature, two recent, monothetic theories will be judged relevant. René Girard's hypothesis of violence as the root of sacrifice and his concept of the surrogate victim, the *bouc émissaire*, will be invoked to illuminate the already indicated status of the female victims as caught "between men." The virgin daughters, as surrogate victims, are then the most suitable victims because the struggle between men does *not* involve them. But the theory falls through when it turns out that the victim, appropriate for its defenselessness, is utterly inappropriate for the nonarbitrariness of the choice of her. Additionally, Nancy Jay's theory of sacrifice as a "remedy for having been born of women" (1985) provides a different motivation, but that accounts in a more central way for the gender-related aspects of our cases. This theory helps understand the motivation of the choice of the victim, but not the violence of her murder. As the third partner in the discussion, Judges shows how the two seemingly incompatible theories each have an insight to offer, but also that sacrifice itself resists its own system.

The Raw and the Cooked

Jephthah's vow concerned a specific kind of sacrifice: *olah*, burnt offering. The burnt offering's meat is not eaten—the entire victim is burnt to ashes. And what motivates such an offering is less specific. The *olah*, unlike the two other expiatory offerings, the *hatta't* and the *asham*, expiates a broad range of sins. While the latter concern pollution and desecration of sanctums, the *olah* may also serve to expiate the neglect of performative commands (Milgrom 1976, 769). It "is all-encompassing: it answers to all the emotional needs of the worshipper" (Milgrom 1976, 769).

Fire is traditionally an important element in Hebrew culture, and in Judges there is more than one significant event associated with it. Passion is the typical compared object of the metaphorical use of fire; fire mediates between enlivening and destructive powers. Many scholars relate the meaning of the Samson myth to this ambivalence regarding fire (Crenshaw 1978). Fire is in many cultures a purifying element, as the practice of burning the dead suggests. Structurally, fire, which leads to ashes, is opposed to the rotting of dead flesh. This opposition is at work in rules on disposing of the dead and in rules on the preparation of food alike: fire also provides a way to prepare food, opposed, by Lévi-Strauss, to the "impure" rotting process (1964) as well as to the "pure" form of rawness which is honey. Cooking relates to purification, even in reality: it kills the germs that effectuate the rotting process.

As a consequence of the features associated with fire, a burnt offering is distinguished from other forms of sacrifice by its radicalness. First, the meat burned is not eaten. This can be seen as a form of generosity: there is no selfish aspect to it, the victim is given to the god in its entirety. Second, it is also an excessive form of "cooking"; the ultimate result of the process is that there is no food left at all. The burnt offering is, therefore, the most radical offering. In the case of human sacrifice, for which, of course, we only have scarce and semirepressed evidence, the burnt offering distinguishes this sacrifice from cannibalism,[4] a crucial distinction for Bath's story; with the slightest taint of cannibalism, the father's heroism would be annihilated.[5]

In order to be able to understand the two other murders in relation to sacrifice, we must deal with the differences that distinguish them. The major difference between the three unquestionable sacrifices—the two proper ones and Bath's—and the two plain murders is most notable in terms of the beneficiary of the sacrifice, or in semiotic terms, the addressee. The beneficiary and potential benefactor of the sacrificer is Yahweh, while the addressee of the murders is either unclear, diffused, or in any case purely secular. Distributing the features of the proper sacrifice among the three cases of female victimization, the following come to the fore. Samson's bride Kallah is executed by fire. Since there is no mention of remains, we may consider her—and her father—as having been completely burnt. The sacrificer, as well as the addressee, are problematic in this case since Samson does not kill her himself. He sets the Philistine crops on fire, and the Philistines respond to that destruction by the murder. The burning of the crops can be related to the nonconsumption issue. In this light, not only the murder but also the crop-burning can be seen as a sacrifice whose actors are mixed up. The Philistines, who are not to eat the crops, are not the sacrificial agents. Neither is Samson, who is to sacrifice his bride, the agent of that sacrifice.

This event is figured by metonymy. The land of the Philistines is contiguous with the sacrificial victim: she lives on it. It is also metaphorically related to the victim: both she and the crops are burnt entirely; they cannot be consumed. Kallah, as opposed to Bath, is not offered to Yahweh. She dies with the father, another fatal metonymy, instead of being given by him to the super-father. The violent selfishness that in modern eyes discredits the story, if not the hero, is far removed from the devotion that we are accustomed to associate with the ritual sacrifice to the gods. In spite of the devotional purpose of sacrifice, performed in order to maintain Yahweh's presence in the midst of the people, it easily deteriorates, in other cultures as well,[6] into a gift offered in hopes of subsequent reward, and although Jephthah's sacrifice is a shockingly violent instance of this modification in the use of sacrifice, we may question whether the criticism on moral grounds is not an anachronistic repression of disturbing aspects inherent in sacrifice. We have already seen that Bath's sacrifice is very much of a trade, while, as we will see shortly, the two "proper" sacrifices are equally "commercial."

The aspect of purification in Kallah's case is obscured by violent passion for which fire is also a metaphor. The destructive aspect of passion desacralizes the sacrifice. This might be because, in Girard's terms, the substitute victim is not remote enough from the real victim, the replaced one. We can interpret the reversal of the metaphor of fire, the replacement of the purifying force by the destructive one, as a systematic relation. However, if Samson, the fighter, is the defiled hero who needs to sacrifice in order to purify himself, the burning of the daughter with the father is a characteristic way for this passionately violent hero to go about satisfying this need. In Bath's case, the need of the hero to purify himself by sacrifice after the defilements of the battle is an obvious one.

Beth, the third victim, is at first sight far removed from the proper burnt offering. Not only is she not burnt, but there seems to be no issue of purity at stake; the relation to nonconsumption also appears to be absent. On second thought, however, one difference may explain the other. There may be no food involved in the sacrifice proper, but the story as a whole is filled by the issue of food and eating. The long eating sessions at the father's house may signify the opposite of abstinence. And that nonabstinence, then, disqualifies the event as a burnt offering. This holds more strongly for the state of the victim. Being defiled, she cannot be sacrificed "properly." Her rape and murder are the systematic *opposites* of a burnt offering. The husband, a Levite, hence a proper sacrificial agent, cuts her into pieces. The slaughter of the sacrificial animal is properly and doubly sacrilegious. We can see here one of the motivations for the ambiguity regarding Beth's state when found by the Levite. Is she alive? Then he slaughters her, but not for Yahweh. Is she dead? Then he, a Levite, should not touch her. Not only does the Levite, a priest, handle the defiling body; but also instead of offering the pieces to Yahweh, he sends them to his brothers. This replacement of the vertical relation by a horizontal one will prove characteristic of Manoah's failure.

Of the three women victims, then, two are "cooked" and one is "raw." Two are related to nonconsumption, one to overconsumption. Excessive consumption defiles, makes the victim "improper" for sacrifice by fire. It makes her the object of a mock sacrifice that is not given to the father but to the sons[7] and that leads to war, not peace. Instead of reducing the victim to a-semantic ashes, it scatters her into a multiple message—a message of violence and sacrifice.

In the Name of the Law: Proper Sacrifice

In the book, the two sacrifices that are the paradigm of the genre[8] are Gideon's and Manoah's. Both are meant to provide evidence of the election of the agent or his son as a god-inspired hero. Gideon's is much more proper than Manoah's. It is proper for the occasion, it is properly executed, and it is properly acknowledged. Yet it is not without an indirect relationship with Manoah's more disturbing case and, via Manoah's, to the other cases which can be more directly linked to the murders. Gideon's sacrifice deserves a careful analysis because, as we will see, it is not only motivated by Gideon's insecurity about his status as the chosen *gibbor*, but also because it thematizes the intimate relationship between sacrifice as a cultural, ritual act and sacrifice as a semiotic demonstration of the power *and* the problematic of meaning.

Gideon, in his communication with the divine messenger, offers a kid and some bread. The combination of meat and cereal produce reminds us of the case where these two kinds of sacrifice were separated. The story of Cain and Abel in Genesis 4 suggested that the cereal offering is not just a poor man's replacement of the unaffordable animal. Indeed, the story is about violence, the violence of brother against brother that Judges 19 also thematizes. Girard's hypothesis of violence as the root of sacrificial practice (1972) comes to mind here. If read with this hypothesis in mind, the Genesis story becomes paradoxically reversed. Abel's offering comes to imply killing while Cain's does not. According to Girard's view, then, only Abel's sacrifice makes sense as a cathartic experience. And indeed, the violence exorcised by Abel is still in Cain's heart. Abel's offering is not more "proper" because the gift is more precious—the relation is semiotic. The gift has to represent the giver; it has to stand for him on the basis of existential contiguity. Cain, being a farmer, gives what is metonymically linked to himself, as does Abel the shepherd. In that respect, both gifts have a similar value. For Girard's theory, however, the point of the sacrifice is in the violence which serves to protect the subject against it. The choice of the offering is relevant, not because of the inherent value of the object, but because of the action it imposes on the sacrificer.

The ensuing violence, Cain's killing of his brother, shows the difference between acceptable and unacceptable forms of violence. Cain's violence is revenge. But in order for violence to become sacrifice, the victim has to stand for the giver. For Girard, sacrifice replaces revenge by a reversal. In the case of revenge, the victim stands in for the antagonist. Hence, his or her death triggers new revenge, and the spiral of violence only arbitrarily comes to an end. The fundamental change that sacrifice brings about in this scheme is the reversal of the victim's position. In sacrifice, a victim that is, or is metonymically linked to the other instead of to the giver's self, has no value as replacement, as sign. Girard claims that revenge is unacceptable for a social structure because of this lack of semiotic status of the victim. It triggers an endless process of similar acts of revenge. This chain can only be broken by the split between violence and motivation brought about by the irreducible gap between sign and referent.[9] The victim of the violence must *not* be guilty of the event that motivates the violent action (1972, 29). The function of the substitute victim is to interrupt conflict between close relatives. The victim, for Girard, is typically one who poses no danger because nobody would adopt its (her) cause. Cain's mistake, then, is not to slaughter—an action that was approved from Abel—but to slaughter his envied antagonist, his brother, instead of the "safe" victim whom no solidarity will protect.[10]

Gideon sacrifices exactly the way the messenger told him to offer. He brings the offering on his own initiative: a kid and bread. The kid allows the sacrificial catharsis to take place. This seems sensible before a battle: once the irrational violence is exorcised, the leader is more fit to devise for military strategy. The sacrifice also includes bread. Unleavened (pure) bread is an accessory of the whole ritual (Exodus 29; Numbers 15), but when regarded in the light of Genesis 4, it may be seen as a supplement: it makes the sacrifice complete. Given the thematization of bread in chapter 19, Gideon's bread also helps to structure the relation between this sacrificial bread and the profane bread that the father used to compete with the husband and that, in its turn, mirrors the Philistine crops destroyed in chapter 15.

Gideon is appointed *gibbor* by the messenger of Yahweh (6:12). He is nevertheless far from sure of himself. He repeatedly asks the messenger and Yahweh himself to prove that, in spite of the earlier refusal to help, the latter will, this time, deliver the people and that he is the leader chosen to do it. His doubts are not presented as negative; three times, Yahweh does indeed give him the sign designed by Gideon himself.

Gideon's *gibbor*-ship is emphatically not self-evident. The need of repeated evidence that he is God's chosen deliverer enhances the basically arbitrary character of election that many biblical stories thematize in different ways. Within the patriarchal stories, the election of the younger son over the elder is the best-known device used to drive this point home (e.g., Nohrberg 1988). In the book of Judges, the chosen deliverers are never "natural" choices. They are not the descendants of a patriarch, as the Genesis heroes were. This difference changes the concept of the hero itself. Heroism becomes a much more individual and unpredictable trait. This arbitrariness of the choice is a recurrent source of tension, even of anxiety, in the *gibborim* and in the stories about them. But there is a relation to fathers and to descent in Judges, too, and it is in sacrifice that it is signified.

According to Jay (1985), the practice of blood-sacrifice is a ritual way to establish patrilineal kinship: a remedy to being born of woman. Jay makes a convincing case for her thesis on the basis of the practices and the details of the ritual, considered strictly as a social practice. The most immediate argument is, of course, the fact that all over the world, the sacrificial agent has to be a man, generally a father-figure. The priests who, in many cultures, are in charge of the sacrifice receive a paternal, leading status *because* they handle the sacrificial victim. Where women perform sacrifices, there is either no blood sacrifice or the women are postmenopausal. In no known culture is a still fertile woman allowed to practice blood-sacrifice. The sacrifice becomes an alternative way of establishing existential contiguity. That is why the relations between agent, antagonist, victim, and addressee are subject to very strict and specific rules.

Reading Gideon's sacrifice with Jay's theory as subtext, we are surprised at Gideon's insistence that the election must be a mistake. His first reponse is incredulity: Yahweh has been a bad father, he has not fulfilled the promise "which our fathers told us" (6:13). Why should he start now? As if to confirm his good care, Yahweh then replaces the messenger as spokesman and confirms that it is in fact he who sends Gideon as a deliverer. Gideon turns now to his own status and questions his ability to become the *gibbor* of the first address (6:12). Significantly, he refers to the double misfit of his familial background: his family is "the least in Manasseh, and I am the youngest in my father's house" (6:15). In his use of social and familial terms as synonymous, he affirms his status as the doubly "youngest" in the paternal line. After Yahweh's repeated affirmation of Gideon's election, the hero-to-be still asks for a sign. The sacrifice intervenes at this point: as "my gift" (minḥathi, 6:18).

The exchange of a sign ('oth) against a gift is what must establish Gideon's status as gibbor. The sign is to mark him, provide him with the distinctive features that show, without further doubt, that he is the chosen one. The father-God, then, is to replace the earthly father, who cannot provide the son with the distinction he needs. The sacrifice is a gift in the anthropological sense (Hyde 1983) of an object with neither practical use nor stable value that is used to establish a relationship between persons. More specifically, the relationship the sacrifice is to bring about is that with the father, the insertion of the humble boy in the mighty paternal line. This meaning is confirmed by the very fact that this "youngest of his father's house" is to be the sacrificial agent. He becomes the subject of an action that is reserved for the fathers, whether social (priests) or familial (patriarchs). If Jay's theory makes sense, then the sacrifice of Gideon has to be the perfect sacrifice, the model that sets the norm. But if it is normative within the structural composition of the book, it then must have problems: it must have the incredulity, the fear, that connects it to the other sacrifices, and it must have an explicit mention of the election that signifies, metonymically, the purity of patriliny. Through its problematic aspects this sacrifice is betokened as a model, a model which conveys its instructions for use as well as its motivations.

In Jay's theory, the bloody aspect of the sacrifice is explained in various ways. Psychologically, it signifies the deliberate act of deciding between life and death, as opposed to its "natural" and "passive" counterpart, birth-giving. It is suitable precisely because it is also on the nonsymbolic level the counterpart of birth-giving. Again, a metonymic relation between sign and referent is required. Real blood is a sign of life-giving and life-taking, which are two typical forms of power, each linked to a view of power itself as rooted in a subject. If life-taking is seen as empowering because it relates the subject to the father-line while opposing the mother, it is so within a specific view of power that, in its opposition to life-giving, can only be purely negative.

In this sense, the two subtexts, although incompatible as theories, meet over the victim's blood. The primary, founding violence suggested by Girard is unavoidable, the more so since it is also directed against the sacrificial subject himself. It is related to the need of empowerment that cannot but derive from a feeling of powerlessness inherent to a system—patriliny—that is unable to avoid the detour through the mother, thus coming, at each occurrence, dangerously close to the rival system, matriliny, of which patrilocal marriage is a close neighbor.[11] The struggle patrilocal marriage has to, but cannot really, win is that over descent for the father.

If it is to be the model sacrifice, Gideon's has to be a "pure" one, namely, a burnt offering. Indeed, the first of the series of signs that he receives is the one of spontaneous combustion. The messenger *touches* the gift with his staff and disappears; Gideon is scared because he has *seen* the messenger of Yahweh *face to face*. This fear, which must be dispelled before the *gibbor* can accede to his power, is caused by the two details of the event that entail bodily contact: sight and touch. These features of the sacrifice deserve a semiotic analysis.

There is an interesting tension, in this passage, between different semiotic forms. The exchange of gift and sign was designed, by Gideon, on the *symbolic* level. In the terms of Peircian semiotics, a symbol signifies on the basis of an arbitrary—unmotivated—but conventional relation of signification. The convention rests in this case upon agreement between two—male—subjects. It is not only possible, but necessary, that the relation be arbitrary. It is paradoxically only on the basis of arbitrariness that the subject can rely on the convention. Touching the meat and the bread with his staff in order to set them on fire is, in contrast, an act of *indexical* signification: the touch causes the ignition and therefore stands for it. The relation becomes metonymical, its basis existential. The contiguity comes close to the contiguity that defines birth-giving. In this light, we could say that the messenger teaches Gideon what the more important issue of the sacrifice is.

Seeing "face to face" the messenger of Yahweh is almost a transgression of yahwistic anti-iconism. *Icons* are proscribed from worship precisely because they initiate the dangerous identity between deity and humans that terminated the sojourn in paradise. *Icon* is also the third of Peirce's three classes of signs, wherein the sign receives meaning on the grounds of resemblence or analogy with its object. The rule of anti-iconism thus coincides with the semiotic preference for symbolicity. In the paternal ideology, both index and icon are considered "weak,"[12] that is dangerous, grounds of signification. Since they dispense with the convention—in religious terms, with the covenant— they allow for the bodily contact of maternity to enter the semiotic space.[13] The implied reversal of giving and taking life is worded by Gideon: the killer is in fear of dying.

This tension opposes the tendency to prefer arbitrary, pure but unmotivated, ungrounded signs that represent fatherhood as opposed to motherhood on fatherhood's own terms, and the preference for metonymy that replaces motherhood on motherhood's terms. We will see that this tension is represented recurrently in Judges's murder stories. The tension is acted out in sacrifice in all its possible forms, "proper" and "improper," and in the slippage from the one to the other.

Gideon's sacrifice is, then, not only encompassing in its object and typical in its subject; it is also a model of the range of possible relations of signification that the book struggles with. The fear of the *gibbor* is as indispensible an element of the model as is the killing of the victim, the displacement of the violence, the anxiety about patriliny and the reassurance about it. We will now examine to what extent Manoah's sacrifice displays the same features and where it deviates from this model.

Manoah's Failed Fatherhood

Manoah's weakness as a husband has been discussed in the previous chapter. Unable to take his place in his wife's life, he has to leave the act of fathering to the messenger of the Father. We will see, here, that his sacrifice mirrors this primary weakness. As such, it confirms the relation between blood sacrifice, patriliny, and primary violence.

Manoah has finally obtained, be it ironically through back-reference to the communication between the mother-to-be and the messenger, disclosure of the conditions of Samson's life. His first gesture, now, is to invite the messenger for a meal. But the community that is established through a common meal is not what the messenger is interested in. The attempt to place both men on the same level— that of the husband—ignores the basic difference in generation between the failed father and the true father. The messenger has so far carefully kept his distance from Manoah. He will not fail to maintain this distance now that the primary act of conception has taken place. This care is necessary now in order to establish the right "patriliny" of the chosen: divine election.

Manoah offers to prepare a kid; the messenger refuses to eat "of your bread" (13:16). And he adds, "If you will prepare a burnt-offering, you must offer to Yahweh" (13:16). The narrator comments, "For Manoah knew not that he was a messenger of Yahweh." Boling and Soggin translate *lehem* as "food," while Slotki comments that the word, which the JPS translates as "bread," means food in the wider sense. These interpretations are certainly possible, but we may also keep "bread" in order to assess a possible literary function of the word. The double allusion to Gideon's model sacrifice and its encompassing objects on the one hand, and to Abraham's hospitality to the three messengers of Yahweh who do accept the meal—including bread—on the other hand, makes the word "bread" very pointed. Both intertexts underscore the details of the event that further determine the *gibbor*'s status. As was done for Gideon, the messenger will light the fire; as in the case of Abraham, the conception of a son is at stake. Like Gideon, the child is to be *gibbor* and to deliver the land from its enemies. Like Abraham, Manoah has problems keeping his wife "properly" obedient.[14] Like Gideon, Manoah is incredulous; but Sarah, too, shares this feature. Like Gideon, finally, Manoah will be scared. But, and here the two cases differ radically, it is not Yahweh but the woman who reassures Manoah, and she soothes him not by the ritual expression "fear not" but by logic.

The logic the woman uses is not only theo-logic but narrative logic as well. Not only does she show that her faith commands confidence, she also shows that the narrative requires the line from prediction to fulfillment. The untimely death of the characters would be narratively untimely. She places the argument on all three levels of narrative structure as laid out in the Introduction. The event, on the level of action, is the acceptance of the offering. The view, on the level of focalization, is expressed in her words: "He would not have shown us all these things." Speech, on the level of narration, of telling, is the last and most convincing argument. Unlike Gideon, whose fear was necessary to connect his sacrifice with Manoah's, the latter is not excused for his lack of confidence. His triple failure to accept the limited role assigned to him leads to the unavoidable priority of the woman in the genesis of the *gibbor*. After the woman's conclusive logic, the next verse names only her: and the woman bore a son, and she called his name Samson.

Within the countercoherence I am trying to build up, the last part of the messenger's speech in 13:16 must be reconsidered. Slotki (1980, 266) explains the insistence on the "proper" addressee thus: "Because many of his contemporaries were offering to idols. Hence the warning." It is not only the addressee, however, who is part of the opposition here. The bread, translated as "food" and thus losing its specific meaning, is opposed to the burnt offering as the messenger is opposed to Yahweh. The messenger refuses the community with the husband because the father of the *gibbor* is the true father, the one through whom the patriliny of election must be established. Communicating the line directly from father to woman, the son will be born as a "patrilocal" son, only temporarily sent out to the virilocal husband.

The meaning of the nonconsumption of food implicit in the burnt offering is located in the triple opposition bread/community//meat/consumption//vertical relation/burning.

Thus the event opposes the failing father to the successful father. Manoah's failure to accomplish his goal, to become a father, is confirmed and enhanced by the explanatory sentence that follows the messenger's command: "For Manoah knew not that he was a messenger of Yahweh." The lack of knowledge can be read, within the isotopy of conception, as a lack of sexual knowledge, in other words, he knew not that the other "knew," that the conception had taken place through the other man, the deputy of the father. His indiscrete attempt to "know" (the name) is immediately criticized. "Why do you ask my name, wondering that it is hidden?" Although he cannot have the (sexual) knowledge that is needed for "proper" conception, he can at least have the insight to understand his situation, and show the appropriate reaction: wonder. Failing even there, Manoah is decidedly disqualified as father.

Although the sacrifice of Gideon was ignited by the messenger while Manoah sets it on fire himself, there is, here too, a contiguity between the fire and the messenger. This time, he does not use his staff to set the meat on fire, but he does disappear in the fire. The bodily aspect of the messenger vanishes at the very point where the concrete sacrifice and its abstract meaning converge. It is thus that the paradox of both sacrifice and patriliny, as well as the bond between them, is signified in this failing father who offers—though not on his own initiative—the comprehensive sacrifice. The bread and the victim, the pure burnt offering offered to the proper addressee: Manoah ends up, after all his failures, showing respect for the proper hierarchy. Sharing his fear with Gideon, he has, in relation to the latter as *gibbor,* only a limited, if indispensible, role to play: he will become the *gibbor*'s foster father.

In the Name of the Vow: Improper Sacrifice

These two sacrifices have in common that they were instigated by the divine messenger or divine voice and not by the subjects who act as sacrificial agents. Bath's sacrifice is also initiated by a voice—not the voice of the deity, however, but a voice addressed to the deity. Gideon was involved in negotiation. He took the initiative of the offering himself, but in interaction with the divine voice; Manoah did come up with the proposal of the meal, but the meal was rejected by the messenger who proposed a sacrifice instead. Between the deity as the initiator, the claimer of sacrifice, and the man, father or *gibbor* who proposes it, there is a common interest. Both parties need to establish the relationship between them that the gift is meant to bring about or to strengthen and that, in the biblical context, is the ever-vulnerable covenant between the divine and the earthly father.

The common interest, the need on both sides for perpetual confirmation of the covenantal relation, makes the "commercial" aspect of the sacrifice not only acceptable, but basic to the relationship itself. Seen in terms of Bremond's narrative cycle (1972) which proposes a structure based on repetition, the book is nonchronological. The repeated series—transgression, oppression, and deliverance—is not so much the content of the book but its elementary pattern, the structure that accommodates the stories as its semantization.

Jephthah's vow is the initiative of a gift, but a conditioned one: he does not yet name the gift. Two aspects of the vow specify, however, that it will fulfill the requirements of Girardian sacrifice. The term "burnt offering" excludes the communal "fellowship" meal. And the active verb of the conjectural description of the victim excludes the bread and guarantees the primal violence. The phrase "whoever comes forth out of the doors of my house to meet me" implies a living being; hence, the sacrifice will involve killing. Promising, verbally, to exorcise the desire for violence not on the enemy but on a scapegoat makes military strategy possible as the alternative to brutal slaughter. This is how the vow makes the victory possible.

Compared to Gideon's sacrifice, there is the same sense of doubt and demand for reassurance in Jephthah's. But Jephthah's promise of sacrifice suggests impropriety. It is not so much the "commercial" character of the vow—if you give this, I will give that—that is improper. Gideon, too, required evidence of success before the battle. It is, rather, the verbal, symbolic aspect of Jephthah's vow that is suspect. Gideon acted before he demanded; coming out with the offering, he acted rather than talked. But where he established, through the gift, the relationship with Yahweh that made his demand an acceptable part of the relationship itself, Jephthah gave no evidence at all of his good faith before the result of the vow was, not only assured, but actually carried out. This, in fact, disrupts the syntax of the sacrifice as a gift. Why is this truly improper?

As Jay has suggested, the sacrifice has to accomplish what fatherhood, seen as a nonnatural, conventional relation, cannot bring about: a mediation between the symbolic, conventional, and the "natural" indexical bond that is considered the prerogative of motherhood. The spontaneous, "natural" combustion of the sacrifice in Gideon's case, as well as the disappearance of the messenger in the fire in Manoah's offering, actualizes that mediation. Sacrifice is both purely conventional and, through its material aspects related to food and its destruction, indexically related to both agent and addressee. Jephthah's sacrifice before the battle is totally symbolic: only verbal, it does not exist until its material, metonymic bond is established; that is, it does not exist until Bath's immolation. This mistrust of performative speech-acts as a sufficient compensation for patriliny can only be made up for in a radically material form of acting out.

The language of the final verbal repetition confirms this interpretation of Jephthah's impropriety. The phrase burnt offering is not repeated. In a pleonastic expression that some consider motivated by discretion, the narrator says: "And it came to pass at the end of two months, that she returned unto her father, and he did unto her the vow which he had vowed" (11:40). It is not in order to cover up the crudeness of the event, in my view, that the word sacrifice does not reoccur. Repeating it would undo the vow of its fragile performativity. It is only through this follow-up that the *word* sacrifice becomes a *deed*. The common translation "he did to her *according* to the vow" erases the very performativity of the vow as a speech-act. *Doing* the vow which he had vowed is the only adequate way to say that he burnt his daughter to death, to ashes, as indeed he had bound himself to do.

At the same time, however, it differentiates "proper" from "improper" sacrifice. Sacrifice is a deed of gift, prior to its reward, while a vow promises a deed, without or, as in this case, after the reward. There is no reason to question the sacrifice itself, as some critics have attempted to do (for sources, see Trible 1984, 116). On the contrary, the repetition of the word "vow" and the repetition of the father's military successes warrants the realization of the vow. Yet it is an improper sacrifice, not in the eyes of its addressee, as some (Trible 1984, 115) in an attempt to redeem, if not the *gibbor*, then at least his divine counterpart, would have it, but in the eyes of the daughters of Israel and of others, to whom I shall return later.

The point of Bath's sacrifice is for me to show the possibility of improper sacrifice. It is not improper because it is human. The victim is "only" a virgin daughter of a father whose descendance is hopelessly "lowly"—improper—in any case. The causal logic has to be reversed. *Since it is improper, it can as well be human.* Once flawed, more flaws are generated by its initial impropriety. Traditionally, Bath's case is compared to Isaac's near-offering in Genesis 22, but there is really a clear-cut opposition between the two cases. Again, however, it is not so much the humanity of the victim that makes for the difference. Instead, as we will see, the network of oppositions is much more subtle.

Bath-Jephthah versus Ben-Abraham: A Case for Separation

Abraham obeys when God commands him to sacrifice "your son, your only one Isaac whom you love" (Genesis 22:2). Whether this obedience deserves the praise it usually gets or whether, rather, it may be criticized as blind submission, at least the patriarch does not volunteer for the deed like Jephthah. We have already seen the slight but significant difference between the formulations that describe the two victims. The similarity (your only one, his only one) establishes an intertextual relation that enhances the oppositions. First of all, the narratorial form differs. In Genesis, God speaks directly to the father. In Judges, the father speaks directly to God. But in both cases the descriptive phrase is embedded in character's speech. The direct address to Abraham is the more poignant, the indirect description by Jephthah the more rhetorical.[15]

The complement "the only one you love" is absent from Judges. "Love," whatever the word may mean, ultimately protects the son as its absence condemns the daughter. But there is "love" on another level, too. Abraham sacrifices willingly, for the "love" of the divine father. Utter submission is, then, one form of love. Isaac repeats it in that he as willingly plays the lamb's part as Abraham plays the son's part. In Bath's case, there is no "love" at stake, neither on the one level, since she is not described as the one her father loves, nor on the other, since the deity has not, by requiring the sacrifice, warranted the relationship between the son-father and the father-father.[16]

As Scarry's remarks suggest (1985, 204), there is a deeper sense to this difference between the two sacrifices. The sacrifice of Isaac describes the structure of belief, "the taking of one's insides and giving them over to something wholly outside oneself." This metonymical view of belief is visualized in the form of the altar which, unlike Jephthah, Abraham is explicitly said to build. The form "externalizes and makes visible the shape of belief." The reversal of inside and outside is exemplified in both birth-giving and "hurt." Scarry's theory of biblical theology as based on the separation of voice and body seems, indeed, appropriate for the case of Isaac. The divine voice interferes throughout the story, and Abraham's identification with the divine father is stressed by his repeated "here I am," an attempt to connect voice and body.

In Jephthah's behavior, we notice a misplaced appropriation of the voice that entails a reversal of the structure of belief. This is yet another sense in which Jephthah's is an improper sacrifice, not because sacrifice has to be initiated by God, but because the speech-act, the conditional vow, presupposes the predominance of the voice over the body that is reserved to the deity.

Both Isaac and Bath go to the mountains, to the wilderness of transition. The representation of Isaac's near-sacrifice takes the form, indeed, of a transition rite. As in many communities where the rite of passage takes some importance, the excessive cruelty of the older men, the fathers, toward the sons constitutes a test of virility (Dillenberger 1985). Living through the anxiety, which cannot be provoked but by the threat of being killed by their own fathers, makes the boys fit for a social life where fearless fighting is the male's part. The voyage to the wilderness, then, has to be carried out *with* the father, that is, with the personification of danger (van Gennep 1960; Turner 1969), and it is thus represented in the story. Bath, the daughter who cannot claim the "love" of the father, is said to undertake the transition rite herself. In the case of girls, the loneliness of the wilderness prepares her to accept the insecurity in confinement that her adult life will hold. If we take, as I think we must, these two stories as meaningful representations of meaningful practices known and understood in the culture, we can see the similarity in the difference. In both represented rites, the point is to go through anxiety in order to accept the hardships of life after the rite. That for Bath there will be no afterlife is, as I have suggested, not so much her concern as her father's. On the level of the ritual, there is no future; time is cut off. This a-temporality and this divergence of concerns are, I would contend, what make the representation at all possible and acceptable.

The major difference between the two accounts is a narrative one. Where Isaac's near-sacrifice is narrated in full, Bath's actual sacrifice is only summarized in the fatal words: he did the vow that he had vowed. Given the intertextual relation, it is appropriate to read the story of Isaac as complementary to Bath's,[17] as the more proper and the more acceptable case. It supplements the minimal representation of the unacceptable sacrifice. It is this scene that has been so often depicted by painters, while Bath's similar but more radical experience is *never* depicted. If we fill the daughter in where the son is mentioned, we can see what happened. Jephthah, we then would read, "built an altar there, and laid the wood in order, and bound [Bath] his [daughter] and laid [her] on the altar upon the wood. And [Jephthah] stretched forth his hand, and seized the knife to slay his [daughter]" (adapted from Genesis 22:9–10). This scene, which is the systematic opposite of the one where the groom lays the bride on the marriage bed, is what we imagine when we read that Jephthah "did the vow that he had vowed" (see Alexiou and Dronke 1971). There is no divine voice to stop the narrative. The only voice that follows is the narrator's, which says, "and she had not known man."

This final complement can, in its turn, be set off against the follow-up to Isaac's initiation. The motivation for stopping the sacrifice that, as a test, initiated both father Abraham and son Isaac in the same confrontation is indicated in two terms. First, there is a parallel between "lay not your hand upon the *lad*" and "he did to *her*." The gender of the victim seems decisive. The explanation is in the second relevant statement. As a reward, Yahweh says to Abraham:

> In blessing I will bless you, and in multiplying I will multiply your seed as the stars of the heaven, and as the sand which [is] upon the seashore, and your seed shall possess the gate of his enemies; and in your seed shall all the nations of the earth be blessed; because you have obeyed my voice. (Genesis 22:17–18)

This unrequested but already promised reward, the multiplication of the male's offspring, stands in sharp contrast to the killing that was Jephthah's required "reward." The "lad" is the one capable of providing the father with virilocal offspring. As we see in Genesis 24, the institution of virilocal marriage, hence, the acquisition of virilocal offspring, is a great concern to this father. When Abraham sent his servant off to woo Rebekah, this man raised the possibility of uxorilocal, in my terms: patrilocal marriage.

> If it happens that the woman will not be willing to follow me to this land, must I if necessary bring your son in turn to the land from where you came? (Genesis 24:5)

The land the servant is sent to is the land of Abraham's relatives. There is no reason, one would think, for him to panic at the prospect of his son returning there. However, the prospect is abhorrent to Abraham: "Abraham said to him, beware that you bring not my son back there" (24:6). The father is upset by the consequence of such a move, which would be, precisely, patrilocal marriage. His son would then live, and engender, under the power of the other father: the woman's father. For since daughters of his are not mentioned, being either absent or irrelevant, it is only through virilocal marriage that Abraham's seed can multiply as the stars in heaven.

Compared to this splendid promise, Jephthah's situation is clearly hopeless. He is the son of a "harlot." Unlike the other wives of Gilead, who lived with their husband, Jephthah's mother stayed with her own tribe. This is why, in the current translations, she deserves the title "harlot." As the rest of the story shows, the issue is the spatial separation. The brothers say to Jepthah simply: you shall not inherit in your father's house, for you are the son of *another* woman. This makes no sense if we take it as it is traditionally interpreted, as a modern case of marital infidelity and the illegitimate status of the son that results from it.[18] For the noun ʾishah is the same when it refers to Gilead's wife and to the "other" woman. Either they are both wives or neither of them is. Also in the case of harlotry in our sense, the identity of the father would have remained unknown. The meaning becomes more pointed when, again, we translate as "another [kind of] wife." It makes sense, then, to refer Jephthah back to his own background. The issue for Jephthah becomes vengeance for his rejection from the virilocal house. But he cannot, as Abraham did, expect anything from descendance, for the fatherline is already broken.

His other alternative is to establish himself as a *gibbor*; then he, too, can insert himself meaningfully into history. He negotiates, with apparent talent, over the position to become, not temporary deliverer but permanent *head*, chief, of the clan from which he was rejected.[19] Jephthah becomes a master killer and a killer who uses his head, his brains, and his mouth to kill. If his seed cannot be multiplied, his *head* can multiply the dead.

If the prehistory of Jephthah disqualifies him as a patriarch, a founder of a fatherline, his descendance is equally unfit, for he has no son. Hence, there is no way for him to establish a virilocal patriliny. The only recourse is to negotiate his daughter and fall back on patrilocal marriage for her. Hence, he does not feel like giving her away. As there is not even a mention of "love" in this story, Jephthah is locked up in a logical aporia. As a *gibbor*, he should deserve a wife; too insecure, he appeals to a helper. But as soon as he invokes help, he must give his daughter away. Rather then giving her away to a husband who would not only destroy his chances of patrilocal descendance, but who would also signify the victory of the brothers in the patriliny of the virilocal house, he gives her up to the father above him, becoming a son again, just like Abraham. His rage over the humiliation of his rejection by the father-clan motivates the position he takes as Abraham's opposite.

Both sacrifices figure the rite of passage that initiates the separation between father and child. In the case of father and son, the common interest of the establishment of patriliny helps them solve the problem, dissolve the anxiety caused by the threat. Submission and courage for both result from the ordeal. In the case of father and daughter, there is no such common interest, only separation. The giving up of the daughter is the giving up of self, as long as virilocal patriliny is the motivation that generates the stories. Jephthah's fire is futile. No patriliny can be established through it. In Jay's sense, this makes the sacrifice not only improper, but also irrelevant, hence doubly improper. The virgin vanishes into nothingness.

Dreaming Fire: Violence without the Sacred

Kallah's death is the subject of this section. She dies in flames, with her father in her father's house. Flames are, indeed, a recurrent motif in the Samson saga. We do not need the relation between the name Samson and the noun *shemesh* ("sun"; see van Dalen 1966) to realize how frequently fire, figuratively and literally, occurs in the story. From the sacrifice that generates the hero's birth to the Philistine sacrifice to Dagon that generates the final catastrophe (16:23), the use of fire and the destruction it brings about—figuratively as the violence of passion, literally as its metonymic extension—punctuate the story's development. It is precisely the framing of the scenes of Samson's life by the two sacrifices at its beginning and at its end that connect the motif of fire and the act of sacrifice.

We have seen already that Manoah's sacrifice, the one that begins Samson's life, if basically "proper," is not without flaws. There is the failed attempt to turn it into a fellowship meal, the indiscreet attempt to communicate with the divine messenger on a level of equality, the lack of faith that makes Manoah a particularly unsuitable agent for the sacrifice that is supposed to embody belief, the attempt to eliminate the woman from the genesis of the *gibbor,* and the misplaced fear at the end that reestablishes the mother's control. The Philistines' sacrifice, the one that ends Samson's life, is by definition improper, since it is devoted to a rival deity.[20] It is also improper because Philistine sacrifice is not a vertical gift, but an emphatically horizontal fellowship sacrifice. The sentence that describes it has: "and the lords of the Philistines gathered them together to offer a great sacrifice to Dagon

their god *and to rejoice*" (16:23). The juxtaposition "and to rejoice,"
typical of biblical Hebrew, slightly obscures for us the specifying function of the third verb. Sacrificing and rejoicing are not two separate
activities; the form the sacrifice takes is joyous. The fact that the sacrifice celebrates the victory over the enemy of the (Philistine) people
turns it into an ironic commentary on Jephthah's sacrifice. There, the
joy that victory should have brought is turned into mourning because
of the impropriety of Jephthah's verbal behavior and because of his
overtaking the initiative of the deity. Here, the "proper" order is re-
stored, but the proper deity is replaced by an improper one. Hence, the
game that accompanies the sacrifice is cruel and frivolous. Mocking
Samson, the event mocks Jephthah, too.

Although the Philistine sacrifice and the subsequent scene of
mockery are situated in the temple, it is clear that the whole event
has nothing sacred about it. The hearts of the Philistines become
"merry"—an expression that occurs repeatedly in the hospitality scenes
in chapter 19—and they make Samson perform like a circus animal. It
is Samson himself who, wiser now and once again long-haired, reverses the situation by a speech-act that allows him to turn it into
something both negative and sacred. He speaks to God and speaks
well: his unconditional request will be rewarded. Killing the Philistine
crowds in their own temple becomes the ultimately God-approved sacrifice that redeems the hero's earlier failures. The last sentence of the
story becomes more meaningful when we see it as the expression of
Yahweh's approval: "Then his brothers and all the house of his father
came down, and took him, and brought him up, and buried him between Zorah and Eshtaol in the burying-place of Manoah his father"
(16:31). Killing the tribe of the patrilocal wife, Samson becomes the
hero of the new institution. In the light of this final event, which post-
humously reabsorbs the fatherline that Manoah was unable to establish, the death of Samson's first wife comes to stand between the social
competition and the ritual of sacrifice that begins and ends the story.

Samson's violence is extreme. His relationship to the body stands
at one end of the dialectic of body and voice that Scarry describes so
well (1985, 181–220). Samson speaks to God only twice. The two addresses are both requests for help, one for survival after manslaughter,
and one for strength for slaughter. Nowhere in the story does God
speak to him. In all his other adventures, which all imply some form of
violence, Samson needs no divine help. Either he gets it without asking—the spirit of Yahweh comes upon him—or he can do without.

Samson has often been described as a hero of mediocre intelligence and faith (Naastenpad n.d.). Nowhere in the story is there ex-

plicit evidence of Samson's stupidity. Such qualifications are more often than not derived from an implicit opposition between strength and intelligence, in other words, between body and mind, or between nature and culture. Such dichotomies do sometimes apply to Hebrew scripture, but if we defamiliarize ourselves from them, the story gains in interest. The story is, then, simply not "about" his mind. It is, however, "about" his bodily strength and the ways he uses it for certain purposes, some approved, some not approved by the subjects of the text. The scene of Kallah's death, too, must be seen in the light of the gibbor's violence and strength; no judgment on it is given.

Samson does not kill Kallah with his own hands. Her death is situated between the confrontation of father and husband in 15:1–2 and the actual burning by the hand of the Philistines. The struggle between men that causes Kallah's death is the more interesting if we realize that the beginning of chapter 15 is the clearest reference in Judges to patrilocal marriage. Although Samson left the house of Kallah's father in anger after the revelation of his riddle, he seems not to hesitate in regards to the appropriateness of his visit to "his" wife. The visit is neither questioned nor criticized. It is presented as "normal," as according to custom, that is, that he comes back "after some time" to "go in to her in the chamber." The father, who confesses that he had assumed that Samson had given her up, does recognize the hero's rights: although he does not let him sleep with Kallah, he tries to compensate for the loss of Samson's apparently "legal" rights. His explanation for having ignored those rights ("I did think that you utterly hated her; therefore I have given her to your companion") sounds plausible and is followed by an apologetic counteroffer. We may assume, then, that the marriage itself is not questioned, but only the hero's willingness to really keep up the patrilocal relationship. His departure has been interpreted as a rejection of the patrilocal bride. The younger sister, object of gift like Kallah and probable covictim, is not even explicitly rejected by Samson. The episode makes clearer than any other how irrelevant the woman herself is when the competition between men is being acted out.

The question is not whether or not the younger sister is indeed, as her father suggests, "fairer than she." Ignoring this question, Samson immediately changes discourse; he no longer addresses the father but the tribe as a whole, as the narrator before him indicates by switching to the plural pronoun: "And Samson said to them: 'This time shall I be quits with the Philistine when I do them a mischief.'" This response shows that more is at stake than the loss of a woman. The honor of the husband as challenged by the power of the father is what concerns

Samson; it is that loss of honor which the loss of the woman entails. The father's mischief will be repaid by violence against the patrilocal tribe.

At this point, Samson alters his behavior. Instead of merely displaying his supernatural strength as he did when threatened by a lion, and as he will do again in several other episodes to follow, he sets out to accomplish his revenge in a very elaborate manner. Rather than slaughtering, by hand, the number of Philistines he may wish to kill, he catches three hundred (!) foxes, binds their tails together in pairs, puts a torch between the tails, sets the torches on fire, and sends the foxes into the fields of the Philistines. The elaborate nature of the attack shows that brutal force and stupidity are not the issue.

First, he does not kill. If "sacrifice" there is here, it is vegetal, not bloody: a Cain-style one. Second, the attack is not directed toward people but toward their land. The crops that he destroys may represent the agricultural accomplishment of the enemy. Attacking the token of the Philistines' superiority that enabled them to act as hosts for patrilocal marriage is one way of questioning the institution itself. Third, although he does use fire, the fire does not kill an animal; the foxes are simply used to set the fields on fire. The relation between fire and animal becomes metonymic rather than metaphorical.

In "proper" sacrifice the victim stands in for the antagonist; any metonymic connection between the two endangers the "propriety" of the sacrifice. Metaphor, the mode of signification based equally on similarity and on separation, is the preferred relation between victim and antagonist. This reversal in the relationship between victim and antagonist in the above "sacrifice" is paired with the reversal of the destruction itself. As a symbolic act, setting the fields on fire expresses Samson's deepest desire: as a Nazirite and bound by the purity laws attached to his status, he wishes to purify the Philistine land of "wrong" institutions so that he may, without any harm to his fatherline, fertilize it; that is, fertilize its female inhabitant. This, however, cannot be done because Samson is overly hasty. He cannot purify the Philistine land as long as his status as husband has not been acknowledged. Had he tried to take Kallah with him to his father's house, he might have run into trouble similar to that described in chapter 19, but he would at least have taken one step in the direction of virilocality. Here, his deed can only misfire.

This symbolic interpretation of Samson's revenge rests on the assumption that it is not "pure" revenge. I derive from the subsequent episodes the character's penchant for slaughter, and I find it surprising that Samson does not kill in a situation so crucial for him. Burning the crops in the field, therefore, must be a symbolic act, as is suggested by the fanciful engineering and the careful preparation for this reversed sacrifice, where the animals are the executioners—they literally *lead to* the executioners who will kill Kallah—and blood flows only "by procuration."

The sacrificial flavor of the scene can be projected on its sequel. The Philistine inquiry, "Who has done this?" is answered with the relevant information: "Samson, the son-in-law of the Timnite, because he has taken his wife and given her to his companion." The kinship terminology used shows that the act to be revenged by Samson was, according to this statement, the use of paternal power over and against the son-in-law's. The Philistine response, then, can be equally sacrificial: where institutions are at stake, personal slaughter is not efficient as a reply. The Philistines' action is incomprehensible without such a socially polemic context. Why should they otherwise kill their own kinsfolk, rather than the criminal? The challenge to the institution, already threatening in Samson's attempt to take power in the wedding scene and similarly responded to by the threat realized here, has to be destroyed thoroughly at its source: the house where the challenge has taken place is to be sacrificed in order to exorcise the seed of impropriety, to purify, in turn, the land of the traces of the opposite "wrong" institution.

On another level, the scene that depicts that the Philistines "burnt her and her father with fire" takes its place in two series. One is the series of problematic marriages that end by the death of the woman. In this series, the death of Kallah refers to Bath's solitary death, not *with* her father but by his hand. Kallah's father, again, is reluctant to give his daughter away, but rather than give her to the super-father, he gives her to the super-son, the young companion of the wedding, presumably a bachelor who will accept patrilocal marriage. If we look in the opposite direction, we see Beth, a patrilocal wife like Kallah, but one whose husband manages at least to get her out of the father's house.

The other series of which this event represents one phase is the intratextual series of attempts at sexual relations that Samson undertakes. The episode of Samson's marriage represents the first attempt. The failure, in that case, displays the *gibbor*'s lack of maturity. The burning of the house where the attempt went wrong is thus one way of allowing Samson to start over. As the subsequent episodes show, the *gibbor* takes a long time to cure himself of improper, patrilocal tendencies. Both the "harlot" of Gaza (who may be another patrilocal woman) and Delilah are Philistines, or at least other-tribe women, whom Samson visits but does not take with him. Here may very well lie the deeper meaning of the destructive fire of Samson's passion. Failing to preserve virilocal purity, he falls victim to what he somehow seems unable to avoid. Samson is a dubious hero, not so much because he privileges the body over the mind, but because he privileges exogamy over endogamy, patrilocality over virilocality, and nomadic wandering over agricultural stability. The sequence of tests that he has to go through can be seen as a slow development toward virilocality. The last verse of the saga, at least, suggests this meaning.

Both Bath and Kallah, as opposed to Beth, die in fire. Theirs are more clearly sacrificial deaths, as they are both offerings burnt on account of the *gibbor* himself rather than on behalf of the god. And they are both improper sacrifices. Beth, as we shall see shortly, represents the systematic opposite of the burnt offering, while Bath and Kallah mirror each other. The father kills the one and is killed with the other. In this scene, the problem raised by Bath's death—how to get out of the dilemma of the possessive father—is "solved" by Kallah's death. She dies *with* her father because only the father's death can eliminate his resistance. But then, the way out is a dead end. Violence without the sacred dimension that implies both a divine addressee and the substitution onto the innocent victim of the violent anger is nothing but murder.

Jephthah's sacrifice did have a "sacred" dimension in that it was offered to Yahweh. There is no mention of the deity's refusal of the dubious gift. But it was, as we have seen, a thoroughly improper sacrifice. Hence, there is no perfect symmetry between Bath and Kallah's burnt offerings. Though both are "cooked," the two victims are too closely bound to the sacrificial agent on the one hand and to the real rival on the other. If Bath is given to the very "husband" who deserved her, Kallah is killed by her own kinsmen, with her own father, by the doing of her own husband. If the opposition between the "raw" and the "cooked" signifies the transition from nature to culture, then these two "cooked" women signify two stages in a return to nonculture. The rules of sacrifice cannot be amended without costs.

The Body Becomes Voice, or the Reinforcement of Culture

The ambiguous mode of Kallah's death, between sacrificial and arbitrary violence, is still clear enough as a negation of the negative sacrifice of Bath through the relation to fire. We will now see that even this double negativity can be doubled in the "rawness" of the sacrifice.

Beth's death will be seen here as a mock sacrifice, as an extreme case of violence without the slightest token of propriety, as the paradigm of cultural regression. It is not a pleasant task to analyze in detail the fate that befalls this female character. Such is, nevertheless, the goal of this section. The extreme violence can only be mastered if it is understood.

As opposed to Bath and Kallah, Beth's death is described in its successive stages in so much detail that it is almost not represented in itself. The gift of her, the rape and torture, and the dragging of her (body) on the donkey, and the slaughtering are the four major phases of what we can only refer to as Beth's murder. All four *are* the murder; therefore, the question of the exact moment of her death is irrelevant. The following analysis is meant to point out the ritual aspects of the treatment, the systematic relation to sacrifice it entails, and the ultimate resolution of the opposition between body and voice that is one of the founding figurations of biblical theology (Scarry 1985). As a parody of Girardian sacrifice, each of the four phases is characterized, not only by the countersacrificial aspects, but also by the violence practiced on a stand-in victim and by violence for its own sake. I will map out the two sets of aspects, sacrificial and violent, for each of the three stages of Beth's cruel execution.

Giving Beth Over

Each of the three stages is in itself elaborated with the deliberation and detail characteristic of sadistic discourse. Giving Beth over is in its turn a complete narrative cycle of opening, development, and closing of the sequence. As a first response to the knock on the door and the threat of homosexual rape, the host acts. Posing as a father, he offers the two young women, his own daughter/property and the other man's wife/property, as a gift to the rapists. His speech-act is the counterpart of Jephthah's vow. Both acts are conditional gifts. Jephthah requested victory over, safety from, a collective enemy as a condition for his gift. This father requests safety from a nonmilitary equivalent of a collective enemy. This is, therefore, again a moment where the political coherence shifts into the countercoherence. Jephthah offered an unknown person, but one who had to be his nubile daughter. This man offers a known set of persons, two equally nubile women, one of each sexual institution, a daughter and a wife: the one still the exclusive property of the father, still available for patrilocal marriage, the other, on her way to becoming a virilocal wife, yet resting in a patrilocal house. But Jephthah offered the gift to his helper, the *gibbor* who would provide the victory. This man offers the woman to the enemies themselves,

thus stripping from the sacrifice its central feature, the divine addressee. It is, therefore, a sacrifice, but one even more improper than
Jephthah's.

As a second phase of this first sequence, the man takes hold of his
wife. Grammatically, the sentence is ambiguous. It is not absolutely
clear which of the two men does this. The representational mode of
the story, however, gives some indication. If we look at roles, the
husband is the only male participant who is only referred to as "the
man"; the others have more specific "names." In terms of positions,
the man is struggling to pose as just a *man*, an independent husband,
rather than a patrilocal son-in-law. Moreover, the antecedent of "his"
in the phrase "his [patrilocal] wife" is clearer when we assume that the
husband is the man referred to. Moreover, as an agent in the fabula
the husband is the subject of the act of "taking hold of her," a phrase
repeated three times in the episode. The episode, then, depicts the
act of turning a subject into an object, hence, a potential sacrificial
victim.[21]

The act is the equivalent of Abraham's binding of Isaac. Again,
as in Jephthah's case, the husband is motivated to the act by a desire to
protect himself from the danger represented by the group of male enemies outside. Where the voice of the host fails to be effective, the husband hopes that the body of the woman will have the desired result.
The meaning of this act is the same as that of Jephthah's: a gift as bargain. But a gift is meant to establish a relationship; this one only serves
as a protection, through separation, from a negative relationship.

Although, again, the addressee characteristic of sacrifice is replaced by an "improper" addressee, a nonsacred one and one too close
to the sacrificial agent, the sacrificial aspect of the gesture becomes
clear when we compare it to the gift of young women, occurring in
many myths and folktales, to an outside enemy like a dragon or some
other monster. The film *King Kong*, despite its parodic aspects, confirms that the basic structure of the gift of a woman to an enemy is
sacrificial. Instead of fighting the enemy, who is considered impossible
to fight, the giver hopes he will be satisfied. The gesture is based on
magic: the partial satisfaction is hoped to ward off the real, uncon-
trollable danger.

The third and closing phase of the sequence is the acceptance of
the gift. It raises questions that no commentator so far has been able to
answer. Why would the rapists, who refused to be satisfied with the
offer of the two nubile women, accept the gift of only one? This is a
major argument in favor of my interpretation of the story. Taking the
two women would be pointless, since it is the man not the father who

has to be punished. The rapists are not interested in attacking the father's property. Rather, they want to eliminate the threat represented by the new institution that the man stands for. Taking the father's daughter *and* Beth would obscure their message. Taking only Beth, the token of the new institution, makes the man "normal," harmless; it strips him of his otherness. Seeing their acceptance of Beth in this light further supports the idea that the whole episode is to be seen as a ritual. The choice of the victim partially supports both Girard's and Jay's views of sacrifice. For Jay, it represents the issue of lineage, although the straight shedding of blood will soon be replaced by a still more direct attack on birth-giving. For Girard, it represents the scapegoat: the victim whose side nobody will adopt in protection, although the scapegoat is not arbitrarily chosen nor completely without relationship to the culprit. The rapists want precisely that victim who stands in for, who symbolizes, the threat to the social order. Either the man or the wife will serve their purpose, but the wife even better since she is *not* guilty (Girard) and since she bodily represents the issue (Jay). The host's daughter does not serve the purpose.

The sacrificial aspects of this first sequence are complemented by aspects of naked violence that turn the sacrifice into a parody, an excess, of Girardian sacrifice. The first phase, the opening of the sequence, is poetically designed to underscore this relationship between sacrifice and its parody. Verse 23 begins with the narrator's voice describing the subject as "the man, the master of the house," enhancing the position of power this father holds when the master *of the house* goes *out of the house.* Transgressing the limits of safety that the pounding on the door had already *entstellt*—displaced—the direction of the master is away from the husband and toward the aggressors (as opposed to Genesis 19).

The narrator's statement is followed by the host's speech. Being the master, the local figure, and the host, it is appropriate that he use his voice to protect his guest's body. His first word is "*do not.*" "Act not so wickedly," he says. The ground for the host's expectation that the mediating argument might be effective cannot surprise us anymore. The fact that the man has come into a father's house indicates that he has given up his attempt to establish the new institution and has submitted to the old one. He has dwelled too long in the father-house, eating the bread of communion, both in Beth's father's house and in this host's patrilocal house, to be able to stand for virilocality, in spite of his attempt to do so by taking Beth to his own house. Beth's father, warning him that the day was already weakened, had predicted this contamination. Therefore, the host has power over the daughters, over his own, but also over the wife who does not belong on the road with a stranger, but who belongs in a father-house.

The end of verse 23 initiates a figure that encompasses verse 24 and that I call a chiasmus of entanglement: "Do not do this wanton thing," mirrored in the encouragement to do "what is good in your eyes." Seeing is the key that turns the bad into the good. The phrase comes straight from chapter 11: "behold my daughter" recalls the crucial phrase "behold his daughter" uttered by the narrator at Jephthah's confrontation with his victim. What Bath herself added in her story is here added by the father: "nubile." He thus turns her into an absolute object—"Behold my daughter, nubile, and his patrilocal wife [equally nubile]." The term that signified a future-oriented life-phase in the female voice becomes a synonym of rapability. *Behold* stands between two other occurrences of the act of focalization—"since [= seeing that] this man has come into my house"—"behold"—"do to them what is good in your eyes." The first focalization draws attention to the *act* of the man who is the subject of submission to the rules that his act signifies. The second one represents the objectification of the woman. After that turning point, the next focalization becomes the freedom of anarchy: submission to the rules on the one hand, free disposal of the objects on the other. The chiasmus reveals the reversal of values entailed by the difference in gender. Not only is the man subject and are the women objects, but the "wicked thing" becomes "good" when it is a humbling of the women. The sequence "do not do the wicked thing"—"humble them"—"do what is good in your eyes"—"do not this wanton thing" figures the ideologeme that differentiates values on the basis of gender.[22] Chiasmus being a figure of entanglement, the very fact that the ideologeme is expressed in such a figure further develops its meaning. It entangles within a causal relation the two aspects of rules and anarchy according to gender. The two sides of the dichotomy presuppose each other: rules can be enforced, but only at the price of freedom. Men can be protected, but only at the price of women. Such is the deeper meaning of the so-called "study of hospitality" that is enacted here.

The rapists, however, do not listen to the voice of the host. They do not want words, they want a body. Wounding the body is the affirmation of mastery they are seeking. The inefficacy of the father's voice inaugurates the next phase of the violence, but it is the husband who makes it possible. The man who failed to make it to his own house hands over the object of contempt and of contest: the woman.[23] Beth is given up in an ultimate act of power and of violence. The man lays hands on her, and throws her out into the night.

Overconsumption of Beth's Body

Once handed over by the husband, Beth is nothing more than an absolute object, a token of the man's/men's power to reduce her to that
state. She will be raped and tortured all night, until the morning. The
sacrificial meaning of this durative event[24] is antithetic to the prescrip-
tions of the burnt offering. The interdiction against consuming the
body of the victim is transgressed to excess. The collective rape is a
collective sacrificial "meal," a fellowship meal of male bonding, wherein
men, in solidarity with each other, share the consumption of the
"other," the victim who does not belong to the group that the meal has
the function to constitute.[25] As Jay (1985) points out, every negative is
boundless, since its only feature is to be other than its positive. The
opposite of the burnt offering, then, is dangerously close to the absolute impropriety that negates it: the absolute consumption of collective rape.

The third feature that turns this event into a systematic anti-
sacrifice is the defilement that is rape. Where fire purifies, rape defiles,
and the desacralization of the victim it entails is a comment on the
desacralization that is, in the eyes of the patrilocal town, the attempt
to defy the institution. The addressee of this act is not God, but society
itself. And in a sense, society is as sacred, as vital, as the life-giving
god. The woman who is unfaithful (zanah) to her father by following
her husband becomes common property of everyone. For the opposite
of the father, the nonfather, is a random category without positive
limits.[26]

There is some narrative logic in the fact that this horrible response to the first and so far only action whose subject is the woman,
the action of zanah, is in its turn followed by her second and last action. The sacrifice that, instead of providing light, took place during
the dark night, ends, again, with an anti-sacrificial aberration: the victim is released. We cannot say: the woman is released, for she is a
woman no more. She cannot really act. Her death is already occurring;
only, it takes more time.[27] The woman who was able to be "unfaithful"
to her father[28] and visit her husband in verse 2 is now, toward the end
of her story, a dead body that can only drag herself, of all places, to a
father's house.[29]

This gesture has been widely acclaimed as utterly dramatic, often
taken to redeem the story's morals, which are otherwise so shaky. For
the purpose of the present discussion, it suffices to take her gesture as
ritual, as the final gesture of her dying body. Lying down at the door of
the father's house, the institutional context which caused her death,

Beth's ultimate gesture resacralizes her as a sacrificial victim who, like Isaac, submits to her fate. While Isaac's submission saved him, Beth's does not, although it should. Because of its multi-indexical meaning, Beth's gesture is dramatic indeed, but not necessarily redemptive of the story. In its attempt to reach the house of safety, the hand designates the cause of her death: the father and the husband, the two competing men who found safety inside the house at the cost of her expulsion.

We can be brief about the violent aspect of the sequence. It is obvious that rape is not one form of violence, but a basic one. Penetrating the body, not with "the mouth of the sword" but with *zachar*, with masculinity itself, is inflicting an incurable wound, incurable, precisely, because it can never be forgotten: *zachar*, memory is the wound itself. Moreover, rape attacks, not the body in general, but the female body as female, the woman *as* woman, for her femaleness. At the moment of her undoing, Beth becomes the personification of femaleness: the pierced one, *neqebah*. Inflicting the memory of maleness, not *on* but *within* her body as the deadly wound that undoes her subjectivity—that is rape.

"They raped and tortured her": are these different acts? Torture is, according to Scarry (1985, 27–58), an attempt to unmake the victim's subjectivity by, first, unmaking her world. The bodily pain, next, is denied and translated into power. Rape, on the other hand, is an exercise of power. If rape is the destruction of the subject through her inside, torture starts at the outside. The two meet inside the body that ceases to be a body, because there is no subject left to experience it as her body. Both verbs, rape and torture, occur because in the compulsion to tell, the text needs to voice the body's experience, to express all the phases of the process of total destruction of a human, female being. The narrative compulsion uses all the means at its disposal to accomplish this impossible aim.[30] The two verbs are presented as durative and repetitive at the same time. They all raped her and tortured her, again and again, all night. Is Beth dead when the morning comes, and when she is, ironically, "released"? It does not matter, and of course she is.

Slaughter and Shattering

The final stage of the sacrifice of Beth starts when dawn chases the night away. The image of the woman lying on the threshold emerges from the dark; the narrative becomes more and more visual. This image forms the transition from the middle stage of the story to the final one. For the reader it is the most moving image of the whole story; not so for the husband, however. He literally steps over her body. As verse

27 has it, "he went out to go his way" before he even sees her. His purpose is to go his way in order to have his way. It seems that the whole event was just a bad dream, or, worse, has not affected him at all. But he cannot escape focalization: "Behold, the woman, his [patrilocal] wife, fallen down at the door of the house, her hands on the threshold." Her last act, her ritual gesture, is repeated, so that her husband cannot ignore her state, her request, and her accusation.

The man is, however, insensitive to the solemnity of the gesture. He who, during the night, had lain hold on her and thrown her out, repeats his authoritarian behavior: "Up!" is his command. And as if between them there had not been this irreversible verticalization of relations, he continues: "Let *us* be going," going *his* way. The response, however, is: "And none answered." Brought from one house to another, traveling from man to man, the woman can only refuse interpellation now that she has ceased to exist as a woman. Her answer is not "no"; there is no woman, "none" to answer. She has become voiceless. For the second time, then, the husband "takes hold" of her, more precisely, seizes her, as he will later seize the knife. Made an absolute object, she is now thrown over the donkey like a package.

Although failing to grasp the ritual significance of the woman's final gesture, the husband does participate in her sacrifice. The narrator uses sacrificial language, the language we know from Isaac's near-sacrifice, to make this clear. Once in his place—the word house, significantly, does not occur here—"he seized *the* knife." The definite article is replaced, by both the JPS (Slotki 1980, 303) and Soggin (1981, 289), by the indefinite form. Thus the commentators decline to respond to the intertextual reference to the other sacrificial text. Seizing *the* knife is, indeed, starting the sacrifice itself, for which the previous part was the preparation. But there is no divine voice, here, to intervene.

For the third time, the husband lays hold on his patrilocal wife—this time in order to put an end, if not to her life, in any case to her existence. Her bodily integrity, so effectively destroyed already by rape and torture, is further sacrificed, disintegrated: "He divided her according to her bones." The terminology is technical; it refers to butchery, to the slaughter of the sacrificial animal. Her body will be shattered, not like ashes on the wind, but like rotting flesh, not purified but defiled, and, according to the purity laws, doubly so. The raped body is now an untouchable, defiling body, an *abjection* (Kristeva 1982). The Levite, the priest who is supposed to be the "proper" sacrificial agent, is the executioner of this anti-sacrifice that reverses all the rules.

Already defiled, the body is now defiling, and the woman becomes after death the unwilling agent of the subsequent collective butchery of intertribal war. Beth's end comments on the dialectic of body and voice (Scarry 1985). In a book where a man's voice can be deadly to the body, the woman's body becomes voice. In this final event, the sending out of her remains "throughout all the borders of Israel," the anti-sacrifice becomes the exemplary content of the refrain that begins and ends the story: "In those days there was no king in Israel."

With the husband as the final subject of violence in this episode, the sequence of subjects is a meaningful one: the father, the community, the husband. The latter's violence resides in all of his five actions. Speaking to her with a command is, in view of what he *sees* ("behold"), a first violence done to her state. Not responding to her triple signifying gesture is denying her in this her ultimate moment of being. Denying her, indeed, is what the rapists have been utterly preoccupied with doing and what is the very act of rape,[31] and the husband, repeating it, consecrates their deed, as *their* priest. "Taking" her is again confirming her state as absolute object; it is the arrogant mastery of man over things[32] that—in gender-relations, in relations between man and nature,[33] and in relations between parents and children—destroys the integrity of the other. Using the knife against her is participating in the torture that befell her the previous night. Cutting her to pieces is going even further.

Dismembering her dead body is not only a desacralization but also an erasure of all her remaining humanity. It is as if the man is trying, in overdoing the violence already done to her, retrospectively to affirm *his* mastery, as against the mastery of the rapists, over her. Even at this poignant moment, the moment of Beth's dismemberment, the men compete.

Sending out the pieces of what was once Beth, the man denies she has ever existed. For the pieces of her body are, in a last and ultimately violent lie, used against her. They are used to cover up his own violence against her by the accusation of the violence done by the rapists that, for all its horror, is outdone by the man's secret, private actions. Ironically again, and irony is the only possible mode left after the silencing of Beth's voice, the public act of sending her body out is a way of hiding, of not proclaiming, what has really happened. Moreover, it is an ironic reversal of Abraham's multiplication. The woman who could have provided this man with multiple descendants is destroyed by multiple men and then multiplied. This is a different kind of multiplication indeed.

After Gideon's sacrifice in chapter 6, no sacrifice is truly proper. Some of them are proper but ineffective because they are not initiated by the subject, like Manoah's, while others are both ineffective and improper. Beth's sacrifice can be read as a systematic critique of the social chaos of the period. It is an anti-sacrifice in that it is anti-sacral and de-sacralizing, in all its details. It is not a burnt offering but a "raw" sacrifice. Instead of pure ashes, rotting flesh is scattered—not vertically, given to the deity, but horizontally, sent to the tribes. Within the isotopy of Lévi-Strauss's opposition between "raw" and "cooked," it represents a regression, backward, away from culture. Within Scarry's view, it represents the unmaking of the world. Where non-use is required of the "proper" sacrifice, Beth's body is used over and over again, for competition, possession, rape, torture, and for messages written in body language, to be sent out where verbal language has failed.

The sacrifice is not followed up by a redressing of the crimes. It is followed by more crime. The competition cannot but go on, and go on in violence. The two scenes wherein the eleven united tribes are so concerned about the fate of Benjamin, the culprit that we might be moved by their generosity, receive a different meaning within the social structure that I have chosen as the basis of my reading. Saving the tribe, saving the integrity of the "body" of Israel, that is, may be one motivation. But making the Benjaminites adopt, by force, the new matrimonial institution is certainly a way to combine the rescue of the tribe, the revenge against their transgression, and the enforcement of the new order.[34] Indeed, the Benjaminites are forced to "take" wives, to abduct them, to take them to their own houses. The integrity of Israel is not only threatened by the lack of wives, but simultaneously threatened by the Benjaminite deviation from "proper" virilocal marriage. The issue, then, is patriliny, and patriliny being "unnatural," the basic cultural act of sacrifice must reconfirm it over and over again. As long as voice and body are opponents in the struggle for the enforcement of culture, women will "lift up their voices, and weep," even in death.

CHAPTER FIVE
THE SCANDAL OF THE SPEAKING BODY: FROM SPEECH-ACT TO BODY LANGUAGE

The notions of integrity and closure in a text are like that of virginity in a body.
Jane Gallop

How can a dead woman speak? Why does she have to be dead in order to be able to speak? And what is speech in a book of murder? How does speech relate to action, affect lives, and bring about death? How does speech relate to the body, and how does the view that emerges from these questions affect the status of the text itself as speech?

At many different levels, we have seen the power of words at work. Not only were Jephthah and Beth's husband able to dispose of women's lives through the use of words, but we as readers of the stories about those speech-acts have also been able to subvert the common readings through the use of words and meanings—the dictionary and narrative theory. Thus, Beth became a patrilocal wife, and the powerful father was affected by this reversal of his daughter's status. The very enterprise of biblical writing and exegesis is based on a belief in the power of words. The attempt to deconstruct the traditional meanings attributed to words rests, in its turn, on a suspicion of the abuse of that power to attribute meaning. This position leads to a paradox that lies at the heart of speech-act theory.

The critical feminist enterprise acts upon exegetical traditions in order to affect not only meanings, but also the status of meaning itself, its delusive stability. It will challenge every claim to semantic certainty by pointing out the motivations for the attribution of meaning, the force that guides it. One of the meanings it challenges is the status of the "original" text itself. As there is no original text, but only prior attributions of meanings to whatever the text represents, there is no

129

utterance whose meaning is not primarily determined by its own force, the motivation that brings it forth and that leaves its traces in it. Meaning cannot be "pure," while the force that affects it cannot be grasped otherwise than *as* meaning.

A feminist analysis has to bring to light the force that underlies, determines the constative illusion[1] itself—that is, the illusion that meanings can be isolated, determined, and fixed—as well as the interests which motivate that illusion. The combination of interest and motivation makes for a push, an urgency that I call *force*. But, and herein lies the paradox, there is no other way to reach that force than through meaning, through the constative mode of discourse. This paradox causes the aporia inherent in the attempt to establish alternative meanings as a way to deconstruct the meanings in question. The only way out of this logical impasse is to rethink meaning, to reconsider meaning within its social functioning: to look at meaning *as* force.

The Book of Judges provides many examples of powerful speech-acts, indeed, of the overwhelming power of speech. In this chapter a few of those cases will be studied, this time with special attention to the problematic of meaning, force, and the social interaction which language in those cases produces and represents at the same time. As is typical of linguistic studies, speech-act theory has been developed around a few core examples. For Austin, its initiator, the favorite example is marriage, where the utterance of the word accomplishes the deed. The choice of this example nicely illustrates one of the major tenets of the theory, namely, that speech is historically and socially determined. Felman, who takes Austin beyond the amendments by which his followers and opponents tried to strip his theory of its radical sting, works with the example of seduction. Her seductive book *Le scandale du corps parlant* (1980) will be the central subtext of this chapter.

The study Felman provides is seductive not only because it is beautiful, but also because it offers a promise. The reader ready to believe in its basic theses is promised social promotion: the believer will gain status as a progressive and radical person. The study is also *about* seduction as the core speech-act at stake, the emblematic one that encompasses all others. And it is based on the seduction, by Austin, of its author who, by letting herself be seduced, steps into the socially female role of the seduced object (her primary subtext is Molière's *Don Juan, ou le festin de Pierre*) only to subvert it and become the reader's seducer. Seduction, then, has, in Felman's study, a triple function that will turn out to provide the key to its own limits.

Similarly, in this chapter there will be a central speech-act. The speech-act in question is not one but many; it is both central and decentered, less clear as a *case* than seduction, although more "cutting"—*tranchant,* as the French would say. The speech-act I will focus on is one that questions meaning, while being excessively meaningful; it is the one that is overmotivated and whose force is more central than, in fact, *becomes* its meaning. It is a speech-act that hovers between the *riddle* and the *vow,* while exploiting the ambiguity of both.

Judges is full of riddles, the speech-act with a deficit of meaning. Riddles ask for meaning because without the answer, they don't have any. Samson's riddle at his wedding, for example, hardly conceals its sexual meaning. It rests, however, on a confusion—a who is who?—that questions this meaning. Hence, there is no meaning in the riddle that we can rely on. The subjects of the performance that is at stake in the riddle are, as we will see shortly, anything but clear. And that lack of clarity is at the same time the riddle's force: it is the motivation of its utterance whose trace the riddle *is.* It is this disproportion between a lack of meaning and an excess of force that makes the riddle the emblematic speech-act through which we will explore the power of language and its relation to events, to history, and to narrative.

On the other side, speech-acts based on an *excess* of meaning exemplify the power of words in the most radical way. Their meaning being death, they bring death, they kill. The opposition between the fatal word and the speechless, powerless character that is killed by it drives the proportion between force and meaning into radical dissymmetry. But the excessive meaning that kills is at the same time motivated by a need to establish the overwhelming power of meaning, that is the underlying force of the act. Again, there is no way to tell the force from the meaning.

The difference between riddle as a deficit of meaning and the fatal word as an excess of meaning breaks down in a case that will be the central and at the same time the decentered example here: the *vow.* Denoting an as yet unknown, hence, nonexisting victim, the vow belongs on the side of the riddle. Killing that unknown victim, however, renders its meaning excessive and at the same time instigates the radical dissymmetry of power between speaker and victim. Hence, it is an act whose meaning is excessive and whose force is no less excessive. Thus, it challenges the assumption that the force and meaning of utterances can be somehow distributed, that they are proportionate, that they are different, distinct aspects of the speech-act.

While seduction rests on the capacity and power of the victim to misunderstand,[2] hence, to participate, be it perversely, in the speech-act, the vow, or the promise of gift, eliminates the victim from the linguistic process. That is why, in chapter 19, Beth never speaks until her victimization is completed. Therefore, in this chapter Beth's speaking body will exemplify what Don Juan's petrification[3] could ultimately not demonstrate:[4] that speech-acts are material, bodily, and irreducibly communicative. That the speaking body is, in Beth's case, a dead body, and that the vow is a speech-act done over dead bodies is precisely the scandal.[5] The difference between seduction on the one hand, and rape and murder that is the vow on the other, is the difference between the exploitation of the victim and the destruction of her. The exploitation is based on the constative fallacy, the illusion that the promise of seduction has a meaning other than its force. The destruction is a way to go beyond that misunderstanding. By making meaning so absolute, while on the other hand making it stand for force, the speaker strips the ensuing violence of any meaning besides force.

Speech-acts: The Word Become Flesh

When the spirit of Yahweh descends upon the body of the *gibbor*, the would-be hero, judge, or savior, the result is typically a speech-act. Therefore, speech-acts are central in Judges. The theory of speech-acts is concerned with the question, how can one do things with words? At first sight, this question means: how to do things with language? But words are also uttered by the mouth of the speaker, a mouth that is itself signified in the speech *as* speech. The mouths are literally uttering body language. That is precisely why speech-act theory is a materialist theory.

No speaker shows this inextricable mixture of language and body better than the *gibbor*, the hero of the Book of Judges who either speaks and then acts upon his words, or, in contrast, acts and then speaks upon his actions. In both cases, he acts out what the conflation of divine spirit and human body is able to perform. The *gibbor* is exemplary, also, insofar as he always fails in some sense to accomplish the perfect match between spirit and body, between language and event, between vow and fate. Thus, he embodies the dimension of failure that is, according to Felman, the most radical innovation of speech-act theory.

The materiality of speech-acts receives its most concrete expression in what we may take as its metaphor: the Hebrew expression "the mouth of the sword," and the play on the word "mouth" which it allows. The mouth that speaks is extended in the mouth that kills through the killing speech-act that is the vow. The seemingly innocent phrase "how to do things with words?" then becomes quite gruesomely guilty in the case of the ever-speaking *gibbor* Jephthah who could ex-

plain how to kill with words. We can take it one step further and consider Beth's dismembered body a speech-act. The text that represents
the response to this speech-act explicitly invites us to do so. The question can then be reversed: how can we turn killing into speaking? or
how can we return from (un)doing things to words?

Killing speech-acts are rooted in desire; hence we have to bring
in another subtext: psychoanalysis, that theory that is so intimately related to speech-act theory. The relations between speech-act theory
and psychoanalysis are multiple. Felman elaborates the common features of both disciplines' conceptions of the referent, of knowledge,
of what the discourse is supposed to be "about." But the discourse of
psychoanalysis also displays its own performative aspects, thus demonstrating both its "truth" and the impossibility of reaching that truth
constatively. The analysis of Freud's essay, "The Taboo of Virginity,"
has shown this paradox. The first effect of the essay's performativity
was a displacement of the "truth": it reveals more about men than
about virgins. What it informs us about is the taboo, not about virginity, and that is precisely what its title promises: being taboo, virginity is unspeakable. But Freud's essay does not talk "about" the
taboo, it acts it out. The taboo disappears as meaning, only to reappear
as force.

Both speech-act theory and psychoanalysis have a materialist
conception of knowledge, of the domain of the real the discourse aims
to represent. Knowledge is not *about* reality, about a distinct, separate
entity called "the real," but it is contiguous to, it touches, the real.
The referent of language is not a preexisting thing, but an act, a modification of the real. In this sense, the model of the ideal act would be
maternity and of the ideal speech-act, the miracle. Judges has mir-
acles, both repetitive,[6] in the spirit of Yahweh coming upon the *gibbor*,
and singular, in the genesis of the *gibbor* Samson, for example, or in
Gideon's test, or in both *gibborim*'s performances. Maternity, on the
other hand, the act that radically modifies reality, is represented ambiguously, and in modern interpretations, as failure. Samson's mother
failed to give her husband children in the "normal" way; Jephthah's
mother is a "harlot"; Abimelech's mother is a "concubine"; and in
both cases, the problematic descendance leads to the *gibbor*'s rejection
from the father's house. The victims of the fathers have no mother.

Yet, the book seems to demonstrate that the relation between the
most important speech-acts and the issue of paternity needs enhancement. Is the *act* itself, as a modification of the real, to be established
through language? Is speech the means to establish paternity?

The second aspect that both speech-act theory and psychoanalysis have in common is the dialogic nature of the real the discourse is "about." There is always an excess of enunciative force that cannot be confined within the limits of the enunciated—hence, the idea of illocutionary force. The force that motivates psychoanalytic speech-acts like slips partakes of excess as well. Excess leaves traces, and traces are writings, and writing yields meaning: force, in the final analysis, is not the leftover of meaning, not even its excess, but its foundation. This view of speech-acts entails an analysis of narrative, the narrative that is so central both in the psychoanalytic cure and in ideological literature.

With its objectifying form, its mission to produce the real, narrative helps the constative fallacy function. Narrativity is the force that motivates the ever-dynamic meaning both to occur and to present itself as fixed. It is on the basis of that illusion that the dialogue of speech can take place. Narrative is needed for the basically dialogic process of the cure to occur. To speak is necessarily to speak to, and to speak to is to affect, to modify the real within which the dialogue takes place and which the narrative is about. This aspect of narrative as dialogue is acted out not only *in* the stories but also *with* the stories, between them and the reader. Not only the commentators' slips but their very enterprise is based on it.[7]

The third aspect that both speech-act theory and psychoanalysis have in common is the dimension of failure that is for Felman the key to the radicalization of Austin's theory. Both speech-act theory and psychoanalysis founded their verification procedure on failure. It is only when a speech-act fails that we can be certain we will be confronted with a performative speech-act; it is only when a subject of psychoanalysis performs a slip that we can be sure something is happening—something that modifies reality, a speech-act, has occurred. It is failure that allows us to see force in meaning, to see the modification of the real being *done.*[8] In the triloquy between the text, the commentaries, and my own discourse, the critical dimension is also located in failure. It is only when the commentators fail to be convincing that we can be sure they were trying to be; when they fail their speech-act, we know there is one. My own position is not safeguarded from this risk; it is up to the readers of this study to point out my slips. The excess or lack of arguments points to the attempt to impose meaning; hence, they signify force. Failure, then, becomes the model speech-act that displays the anchorage of meaning within the motivating force and the enactment of the attempt that fails. As Felman writes, "Failure refers, not to an absence, but to the enactment of a difference" (1980, 115).

The materialism inherent in speech-act theory makes it impossible to define psychoanalysis outside of it: psychoanalysis *is* a speech-act theory. But also, the discourse of psychoanalysis is, as we have seen, a set of speech-acts in its own right, including, we can now add, the failure. Indeed, Freud's struggle with the distinctions of gender and subjects in his account of virginity illustrates the status of his own theory. Rather than being able to define the meaning of the taboo, he could only, in keeping with his own theory, enact its force in his very failure to do so. But since the force encompasses the meaning, indeed, produces it, the essay was more illuminating than we might expect from a failure—yet for the meaning to be found, we had to seek for it inside the force, not apart from it. The essay helped us understand the taboo, its extent and its modes, and thus, it helped us see the taboo at work in both Freud's and Jephthah's slips and failures.

In this analysis, speech-act theory and psychoanalysis together show a common concern for what their own discourses display about their subjects. They are theories of the subject in the same sense that narratology is a theory about the subject thematized in relation to its acts of self-reference. Narratology thus conceived overcomes its own limits: concerned with a mode of discourse that has objectification of the object as its basic stance, the focus on the subject strips meaning from its pseudo-objective status. The subject is what relates the act, less to its result than to its source, process, and matter. In order to understand the events of Judges in their performative aspects we must bring the relations between the events and their sources, processes, and matter to light as explicitly as possible. Samson's riddle shows this need most clearly: without the subject's awareness of both riddle and narrated/hidden event, there is no way to answer the riddle—that is, to understand its meaning.

Samson's Riddle: The Word Become Woman

During the seven-day party preceding his wedding, Samson "put forth a riddle" to his thirty Philistine companions at the feast: "Out of the eater came forth food and out of the strong came forth sweetness" (14:14). As a speech-act, the riddle is based on a position of power. The subject who proposes the riddle knows the answer, while the addressee does not. Moreover, there is power in the initiative itself. It presupposes the right to be listened to, the obligation on the part of the addressee to invest the effort to find out the answer. In the case of a wager, the power is betokened by the possession of a stake. There is a conditioned promise involved which, we might suggest, is a form of seduction. All these aspects are explicit in the speech-act that precedes the riddle itself—its staging:

> Let me now put forth a riddle unto you; if you can declare it to me within the seven days of the feast and find it out, then I will give you thirty linen garments and thirty changes of raiment; and if you cannot declare it to me, then you shall give me thirty linen garments and thirty changes of raiment. (14:12)

The companions accept the challenge. Thus they submit themselves to the power of the addresser, hoping or trusting in their own power to reverse the situation.

When the answer is later revealed, it turns out to be a "bad" riddle, a riddle that cannot be "found out" at all by anybody else but the addresser. The riddle's answer/meaning is Samson's secret performance and transgression, the killing of the lion and the eating of honey out of the corpse's belly. The event is fraught with ambiguities, too many to allow for a straight answer to the riddle, anyway. The distinction between the general and the particular has not been respected. The riddle turns out to be based on an event that has been told by the narrator to the reader, but not by Samson to his companions. Without that narrative act, the event remains particular and cannot be "found out."

The riddle as a genre is based on another impossibility: although it must be understandable *after* explanation, it cannot be before. The explanation turns the arbitrary into logic. This generic impossibility is based on an incongruity other than that of Samson's particularizing riddle. While the latter plays on the dialectic between the secret/private and the known/public, "proper" riddles turn the initial arbitrariness into retrospective logic by generalization. Thus, the creature who walks on a variable number of legs in the Sphinx's riddle to Oedipus becomes "man" in the answer. Impossible because arbitrarily particular in the riddle, it becomes, retrospectively, logical, "natural." Its understandability in retrospect is a generic requirement. Given these conventions, we can at this point already predict that the companions need to appeal to resources other than their own inventiveness to find the riddle out. And, given the structure of power involved, we can foresee that the revelation of the riddle, which is inaccessible, must cause a crisis. And indeed, that is what will happen.

Samson's trap is concealed in his initial statement. The figure "thirty" is ambiguous. On the one hand, it enhances the promise of the stake. Since Samson is alone while the companions are thirty, it seems "natural" that they will win the stake, for which Samson will hardly have much use. On the other hand, providing the stake is much more difficult for Samson, since he has to give thirty sets by himself while his companions will only have to give one set each. The interest that motivates the contest is therefore hard to understand. Here, as in the riddle itself, there is a tension. In both cases, the narrative development, whose motor is Samson's bodily performances, heavily depends on that tension. The arrangement of the contest—the figure thirty—sets the stage for the contradiction between promise and threat that the scenario of the riddle will display.

In order to understand the riddle, we must first compare it to the vow, its fellow example here. The basic grammatical criterion for performative acts to occur is the asymmetry between the first-person, present tense of the indicative mode, on the one hand, and the other persons, tenses, and modes on the other (Felman 1980, 19). This criterion, however, fits Felman's example of seduction more convincingly than it fits our example. Seduction takes place in the present: either the victim is actually seduced or there is no seduction. The problem is in the criterion, which pays no attention to the disturbing centrality of the future tense in the meaning of the promise/vow. True, the speech-act itself can only be performed in the present, but the linguistic use of tenses does not refer to that *hic et nunc* situation. The tension between time and tense, between the moment of utterance of the speech-act and the duration of its consequences, is inherent in the speech-act: therein lies its effect on the real that it "touches."[9] The core examples of both theorists, Austin and Felman, point at a difference. If it is true that marriage is accomplished in the present tense, the promise that is the basis of seduction is, as a present-tense act, basically incomplete. Marriage *is* accomplished by the "yes," and whatever happens in the future, there is no way to deny the married state after the utterance. There even exists a "promised" state, the state of engagement to marry, that is, precisely, a rehearsal of marriage whose ceremony is similar: it doubles, as if it distrusted it, marriage itself. But the promise, unlike marriage, is open to permanent revision. The conditioned promise that is the vow exemplifies that difference by making it explicit. The supplement "if" specifies how the future is involved in the act. At the same time, it makes the promise in a sense more binding: the other party, the addressee who becomes the subject of the condition, gains some power. The condition makes the fulfillment less certain, while strengthening the obligation to the subject in the view of the addressee. In other words, while saying "yes" is to marry when spoken under the appropriate circumstances, saying, "If you sleep with me, I will marry you" is not. The promise accomplished in the present time is, significantly, phrased in the future tense, and the indeterminacy that tense introduces is added to the uncertainty presented by the condition.

The vow, in this context, is the conditioned promise of something else. The stake is, typically, not the subject itself nor the addressee, but a third object—or a third person, for that matter. This introduction of the third person in the process is what distinguishes the vow from many other speech-acts. The obligation that it entails not only compensates for the indeterminacy implied in both conditionality and futurity, but it is in turn compensated for by the derivative third object, stake, or victim. Unlike the seduction as promise of marriage, the vow involves an objectification that excludes the object from the process. The victim of the vow does not have the option of accepting or rejecting the deal. Her collaboration in the speech-act is not conditional for its "felicity." The asymmetry, then, becomes a dissymmetry, a power structure that radically separates the third party from the process as a nonparticipant, while being the party most thoroughly affected.[10]

The riddle predicts that dissymmetry. The proposed stake, as we have seen, is the symbol of the power structure that Samson tries to establish through the riddle. The all-male company in which the speech-act is accomplished, together with the generic feature of insolvability, the use of the future tense that points to the future wherein the wedding-to-come must necessarily break the unity of the group by the introduction of the woman, and the crisis that cannot but break out because of the dissymmetry of interests all suggest a problematic of possession in the future where a woman is at stake. Is she, also, the stake?

A second characteristic of performance is the asymmetry between force and meaning. The riddle has a meaning that is its answer; it has a meaning *as* riddle, and the act of proposing it has a meaning. The analysis of these three semantic aspects shows that the distinction between force and meaning not only fails, but also that its failure itself is thematized *in* its meaning. The answer to the riddle is given by the companions, who have used Kallah, by promising to murder her, to get the answer from Samson himself. Hence, the riddle's meaning is self-referential. This self-referentiality is appropriate, as the answer reveals: "What is sweeter than honey? And what is stronger than a lion?" (14:28). Samson, the hero of strength, signifies himself in the riddle. The first meaning of the riddle, then, is its answer, which makes the private experience public. Whatever the precise meaning of the answer will turn out to be, it encompasses strength: force. The second level of meaning, the form of the riddle as speech-act, is embedded in a problematic of power relations—relations wherein force, again, precludes meaning.

A second feature of the meaning of the riddle-and-answer combination is the paradox in the riddle and the banality of the answer. This points to a problematic of "speciality." Samson's extraordinary strength is the semantic core of the answer to the riddle and the concealment of that answer. The *gibbor*'s encounter with the lion in the previous episode has encouraged Samson in his attempt to be someone very special by suggesting his own power to him, and hence suggesting his riddle. The power of his special strength is, however, by definition secret, hence not necessarily available in all circumstances. Proposing the riddle, then, is not only using that power; it is also making that power known. But, paradoxically again, the game depends on secrecy, and the revelation of the answer destroys the power. The subject is entangled in a logical conflict that leads, ultimately, to the failure of the act.

The very form of riddle and answer shows a problematic of power relations at work. The question of the subjects of speech and the mode of discourse they use is again revealing. Samson took power by proposing the riddle; but he gave it the form of a statement, that is, the form of an answer, not of a question. The companions do answer, but they give their answer the form of a question. Thus, the question that is conventional to the riddle is referred back to him, and he is then placed in a position to answer riddles rather than propose them. As a matter of fact, the riddle and the answer can be easily reversed without losing riddle-logic in the process. As a groom, on the eve of sexual initiation, Samson, indeed, is overstating his position. The companions, on the other hand, are on native ground, in native company, and, as we have seen earlier, conceiving of the wedding in a different way: they are in a native tradition of marriage.

The answer, as already suggested, cannot be found out without the help of a mediator between subject and addressee. Samson has to reveal the answer himself, and the question is, how can this self-referentiality be broken open in order for the companions to have access to the knowledge? The meaning of the riddle as revealed in the answer is the combination of sweetness and strength. But the site of strength, its symbolic subject, is not, as is generally assumed, Samson himself; at least, not univocally. The lion, in the founding scene of the riddle, does not represent Samson but his antagonist. For the lion was his antagonist in the first place; he was the other who forced Samson to discover himself. Another antagonist whose belly also yields sweetness like honey and who is also combined, conflated, with the strong one is the woman in marriage. The first meaning of the riddle is, then, the formidable woman.[11] The identification with the lion does not predict much good for her, however; the lion can only yield sweetness when dead.

On the third level of meaning, to propose a riddle is, as I have already suggested, to usurp a position of power that the subject Samson may not (yet) deserve. The conflict that ensues from that usurpation is signified in the generic properties of the riddle itself. The companions, then, need to go and find access to the subject's mind. They go to the most obvious candidate: the woman. The choice is obvious not only because of the wedding situation, but also because, as I have argued, the identification between sweet and strength, in the riddle, signifies the initiation of marriage itself and proposes that conflation as its meaning. It expresses, in fact, Samson's view of marriage. Samson will be subjected, then, to (part of) himself in order to reveal, instead of conceal, that part. The dialogic speech-act that is the combination of riddle and answer, then, requires a third party, an "excess" whose trace remains in order to betoken the force at stake. That violence will be used to erase that trace—a violence that, as another aspect of force, will leave its trace in its narrative account—is therefore unavoidable.

But how can we talk about these meanings at all? We can do so on the basis of narrativity, on the basis of the presupposition that there is a sequence of events that not only triggers or motivates the speech-act, but also determines its meaning. Without the event with the lion, known to us but unknown to the participants, hence, without its secret within the narrative, there is no meaning possible in the riddle. There lies precisely its generic flaw: riddles are supposed to be generalizable. This narrative anchoring in the particular story of this particular *gibbor* is what makes it, as a riddle, both impossible and typical of the series of riddles in the book. It brings it close to the speech-act of the vow. The outcome of the riddle is equally narratively embedded in the whole story. That embedding determines its status as a particular type of speech-act: the one that lacks meaning. It has no meaning outside the sequence; hence, its motivation and meaning are but one. Narrativity produces both the riddle and the answer, and the latter requires the narrative. The metonymic relation between narrative and riddle is the *slip* of the speech-act. As in psychoanalysis, the slip is not the excess of the narrative, but its motor (Brooks 1983). As such, it motivates, energizes, *is* the narrative. Hence, on this level too, force and meaning are conflated.

If this is the case, then, we must conclude that the riddle, as the motor of the narrative, already signifies the end of its plot(ting):

Kallah's death. The force of the speech-act is motivated by the need to undo the woman who will mediate between the subject and the addressee and who is, ultimately, the stake. The sequence that the riddle constitutes by linking the lion episode to the wedding-feast episode follows the line of increasing violence, only to end in Kallah's death. This linear movement is itself signified in nonlinear predictions; the meaning that is her death is predicted much earlier. The dead lion prefigures it, the companions announce it, and Samson triggers it. When they try to find out the riddle, the companions say to Kallah: "Entice your man that he may declare unto us the riddle, lest we burn you and your father's house with fire. Have you called us hither to impoverish us?" (14:15). The first sentence, here, signifies the conflation between Samson and Kallah; it is obviously she, not Samson himself, who must declare the riddle to them, after getting the answer from him. The second part of the sentence predicts Kallah's death, as the bride living in her father's house. The death, conditionally promised, equals the vow in the proposition of the riddle, for we have seen that the contradictory interests involved make a satisfactory outcome impossible.

The second sentence provides the vow with a motivating force that is the attribution of guilt. The reversal of guilt and punishment betrays the arbitrariness of the attribution. They want her to do their errand, they want to force her to do it, they threaten her, and then, as an afterthought, they come up with her guilt. Now, if we look at the passage that precedes the wedding, we see that the subjects who "called him hither" are, again, both Samson and the bride's tribesmen, not Kallah. It is significant that throughout Kallah's story the agents are thus conflated.

What interests me here is that the force of the speech-act, the excess that is outside the force, and the choice of the semantic of strength as the core of the riddle, seems to thematize that overwhelming predominance of force. As in psychoanalysis, where there is no story without its motivation, the force that pushes the subject to tell the story and that lies both in the past and in the present of the speech-act, there is, in Judges in general and in this riddle episode in particular, no riddle without the story, and no story without the riddle; no present tense without a past that predicts the future. It is in the future that the word of the speech-act becomes flesh, burned flesh; and the flesh is female.

This leads us to the third aspect that characterizes the performative speech-act: its failure. There is, as we have seen, a dimension of failure inherent to speech-acts, and that dimension is the most fruitful one for the theory. It has a capacity for specification, for information that is hard to find elsewhere. The fact that a speech-act may fail is crucial to our understanding of the riddles and vows in Judges. If the book were to consist solely of monologic narrative, dispensing with the speech-act of Samson and the companions, there would be no way to measure the failure that keeps the story in movement.

Following Austin, Felman (1980, 18) distinguishes two modes of failure: misfire and abuse. Misfire occurs when the circumstances of the speech-act are inappropriate for its success. Someone who is already married cannot marry in a monogamous society, however hard she or he tries and says "yes." Abuse occurs when the subject knows very well that she or he is not going to fulfill the promise. In other words: the difference between the two categories is based on the subject's implication. In the case of misfire, the circumstances may be outside the subject; there are "facts," rules, situations that do not enable the subject to perform successfully. Abuse depends more heavily on the subject who is fully responsible for his or her inability to fulfill the promise. When it comes to abuse, Austin works out, in his characteristically humorous way, the impossible differences between committing abuse "intentionally," "deliberately," or "on purpose." These terms would be out of place where misfiring is at stake.

Can we now answer the question whether the contradiction inherent in Samson's riddle is based on either of these two modes of failure? Proposing a riddle whose answer is impossible to find out because it is not generalizable seems to be a case of misfire. Proposing a riddle as an exercise of an authority one does not possess seems closer to abuse, although there are other circumstances involved as well. Proposing an impossible riddle that implies a promise of gift while one is not the possessor of the gift is clearly abuse. There can be no serious intention of fulfilling the promise. Or can there? In other words, Samson could very well be so caught in his own riddle that he is not aware of the real stake he is proposing, and indeed, the following episode points in that direction. And, finally, since the impossibility is already part of the meaning of the speech-act, Samson cannot even be accused of lying.

The Riddle as Vow and the Vow as Riddle

We have seen that the riddle was proposed within the context of a secular vow: a conditional gift. [12] The basic feature of the riddle, its concealed meaning, made it possible for the narrative logic to produce a third party, the mediator, object of violence toward which the sequence leads, as the ultimate object of the conditional gift. This turns the riddle into a vow, a vow like Jephthah's: one that promises to give what the subject does not *know*.[13] In this section, the relations between the seemingly innocent game—the riddle—and the deadly vow will be further explored through the analysis of a larger number of riddles and vows than the two founding ones we have seen so far and which will guide us as subtexts.

Riddles have a specific relation to the reality in which they interfere. They pose, and dispose of, the unknown; so do vows. The first vow of the book is a case we have not paid much attention to so far: the conditional gift of Achsah, chief Caleb's daughter, to the prospective conquerer of Kiriath-sepher, the city of books. This vow is the example of a "proper" vow: although it disposes of the daughter in a way we would, today, not rave about, it is in accordance with the tradition it signifies, and the following episode shows that it is, within the context, "proper" enough to serve as a model.[14] The vow is carried out, and its beneficiary is generally considered the ideal judge. The vow leaves no "rests": nothing to regret, to blame, or to guess. At the outset it also has aspects of the riddle. The question that is asked like a riddle is not "who is the object of the gift?" but "who will be the subject of the conquest?" The difference is significant and determines the acceptability of the gift. The giver/vower does not fail his speech-act by abuse; he does have both the power to fulfill and the intention of fulfilling his vow.

Like negations, however, questions are intrinsically indeterminate. One question implies another: to whom will Achsah be given? In other words, the very form of the riddle combines the public and the private domains, and determines the fate of both city and daughter; it defines the status of the *gibbor*, whose name is the riddle's meaning or answer, while the hopeful anticipation of his action is its force. In comparison to Samson's riddle, this vow/riddle makes explicit what the other one tried to conceal: the identity of the third party, the stake, she who has no participation in the speech-act while yet being its object.

The vow modifies the real in that it triggers a narrative sequence: first, the *gibbor* qualifies for the award, changing the situation of the city; then, he receives the award, changing the situation of the daughter. Achsah becomes, through this narrative, an *ʿalmah*. She accedes to the third of the three phases of female ripeness and is thus separated from her father.

Riddles establish truth. Truth is a perfectly adequate relation between a statement and its referent, between language and the reality it represents. Riddles conceal that reality, but their answers, which are always, typically, the only possible answer, are undeniably true. One does not challenge the answer to a riddle. The same holds for vows. The vow promises the gift of the unknown object; once the identity of the object is revealed, there is no possible challenge to it. If the gift of Achsah to Othniel is the "natural," true consequence of the riddle-and-answer of Caleb's vow, so is the gift of Bath. Her identity as the object whose existence the vow radically changes is not questioned. Only one being can be the first one to come out of the house and meet the victor. Hence, the description of the object in the speech-act is necessarily perfectly adequate, hence, true.

This feature of the riddle is interestingly exploited by Yael in verses 4:20–23. The exhausted chief Sisera, on his flight after the defeat of his army, is invited by Yael to seek refuge in her tent. As he prepares to go to sleep, Sisera gives Yael an order: "Stand in the opening/door of the tent and it shall be, when any man comes and asks you and says: 'Is there any man here?' you will say: 'None.'" Is this speech-act a riddle, a vow, or something else? It is in the first place an order. But as an order, it misfires. Sisera's circumstances do not give him the authority required for ordering. The failed order embeds in itself a question. At first sight a question of presence, its ambiguity allows it to be interpreted as a question of identity that assimilates the order to the riddle. The question is not, this time, *who* the man will be, but *what* he is: a man or not a man. Typically, the negation allows for indeterminacy, and in the space created by that property, both characters respond to the speech-act in a different way. For Sisera, the answer was obviously meant to deny his presence; it was an order to lie. For Yael, the speech-act was a riddle, and riddles have perfect truth-value. Hence, the answer meant for her: no man. The riddle consists, then, of finding out how a man can be no man. Her answer is, by being a dead man, and she acts upon this answer.

This can be read as a response to Samson's riddle: How can a strong lion/woman yield pleasure? Answer: As a dead lion/woman. Sisera's involuntary riddle shares properties with the vow as well. It is emphatically phrased in the future tense, the object is not participating in the dialogue, and, as is systematically the case with vows in Judges, this leads to death. Turning the misfired order upside down, Yael "obeys" it, but turns the lie into a question of identity.

Riddles have a specific relation to desire. They stage the desire to know, which is, as we have seen, the erotic desire of the Hebrew male. Proposing a question is proposing, for the addressee, the possibility of knowing: knowing the object of the desire to know, enjoying her as the stake of the game. Samson's riddle, caught in the web of the narrative that produced it and was produced by it, was about the desire to know what yields pleasure through violent appropriation, and that is precisely the view of eroticism that the book exclusively represents. Jephthah's vow was equally "about" the exclusive possession of the daughter that Freud described as the "essence of monogamy." The riddle that becomes the interpretation of the negative vows and the threats that we also find in the book have a similar relation to desire. Two examples suffice, here.

When Barak does not take Deborah/Yahweh's promise of victory at face-value, in 4:8, it is because, like Jephthah, he needs help from a real *gibbor*, someone unlike himself. Deborah turns his vow ("if you will go with me, I will go") into a riddle when she responds with the negative promise: "I will surely go with you; but the road you walk shall not be for your glory; for Yahweh will give Sisera into the hand of a woman" (4:9). As a reversal of the daughter-of-the-chief, Sisera, the chief of the enemy army, will be given into the hand of the real victor: a woman. The riddle that ensues from this threat is, of course, the identity of the woman, who is, however, this time not the object but the beneficiary of the gift. Typically, there is no way to find out the riddle beforehand, while its retrospective "logic" is obvious. Since dishonor for Barak is part of the threat, it cannot be his respectable colleague Deborah; it has to be some woman who would bring utter shame to the failing hero. Hence the choice is Yael, a woman who is hardly Israelite and who lives inside a tent, rather than participate in the battle that is the stage of the political coherence. But again, the sexual aspect of the riddle is another part of it. The woman can only "get at" the fugitive through seduction, through the promise of safety and comfort in her tent, in her bed. Giving him into the hand of a woman is, then, nothing other than what the custom prescribes: giving in marriage.

The second example is the negative vow, toward the end of the book, to give no daughters as wives to the Benjaminites; this negative vow leads to a question that shows again the sexuality inherent in riddles. The vow threatens to exterminate the tribe of Benjamin, hence, to destroy the wholeness of the people. The riddle it entails is, then: how can one provide wives to the Benjaminites without breaking the vow not to give them? The question of identity is implicit: who can these wives and nonwives be? But again, the indeterminacy also allows for the other possible question: how can they be Israelite women, in spite of the vow? Again, the truth of the riddle, the reality-changing aspect of the vow, cannot be questioned. And again, the answer is logical in retrospect. The issue of the riddle is neither in the gift nor in the identity of the object, both being determined by the vow and the law. Instead, the issue turns out to be, "How can we avoid giving?" The objects of gift, women, and more precisely, women who will guarantee ethnic purity through endogamy, will not be given but stolen, abducted—certainly, in our understanding, raped.[15] The example brings us back to both Austin's favorite example and Felman's definition of seduction. The negative vow concerned the refusal to give, not the promise to give what one does not own. The speech-act that becomes impossible, then, is marriage. The description of the women to be stolen, in the speech-act of the leaders who solve the problem, is the one already quoted in chapter 3: young girls, marriageable, who have not known man by lying with him. The order is, as is typical of the riddle, to produce such wives. But they can only be produced by murder, not by birth-giving. They will be produced by the killing of all the subjects who do not fit this description. The negativity of the description matches the negativity of the production: only by killing those who are *not* the objects of the riddle can those objects come into existence.

If desire is acted out in such negative, destructive ways, we must conclude that there is hardly any difference left between desire and violence. The violence the riddles in the book result in is the form taken by the appropriation that, according to Felman, seduction implies. The riddle-as-vow and the vow-as-riddle both explore the modalities of appropriation by language, that is, by the power relations involved in speech-acts. The playful reversal that seduction allows and that Felman's own text so beautifully illustrates—the reversal that gives the addressee the possibility of escaping the status of object and of gaining that of subject—is strictly impossible in the case of the fatal speech-acts, riddle and vow. The appropriation of the stake is performed outside of the object's participation. The appropriation is therefore radical, deadly.

Some of the examples quoted in this section presented a riddle/vow whose subject was a woman and whose object/victim was a man. Samson's mother presents the limit of this speech-act. We have seen how she, not her husband, was addressed by the messenger of Yahweh who stipulated the conditions for the gift of the son, hence, for the vow. The difference between this vow and the other ones is that the object of the gift is himself the alleged subject of the condition. The mother, too, is asked to observe the appropriation rules, but the Nazirite status assigned to Samson prescribes a specific behavior on his part as well. More strikingly, the mother, addressee of the gift, takes it on herself to have more responsibility for the condition than the subject of the vow intended. While the messenger does not specify the duration of Samson's Nazirite status, hence, of his commitment to the rules, the mother extends that indeterminate period to "the day of his death" (13:7). By offering this interpretation, she shows that she understands the absolute character of riddle and vow. There is no relative, unverifiable truth, only an unexpected one.

But her autonomous behavior creates a new riddle. The rule she establishes has no clear subject. She repeats the speech of the messenger, and it is within that repetition that she adds the new element. As in the case of the curse of Benjamin, the riddle concerns the question of how to get around the contradiction that is now inherent in the vow because of its imperfect doubling. Again, the narrative provides the answer. Samson will die and not die from his transgression. He will die as a consequence of the haircut, but not on the same day. The "day of his death" is retrospectively interpreted as the day that causes his death, and, again retrospectively, the logic is flawless. Lack of meaning becomes excess of meaning.

The linguistic behavior of Samson's mother shows the gesture of appropriation inherent in performatives. The difference that characterizes this vow as opposed to the others, Samson's own participation in the fulfillment of the condition, differentiates this female appropriation from the male ones. Similarly, Sisera himself posed the riddle that Yael used to appropriate the victory. Compared to Jephthah's vow the difference is striking and is related to the difference in power between fathers and mothers. The question that arises, then, is whether fatherhood as such has a relation to speech-acts, specifically to the riddle/vow act. Is knowing and not knowing, the issue of fatherhood and of riddles, also the key to speech-act theory as a materialist view of language?

The Daughter's Body Language as a Challenge to Fatherhood

As a son, Samson strikingly resembles Felman's emblematic character, Don Juan. Interpreted by many as the hero of passionate love, Samson features the plurality of desire that Don Juan stands for. Although less prolific in this respect, Samson also breaks promises and vows, and he too is killed by stone. Like Manoah, Don Juan's father is not very successful. He complains about the ordeal of the fatherhood that has not kept its promise. He has no power over his son—specifically, no power over the son's promises. Felman's comment on the father's complaint holds strikingly well for the failing father in Judges:

> En tant que promesse non tenue, Don Juan emblématise la rupture et le décalage entre conscience paternelle et performance paternelle, la discontinuité entre intention et acte: le non-savoir-de-soi de l'acte même de la production de sens; le «malheur» ou l'échec du Père en tant qu'autorité constative, cognitive. (1980, 51)

The father who represents the failure of the constative, the overwhelming priority of force over meaning, is not the same character in Felman's narrative as the performative hero, the seducer. In Judges, however, it seems to be primarily the father who performs the crucial speech-act of the vow. The case of Samson is, significantly, a deviation from this rule, as his participation in Kallah's death partakes of that same lack of clarity. Jephthah resembles Don Juan's father in his despair over his cognitive failure. Not knowing whether or not he will qualify as a *gibbor*, he gives away what he does not *know*. His fatherhood being what he gives away, it is, in this sense, as insecure as is Manoah's. Both fathers speak too much and are punished for it. If Manoah is corrected by the messenger, Jephthah, however, never learns the lesson. He seems to be a compulsive speaker, and, moreover, he seems pretty good at it. His success in the negotiations over his position as leader (11: 6–11), his shrewd device for telling an Ephraimite from a Gileadite (12:5–6), and his tendency to negotiate before fighting show that for Jephthah the mouth that utters words and the mouth of the sword are closely related. The lethal quality of his words adds to that effect. The question that arises from that relation has already been suggested in the previous chapter: Is there a bond between speech and violence, and is that bond a polemical response to the failure, inherent in fatherhood, of reaching material contiguity with the daughter? In order to answer that question, we will first look at the daughterly speech-acts which are, typically, acts of body language.

Achsah is the first individual woman in the book, the token daughter who is given away in the "normal" ritual of welcoming the victor, in a "proper" vow that fits into the social practice of the day. Narratively, she is the female figure who holds, in a condensed form, all features of the other daughter-stories. The "property" of her fate is betokened by her relation, not to sacrificial killing fire but to life-giving water. Like Beth, she goes through a confrontation with her father at the moment of her marriage to the victor, and interestingly, she is the subject of an act of body language[16] that has confounded philologists. The confrontation between her, the husband, and the father seems therefore a significant counterpart of Beth's final speech-act. The comparison between this initial act and Beth's concluding act of body language may reveal the underlying interests that establish the gender-specific relation between speech and violence of which Jephthah is the most competent performer.

The gift of Achsah, the daughter of Caleb, to the victor of the city of books is promised in a vow that functions as the perfect riddle: its outcome is unpredictable while its answer, in retrospect, produces the *gibbor* who is to be the model judge. The military issue is "proper": the city to be conquered is part of the promised land, and its conquest is part of the project of establishment of the people. The gift is also "proper" on the level of sexual relations, since it is not only endogamous within the tribe, but even within the clan, the family, Othniel being Caleb's younger brother. Chiefhood is thus handed over from elder to younger brother. In this respect, the marriage between Achsah and Othniel is a model also in that it avoids the problem of the conflict between patrilocy and virilocy, both brothers being of the same clan.[17] A-conflictual, the gift is triply proper and can be seen as the core which generates, by antithesis, the problematic cases that elaborate on each of this gift's "properties."[18]

This short story (1:12–15) has one problematic passage, however. On her way to her father or her husband, Achsah addresses her father with a strikingly self-confident, assertive request. There are two verbs in that passage that raise problems to commentators. The one, "to entice" or "to incite" in 1:14, whose meaning comes close to seduction, poses the problem of the subject—who entices whom? The verb form suggests that Achsah entices Othniel, but since she is the one who will make the claim, the reverse has also been proposed— while the other, the verb that describes the action resulting from the enticement, poses the problem of the nature of the act.[19] One more brief exercise in philology[20] will help us assess, not only the text itself, but also its treatments in commentaries.

The verb form *vathiṣnaḥ* describing Achsah's introduction to her request for wells in Joshua 15:18 and in Judges 1:14[21] is the same root which in 4:21 describes the tent-pin going through Sisera's temple right into the ground, or, in a different interpretation, of his brains oozing into the ground. Unfortunately, nobody knows what the verb means exactly, and the coincidence of the occurrences in such different situations is the more disturbing since in both cases there is a woman's insubordination at stake. The latter aspect of the problem, however, tends to be overlooked by philologists who nevertheless confess their powerlessness to explain the word. The philological problem about the meaning of the verb might be in itself evidence of the force involved. The verb *affects* the scholars because it does not yield transparent meaning, but also because, as if to confuse reassuring distinctions, its most likely meaning is *force*.

A detailed discussion of the verb is led by E. W. Nicholson (1977). It starts with James Barr's critique of the *New English Bible* translation of the passage as "she broke wind," which Barr found "an invitation to ridicule" (1974) and which goes back to Driver's argument based on the Accadian *shanahu* (1957). Nicholson convincingly refutes this Driverian argument. The Accadian "to void (excrement)" does indeed belong to the semantic field of which "she broke wind" is a part; this semantic field, however, has a more specific verb for "to break wind," and therefore, extension of the verb is not called for. Nicholson's conclusion that there is no solution to the problem since no suggestion is compelling, hence, that we simply do not know what the verb means, seems justified. From there to the next step, which is to retain the traditional rendering of the verb as "she alighted from her ass," however, is a symptom of the limits of philology.

Two factors can be helpful, if not in solving the problem, which cannot be done anyway, then at least in providing suggestions for a more specific understanding of the verb. One is that the problematic word clearly refers to a gesture, a physical action. Therefore, looking at anthropological material, specifically the material of symbolic anthropology, is worthwhile. The second factor is that the word occurs within a narrative, a short story, whose structure can be illuminating. The typical limitation of philology, which tends to ignore these contextual possibilities, leads to conservatism (the advice to keep the traditional interpretation). A confrontation between subject and act can be revealing. Whether or not the act signified can be considered a speech-act has to be examined carefully, since the traditional rendering of the verb does not cover that usage.

The state of the interpretation of this verb is as follows. Nicholson does not pay attention to one feature in Driver's argument. The translation "she broke wind" is interpreted by the latter as symbolic. The act expresses contempt or anger. The new translation, therefore, has the advantage over the traditional one of accounting for the father's surprise, revealed in the next phrase. This aspect shall have to be retained; I will integrate it in the narrative analysis of the episode. There does not seem to be a compelling reason why anger or contempt should be assumed, although the fact that until this point her father gave her only useless dry grounds may be a good reason. I would picture a more self-confident Achsah, who just claims her due, without emotional outburst.

Although I do agree with Nicholson that the idiom of the semantic field in Accadian does not call for Driver's extension of the verb's meaning, the idea itself of envisaging a possibly symbolic meaning for whatever gesture is worth retention. It suggests we look further into Koehler and Baumgartner's proposal to translate the phrase as "she clapped [hands]" (1958, 808). Not only does this proposal, which Nicholson mentions without further examination, have plausible philological support, it also offers the possibility of symbolic interpretation. The translation is based on the Arabic root *shahana* "to strike," by metathesis.[22] It has the additional advantage of being applicable to both cases: to strike one hand to another in Achsah's story; to strike the tent-pin through Sisera's head in Yael's story. In both cases, the verb implies force.

Although Gibson analyzes Driver's argumentation in much more detail, his reasons for accepting the traditional interpretation are equally weak. Without avowing overtly philological limits, as we can at least praise Nicholson for doing, Gibson comes up with extremely weak contextual arguments by drawing upon cases where similar circumstances occur with different verbs: a female subject and a bestial noun provide enough reason, in his view, to conclude with the contradictory statement: "It is a semantic possibility arising from the texts that the structure is a *rare* but *standard* mode of description of the same circumstance" (Gibson 1976; my emphasis). Where philology must stop, literary analysis may be helpful.

However brief, Judges 1:14–15 form a story—the story of Achsah—or a drama—the confrontation of Achsah and Caleb over her possessions—or a poem—the one presented as such by Boling (1975, 51) on the basis of Albright's account (1968, 48) of the passage's rhythm. The metrical form indeed argues for a relatively isolated, autonomous position for this mini-story. It may therefore be one of the many cases of the insertion of older, available lore into the edited canon. In that view, it receives the same "glacial" status as Bath's view of self.[23] It stands separately in the chapter because of the alternation of battle accounts and individual encounters. In chapter one, there are three such encounters: one with the lord of Bezek, one between Achsah and Caleb, and one between the scouts and a native informant. Each of these can be analyzed as stories, although their place within the overall account of the battles is not problematic in the two other cases while it is slightly so in Achsah's case.[24] The episode has been explained by Slotki (1980, 160) as a motivation for Othniel's later possession of the lands, or, differently, for Caleb's descendants' claim to it. Slotki does not seem to realize that the alternative between his two options implies the difference between patrilocy and virilocy; moreover, these later claims are nowhere evidenced in the text.

Achsah enters the text as the object of the verb "to give," with a future aspect: a vow. The addressee of the gift is not yet known. In the next verse, she is again the object of the verb "to give," now in the present tense and with an identified addressee: Othniel. The first time she is the subject of a verb, it is in a participle: "in her coming."[25] The verb creates problems, since she is already assumed to have been given. Instead of supposing that she has been hidden for reasons of safety (Slotki 1980, 159), it seems more consistent with the nature of the act of promising to take "to give" in the verbal sense, as a performative symmetrical to "to promise." It relates Felman's favorite example to Austin's. As a speech-act, then, the gift is as yet a purely verbal matter, the realization of which is heavily dependent on Achsah's collaboration. This makes her position in relation to the request much stronger.

The next verb has been hotly disputed regarding its subject.[26] Many scholars attribute the subject-position to Achsah, following the Masoretic Text. Boling translates the phrase as "he nagged her" and is suspicious of the other possibility, "she nagged him," as a tendentious translation that tries to save the integrity of the first and ideal judge. And indeed, Slotki's comment suggests that the propensity to tendentiousness is real.[27] The assumption that the verb means "to seduce" since it has a female subject is both common and ideologically biased.[28] It becomes quite ironic in the light of Felman's hero Don Juan, the model subject of this verb. Soggin (1981, 22) is even more explicit. As he does quite often when it suits him better, he amends the MT and he adopts the choice for Othniel as the subject of the verb. But then, he has to change the meaning of the verb: "The verb here has a somewhat obscure sense: normally it means 'seduce,' 'tempt,' always with decidedly pejorative connotations. *So* while we cannot accept MT because it is *manifestly absurd* [. . .]" (my emphasis).[29] The italicized word *so* shows that there is a link between the moral opinion about Othniel and the logic of philology. The logic itself remains implicit, but can be translated as follows: because the verb has negative connotations, the Hebrew text that ascribes it to Othniel *must* be corrected because it would ascribe the negative act to a male subject. "Absurd" here means, clearly, not flattering to a male character. The very gesture suggests that there may be an interesting issue at stake in the episode. Soggin's note can be described in terms of the present chapter as a wonderful example of a speech-act that lacks meaning (riddle), a lack which, through its forceful motivation, receives excessive meaning (vow) through its impact on reality (ideology).

The infinitive that follows is equally ambiguous, but the next phrase shows that Achsah is the one who actualizes the request. This is no evidence, however, for the assumption that Othniel nagged her to ask; the reverse is not excluded, but the question is beyond decision. A third possibility, namely, an impersonal construction to be translated as "she or he moved him or her to ask = that they ask" is not to be discarded either. Slotki, whom we saw already preoccupied with the question of permission, insists: "Achsah makes the request, but only after obtaining the full consent of her husband" (p. 160). The problems raised so far by critics produce a sense of gender problematics. It seems painful to acknowledge Achsah's autonomy as a full subject of speech and action. Therefore, the problem of the enigmatic action she performs "from upon her ass," its status as a possible act of body language, might be related to this problematic.

Since the evidence collected by both Nicholson and Gibson against Driver's suggestion seems convincing enough to discard the obviously disturbing translation "she broke wind,"[30] I suggest we look at the *action* in the sense of "narrative unit." The verb is the only one that refers unambiguously to Achsah as its subject before the verb "to say" appears in verse 15. It can mean, so far, "she alighted [from her donkey]" or something like "she clapped [her hands]." The first, traditional translation leaves Caleb's surprise ("what unto you?") in the next verse unexplained. The second one does explain it: Achsah does something unexpected. Both translations account for the following double preposition "from upon," the traditional one most obviously, the other one in a less conspicuous, but narratively more interesting way. The preposition must be considered in the light of focalization.[31]

The next phrase, Caleb's exclamatory "what unto you," is a *shifter,* an indicator of focalization by a character.[32] In other words, it appoints Caleb as the focalizer of the preceding action, since he responds to it. If one imagines the scene, which is certainly dramatic, one sees Achsah, probably in a wedding outfit, sitting on her animal, and the sound produced by her clapping hands does come from *upon* her ass *down* to Caleb. The symbolic meaning of clapping hands is not specifically clear, but that it is a way to attract attention is most plausible. It may indicate the prelude to a request or, rather, a claim.

Now we must see why the traditional interpretation would not do equally well. It too accommodates the double preposition. It does not entail the specific narrative situation I have just described, nor does it have to do so. The descent "from above" the ass is generally considered in the light of similar situations, specifically those where a woman descends (e.g., Genesis 24:64). In those cases, however, there is no subsequent request or claim involved. Some scholars comment that descending is a mark of respect, a "normal" action preceding a request (e.g., Slotki 1980, 160). The weakness of this interpretation lies precisely there: it does not explain Caleb's surprise, nor does it accommodate Achsah's wording of the request.

The request itself creates an opposition between what Caleb had given her and what she wants. He gave her the land *negev*, translatable as Negev, as "south" or "dry." The latter translation introduces the opposition: Achsah is not satisfied with a useless piece of dry land; therefore, she wants the wells. Conceived of in this way, her request comes closer to a claim. The tone of her sentence can be imagined as slightly irritated, perhaps angry, an emotion that Driver must have had in mind when he decided that the action from above the ass expressed contempt. This part of his suggestion is thus confirmed by narrative structure. Additional evidence for the opposition is in the chiastic structure (Boling 1975, 57) and in the conjunction "for" that links the already received to that requested.

When we go back, now, from the content of Achsah's words to the gesture with which she introduced her speech, we move de facto back from narrative theory to symbolic anthropology. No one would deny that the problematic verb points to some symbolic gesture; it is the gesture's symbolic nature that is problematic. The meaning of that gesture should explain the relationship between it and Caleb's surprise, the subsequent speech and the success of the request. These relations are important in that they are inherent in the idea of body language itself. No gesture meant to be meaningful stands alone.[33]

I propose to interpret the verb as follows: the gesture is a ritual way of instating the *phatic function*.[34] As such, it is pure performativity, pure force: its meaning is to enhance the force of the following statement. Achsah shows that she has something to say, something important and bearing consequences for her relationship with both father and husband. The following words spoken by Caleb serve to acknowledge the establishment of verbal communication. Caleb's words allow Achsah to speak and show that he realizes the importance of what she will say.[35] He can be imagined to await her words with some anxiety. Therefore, he is prepared to give in immediately. This success of the speech-act is more plausibly prepared for by the meaning "she clapped her hands from on top of her ass" than by "she alighted from her ass."

My conclusion is that the translation "she clapped [her hands]"

has to be recommended. This is not because there is stronger philological evidence for it than for the traditional translation. It is in spite of
philology, or rather, in response to this discipline's limits, that it is to
be preferred. Arguments in its favor are:

(1) it explains and enhances the narrative structure of the story;
(2) it adds an interesting case for the study of the anthropology
     of gesture in the ancient Near East, and hence, it extends
     our understanding of the culture in question (Gruber 1980);
(3) it explains why other cases where a person dismounts to
     extend a greeting use a different verb;
(4) it provides insight into the particular kind of body language
     used by the daughter in addressing the powerful father
     whose object of gift she is;
(5) it enhances the performative aspect of a symbolic gesture
     whose phatic function relates physical to verbal language,
     and hence, it exmplifies the materiality of speech-acts.

Achsah is not only a model as the daughter who, given away, yet
assumes a subject-position. Her story reveals that she is also a model of
daughterly speech-acts. Her request must be situated within the thoroughly patriarchal structure where daughters are promised as conditional gifts, as stakes for military bravery, where they are the shifters
between the two coherences. She too is vowed away for the sake of
"higher" interests: war and "national" unity. But within those limits,
she shows what language, if "properly" used, can perform: it can gain
water, rather than fire. In the interpretations of her story, it is often
assumed that its etiological function explains Achsah's descendants'
claim to Negev (Cohen 1980, 160); she asks for the wells which "by
their situation seemed naturally to belong to Caleb's descendants."
The assumption that there is a conflict at all between the groups is opposed to the self-evidence of virilocal marriage and the patriliny that
excludes the daughter's father. We have seen with ample evidence that
such is not a self-evident setting. I suggest, indeed, that the claim for
her own descendance must be seen in the light of the non-self-evidence
of virilocy. If Achsah claims the wells, she seems to behave as Beth's
sister. Her initiative may cause surprise precisely because it is not so
"natural" that her descendants be treated different than Caleb's. The
etiological function receives, then, a much more profound meaning:
the claim is not just a matter of personal ambition but of social transition. Othniel has so much interest in this issue that it seems more than

plausible that he is, indeed, the subject of seduction, a seduction that typically leaves the subject-position of its "victim" intact.

If patrilocy *versus* virilocy is, indeed, the underlying issue of the conflict, the body of the daughter, as the material mediator of the line of descendance, is the site of the struggle. It seems appropriate then that the language used is body language. The daughter, by using body language in her address to her father, acknowledges the function that is assigned to her. Since the father, in his vow, disposes of her body, her taking some distance from him in following a husband is acted out in the semiotic use of the body. Speaking through her body, she signifies its performative power: it has the force of a speech-act. Thus recuperating a subject-position for her *as* body, Achsah's gesture sets the limit to the father's absolute power. That limit is the body as producer of descendance, life. The water she claims is the indispensable material support of the life whose production saves her subjectivity. At the same time, the bodily nature of her speech-act enhances the materiality of the daughter's way, as opposed to the father's, of establishing descendance, albeit for him: through her body. Her daughterly submission also implies her future motherhood. Moments such as this display the utter necessity of the daughter's contribution to the production of the father's descent; the peculiar interest of patrilocy, which is the direct bodily contiguity between father and descent through the daughter he owns forever, can be understood in this dramatic confrontation.

At the other end of the book, Beth's body language sadly echoes Achsah's. Where Achsah's father responds to her gesture with the acknowledgement of her right to speak, to desire, to be, the husband of the already-destroyed Beth responds with the opposite attitude. Instead of the question "what unto you" (what do you want? 1:14) he gives the order "up!" Beth's gesture is not acknowledged as an initiator of the phatic function. The hands on the threshold that both accuse and implore are ignored by the husband to whom they are addressed. Beth's claim to safety in the house is countered by the husband's final attempt to take her to *his* house. In some sense, however, her gesture is similar to Achsah's. Both women are addressing the men who gave them away. Both choose to follow the husband and leave the father; Achsah does so peacefully because the two men are brothers, Beth does so with conflict because the men are unrelated. But while Achsah addresses her father from above, Beth addresses her husband from below. The gift of her was improper; instead of assessing her subject-position, the gift of her destroyed it. While Achsah's father faces her, Beth's husband steps over her. When in the morning Beth's husband opens the door, the verb used is *yiphthah*.[36] And indeed: "Behold, the woman, his [patrilocal] wife." The language is that of visuality, of voyeurism, of one-sided power relations. It is here that the hands on the threshold, Beth's final, powerless act of body-speech, are mentioned, and ignored. They misfire. Like Achsah, Beth speaks within the limits assigned to her: as body. But where Achsah, whose daughter-position was "properly" acknowledged, could add verbal speech, Beth can speak no more.

Beth's story does not end with this gesture. Her body is put to further semiotic use. The peaceful deal between Caleb and Othniel was possible because their blood-relationship allowed them to overcome or, rather, to ignore the virtual conflict between patrilocy and virilocy. It was mediated by Achsah's request for the life-source. This deal is inverted into an ever-increasing mechanism of violence brought about by a deal that betokened the refusal to respect the bodily integrity of the daughter. Beth's body will be used to speak, but it is no longer Beth who speaks. Her body is "divided, limb by limb, into twelve pieces, and he sent her throughout all the borders of Israel" (19:29). The totally destroyed subject becomes the speaker to the whole nation. The obscure, anonymous husband gains, through the use of her body as language, a position that comes close to being that of a *gibbor*. This act turns a domestic conflict into a major political issue. [37] But unlike Othniel, who also used Achsah to establish himself as a husband as powerful as the father, this man gains his position through the destruction of the daughter/woman whose body could bring him life. Beth's dead body can speak, but by a perverse twist, it is the man who totally subjected her, not herself, who speaks. In order to assess the meaning of this difference, let us return briefly to the rape.

The meaning of the particular punishment inflicted on those who attempt to establish virilocal marriage has been understood in various ways, none of them satisfactory. Although the threat of homosexual rape is interpreted as a challenge "to standards of proper cultural civilized behavior, as the Israelites would define such behavior" (Niditch 1982, 367–68), hence, as a symbolic gesture, its meaning in relation to the other body-speech-acts of the story is not examined. The oblivion of its relationship to the other body-speech-acts leads to astonishing gestures of repression on the part of the commentators. Alter (1984, 132) gives a clear instance of this repression. He qualifies the story of Judges 19 as a "heterosexual companion piece" of Genesis 19. The threat of homosexual rape is here separated from the "real" heterosexual act of rape in a way that conceals the *language*: force and meaning together. [38] In a sense, rape is the bodily speech-act *par excellence*. It is well-known that rape victims experience the act as one of aggression, not lust; no real rapist confirms the image of the frustrated man longing for sex that sexist ideology presents in order to justify rape. He appears rather as a hate-filled misogynist. Homosexual rape is equally motivated by hatred of the object, and it is "logical" that it is often committed by heterosexual men.[39] Since rape is the expression of hatred, it is not surprising that the act is often accompanied by (or should we say accomplished through?) offensive verbal language. Why, then, is there so much hatred, on the part of the inhabitants of Gibeah, and why is it addressed to the man? Why is this particular body language of sexuality chosen to express it? The first of these questions has already been answered. I have suggested that the rapists can be, and were doubtlessly by the ancient audience, assumed to hate the man for challenging their institution of sexual relations.[40] That the punishment has to be sexual is already motivated by this contiguity between crime and punishment. The issue is the "natural" right of physical property of the father over the daughter which is part of his attempt to make fatherhood "natural" by imposing bodily contiguity as its basis. The language of rape can be seen in the light of this obsession. The aggression of rape is the speech-act of contiguity *par excellence*. The hatred is spoken *by* one body *into* the other. But there is more to it. The threat to rape the husband is the threat to turn his body into anybody's property. Thus the rapists signify the insult against the father's property rights of which the man is guilty. The daughter "naturally" belongs to her father; this is the only accepted and culturally sanctioned contiguous bond. Going away with another man, going astray, she is going to be any man's property. Any man—the arbitrariness of signification of relations that is so hard to accept—is understood as "every man." Between the "natural" owner and "any man" there is no difference; as long as the daughter's choice is not acknowledged, her subject-position is ignored. It is the man who, by taking away the daughter, is responsible for her being anybody's, everybody's property. The gift of Beth, her rejection by the man, and her abandonment to the rapists acknowledge that meaning.[41] The Levite will take her home later, but only as the woman already destroyed by everyman. Beth's abandonment is the gesture by which the Levite submits to the other institution.

If the homosexual rape is thus the equivalent of the heterosexual rape of Beth in the night-long torture session, the host verbalizes this equivalence very pointedly. To rape is to humiliate, and that is to be done, not to the man, but to the daughter. This is not simply so because men are more valuable subjects and, hence, have a primary claim to protection, for the murder of men is not precisely shunned in the book. It is, more profoundly, because raping him would be a symbolic gesture, based on the responsibility of the man for the daughter's alienation from the father, while raping her does more. It also partakes in the contiguity that is so basic to fatherhood. That is why the rapists do accept the gift of Beth, while they refuse the gift of the two daughters that was interpreted as a simple compensation.

In the light of this interpretation, both Alter's attempt to strip the event of its homosexual component and Niditch's emphasis on the homosexuality are arguably androcentric. Alter just ignores the transition from one form of punishment to the other, while Niditch excuses it. In a most surprising discussion, she alleges three excuses for the husband. First, the "concubine" caused the trouble since she was the one who left him to go back to her father in the first place; I have discussed the bias underlying this interpretation in chapter 3. Second, heterosexual rape is less serious than homosexual rape. This may be so in the context of Judges, in which case the ideologeme should at least be criticized, but it does not explain why the husband later lies about the dangers incurred. Third, Abraham and Isaac also gave away their wives in order to save their own lives.[42] This is indeed the case, and Niditch rightly shuns cheap indignation motivated by anachronistic ethnocentrism; for the same reason, Achsah's gift is, within the represented context, acceptable. Beth's, however, is not, and it is condemned by the very contextual evidence that, for Niditch, excuses it. Significantly, she eliminates the telling ambiguity in verses 27–28 when she states: "she lies dead at the door" (1982, 370). Thus, she denies the symbolic meaning of Beth's gesture, its status as body language and as speech-act. Hence, she partakes of the husband's blindness. She further adopts the position of the husband when she defends his half-hearted account of the event in 20:4–5. Rather than acknowledging his cowardice, she attributes it to shame: shame about the homosexuality of the threat. This apologetic attitude shows the strong inclination, visible in many readers' responses, to identify with the party that holds up the standards of idealized Israel. The troubling fact that the Levite, an Ephraimite, is as much or more of an outsider than the Benjaminites who, as a full Israelite tribe, commit the abomination is thus repressed, while it is precisely Benjamin's belonging to Israel that starts the intertribal war, the negative ending of the book. It is revealing that the party to be justified is the *individual man*, as opposed to the collective men (the rapists) or the individual woman (Beth). This individualism partakes of the ideology of narrative as it is used in historiographic ideo-stories. The historiography of the people can only be turned into a seductive story—seductive because a story—on the condition that the individual man, the *gibbor*, is its leading actor. Both critics try to escape the question of the status of rape as a symbolic act, as an utterly bodily speech-act, significant in relation to the other bodily speech-acts represented in the book.

Again, the speech-act performed by the daughter is embedded in the limits of the subject-position assigned to her. Like Achsah, Beth can only speak as far as her speech is acknowledged. Unlike Achsah, the value of her body, within the interests of the father and husband, is undone. Her gesture at the door of the house is already not hers, since she was only able to fall down, not to act fully. That the story takes over and speaks for her seems to show that there is some awareness of her humanity. But when the husband "divides" her, he signifies, again and more radically, his acceptance of the law of the other group, to which he does not belong but by which he is overruled. Scattering the daughter's body throughout the land is another way of speaking rape: of symbolizing her body as every-body's through wounding it from within and from without.

Judges 19 ends with an imperative: "speak," a masculine plural response to the mute speech of Beth's divided flesh. Just as the husband did respond to Beth's gesture, not by listening to her as Achsah's father did, but by seeing, by the act of focalization followed by an order, just so the tribes respond to the message they see ("all that saw it said") by the order: Speak. As speech-acts, both orders fail, the first one by misfire and abuse, the second one by abuse. The husband's speech-act misfires because the circumstances are, to use Austin's happy term, "infelicitous": the order presupposes a subject able to obey. He abuses, because he has given up the authority that the order presupposes he has. The tribes do not misfire: the violent nature of the speech-act makes the violent response of the call to war appropriate. They abuse since they address their order to speak to the husband, not to the "speaker." The speaking body is ignored. In other words, the tribes, just as the majority of later commentators do, blame the Benjaminites exclusively, not the husband and what he stands for. Thus, the speaking body fails to speak because it is not listened to. There lies the deepest scandal of the speaking body: it is denied speech.

The daughters in the book speak through their bodies, thus showing the materiality of speech in its specific socially determined framework. Their speech-acts reveal that it is their bodies that are the stake of the speech-acts that circumscribe them. Their bodies produce, in the men between whom they are defined or crushed, the identity that is indispensable to the construction of the *gibbor*. Full possession, full power of disposal over the daughter's body, is what they desperately try to come by. The materiality that seems to be lacking in their relations to their offspring is produced by the contiguity they seek. Contiguity, and its linguistic figuration, metonymy, is the foundation of the speech of the daughters. The question that then arises is: How do the fathers act as speakers in their striving for materiality?

The Mouth of the S/Word

One of Austin's favorite metaphors is fire; one of Don Juan's characteristic assets is his sword. Felman points out that the interesting ambiguity implied in fire is that it is impossible to decide whether it is a thing or an event (1980, 151). The same can be said of the sword, the instrument of "rupture," of the breaking off of relations, and of "coupure"— cutting: penetrating and dividing. The same can be said of words. Are they things to be placed in a sequence and to be read by innocent bystanders or are they events that *are* not things but that *do* things? In other words, how material are words in the Book of Judges? Jephthah, the master of manipulation of the sword, word, and fire, has to be our central character once more.

The language of the fathers is a language of power. It is through that language that Jephthah establishes himself as the head of the Israelite people in his negotiations with the elders of Gilead (11:6–11). The central element and stake of the negotiations is Jephthah's sword: he requires appointment, not as a temporary, military *qaṣin*, but as permanent head, *rosh*, after the victory. But negotiation is not only about or *for* power, it is also based on power. Thus Jephthah negotiates for his own status as leader over the people who had expelled him as the son of "another woman," a "harlot" or patrilocal wife, on the basis of his power as a master of the sword. The term "head" seems appropriate for the hero of the mouth: to be "head" compensates on more levels than one for the expulsion from the father-house, from history, from contiguity with forefathers and offspring. In his subsequent speech-act, his message to the king of Ammon, Jephthah further strengthens the position he has newly acquired: the land becomes "my land" (11:12). The message is a long enumeration of wrong done to "my" land in the past; in this way, Jephthah reinscribes himself into history. The message ends with an appeal to Yahweh: "May Yahweh, the judge, judge today between the sons of Israel and the sons of Ammon" (11:28). Jephthah, who has been introduced into the story as a *gibbor ḥayil*, a hero of might, establishes here a distinction between *gibbor* and *judge*. He may be the head of the people, but he is not their judge. He has not finished negotiating, however. Although the spirit of Yahweh comes upon him, producing his power, the habit of negotiation that characterizes his character is compulsory. The fatal vow, utterly futile since the Judge has sent his spirit already, displays Jephthah's addiction to negotiation, the speech-act of and for power. We may wonder why the repetition-compulsion is so insistent. Negotiation is based on power; the one who has none has nothing to negotiate with. But it is also a recognition of the limits of power; the negotiator both has something and lacks something. Jephthah, the head of the people to be, hero of might, has the power of his s/word, but he lacks some other power, the power that would give him security, certainty about his victory. If the judge is appealed to here first to decide, then to accomplish, the victory Jephthah is hired to perform, it is because the negotiator, the man of speech, recognizes his fundamental lack.

If we return to the opening of the negotiations over Jephthah's position, the questions he asked the elders of Gilead appear less rhetorical, more real, more material, than they first seemed to be. He asks, "Did you not hate me, and drive me out of my father's house? and why did you come now to me, being in distress?" (11:7). The first question refers to the beginning of the story, where it is said that Jephthah was driven out of his father's house because he was the son of another, a different woman. This speech-act, like Samson's riddle, is anchored in the narrative sequence whose meaning culminates in the character's speech. He was not allowed to "inherit in our father's house." What inheritance is referred to remains unclear; is it material goods, or participation in the fatherline? Is he denied possessions, or the status of Gileadite? His ambition to become the permanent head of the people speaks to the latter, rather than to the former denial. The second question, if considered rhetorical, blames the men. With this reproach Jephthah opens the negotiation; but its force, its motivation, may be serious anxiety about his status: now that the clan is in trouble, there may be a place for him. Why, for what purpose, with what offer? And indeed, in the previous chapter, the Gileadites had already decided to appoint the deliverer "head" over, not all of Israel, but specifically, of Gilead, the father's house. In light of his later sacrifice of Bath, his patrilocal asset, it seems plausible to put more weight on the specific meaning of "to inherit" as to inherit the (virilocal) fatherline.

Like Don Juan, Jephthah is a master of "rupture" and "coupure." Breaking away from the father's house, he later breaks with his only child, a break that costs him his identity—and Bath her life. His attempts to counter this movement of "rupture," of breaking, by reinserting himself in the line, involve "coupure," killing. The weapon of negotiation, the mouth that must provide him with the position in history for which he strives, is replaced with the specific weapon of killing that is best suited to materialize the fragile, insecure position over the fatherhouse that he has conquered: the mouth of the sword. His basic insecurity betrays itself doubly in his fatal vow: not only is he shown to have no confidence in his own *gibbor*-ship, he also proposes a riddle with a stake that is contiguous with himself. The "comer-out of his house to meet him" is also the materialization of his relationship to his (father's) house. The daughter's body can either secure the fatherline or destroy it, according to his power over her, his "exclusive possession."

It is precisely the exclusivity of that possession that can never be secured. Fatherhood is never certain, the fatherline is always doubtful, as the son of the "other" woman is well placed to understand. The use of the s/word that Jephthah seems a master of is itself not a clear-cut enterprise. The *shibboleth* episode in 12 : 5–6 is, in its ambiguity, a *mise en abyme* of Jephthah's problematics. The situation is war; we are in the middle of the political coherence. The mouth of the sword, not the mouth of the word, is the appropriate weapon under the circumstances. But Jephthah misuses the word; he uses it in inappropriate circumstances. Killing, as he now has learned, is tricky; the sword can kill the self. It is crucial to tell—to know—a Gileadite from an Ephraimite, a member of the father-house from the others. The trick Jephthah devises to "judge"—that is, to distinguish—is verbal: once again a riddle. The question is, who belongs to the fatherline? The criterion is the "proper" pronunciation of the word *shibboleth*, proper being the pronunciation in the father's house. Language determines the fatherline.

Within the framework of the character's problematic of his proper position, the meaning of the word *shibboleth* may have some relevance, not for the participants in the game, but for the story that embeds it.[43] There are many meanings, two of which are key words in the counter-coherence of Judges: "ear of corn" and "stream of water." As usual, commentators tend to choose; like Jephthah, they need to tell the "right" meaning from the "wrong" one. The ambiguity of the word, however, problematizes in its turn the possibility of decision about meaning that Jephthah so desperately seeks. "Ear of corn" as the word that triggers the mouth of the sword's "coupure" seems an appropriate one, ambiguous in its own right. It can recall the crops of corn destroyed by Samson's fire, the vegetal realm that provides food, bread for the mouth. For readers who do not fear psychoanalytic symbolism, the ear of corn is even appropriate as that which is cut off by the castrating mouth; we have seen in chapter 3 that there is some reason to read this into the story. The stream of water, on the other hand, contiguous to the speech-act since the event takes place at the shore of the Jordan, can recall Achsah's request for the source of life. The spatial contiguity becomes in its turn contiguity with the daughter. Food on the one hand, water on the other: the word is doubly related to the material conditions of life. But to the extent that it stands for male (ear of corn) and female (water) materiality, it reintroduces the insecurity of the fatherline.

Materiality is also enhanced in the use of the word *shibboleth*. Its phonetic sound, its materiality *as* word, is decisive over life and death. The "proper" pronunciation, then, reinforces the word's semantic aspect. The proper pronunciation of the crucial word that means water and food, female and male, is the pronunciation according to the father's house: the materiality of the word as word is also the reinforcement of the symbolic bond over the material one. The mouth of the word enables the mouth of the sword to be effective, not the other way around. As such, the episode signifies the priority of language over the body, while at the same time proclaiming the materiality of language, its bodily effectiveness and foundation, its basis in contiguity.

The materiality of the word is expressed in its intranslatability. In order to keep its meaning as speech-act, it has to remain unchanged in translations: *shibboleth*. It is a reversed password, as Derrida writes, a "pass-not-word" (1986, 320), a silent word that has no meaning, that is pure force. Unlike the password, it is not secret. The Ephraimites know it. But knowledge, in spite of the attempts to give it priority over materiality, is not enough really to establish fatherhood. The Ephraimites know, but they lack the potency to do. Theirs is a failed speech-act. The meaning of the word is erased, bracketed, by the question of the men's capacity to "do" right. The word is also significant in the closeness to "right" and "wrong." It is the same word, but just with that very slight difference that establishes the categories. The meaning, if any, remains the same; the whole word remains the same. The tiny difference within sameness produces the group. By the one consonant pronounced "properly" or "improperly," the group escapes arbitrariness. Derrida relates *shibboleth* to circumcision (1986, 341), the cut that divides and defines. Circumcision is not an issue in Judges, but in a sense the cut of the mouth of the s/word replaces it. It is, then, not the male member that is circumcised, but the male word. Derrida formulates it as follows:

> The circumcision of the word must also be understood as an event of the body, in a way essentially analogous to the diacritical difference between *Shibboleth* and *Sibboleth*. It was in their bodies, in a certain impotence of their vocal organs, that the Ephraimites experienced their inability to

pronounce what they nonetheless knew ought to be pronounced *Shibboleth*. The word *Shibboleth*, for some an "unpronounceable name" is a circumcised word. (1986, 344)

That the impotence or potency is situated, not in the male member, but in the male head, the site of knowledge, of symbolization, but also, of the knowledge of the insufficiency of symbolization, is quite appropriate. Jephthah has learned, in his long career as *gibbor*, how to become a hero of masculinity, of paternity: of memory. Memory, the historicization of language, is another form of its materialization. Master-killer, he is also the master-speaker of the book.

Jephthah's mastery of the word and his knowledge of its limits, compensated by its bond with the sword via the mouth, sets the model of fatherly speech-acts in the book. Caleb's appropriate response to Achsah's request has been forgotten now that fatherhood and the subject's place in the fatherline have turned out to be so shaky. Rather than Caleb, the fathers who model their speech-acts on Jephthah's are Manoah, the father of the *gibbor* Samson, and Beth's father. Both struggle, like Jephthah, with the materiality of language, with contiguity.

Samson's father has no daughter; he does, however, have a son who "goes astray," who obstinately turns away from the father's house to go to the woman's father's house. Manoah's position as a father is therefore as problematic as that of the daughters' fathers. Beth's father, the father of the central victim of the competition in the book, is Manoah's symmetrical counterpart. Both struggle with language. Manoah's attempt to instate his fatherhood is acted out in a competition with the mother. The stake of the competition is speech, not the meaning of the messenger's words, for the mother has already secured that by repeating and completing the words for her husband. The stake is the possession as addressee of the speech-act. Manoah wants the words to be spoken to him. The words that spoke the son-to-be have to be addressed to the father, or else, father he will not be.

When the messenger reappears, it is again the woman who establishes the contact; it is to her that the stranger comes and speaks. Manoah's first act, then, is to secure the identity of the man who brought forth the child, to make sure it is the right man: "Are you the man who spoke to the woman?" The cognitive contact, however, is not enough. The contiguity that has to be established requires a material bond— the invitation to share a meal, this improper attempt to establish the messenger as a member of the same group is, as we have seen, corrected by the messenger into a sacrificial offering of *leḥem*, bread. The messenger knows better than Manoah what fatherhood comes to. Saying

"I will not eat of your bread" (13:16) is refusing to acknowledge the father-house as the house of bread. Manoah is once more corrected when he takes the identity of the messenger to be a riddle. The reply to his indiscrete question is: "Why do you ask my name, for it is wonderful?" (13:18). Unlike the riddles, the question of the identity of the messenger cannot be revealed. That is not because his divine provenance is a secret, for it is not. It is because the name cannot be pronounced—neither the divine name, nor the messenger's. Naming is the speech-act of fatherhood *par excellence*: through it, the child becomes the son of the father. Each deviation from this rule is significant. Samson is named by his mother. The father has not succeeded in establishing himself; his is not the house of bread where the child can be kept. Samson will be a *gibbor*, but unlike the patriarchy of Genesis, *gibbor*-ship is not inherited through the fatherline. Manoah's speech-acts are, throughout the story, utterly futile. His speech does not become flesh.

The relevance of naming for the establishment of the father-child relation is very pointed in two opposite cases. On the one hand, Abimelech is named by his father, Gideon, but the name he receives is ironic: it means my father is king. Such a name hardly fits a son whose father declined the offer of kingship and who will have to turn to his mother's clan to claim kingship—a fatal act that causes the death of the father-house.[44] On the other hand, the three female victims are nameless. Not naming, then, becomes an act as significant as naming. If Abimelech's father overdoes the naming, the fathers of the three victims under-name their daughters. Reducing them to the status of daughter, not allowing them to grow into full subjectivity, is reducing them to the resources of body language. If naming is a significant speech-act, not naming is a significant act of appropriation, of taking "exclusive possession": a body-act.

Beth's father confronts the husband of his daughter in his own house, the house of bread. The site of the exclusive possession of the daughter is also the site of the father's speech. After three days of hospitality, the husband prepares to leave the house, but the father will not let him go. He detains him with the words: "Support your heart with a morsel of bread, and afterwards you shall go your way" (19:5).[45] The last part of this speech seems a failure through abuse: the next episode shows that the father had no intention of letting the man go; the promise is no promise-with-a-future. But this may be yet another case of a failure—not of the speaker, but of the addressee, a failure to understand the force of the speech-act rather than its meaning. The question—or the riddle—implied in the speech-act is: what will the husband's "own way" be, after having strengthened his heart with the father's bread?

Like Manoah's invitation, the father's invitation to share a meal is an attempt to establish a group, a community of the father-house. After eating the father's bread, the man is expected to have "his own way" within the father-house. The speech-act is meant to establish, through bread, the contiguity that only the daughter can provide. The failure of the father's speech-act, then, is misfire: the circumstances of its utterance are inappropriate. The father promises with the intention of carrying out his promise, but the riddle is not acknowledged by the addressee. Food, then, is more than the material satisfaction of the mouth. It is also what relates the word to the body. Bread is spoken rather than eaten; as a spoken attempt to establish who belongs to the father's house and who does not, the offer of bread is the offer of con-tiguity, of participation in the material symbolization of fatherhood. Taking the daughter away from the father without providing for her "in his own way," his own house-of-bread, the husband cannot but fail to replace the father. Once at his house, there will be no bread for the mouth, only the mouth of the knife that will cut and separate, not bond and share.

The mouth of the s/word is, in Judges, the site of the materiality of language as a mediation between symbolic fatherhood and its mate-rial anchoring in the daughter's body. Bread, or corn, or the water that allows it to grow, is virtually the positive side of the contiguity to be established, but it is unsuccessful because the speech-act misfires. The sword is the negative side of the same attempt: one group, line, con-tiguity is established through separation from the other. The priority of the word itself, uttered by the mouth of the father who is so forcefully motivated to use force as speech, is betokened in the core speech-act of the failing father: Jephthah's vow, which does not feed the mouth, but kills through it.

Jephthah's *shibboleth* device was an attempt to tell one group from the other. To tell, in this sense, is to differentiate, to discriminate. This act is the one that gave the book its title, explicit in the Greek version: *krittein*, to judge, is also to differentiate, which is the ety-mological meaning of critique. The more usual sense of to tell is to produce narrative, to recount. *Shibboleth* seems, in this light, a failure to match the speech-act of judgment, of differentiation, with the speech-act of narration, the speech-act *par excellence* of memory, the speech-act, also, that brought forth the Book of Judges. That failure is signified in the untranslatability of the word that is its undoing *as* word. If memory is the asset of maleness, if knowledge is the token of fatherhood, judgment is the decisive speech-act that arbitrates between failed and successful attempts to actualize, to materialize, fatherhood. Judgment is the ideal that is replaced, by the powerless father, with the mouth of the s/word. In this sense, the *gibbor* is not, despite his status as head, a judge. *Gibbor*-ship as represented by Jephthah is rather a reversal of judgeship—its impotence.

The cutting quality of the word that is meant to establish contiguity, the contiguity of ideal fatherhood, and which, like fire, hovers between being thing or event, is linked to, placed in contiguity with, the site of "true" or "proper" contiguity: the house. Is the house the word's other side, the materialization of the word whose materiality can only cut, not bond? Is the word's stake, as the site of fatherhood, betokened by the daughter's bondage in it? Or is the word become stone, its unavoidable realization, the hard aspect of the fugitive word used to produce meaning, permanency, memory? In the following chapter, the contradictions of the house in Judges will be examined in relation to the word that calls it into being as the object of narrative and that calls it into relevance as the material support of the word.

CHAPTER SIX

THE ARCHITECTURE
OF UNHOMELINESS

Time & Space are Real Beings. Time is a Man Space is a Woman.
William Blake

Speech, in Judges, is the body of the fabula, the materialization of events. Speech-acts constitute "reality."[1] The question that remains to be answered is: which reality? In other words, how can we read the composition of Judges if its structure does not seem to emerge through chronological continuity, but rather through the undoing of that continuity? Where temporal continuity fails to underwrite the sense of coherence that we as readers need, it may be revealing to look at the spatial construction of the book.

Within the political coherence, the geography of the land to be conquered is the spatial dimension most attended to by critics. In the countercoherence, space becomes meaningful on the smaller scale of individual events: the houses to be conquered.

It has been suggested already that the chronology of the period of the judges is not only impossible to construct, but that the very attempt to do so reveals both a desire to avoid the book's crucial issues and a blindness to the possibility of a nonchronological form of historiography. As the book thwarts a chronological reading, it imposes the spatiality of the fabula if only through the enterprise of conquest represented therein. True, the interest of geographical details has been acknowledged by biblical commentators. The geography of the fabula is, however, usually considered in terms of physical reality. Where do the ancient sites that are mentioned in the book really lie? How did the armies move from one place to another? And how did the tribes unite themselves? Those are the questions that geography elicits.

169

These questions, however, do not provide an alternative to a chronological reading; instead, they support such an endeavor. In asking these questions, the semiotic function of spatial indications is ignored, as is the semiotic structure they help to produce. And where semiotic function and realism clash, no shift in perspective follows. Yet it is obvious at some points that the geographical indications lead to a spatial coherence that is not complementary to the chronological one, but that does take its place. A good example is the transition from chapters 17–18 to 19.

Between the story of Samson and the story of Beth, there is a little known episode of a man named Micah who steals silver from his mother, gives it back, and confesses his theft. The mother, then, uses the money to have an ephod and teraphim made and, supposedly, to pay for a house-priest. Later, there is an oblique threat by armed men, during which Micah loses both the image and the priest. Since the story is not about a judge or a savior, it is considered part of the book's epilogue, the chapters presented under the heading "in those days there was no king in Israel, every man did what was right in his eyes." If we start from the geographical structure of the book, chapters 17–18, on the one hand, and 19–21, on the other, hang together on the basis of the opposition between Judah and Ephraim, or, to be more precise, on the basis of the opposition between the hill country of Ephraim and the town of Bethlehem in Judah. The character of the Levite switches places between those two spatial backgrounds. In chapter 17 Micah, the Ephraimite, receives in his house a Levite from Bethlehem, while in 19, the Levite from Ephraim takes a woman from Bethlehem. The word *Bethlehem* contains also the root for "house." In both cases, the house is not a very stable place, and there is much ado about arrivals and departures. This geographical opposition and the meeting of its two poles in the house suggest a function of the house in the countercoherence proposed by my reading of the book.

The house is the place where the daughters, whose fate is the primary focus of this study, meet their undoing. Significantly, the house motif is absent in the episode of Achsah, our exemplary "proper" story. In Judges, there are houses and there are tents, and the two kinds of dwellings raise the question whether they are just variants of possible dwellings or whether there is an opposition between them that represents some deeper opposition? The house—or tent—is also the place where the interaction between the political and the domestic is located.[2] The problematic of chronological and military history reflects on the interaction between the public/national/political/historical and the private/individual/domestic/contingent spheres. Finally, the house

can be seen as the figuration of contiguity where chronological contiguity is too problematic. In the house fatherhood establishes itself;
the house becomes fatherhood's synecdochic metaphor. In this chapter, these relations between the house and other story elements will be
considered as oppositions, as limits leading to transitions, and as a
dialectic.

Oppositions

It is a common view that houses are one side of an opposition between
public and private, between danger and safety, between freedom and
bondage, between communal and individual. Reading Judges, we
quickly discover that those neat oppositions do not work and perhaps
never do because they rely on the myths we are used to about the
home, homeliness, and the family.
  The oppositions are produced in order to make an unacceptable
division appear acceptable. To that end, the positive and the negative
sides of the oppositions are distributed in a specific way. Although the
public domain is by far the most important one in any historiographic
endeavor, the indispensability of private values as the constituents of
the public enterprise is generally acknowledged. The opposition between danger and safety compensates for the unfair distribution of
power between the two domains. If the performers of public functions
do not have to share their power with those who, in the private house,
provide them with the values and motivations they need, at least they
also incur the dangers related to the public sphere. Thus the third opposition is integrated: if they have the freedom, they also have the
dangers. The inhabitants of the house are not all equally free to move
out of it at will, but they also are not equally safe in doing so. Bondage
is compensated for by safety, freedom bought at the cost of danger. Recent studies of situations where this reassuring distribution breaks
down[3] have demonstrated how closely these oppositional ideas support
myths that do not match reality.[4]
  The most confined category of people, daughters who live in
their fathers' houses, are also the least safe. Danger does not come only
from strangers; within the house, men rape their daughters and sisters,
thus violating the only freedom they were told they possessed, the free
disposal over their bodies (Ward 1985). On the other hand, the military dangers of war are not limited to the political sphere. In an interesting but too brief article, Jean Franco (1985) analyzed the rupture of
the sanctity of houses and churches in recent developments in Latin
America. The historical situation represented in Judges is different

from today's, but the case brought up by Franco and the analysis she offers can illuminate, as a subtext, the contradictions in the system of oppositions constructed in the book, and by its readers, wherein houses seem to constitute one pole. It is significant, for example, that the enemy king Eglon, in chapter 3, is killed by the *gibbor* Ehud, not only in his own house/palace, but in the place of the most intimate privacy.[5] On the other hand it is equally significant that Jephthah becomes a *gibbor* only after having been thrown out of the house of his father. The men have a problematic relationship to the house they come from and go to. The women who kill men do so in the house. The victims are killed in, or in close contiguity to, the house.

Kallah's death shows that houses can only be safe places if they are accepted *as* houses, that is, as the site of the constitution of the lineage. Her death, not only *within* the house of her father, but also *with* the house of her father whose synecdoche she is, shows the intimate bond between the concrete, material space and the abstract, institutional function of the house. Killing her in the house of her father is killing and destroying the house of her father itself, destroying the patrilocal family. As an institutional space, then, it is part of the social organization of the people. So the house, as one pole of the public/private opposition, has to fall apart because the concept of "house" has taken on the double meaning of space and family. It partakes of both sides of the public-private opposition.

This collapse of the opposition is more obvious as the second meaning of "house" is extended, in Hebrew, to refer to the people as a whole. The house is the site, or the signifier, of descent, of patriliny. And it is in turn this patriliny that produces the people by the mediation of the tribes: the sons of Israel/Jacob. But what happens to this rupture in the case of Judges, where patriliny is so problematic, indeed, as to be virtually unestablished? In this case the house cannot extend its significance innocently.

The embedding of the private house within the political warfare is more complex. Samson's struggle with patrilocal marriage is part of his struggle against the Philistines. This very configuration of the fabula bears witness to the book's ideological commitment to replace patrilocy. Bath's death at her departure from her father's house is incorporated into the political war while her identity as the sacrificial victim is not yet known and while her relation to the house is her only known feature. Jephthah vowed to sacrifice, not his daughter as a person, but his house. House and daughter are one and the same. The house as an institution—as patrilocy—is to be sacrificed for the public good. The public welfare requires the establishment of the people in the land as

different from its other inhabitants, and the opposition of patrilocy versus virilocy is the site of definition of the difference.[6] The house and its
structure of descent become the mark of the conqueror.

The opposition between freedom and bondage is firmly asserted
in several of the core stories. Jephthah was free to relate to a group of
people whose affinities were far from clear (11:3); his daughter, by
contrast, only had the freedom to accept her total submission. But
even Jephthah, mightiest of *gibborim*, is initially thrown out of his father's house. His career, like that of Samson, starts with the departure
from the father's house. If Jephthah, as a son, is not clearly enough his
father's son, he takes his own freedom and moves out. Our heroine
Beth, who in the beginning of her story seems to have the freedom to
follow her husband, can only leave the virilocal house at the risk of
being either taken back or killed.[7] Her freedom is the choice between
two forms of submission. Liberation from the father's house brings freedom to sons, danger to daughters. Hence, this opposition fails, too.

The mythical, deceptive nature of the oppositions becomes visible
when we try to establish a semiotic square as their figuration.[8] If, for
daughters, going outside implies danger, then staying inside should
provide safety. If traveling, staying outside, is neither particularly safe
nor particularly dangerous for sons, going inside should not be particularly safe or dangerous either. The semiotic square resulting from this
"logic" runs as follows:

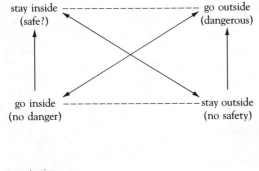

Key

------ = contraries

◄————► = contradictions

————► = implications

The logic does apply, but only for gender-specific categories of subjects.
To stay inside is safe for neither daughter nor father (in Kallah's case).
To go outside is dangerous for daughters (Bath, Beth), but not for sons
(Samson, Jephthah). For sons, to go inside is neither safe (Samson)

nor dangerous (Beth's husband). Both are ambivalently safe inside. Samson *seems* to be safe from Philistine attacks, but is trapped in his illusion of safety; Beth's husband *seems* to be in danger but can save himself by remaining inside while throwing Beth out. To stay outside, too, is neither safe nor dangerous as such. Traveling is dangerous in Beth's story, but it is not while outside that the danger occurs. Jephthah accomplishes his successes outside. Never is he in a danger he cannot escape from, even by means of his "house" lineage.

The oppositions do not work "logically" because houses are of two competing kinds, both equally ambivalent: the patrilocal and the virilocal house. The patrilocal house is the most permanent, stable house, and that may very well be its ideological basis. The father re-mains in his house forever, and so does the daughter. The virilocal house, by contrast, is permanent as to the father's presence, but the daughter leaves it. The difference is basic: as we have seen, the daugh-ter is indispensable for the contiguity that her possession guarantees. A semiotic square representing the opposition of these two houses runs as follows:

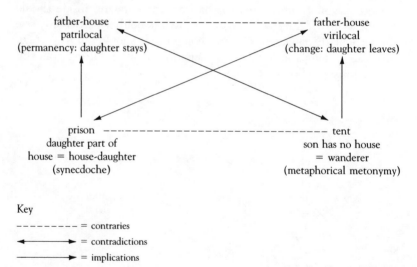

Key

- - - - - - - - = contraries

◄————————► = contradictions

————————► = implications

In both systems, the grown child has an indispensable function in the construction of the father-house, but the basis of that function is differ-ent. The daughter as *part of* the father-house cannot be allowed to leave it radically or the father-house breaks down. The permanency is threatened because, as we have seen in Jephthah's linguistic slip, the patrilocal father can only conceive of his daughter as part/member of himself.

The other side of this obsession is the daughter's imprisonment. The Hebrew expression "closed house" for prison allows for more continuity between a house one is not able to leave and a prison proper than the English expression suggests. As opposed to the patrilocal father-house, the virilocal one, whose establishment is thematized in Genesis, seems slightly more open. The daughter is allowed to leave.[9] When she leaves, however, she also leaves her familial ties, as well as her relative freedom to move around. It remains to be seen if the transition represented in the book is a progression or not. To begin with, there is no symmetry between the position of the daughter and the son in either system. In the patrilocal system, the son moves out and his position in the house of the father-in-law is not very clear. In the virilocal system, the son remains in the clan of his father, and the virilocal father-house can be a structure of paternal domination, at least over a few generations.[10] But the daughter and the son differ in their relation to the father in the two systems. Where, as part of him, the patrilocal daughter is the father's synecdoche, the virilocal son as his successor is his metonymic extension. This difference is best explained in rhetorical terms because the position of the father in the imagination of the people is constructed on the basis of language. The crucial part of speech-acts in the fabula is a function of that epistemology of gender.

The rhetorical difference between the daughters and sons explains why the son can be allowed to leave the house and wander around, indeed, be thrown out, without any harm being done to the father's integrity. The son is the image of the father, and the existential relation of chronological succession is not broken by his temporary departure. In order to become a future father, he has to become his father's metaphor, linked to him as he is by temporal metonymy. The daughter has no such possibility because she is not *like* the father. Where the reassuring metaphor[11] is lacking, synecdoche is the obsessional compensation.

This representation of the basic opposition that underlies the architecture of Judges points out the limits of the oppositional logic that we are so used to. The two systems had to conflict because there is no "logic" in their rivalry. The patrilocal house is a site of tension because there is no real permanency possible. Fathers die, and mostly, the daughter's brother takes over, which may or may not have been the case in the Judges world. There is no evidence of this in Judges, but there may be in Genesis 24. Whatever the brother's position, if the father has no son, the daughter's husband who takes over the fatherly position is the token of nonpermanency. He is arbitrarily chosen. On the other hand, in the virilocal system as represented in Genesis the sons can only become fathers in their turn by submitting to the father's power for a very long time, hence, by spending a very long time as father-sons (e.g., Jacob's sons) or by going away and wandering (Joseph).

The problem of succession so acutely played out in Genesis witnesses to this contradiction. Both forms of patriarchy display the systems' inherent impossibility. Genesis is more concerned with the problems of virilocy, while Judges struggles with patrilocy.[12] The house, therefore, is crucial, not only as a symbolic figure of confinement and expulsion, but as the material basis of this struggle.

Two stories in Judges, Abimelech's and Jephthah's, start with the expulsion of the son from the virilocal father-house. On the other hand, Gideon, Abimelech's father, is said to have "seventy sons of his body begotten for he had many women" (7:30). The two supplements to the sheer mention of the number—the bodily contiguity between Gideon and his sons, and the extensive harem—seem to respond to implicit questions about his fatherhood. The next verse retrospectively undermines those supplements, however. It is translated by the JPS as: "And his concubine that was at Shechem, she also bore him a son, and he called his name Abimelech" (8:31). The first explanatory phrase, "from his body begotten," is not simple insistence on Gideon's paternity. As far as the paternal body is concerned, there is no difference between the seventy sons and Abimelech; the difference comes in the sons' residence. In contrast with the Shechemite son, the seventy live in the virilocal father-house. The paternal body, then, is closely related to, indeed identified with, the paternal house. The status of the woman is here again an issue. The many women stand in opposition to a single "concubine." There is no clarity about the number of wives the Israelites were allowed to have, but "many" is not a reliable guarantee of "legal" matrimony, let alone of the widely assumed opposition between the one favorite, legal wife and the "secondary wives" that concubines were supposed to be. This instance of the notion of "concubine" is again contradictory to the Latinate, and even more so to the modern concept. And again, the only possible meaning is [patrilocal] wife.

The case of Gideon is even more interesting if we take into account the speech-act of naming. It is the father who had refused the office of ruler[13] who names his son "my father is king." Is Gideon provoking or predicting Abimelech's later revolt against the virilocal father-house? Is he, who refused political leadership, reminding his son of his kingship in the house, his rulership over "many women"? Or is he acknowledging the "kingship," the power, of his patrilocal wife's father? [14] For that father is the real, social father of this son; from his body the latter is begotten via the daughter. [15] Whatever Gideon's motivations, the "concubine" is, again, not in the least described as a "lowly" woman. The contrast between the virilocal, patrilineal sons who are said to be "from his body begotten" and the patrilocal, matrilineal one who is the son of a king points to a radical differentiation between two classes of sons. Indeed, the ensuing striving for power is based on the competition between two sides who have an equal claim to power.

The first verse of chapter 9 is one of the most explicit formulations of patrilocy: "And Abimelech the son of Jerubbaal went to Shechem unto his mother's brothers, and spoke with them, and with all the house of his mother's father, saying [. . .]" The son who is not "from his [Gideon's] body begotten" says then to his maternal uncles: "*Remember* also that I am your bone and your flesh" (9:2). [16] The relation between house and body, both materializations of kinship, is established through this formula that, in Genesis, is claimed to mean heterosexual bonding, only anachronistically rendered by the word "love." The belonging to, choosing of, the patrilocal rules of kinship is expressed in a bodily metaphor that responds to the one used with reference to the virilocal father, Gideon. The maternal relatives do make Abimelech king at Beth-millo, a location that can be understood as a cornerstone in the book's architectural design. The place named "house of the fortification," house of the tower that is, could very well be the "tower of strength" that will be the site of Abimelech's undoing.

Jephthah is also a patrilocal son. His mother is referred to as an ʾishah zonah, widely translated as "a harlot." We have seen that the "unfaithfulness" implied in the root zanah can be related to the leaving behind of the father in favor of "any man," or the other way around, and the case of Jephthah further confirms this possibility. The noun zonah hardly fits our view of prostitution; how would it account for the acceptance of the son in a father-house? A prostitute as the term is commonly understood is by definition promiscuous, hence, unable to identify the father of her child. In fact, the only way to provide her child with a father would be to remain patrilocal and thereby to attribute fatherhood to the mother's father. This is one of the ways prostitution and patrilocy may eventually—through the ideological imposition of virilocy—have become conflated. If this woman is a patrilocal wife, the noun zonah could indicate that her temporary "unfaithfulness" from her father's house or her relinquishing of her son, indirectly implied by the fact that Jephthah seems to have grown up in the virilocal house, turns her into a "woman of unfaithfulness" in the eyes of the patrilocal ideology, while her residence in her father's house turns her into a "prostitute" from the virilocal perspective. The term becomes pejorative in both cases, but not in the same sense. The motive the other sons allege for their expulsion of Jephthah is indeed that he is the "son of another woman." "Other" is, then, less an "opprobrious term for concubine" (Slotki 1980, 250) than a quite appropriate term for a woman of the other institution.

Jephthah and Abimelech share an ambition to establish power over the land between the two father-houses. After destroying the virilocal-patrilineal house, Abimelech makes a point of conquering Shechem, the patrilocal-matrilineal father-house, while Jephthah negotiates for power over territory that includes the virilocal father-house. Jephthah, later, kills his daughter, I suggest, rather than give her up to a virilocal man; Abimelech is killed by a woman at the patrilocal site. The house of fatherhood itself is too problematic to allow for either solution, the conquest of the patrilocal house or that of the virilocal house, to work. The crucial opposition that underlies all the others—that between patrilocy and virilocy—breaks down where ambition meets gender or where *gibborim* meet women. The consequence is chaos, and chaos results in violence.

Limits

If the antithetical view of the house as either side of an opposition can only help us realize that oppositional logic is part of the problem of misreading, we can try to look at the house in Judges as an opposition in itself. It is not, then, opposed to something other than the house, but it opposes itself, the different aspects that turn around, in, and through it. The house is represented as what it is not: as door, as threshold, as opening—we recall the verb *yiphthah* in chapter 19—as the place where nothing happens unless one leaves it. The house in opposition to itself becomes the structure to leave behind. Rather than the token of civilization, the house negatively signifies the powerlessness of civilization, or its abuse. As the limit of the political life enhanced by the historiographical project, the house comes to signify the limit of life.

We have seen that Bath and Beth both meet their death at the limit of the house. We can now understand why the vow Jephthah made had to lead to his daughter's death, whether or not he "knew" her identity as the sacrificial victim. As a patrilocal son expelled from a virilocal father-house, Jephthah is torn between the two institutions and the two possible figurations of fatherhood they entail. As a son, he was the victim of the competition between the two systems. He was brought to the virilocal father-house by his "unfaithful," inter-institutional mother, and when he was expelled from it, he belonged nowhere. For him more than for anyone else, then, the establishment of his identity as a father is vital. His ambition to become the "head" (*rosh*) of the inhabitants of Gilead is his response to his expulsion from the house of Gilead, the house of his father. When we meet him again as the mighty *gibbor* who is insecure about his victory, his vow to sacrifice rather than to give away necessarily concerns—condemns—the one person who insures his status as father. To sacrifice her is to escape the need to give her away in virilocal marriage. The daughter is the only possible object of the vow, since her "coming out of the doors of his house" is the threat that weighed on him from his early days on. As the image, not of her father but of her mother, she cannot but be "unfaithful" to her father as her mother had been to hers. Coming out of the house, she is on the verge of becoming a "harlot," a woman who goes away from the father. Rather than allowing that threat to his self to happen, Jephthah must prevent the transition from taking place, in the drastic and magical way we know. To prevent her from becoming a "harlot," Jephthah has to keep her a "virgin." The use of the male expression for ripeness, the one that expresses the negative view of "virginity," is thus directly linked to the establishment and the preservation of the house.

Viewing of the composition of the book as architectural rather than chronological becomes acutely necessary when a chronological reading can only lead to the exclusion of some of the stories.[17] The stories of the Book of Judges are not only not chronologically coherent, sometimes, their coherence is anti-chronological, that is, retrospective. When read with an eye to the book's retrospective logic, Bath's story makes much more sense. Just as Sisera, in chapter 5:26, has to be standing while he is slain because he had to fall in the next, climactic verse,[18] so Bath had to be vowed to death in 11:30 in order for the dramatic confrontation in verse 34 to take place.[19] The climax, here, is the *view* of the daughter coming out of the house as the *gibbor*'s bride: behold his-daughter. It is this view that worked on the audience, that the listeners "knew," that they expected: it was a traditional cultural event, initiating the marriage of the daughter and relating the political and domestic spheres. It is the "wandering rock" that constitutes a generative kernel of the story. It is this moment of intense and dramatic focalization of the daughter coming out of the house—in other words, being unfaithful, leaving her father—that destroys Jephthah's identity. As the slip in the same verse so wonderfully expresses: besides *him*—as a patrilocal father—he was no father, no *gibbor*, no man.

The daughter would have been safer had she stayed inside the house and waited for her father to bring in a man of his choice for her. But as the synecdoche and its rupture in verse 34 shows—besides *him* he had neither son nor daughter—the "exclusive possession" is incompatible with the status of *gibbor* and with the political life that historiography tries to focus on. The house is not as permanent, stable, safe, as the opposition between the two institutions suggests. Kallah's death illustrates that as well: it is patrilocy, according to the ideology of Judges, which must be fought, because it is still very powerful. Bath's virtual "unfaithfulness" can only be countered by violence.

Bath's coming out of the house comes to stand, now, in a parallel with her request to her father. "Leave me alone" is, like her coming out dancing and singing, a ritual of separation from the father. The first time she asks to go, the father is broken, his identity annihilated, and he accuses Bath of the fate he is bringing on her. The second time she asks, he says "go." Within the isotopy of transition that we are looking at, his willingness to let her go the second time can be understood as an acknowledgment of her ripeness. But more importantly, it reflects Jephthah's understanding that she is going, not to a virilocal father-house, but to the wilderness, a nonstructural space of liminality; Jephthah has no competition with that space. After the ritual of separation, she will come back to her father's house: "she returned unto her father" (11:39). The sojourn in the mountains in no way threatens Jephthah's position as the powerful subject for whom the daughter is an object to be possessed.[20]

The dramatic moment of Bath's coming out of the house of her father is so central to the whole story because it functions as a shifter between several isotopies. As the limit between Jephthah's political life as *gibbor* in war and *rosh* in peace and his domestic life as a father, the moment is equally temporal and spatial. The door of the house and her coming out of it—at once a spatial transgression and a temporal transition—is also the definition of Jephthah's fragile identity. The view of the daughter is the view of the open door, of the leak in the system, of the breach in the architecture of exclusive possession. The open door destabilizes the permanency of patrilocy. It literally opens the house, as a piece of architecture and as the system based on it, to the world that does not let itself be defined by one exclusive system. This is also stressed in that poetic echo of the limit that the door represents, in the use of the verb *yiphthah* recalling Jephthah's confrontation at *his* door, when Beth's husband opens the door of the house at that story's climactic moment.

Indeed, the open door signifies the openness, the vulnerability, of Jephthah's position as *gibbor* and father. The castration is expressed in the slip about him; it creates a wound, an opening, a door, in his virile identity. The opening disclosed by his name is a permanent attribute of this *gibbor:* he opens his mouth, he uses the mouth of the sword in order to open bodies, he watches the door of the house open; opening his family-house, he produces the opening in history created by his exit from the door of the virilocal house, the breach in his maleness, as seen within the ideology of the book. The materiality of his speech-acts and the semiotic function of the material house join in this decisive scene of deadly focalization.

Bath's double act of departure from the father's house is echoed in Beth's equally double departure. While Bath was accused, at her first exit, of causing the father's undoing, Beth is equally accused, at least in the traditional translations and commentaries. We do not witness her coming out of the father-house. Since we begin to read her story with the husband rather than with the father, we see her being "taken." While Bath is presented at the moment of coming out, Beth is introduced at a later moment. Her first change of house is only implied. Later, she returns to her father's house. Bath left her father's house for two months, Beth went back to it for four months. It is significant that time, in these stories of female transition, is counted in months. Bath's coming out to meet her father is mirrored in Beth bringing her husband into her father's house (19:3). Her father, rather than rending his clothes as Jephthah did, rejoices to meet him.

The scene of hospitality as it is usually seen is the only extensive description in the book of life inside the house, of homeliness. Since we meet the daughters so systematically at the moment of transition and in the space of transgression, this scene catches attention. But we are disappointed if we expect the life of daughters to become visible. From the moment that she brings her husband in, Beth is not mentioned. The dialogue, the pleasure of eating and drinking, and the competition over the house where the daughter must live: it is all exclusively the business of men. Beth is mentioned again only when, far from home, she and her husband reach an unhomely place to spend the night.

The journey of the husband with his possessions, including the woman who is without status—taken out of the father's house, but not yet integrated into the virilocal house—depicts the situation of the wandering son. Although there is no immediate danger represented on the road, there is no safety there either. Seated at the "broad place of the city," the man is, in his turn, suspended between places, institutions, and statuses. The question the old man asks him, "Where are you going and where do you come from?" can be read on two opposing levels. In terms of the journey, it elicits the answer that the man actually gives: coming from Bethlehem, the house of bread, he is going to the hill country of Ephraim, the pasture land. The answer is a chiastic reversal of the question. The chiasmus shifts a concretely spatial isotopy into a symbolic one. The man gives a double answer, restoring the order of the question in his second answer: "From there I am, and I went to Bethlehem" (19:18). If we read this answer as symbolic, it refers to the attempt of the man to take over the position of the patrilocal father. From the nomadic pasture land, he went to the house of bread. But given the outcome of the attempt embodied in his departure, he needs a third answer: "I am now going to the house of Yahweh and no man takes me into his house." Soggin (1981, 287) follows the Greek text and changes "the house of Yahweh" into "home": I am going home. The argument for this drastic change is that there is no indication of any cultic function which the Levite may have performed. The JPS keeps the Hebrew, though Slotki glosses it as "Shiloh" (1980, 301). If we read the architectural geography of houses, however, we can note an interesting movement from the house of bread to the land of pasture, to the house of bread, to the house of Yahweh, to nobody's house. Ephraim is framed by a twofold reference to the house of bread. The house of Yahweh can be an allusion to both the Levite's status as a priest and his situation: no house, anywhere, but within Israel, the house of Yahweh. If nobody will take him in, he will spend the night in the open. Clearly, this man has a housing problem. The precision of the geographical indications is countered by the imprecision of the actual state of the wandering man.

The vagueness of the spatial status of the man both contrasts with and is similar to the daughter's liminality. We remember that Bath came out of her confinement and met her death sentence at the door. The Levite, in turn, came out of the house to wander around, hesitating between two systems. The limit of the daughter's space—the door—is both similar to and radically different from the transitional situation of the man who is in the open space: the house of Yahweh, of no man. He went out and is now taken in. Bath went out and goes out once more. Beth went out, is taken in, taken out, taken in, thrown out. The door does not have the same function for men as for women.

The men "of the sons of worthlessness" beset the house round about. The house becomes, thus, a closed house, hence, a prison. The men who beset the house become its door. And the door opens in the threat of rape. The man, this second Jephthah, sees his identity again in terms of an open door. There seems to be no way to keep the door of the house closed. So instead, the response to the threat of opening is to open the door himself and to throw Beth out. The images of the threatening men surrounding the house, the enforced opening, the expulsion of the victim become, if we look at them from the perspective of the object of victimization, the very image of rape. The door of the house represents, then, the female body itself; the impossibility of keeping the door closed, the female body's vulnerability to rape; the act of throwing Beth out becomes the act of rape as the enforcement of entrance in the body. But then there is a reversal at play, producing a "dialectic of outside and inside," as Bachelard (1964) would call it. It is this dialectic that drives home the idea of the breakdown of kinship categories.

Dialectic

That lack of safety inside the house is, once we look for its symptoms, present in all of the book's stories of individuals. Even the captive king Adoni-Bezek refers, in 1:7, to a situation in his house that is quite spooky: there, captive kings had to gather food under his table, their thumbs and toes cut off. The house has become entirely political. Achsah, in her "proper" story, is given away, which implies, not so much safety in her case, but the instability of the father-house. Hers is virtually turned into a virilocal marriage by her acquisition of the wells, but given the subordination of the fiancé to the bride's father who is his older brother, the harmonious solution to the institutional conflict indicates the underlying tension in its own subtle way. That Yael's tent is not a safe place to be has been amply argued by the critics. That the tent in question is a woman's space and that the man who enters it is thus transgressing a spatial, institutional limit has not, however, been taken into account. Gideon's call takes place outside his father's house, but in a spatial relation to it. His acceptance of the call puts him in immediate danger. His life is threatened by the men in the city because he cut down the idols of his father (6:25, 6:30). Being the "lowest in his father's house" (6:15), Gideon most resembles the heroes of Genesis. Surprisingly, his father stands up for him, and there is no sign of conflict within the family here. It is only when he himself has become a father that the problem of the house arises again, as we have already seen in Abimelech's story. This does not contradict the conclusions of this study, since Gideon, however much of a *gibbor* he may be, has no individual story, no encounter with a woman, no daughter. He is represented only on the level of the political coherence.

The dialectic of the house is clearly, though briefly, represented in the story of Abimelech. The tragic quality of Abimelech's fate is due to the inaccessibility of the house. He does not belong to Gideon's house. The son whose name is "my father is king" cannot belong to the house of the father who had said, "I will not rule over you, neither shall my son rule over you" (8:23). Going to Shechem, to his maternal father-house, he is accepted as ruler, and the first thing he then does is to go back to "his father's house" and kill it off (9:5). When, after having been made king by the lords of Shechem, he ends up fighting against Shechem, his mother's father-house, the safety inside that house suddenly becomes inaccessible to him. It is significant that the only successful patrilocal son is killed by a woman who stands on top of the "tower of strength" of Shechem—in other words, the fortified patrilocal house. Abimelech's story dialectically figures the conflict that cannot be solved.

On the other side, the daughter's side that is, the three victim-daughters show the dialectic in detail. Among the three, the available positions are distributed systematically. Bath is killed outside the house. She met her condemnation when leaving it. She then left it again, came back, and, given the ritual of sacrifice, we must suppose her actual death to have taken place outside. Kallah, in contrast, met her death inside the house, after also first encountering the tension inside the house, at her wedding. Both Bath and Kallah never went into a virilocal house. Beth alone represents the dialectic synthesis; she has to live through all the possibilities of the opposition. She is the only daughter who did enter a virilocal house, twice leaving her father's house, twice entering the virilocal house. Between the two, there is a mediating father-house: the prison in Gibeah, the house that figures rape both metaphorically in its enforced opening and metonymically in the contiguity between treachery inside and violence outside. This house, as a properly dialectical meeting place, represents all aspects of the conflict. As the site of the climax of violence, it is also the architectural climax of the book.

The house belongs to a father figure, but he is of the husband's tribe. The arrival of the company at the broad place of Gibeah, the announcement that "no man takes me into his house," and the entreaty to the old Ephraimite to invite him in make the reader/listener aware of the dangers attached to the outside. The relief at the invitation to come inside is, however, unreliable. We already know that this couple is somehow condemned to remain unstably settled; no house they have been in together has proven to be permanently theirs. They either come in together and then the woman leaves, or they leave together and then they come in separately, as in the father's house in Bethlehem. According to this logic, Beth can be expected to leave the house alone; it is her turn, so to speak.

The dialectic between inside and outside, between two forms of unsafety, is brought to its climax in 19:27. The man opens (*yiphthaḥ*) the door of the house and goes out to go on his way. But there is an obstacle to his simple forgetfulness of the past. The obstacle is visual, and it forces him to assume his position as the subject of focalization. The obstacle is obstinately metonymical; the house is not an isolated place, but is contiguous to the outside. The obstacle is described in these words: "And behold the woman his [patrilocal] wife fallen down at the door of the house, with her hands upon the threshold" (19:27). This representation derives its logic not from realism, but from its own climactic strategies. The word "behold" stages the scene, the confrontation between the subject of focalization who can freely go and the object he has sacrificed for the sake of his own freedom. The woman is described as what, in this particular story, she so fully is. Thus, "the woman his [patrilocal] wife" is represented in terms of both sex and status.[21] For both these terms account for what has already happened to her and what is still to happen. The fact that she lies there "fallen down" represents the ambiguity of her state. She is physically fallen, a position opposed to the full subjectivity of a standing person ready to "go his way"; she may be seen as fallen in the military sense, that is, dead, or the equivalent; she is in any case fallen out of her status as the man's wife, for she has been used by "every man"; and she has fallen down on her way to the safety inside the house.[22]

The last phrase, "with her hands upon the threshold," embodies the dialectic between inside and outside, between imploring and accusing, between annihilating and symbolizing. The realistic reading falls short, here; the man can hardly have gone out to go his way *before* he saw her with her hands on the doorstep. The architectural reading enhances the poetic precision of the description: on one side of the opposition, the man is in the house; on the other side, he is out of the house. In between is the woman with her hands in the intermediate space, as the synthetic new element that changes and suspends the simple opposition. The moment of this confrontation is constructed upon the spatial isotopy: both time and space converge in the ambiguity of "fallen," which echoes Sisera's fall, while the intertextual allusion of the word *yiphthah* further enhances the architectural composition. This *yiphthah* who was on his way to the house of Yahweh and who delivers his wife on the way can be seen as a commentary on Jephthah's sacrifice. To open the doors of the father-house to let the daughter/woman go away is, in the ideology of the book, to give her away to any man—to every man, that is.

The final entrance into a house is staged as a preparation for Beth's being given as a final gift to every man, her dismemberment in the countersacrifice. The house of the husband is now only a repetitive space of uncanniness. The first time Beth had come there, it was a voluntary voyage. The return to the father-house had been a submission to the patrilocal institution. If it was, perhaps, not voluntary, it was, at least according to the rules, "proper." The third entrance into a father-house was a flight from danger. The fourth entrance was not allowed; it was stopped on the threshold. The last entrance is not hers any longer. Her husband enters her, only to send her out again. The house has become public space. The text says, "when *he* had come into his house."

The story of Beth is the most uncanny story of the book, perhaps of the whole Hebrew Bible. It is so because it contains contradictions that cannot be solved. Attempts to resolve them reveal the desire to dissolve the uncanny effect of the story. I would like to counter this tendency, if only because both sound scholarship and the text deserve better. Instead, I propose to dwell for a while on the uncanniness of the story and to try to read it with Freud's essay on the uncanny as an illuminating subtext.

Freud starts his essay with a linguistic study of the concept of the uncanny, a most interestingly ambiguous word in German: *unheimlich.* The word is constructed on the root *heim,* which means *house*: Beth. Although Freud does not play on this meaning of the root, it is so appropriate in this chapter that I cannot resist translating the word, more literally than do the translators of the Standard Edition, as *unhomeliness.*[23] The attempt to build up the *house,* in the sense of family, via the daughter—who, for the sake of the patrilocal community, has to remain in the father-house and, for the sake of the virilocal community, has to come out and go with "any man" to the virilocal house—falls through when the two systems conflict. Such a conflict occurs when one daughter, Beth, is required to build two houses. The uncanniness or unhomeliness is, in my view, responsible for the violent impression the book makes on the reader, but for which the murderesses are generally held accountable. In order to get a clear view of the meaning of unhomeliness, we must try to visualize the scenes.

Unhomeliness Revisited

Imagine a movie about Beth's story in which the stories of Bath and Kallah are represented as preludes, subplots, or epilogues. We may decide to have the three roles played by the same actress in order to enhance the sameness of their nameless fates. The movie would be frightening. My guess is that the modes available for this story in our present culture would be either pornography or high symbolism. The symbolic mode, which is the one I choose for this imaginary movie, would try to interpose mediating screens in order to avoid direct identification. The best movie would be the one that would bring forth, successively, identification between the audience and the father, the husband, and the daughter—each of them in turn. There would be no dominating identification, no decisive explicit response. Such a mode of representation would be as close as possible to the text while also entailing a level of uncanniness hardly imaginable. In the classic movie *Gaslight*, Ingrid Bergman is persecuted by an unknown murderer; it is her husband, who tries to drive her crazy in her own house. In all the films modeled after this architext, the heroine thinks she is finally safe in her own house, only to discover that the man who wants to kill her is her own husband. We can think of the young girls who are told by their mothers to watch out for strangers, only to be raped by their own fathers. Thinking of them we come close, but not yet close enough, to the feelings aroused by our movie about Beth.

First, the conflict that condemns Beth is institutional; hence, there is no escape for her. No personal qualities or right choices can solve the problem for her. In her version of this story, Doris Day is finally saved by the husband of her husband's accomplice/lover, whom she had thought to be her best friend.[24] Uncanny as it is, this situation allows for a solidarity between two victims, one of whom, being a man and not involved in more than one plot, is powerful enough to intervene. These films in fact try to reassure us: after holding our breath for eighty minutes, the uncanniness disappears when the mystery is solved. We are reassured, not so much because this particular woman is saved, but because there was a solution, an explanation of the problem, and because the problem was individual, hence, far from our own lives. The other situation, that of the raped daughters, is, on the other hand, institutional, hence, general. Once we realize the possibility of such a situation within our own houses—a possibility suggested by the sheer frequency of news items about father-rapists—the uncanniness strikes. But it is still possible to believe that the situation is not institutional, that it could never occur in our own lives, as long as it does not actually occur or as long as we manage not to see it. As the uncanniness surrounding Ingrid Bergman or Doris Day is built up through identification with the victim, the daughter-rape's uncanniness is broken down by careful attempts, in informational texts about it, to enforce identification with the perpetrator (Ward 1985). A movie on the mode of the first but with the thematics of the second would perhaps be effective in producing awareness of the uncanniness in our own homes.

Beth's movie would have to start on the construction of homeliness. The German word *heimlich* means "familiar" as well as "secret." The secrecy can be constructed around, on the one hand, the daughter's personal desires and, on the other, around her confinement to the house. The opposites of these meanings are, strangely enough, each other's opposites as well. Familiar is opposed to strange, spooky: *unheimlich*; secret is opposed to public, open. My movie would play on these oppositions; the house would develop into a spooky place where things happen whose state of reality is unclear—the daughter would have the feeling of being touched without knowing who touches her or of being watched without knowing who watches her.[25] The other motif, that of her public status as daughter, would be developed in terms of matchmaking. But the movie would be unlike most uncanny movies in that the triple perspective would be systematically sustained. It would require much imagination, but it would have to be done: we must understand the father's anxiety at losing his daughter and, hence, his emotion, which focuses on the house. We therefore represent the emptiness of the material house that inspires his fear of death without descendance, a descendance that is connected to him by reassuringly material bonds, bonds which imply bondage. We must understand the husband who, in spite of his revolt against the father and his desire to acquire the daughter, has been brought up to identify with the fatherly position. It is this position that he will occupy in the future. Therefore, when danger occurs, he forgets about the heroism that he was trained to develop as a "hero of might" in order to deserve and conquer the fatherly position. We will understand the daughter who has, on the one hand, no place to be, no position to take, if not in connection with the father, but who, on the other hand, also experiences her subjectivity when she desires to "go astray," to make her own choice or, at least, to change her life, go elsewhere. She receives on her body the blows that the men deal each other because it is over her body that they fight. These three subject-positions enter into conflict with the roles they assign to each other; that conflict is what inhabits the house.

The first symptoms of uncanniness arise when, in the beginning of the story and of our movie, we realize that the husband goes after Beth to take her back, that "to speak to her heart" means, not "to be kind to her," as critics anachronistically tend to think, but to argue, to reason, to convince her to leave with him. The audience's slight feelings of discomfort would be due, I imagine, to the lack of personal involvement with Beth as a subject. The emotional mode of the movie would be utterly flat, represented in the husband's flat, ever-impersonal voice and face. The prolonged scenes of hospitality in the father-house are good for a long stretch of representation. Starting on a note of merry everydayness, this long scene will slowly move into uncanniness, when the insistence of the father toward the husband, the absence of Beth, the lack of openness about the motivation behind the insistence would bring about a split between what the actors do and what they feel. The uneasiness would increase with time; the scene should be stretched out of proportion. The interior of the house, familiar at first, would become strange, estranged. Beth would be there, sitting, waiting, anxious, but uninvolved, uninformed.

The uncanny as analyzed by Freud is characterized by doubleness on the one hand, strangeness on the other. Doubleness and strangeness are somewhat contradictory: lack and excess do not match. They do interact, however, as we have seen in the analysis of speech-acts of lack and excess. The most uncanny aspect of uncanniness is precisely the undermining coexistence of contradictory elements in one and the same feeling (see Felman 1981). The feeling of uncanniness often arises, for example, when apparently animate beings are not clearly alive or, in contrast, when a lifeless object may in fact be animate (Freud 1981, 226). The most uncanny moment, in this respect, is indeed the one we have already appointed the climax of the story and, I would now suggest, of the entire book: the confrontation between the man who steps out of the house to go his way and the fallen woman with her hands on the threshold. If the reader is left in doubt about the question of life and death, it is certainly due to the effect of uncanniness. The attempt to naturalize the scene, to dispel its ambiguity, reveals the effectiveness of the strategy of uncanniness. Slotki states: "He evidently thought that she was alive" (1980, 303), thus separating the reader, who is then supposed to assume that Beth is dead, from the character of the husband who is assumed to adhere to the opposite view. Splitting the two sides of the uncanny doubleness turns the unhomeliness of the scene into tragic irony—a much more acceptable device because it saves the integrity of the reader's isolation and the character's innocence. This is the sort of naturalizing criticism that must be countered in a full re-presentation of the story.

The secret and its opposite, the public, are equally represented in this confrontation. Freud explains the ambiguity of the word *heimlich* by contiguity: "From the idea of 'homelike,' 'belonging to the house,' the further idea is developed of something withdrawn from the eyes of strangers, something concealed, secret" (p. 225). It is dramatic to the extreme that Beth's body, lying outside, in public, is not only not seen by her husband—he first goes out to go his way, says the text, before the obstacle arises before his eyes—but it is also mis-seen once it is seen. He does not see it as what it is. He takes her as alive and capable of standing up. Hence, he denies what has been done to her. The body of the woman, exposed, is still a secret. Attempts to make readers believe she is dead at this point are not only attempts to make the husband appear as innocent as possible, but also to spare the reader identification *with him*. This is a serious loss, for it is that identification that can bring about a working through of the uncanniness of the book, hence, it is that identification that can bring about a catharsis (Dupont-Roc and Lallot 1980).

Freud's example in his essay is Hofmann's tale "The Sandman." Between this nineteenth-century horror story and the biblical narrative there is, of course, an unbridgeable gap of time, context, and effect. Nevertheless, the two stories can illuminate each other to some extent. One of the most uncanny scenes in "The Sandman" is the one where Coppelius, the evil father figure, is imagined as screwing off the young Nathaniel's arms and legs as an experiment. In Freud's terms (1981, 232): "He had worked on him as a mechanic would on a doll." The mechanical aspect of this vision is strikingly similar to the husband's sacrificial act: "And when he was come into his house, he took the knife and seized his [patrilocal] wife and divided her, limb after limb, into twelve pieces" (19:29). The doubleness is again insistent. On the one hand, the act is clearly symbolic; on the other, it is the act of a professional, a butcher or a mechanic, who goes about his business with competence. The definite article with "knife" is not only an intertextual comment on Genesis 22:10 with irony; it also conveys the mechanical nature of the event of her dismemberment, stressing even further the final annihilation of Beth as subject. She is, indeed, no more than a doll here. "The" knife is the knife the man knew he would use; the article connotes premeditation. Contrasting with the horror that the act inspires in those readers who are taken by surprise, the definite article is again a symptom of identification that the translation as "a knife" denies.

But why is the representation of this act of horror called for in the first place? What function can it possibly fulfill within a book that deals with so many aspects of the tension between the political and the domestic spheres? This question touches upon the problem of representation, specifically, the representation of the unrepresentable. Lyotard (1984, 338) analyzes the way the unrepresentable can suddenly emerge out of the "artifices" of old objectifications, calling them into question, unmaking their fixity. This emergence happens in order for something that defies representation and conceptualization to happen nevertheless.[26] The problem of representation, then, is also a problem of chronology, of time, and of the attempt to unmake chronology, to suspend time.

The husband's house was the peaceful setting of the beginning of the story. In our movie, its interior should be materially identical when at the end "they" go back there again. The same space, the same objects, will acquire a totally different meaning: they will go from homeliness to unhomeliness. The sense of time and the suspension of time, both equally acute in this repetition of space, would lead to a still deeper aspect of the uncanny. The return to the place of origin is a crucial aspect of the story, though one that has been suppressed from criticism. The idea of return is itself uncanny. Where does one return to, and who is the subject of return? The latter question cannot be entirely answered; as we have seen, Beth's being neither dead nor alive is necessary to her status as both the raped daughter/wife (her perspective) and as the uncanny (the husband's perspective). The former question is no easier to answer, due to a fundamental repression in the book, to which we will turn shortly.

Freud suggests that the aspects of uncanniness that we have seen so far are related things: both are familiar yet strange, they reveal a blindness to what the eyes see, they entail doubleness and multiplication. He connects those aspects of the uncanny to the body of the mother. Doubling, he writes, is a compensation for the fear of death, annihilating, for the loss of the self.

> Such ideas, however, have sprung from the soil of unbounded self-love, from the primary narcissism which dominates the mind of the child and of primitive man. But when this stage has been surmounted, the 'double' reverses its aspect. From having been an assurance of immortality, it becomes the uncanny harbinger of death. (p. 235)

If we ignore Freud's own strategies to distance himself from the uncanniness of his own theory (the obsession with the temporal perspective, "the child and primitive man" as the subjects of otherness), then we see here a possibility of understanding both Beth's story and the responses it gave rise to, both in the text itself and in subsequent interpretations. On the one hand, the story of the dividing of her body can be seen as the acting out of the man's own fears. Multiplication of her body provides him with additional protection, a strategy which, as the sequel to the story shows, works very well. On the other hand, the denial of the rejection of her body, both in that sequel and in the readings of it, wherein the horror is directed toward the Benjaminites and the husband's collaboration with them forgotten, shows the repression of the other side of uncanniness, the meaning of the multiplied body as the harbinger of death.

The act of multiplying Beth's body and sharing its possession with the tribes of Israel can also be seen as an attempt toward communion that reveals a regressive tendency. Freud relates the feeling of uncanniness with "a regression to a time when the ego had not yet marked itself off sharply from the external world and from other people" (p. 236). This way of putting it leads back to Jephthah, the other opener of doors and of the female body. The narrator's slip on his account—besides *him* he had neither son nor daughter—points to a chaotic, undifferentiated view of self that the "house," in its material as well as familial sense, represents. Beth's husband shares his "house" with the tribes, unable as he is to construct a house of his own. Jephthah, the cutter, cuts off his house for similar reasons. The men in these stories can only regress, can only return to the past. They are not able to enter into a different time, a future.

The Empty House Is Haunted

Freud's definition of the uncanny strikes us as both insightful and particularly male-oriented. Having decided not to shun the male perspective—the better to understand it—I will present it here with the explicit purpose of grasping its weakness as well as its seductiveness—the better to undermine it, later. The juxtaposition of the elements that make up uncanniness in Freud's view is revealing: "Animism, magic and sorcery, the omnipotence of thoughts, man's attitude to death, involuntary repetition and the castration complex comprise practically all the factors which turn something frightening into something uncanny" (p. 243). The inevitable presence, in this series, of the castration complex betrays the orientation. Freud seems to assume that uncanniness is a male feeling. Let us pursue this line for a short while.

The feeling is then characterized by the sense of objectification, of dis-empowerment, that makes for the loss of subjectivity. Although it seems hard to imagine Beth's story as the enactment of the *husband's* fears, the integration of the story in the context of Judges and the po-litical coherence make that interpretation inevitable.

The attempt to understand this man is in no way an attempt to redeem his behavior; nor does it help us to occupy a position of moral indignation that brings sympathy for the victim but no remedy to the social sickness that victimized her. If we try to identify with the man, we may have a better chance of grasping the social problem. If Freud is right that the factors he enumerates are the elements of uncanniness, then in the next step, in acknowledging the idea that the death and dismemberment of Beth represent *his* fright, the story becomes yet more impressive. The acting out of castration anxiety, caused by the imagined omnipotence of the father, takes the following shape. The image of the father, once left behind, turns up again in Gibeah. This involuntary repetition is already uncanny enough: the past becomes fu-ture, behind stands in front, blocking sight of the man's own self. Giv-ing Beth over to the rapists, to everyman, is a first multiplication, dictated by the interiorized indictment of the father: to go with an-other man = to go with any man = to go with everyman. To come home, then, not with the one woman with whom, in the past of verse 1, he had come home with once, but with this multiplied woman who has become properly untouchable, makes for a compulsory repetition of this multiplication, a rejection of the rejection, a defilement of the defilement. The husband's mechanistic competence—*the* knife—is certainly not cheerful, nor is it voluntary. *The* knife is also the instru-ment of the castration inflicted upon him and which he desperately tries to divert onto Beth, just as he did with the threat of rape.

What does the house look like, the house which has now become so spooky we can hardly bear to look at it, yet which remains so famil-iar because we have been there before and keep returning to it? If this episode is seen as a male fantasy, then the first urgency the man feels must be to eliminate the daughter from it. Freud provides an explana-tion for the sense that she, on the deepest level, does not belong in the house:

> Whenever a man dreams of a place or a country and says to himself, while he is still dreaming: "this place is familiar to me, I've been here before," we may interpret the place as being his mother's genitals or her body. In this case, too, then, the *unheimlich* is what was once *heimish*, familiar; the prefix *"un"* is the token of repression. (p. 245)

If the house is related to the mother as producer of life, of the subject, then it is "logical" that the characters cannot be allowed to remain in it. The relentless traveling compulsion of the *gibborim* who are bound to leave the parental house becomes understandable; the impossibility of the daughter remaining in the house once she has reached the age of nubility becomes fatal. The confusion of the temporal sequentiality of the book and its replacement with spatial movement from house to house fits well with the idea of regression to a pretemporal world, a regression to the mother's body.

But, and this is the most interesting aspect of the architecture of unhomeliness, the identification of the house with the mother's body also provides a beginning of an answer to the question I will discuss in the next chapter, a question that has been raised by Marianne Hirsch in a paper on maternal anger (forthcoming) and that must be raised in the perspective of the present study with even more acuity: where is Clytemnestra? Where, in Judges, is the mother, the angry mother who might have protected or, if she could not, have avenged her murdered daughter? If the house *is* the mother, in the male fantasy, then there is no place for the mother *inside* it. And indeed, the mothers in the book are defined as living elsewhere, their identity is the spatial otherness that led to the pejorative titles concubine, whore. Samson's mother conceives her son outside, in the field, while Deborah, "a mother in Israel" as she calls herself in chapter 5, is placed, in chapter 4, not in a house but under a palm tree. The mothers are displaced, removed from the father-house as well as from the virilocal house, and this displacement points to a repression. It is this repression and the return of it that will be the subject of the next chapter.

The perspective of the husband may be illuminated by the Freudian subtext, but the perspective of the daughter is emphatically absent from this account. This gap between the perspectives of the husband and the daughter, the two characters who are engaged in a relationship of some sort, is the more poignant since it is her body that receives the physical incisions, the marks of the castration that the husband fears for himself, and that he fears in relation to the father. From his perspective to hers, we have to jump over her dead body just as the husband stepped over her/it; we have to jump from the unconscious fears that the dreamlike fantasy of the episode suggests to the social reality in which the representation of her takes place. Access to her perspective is blocked by her objectification, her silencing, her object status. If we can see her lying at the threshold, we can grasp more. We see her then, not as an object that is uncannily between death and life—"behold his woman"—but as the destroyed subject who "sees" from *below* the closed, then opened door. We see the man who estranged himself from her by rejecting her. We see the traveling legs[27] of the man that, viewed from below, are detached from his estranged voice—"up!" Then we can grasp what uncanniness feels like for its victim. The night that unmade her can only be imagined vaguely, and yet it is inscribed in the story. We need to unread the tendency of reading, for which the man, in his later account to the tribes, set the example, by representing as concretely as possible the episode as undergone by her, for, as Scarry put it, such is not an obvious mode of reading: "physical suffering destroys language, and moral rightness . . . tends to lie with the most articulate" (1985, 201).

In our effort to linger with Beth, then, we wonder why, from her perspective, there seems to be an incompatibility between her and the house she is confined to, yet thrown out of. On a first level, one which we have explored already, it is her position as house-daughter[28] that is conflictual in itself. Once nubile, she can only stay a house-daughter while producing children for the generation before her. This denial of her autonomy is one way of denying her subject-status; hence, being a house-daughter is an impossible state. A representation of this impossibility would take the form it has here: the daughter is irresolvably linked to the house, yet expelled from it. The image of Beth with her hands on the threshold represents this paradoxical state of being confined to and excluded from the house. The boundary between inside and outside gives rise to "an almost obscene conflation of private and public. It brings with it all the solitude of absolute privacy with none of its safety, all the self-exposure of the utterly public with none of its possibility for camaraderie or shared experience" (Scarry 1985, 53). Scarry speaks about physical pain, which is the next level we shall have to talk about; but the description applies equally well to the place of the house-daughter. More importantly, it connects the physical place to the familial place, *through* physical pain.

We can identify with Beth, indeed, on the level of her physical pain. As Scarry so impressively argues, pain is the opposite of power, and the body as the site of pain is opposed to the voice as the site of power. That is why the fathers in Judges speak more than the sons and the sons more than the daughters.[29] That is why Beth never speaks, but is only spoken through. That is also why physical pain is used as an instrument of power.

Beth's pain and its denial serve a more concrete representational purpose. The relation between inside and outside that is at stake in the setting of the stories within the dialectic of inside and outside the house mediates between the dialectic of the mother's body out of which the *gibbor* came, into which he threatens to be pushed back, and the dialectic, or competition, between the political and the domestic. Access to the world requires the free disposal of a body. Pain, on the other hand, destroys the body while making it a prison, an utterly present and hostile entity. The body in pain blocks sight of the world:

> To acknowledge the radical subjectivity of pain is to acknowledge the simple and absolute incompatibility of pain and the world. The survival of each depends on its separation from the other. To bring them together, to bring pain into the world by objectifying it in language, is to destroy one of them. (Scarry 1985, 51)

The two dialectics involved in the figuration of Beth's pain are emphatically present in the representation. The rape, rightly described in Judges 19 as, and as complementary to, torture, is one way of turning her body into a house and conflating inside and outside. The public aspect of the gang-rape enhances this point even more. The image of the daughter lying at the threshold and denied by the husband is another enactment of the mutual metaphor linking house and body. The house become body, the intimate inside of the body become public, and the public body brought into the house, only to be sent all over the borders of the land: this experience of utter scattering, of denial of wholeness, is the fate of the house-daughter fallen down, between spaces, between institutions, between men. We hardly need a Freudian perspective for this concrete bodily image of the social conflict about the female body. The uncanniness is not evoked by past memories but by present pain.

But if, for the unconscious of the man, the house is the mother's body, then the mother does, in his fearful fantasy, witness the daughter's pain. If the representation of the daughter's experience is not eliminated, but is present as a wandering rock, ready to be repressed, misunderstood, forgotten, yet undeniably there, then the man himself, his perspective, will not be able to completely eliminate the mother whose body is inscribed in the architecture of the book. We will now turn, therefore, from the house-daughter to the mother-house.

CHAPTER SEVEN

THE DISPLACEMENT OF
THE MOTHER

Frequently to be really "scientific" means not pretending to be
more "scientific" than the situation allows.
    Umberto Eco

Where is Clytemnestra?
    The triangular relations, in the three victim stories, between fa-
ther, husband, and daughter, are all structured around the daughter—
unlike the Oedipal model. They exclude the mother. Not only does
the mother not participate in the competition, but no mother comes
to rescue her daughter, no mother avenges the murder of the daughter
by a murder of the murderer. Or so it seems.
    This is not to say that mothers are absent from the book, nor that
there is no view of motherhood represented. But mothers are totally
absent from the stories where patrilocy and the murder of the daughter
go together. Since the mothers that do appear are often related to
patrilocy, it seems suspect that they are so conspicuously absent from
the victim stories. In the Greek tradition, the avenging mother is represented more than once (Simon 1978; 1987). In this chapter I will
elaborate the contention that in the Book of Judges the avenging
mother is no more absent than she is in the Greek tradition. But her
repression here is more radical, leaving only traces that are displaced
and disfigured.
    I will approach the question of the mother from two different per-
spectives. First, I will trace the concept of motherhood in those cases
where a mother is explicitly mentioned. Apart from the evident cases
of Abimelech's and Jephthah's mothers, there are Samson's and Micah's
mothers. But there are two other mothers mentioned in the ancient
and to some extent alien text of chapter 5, the Song of Deborah, both

of whom disappeared *as mothers* from the later version, chapter 4. Second, I will take the six murder stories as the starting point of an examination of the two sets of murders: the murders of daughters *versus* the murders of men. I will look for traces, symptoms, of motherhood in the figures of the murderesses that explain both Clytemnestra's absence and the insistent genderedness[1] of the murders in the book.

The use of the concept of displacement in tracing back maternal anger implies a particular view of representation. The displacement of one problematic—the mother's response to the murder of her daughter—onto another—the murder of a hero for the sake of the people—is the figuration of the return of the repressed in which political interests replace "domestic" interests. The repression at stake is the shifter that allows readers of the book to step over from one isotopy to the other. The shift is also inherent to the historiographic project of which the book is one result. The historiography of the Israelite people is an endeavor that partakes of the larger project of centralization of power and imposition of the state by means of literacy. Part of this enormous project consists of the reversal of priorities between domestic life and politics. The murders of the daughters take place within the domestic sphere, although, as we have seen, they are related to the hero's heroism, or lack of it. Marriage institutions and sexual possession largely motivate the victim stories. The men are killed within the public sphere of politics. But that the heroes happen to be killed in, or close to, a house is indeed a first indication of the displacement I wish to point out in this chapter. The location of all six murders is symptomatic for the architectural composition that underlies the book. Thus, they are themselves, as a set, symptomatic for the repressed spatial in favor of the chronological that represents, in this book, the repression of the description of the life of the people in favor of the foregrounding of politics.

Displacement is itself a spatial concept derived from the German *Entstellung*, a word that means both distortion and dislocation (see Weber's excellent analysis, 1982). But the prefix *dis-* itself already holds both meanings: the disjunctive aspect it introduces represents the result of tearing apart what used to be, or could be imagined to be, together. This insistent double meaning drives the point home that displacement is distorting because it is spatial, that is, because it betrays the spatial aspects of the history whose temporality has been emphasized alone. Displacement, then, is not an incidental figure, but an indispensable commentary on the historiographic project itself. Representation in chronology is not possible, displacement seems to argue, without displacement—distortion and dislocation—of the spatial. We may call such a view a poetics.

Explicit Mothers: Jephthah's and Abimelech's, Samson's and Micah's

The mothers of Abimelech and Jephthah, discredited by the exegetical traditions, indeed appear to have only a negative influence on their sons' fates. Because of the institution they live in, their sons are expelled from the house of their fathers. After they leave that house, their careers, their ambitions, will be, for the rest of their lives, to become a *gibbor* over the house they have been expelled from. The mothers, then, are the motors of their sons' ambition since their status triggers their sons' expulsion, hence, of the fabula that their sons' ambition triggers.[2] Without their "improper" status, their sons would have become ordinary men, not heroes of might. In their ambitious endeavors, Abimelech fails while Jephthah succeeds. The former starts with success and ends by being killed at the very site of the mother's father-house, only slightly disguised by displacement. The tower of Shechem (the mother's father-house) becomes the tower of Thebez. This movement full-circle shows that Abimelech's attempt at kingship is also an attempt to cut across the division between the two institutions.

Jephthah is more successful. But in the first stage of his career, he has to buy his rulership by the gift of his daughter. Giving up a patrilocal father-house as he does at a very early stage, he is more acceptable than Abimelech as a virilocal leader; leaving the father-house, he does not return to his mother's house but remains in a space in-between: the land of Tov. The space is rather vaguely identified, and it seems more interesting, within an architectural reading, to interpret it as what the name means—good. Transitional spaces are good, we could then interpret, as a valuation of the specific transition that takes place therein. The men Jephthah gathered around him are described with the same word as those Abimelech hired in 9:4—empty. A good land filled with empty men: such is the transitional space of Jephthah's initiation, which ironically mirrors the transitional experience of his daughter. She, too, leaves the father-house to go to an in-between space, but she is called back for sacrifice, not for success. On the other hand, she was accompanied, not by empty men but by full women: the daughters of Israel, full of the memory of her.[3] While Abimelech pursues his quest for acceptance in the mother's father-house, Jephthah waits, in the good land, until the virilocal father-house comes to fetch him back, offering him permanent rulership.

Comparing the two cases, it seems obvious that, globally speaking, the ideology of the book supports the virilocal tradition,[4] but also that this priority is not a given but an option that has to be "conquered," with difficulty and at the cost of many relapses, violent struggles, and murders. That is why the gibbor has to start from nothing, from nowhere, that Jephthah have an improper mother and that he first be expelled. The "improper" mothers, similar in their patrilocal background, different in the stage of the development toward virilocy that their sons represent, are indispensable to the stories of ambition that turn the ethnographic issue into a political one. Dealing with spatial displacement in terms of the symbols of the life of the people, the stories start with the "improper" mother to be displaced—the "other" woman, as 11:2 has it—which figures the basic displacement at stake in the book: the repression of the life of the people by its political life.

Before Samson was born, his mother was the most powerful figure in the house, or, to be more accurate, around the house. The space where her conception and the stipulation of the rules of her son's Nazirite vow happened is not the virilocal house itself, but the contiguous fields around it. This mother is not an "improper" mother, but her acceptance of the virilocal space is not complete. She took it on herself alone to communicate with the messenger who "fertilized" her. She also put the verdict on her son's life, stipulating that the Nazirite vow hold, not only "from the womb" but also "until the day of his death." By contrast, Manoah hardly has any claim to fatherhood. And from beginning to end of Samson's genesis, Manoah blunders by mistrust, lack of understanding, and fear. It is the mother who names the child, and in naming him, completes the determination of his future life she undertook at the time of his conception. Giving him a name that is, as is generally assumed (Dalen 1966), related to the sun, she instills in him the fire that will eventually kill Kallah.

The power of the mother is slowly undermined in the course of the story. In 14:2, when Samson desires the Philistine woman he had seen at Timnah, he comes to his father and his mother. He addresses both, and both answer negatively. The subject-position of the mother is thus confirmed in her parental role of judgment. But Samson then addresses his father alone, as if more meekness could be expected there. Instead of a renewed answer to his request, we read the narrator's explanation of the conflict: "His father and his mother knew not that it was of Yahweh; for he sought an occasion against the Philistines.

And at that time the Philistines had rulership over Israel" (14:4). The verse is, of course, a sign that the story to follow is part of the divine project. But that implies that the divine father of Samson wants him to live in a patrilocal house. The preceding analyses have shown that the dominant ideology of the book clearly supports virilocy, albeit by representing the difficulties of the transition. But where Yahweh stands, and whether he always stands on the same side,[5] is not so clear. In a sense, the rejection of Manoah as the father is reconfirmed here. Like Jephthah, it is important that Samson's *gibbor*-ship come out of an active conquest of the virilocal father-house,[6] accomplished only through death, not out of a patriliny that would guarantee heroism by birth.

Both parents go with Samson to Timnah, and after the incident with the lion, it is again said that he did not tell "his father and his mother." When he commits his first major transgression of the Nazirite law, eating honey from the dead body of the lion, he offers the honey to both parents, without telling them where it came from. Both the secrecy which, along with his force, is his major asset and the transgression itself are indications that he is trying to emancipate himself from his parents' authority. The trip to Timnah is a transition rite. Samson's deviation from the straight path to his marriage takes him into a wilderness where mortal danger threatens. His killing the lion is the performance that qualifies him for adulthood by bodily power: *gibbor*ship. But the transgression of the Nazirite law is more specifically a revolt against his mother. It was she who stipulated the duration of the law. This revolt is appropriate for a young man who is on his way to patrilocal marriage.

The mother who acted so autonomously at first, and has next been coupled to the father, is entirely repressed from here on. It is the father who "went down to the woman" to arrange the marriage, and after his failed attempt to marry patrilocally (14:19), it is to his father's house that Samson returns. He tries a few more times to return there, hesitant as he is between the two systems. And after his heroic death, "his brothers and all the house of his father came down, and took him, and brought him up, and buried him between Zorah and Esthaol in the burying place of Manoah his father" (16:31). Samson's course from the power of the mother to the grave of the father has been a long, difficult and deadly one, his adherence to patrilocity becoming his undoing in the house of Delilah, after a narrow escape from the house of another woman.

Samson's first attempt at liberation from the power of the mother led to Kallah's death in the patrilocal father-house. His two other relationships to women, the brief one with the "prostitute" in 16:1–3 and the crucial one with Delilah in 16:4–20, also fit into the architectural view of the book. Both the second and the third women are different from the first one, Kallah, in that there is no father mentioned in their houses. But they are also similar in that their relationship to Samson is staged inside their houses. The word for prostitute has been used elsewhere to refer to the patrilocal wife. The Hebrew has, as usual, "a woman zonah." It is worthwhile to pursue the hypothesis that the "prostitute" at Gazah is, then, simply a patrilocal woman or rather, an "unfaithful," nonvirilocal one. She receives a lover in her own house. She does not necessarily live with her father; probably, any woman not living with a virilocal husband ended up being called a zonah.[7] There is no way to tell the difference between the categories of such women as they were distinguished at various moments.

The Gazites are aware that Samson is in town, and they are prepared to take him when morning comes (16:2). After Samson's failure to enter into a sexual relationship in Kallah's patrilocal father-house, the "kindness" of letting him go through his sexual initiation before capturing him indicates an awareness of the connection between his legendary strength and sexual arousal. But his departure at midnight makes sense as yet another moment of hesitation, an incapacity to decide for either institution. The power of the mother, as determined from the very beginning of his life, cannot be easily undone. Leaving the woman's house before midnight, then, can be read as yet a further reticence to establish his adulthood, his sexual maturity, a further reticence to separate from the mother. Samson is then a representative of the people which created history, a screen onto which the people projected its own fantasies.

Delilah actually commits for Samson the rupture of the Nazirite law by having his hair cut off. She undoes what the mother had determined, replacing the mother and mothering him herself. It is clear that his *gibbor*ship largely depends on his sexual immaturity. He tries to make sexual decisions that will free him from his mother's influence, but he is unable, or unwilling, or both, to carry them out. He tries to free himself from the mother's influence by breaking her rules, but by not telling her, he does not arrive at a break with her. His final success in breaking with her not only entails his own undoing; it also depends on his acceptance of Delilah, an "other" woman, the other mother.

The character who is the most obvious hero, the hero who has bodily strength as his major asset, is also the hero who operates on the basis of secrecy and the one who relates to women in the most insistently problematic way. The relation between bodily strength and sexuality on the one hand, and between secrecy and sexuality on the other, are thematized as early as the riddle episode. The tearing apart of the lion while on his way to the first woman, as well as the performance with the doors of Gazah after his visit to the second woman, both point to a view of sexuality as bodily strength—and more specifically, of the latter as a precondition of the former. At the same time, through the dialectic of fear, the former threatens also to be fatal to the latter. In brief, the *gibbor* whose life is so strongly predetermined by the mother—but a mother in a virilocal house—is strongly intent on, yet insecure in, his sexuality. The institutional change that seems to underlie the book is the quicksand on which Samson establishes his life. The contradictions between his incredible strength and his sexual insecurity (see Bal 1987) can be explained within the framework of his difficult emancipation from his mother. As a virilocal wife who kept an unusual degree of autonomy, she represents in her turn the insecurity of virilocy by conceiving, determining, and naming her son outside of the house of the official father. In a slightly different setting, and with a human "fertilizer" instead of a divine messenger, this mother would most likely have been called an *ʾishah zonah*, an unfaithful woman, or, in the more common translations, a prostitute.

The story of Micah, generally considered to be part of the book's epilogue, is much less known than Samson's, but his mother certainly resembles Samson's mother in some ways. Her motherhood is also defined by a predetermination of the life of her son. By extending the Nazirite vow, Samson's mother de facto cursed her son. Micah's mother in turn cursed her son by cursing the thief of the silver, which he was. There is no mention of a father in Micah's story. If it was the mother who named him, she predicted the son's future life, just as Samson's mother did. For his name, whose longer form is Michayehu, might mean "who is like god" (Slotki, 1980). The transgression of the absolute boundary between deity and humanity is the most heinous sin in Judges.[8] Slotki (1980, 286) interprets the implications of the name differently when he says: "It is strange that a man with such a name should be the patron of an idolatrous image." Micah will patronize idolatry, as a typical anti-hero in Judges, because his name predetermined him to do so: to be like god is presupposing that God can be likened. If Samson went astray after "other" women, Micah went astray after "other" gods, images of god being by definition alien, other, than the god whose image was forbidden. Whether or not his mother actually gave him the name, she did have the idols made (17:4).

The curse mentioned in verse 2, then, is carried out, in spite of Micah's attempt to escape it by confession—the opposite of Samson's secrecy. His confession, as an attempt to counter the motherly curse, resembles Samson's attempts to escape from the motherly power. But in Micah's story there is a different representation of the subjectivity of the power of the mother. When he restores the money, he says: "The eleven hundred pieces of silver that were taken from you, about which you uttered a curse, and you spoke in my ears, behold, the silver is with me" (17:2). The curse and, hence, the power it presupposes exist to the extent that the son focalized it. If Samson's struggle for liberation focuses on sexual relations with foreign women, Micah's concentrates on foreign gods, the other interdiction presented in the book's introduction. The man who is "like god" pushes the realization of his name further, when we read: "And it [the images] was in the house of Micah. And the man Micah had a house of god, and he made an ephod, and teraphim, and consecrated one of his sons who became his priest" (17:5). Not only did he create the idolatrous images, but he also has a house of god, juxtaposed to or identical with his own house. And as if that architecture of idolatry were not enough evidence of his god-likeness, he consecrates his son to be his priest. Thus, if the name does make sense, Micah actualizes his mother's predictive power.

His next fairly enigmatic act is to appoint another priest. Why is this second priest better than his son? When we recall that the traveler who comes by Micah's house in 17:8 is a Levite coming from Bethlehem in Judah and that Micah himself was from Ephraim, we immediately see how the situation is symmetrical to the one in the next story, the story of Beth, the story without a mother. The traveling Levite is asked to "dwell with me, and be unto me a father and a priest" (17:10), an invitation which is readily accepted. Why does Micah, who already has a grown son, need a father? This unexplained detail may refer to the same tension between fatherhood and motherhood that we have seen at work throughout the book. The new priest delivers Micah from the power of his mother by replacing her. Strangely enough, the Levite is several times referred to as a young man. Fatherhood, then, emphatically refers to some kind of social fatherhood here, the leadership that counters the domination of the mother. Micah's success, however, is highly dubious. The "young man was unto him as one of his sons" (17:11). Having started as an emulator of God, Micah is not allowed to escape his fate. The father he had chosen for himself has become a son, the reversal using familial roles as metaphors of social roles.

Micah's story ends with the abduction of the idols, and we hear from him no more. Once his idols are taken away from him, he no longer exists as the godlike man. His story has little bearing on the view of Judges that circulates in modern culture. Perhaps it is because this story does not have the extreme violence, the individual encounters between the sexes—except, of course, for the confrontation, half told, half repressed in the retrospective mode, between mother and son. But if we take it that the book's so-called epilogue should be considered a crucial part of it, Micah's story comes to function in different ways. It partakes of the architectural composition of the book, thematizing the house and the geography of the land. Relating to the previous story via the tribe, the Danites, and to the next via the Levite traveling between Ephraim and Bethlehem, it seems indispensable as a symptom of the problematic of motherhood. The link between Micah's mother and Delilah via the silver, and between Micah's mother and Samson's via the curse strengthens the connection between Samson's mother and Delilah. But most importantly, the two transgressions that the introduction to the book describes, going astray after other women and going astray after other gods, are exemplified with much emphasis in the three final stories.

Samson's promiscuity was sexual, Micah's religious, while the story of Beth and its aftermath focuses on sexuality once again, thereby taking Samson's and Micah's transgressions to the extreme in Beth's story. In both Micah's and Samson's stories, the mother pushes the son toward the transgression by naming and/or cursing him and by inscribing, in the names of their sons, the need to free themselves from her. Micah's idols are taken away by others, hence, becoming anybody's, everybody's. This is the religious variant of Beth's being taken away, hence, becoming anybody's, everybody's. If Micah's story is less appealing than Samson's in the memory of modern culture, it is not only because it reminds us of the close relation between both types of promiscuity and because it refers us to the horror-story of Beth at the end, but also because it stages most explicitly the power of the mother. These three equally disturbing aspects are all, therefore, candidates for repression. But repression leaves its traces; if the story is in the canon at all, if the book builds its architecture on it, it is simply because the mother is there. Pushed out of the final story, she had to be placed, displaced, somewhere else. The mother of the sexually abused daughter in chapter 19 is replaced by the mother of the man who abuses less horribly, but with equal strength, the divine law. The mother curses the son. Micah's story, then, is no less transgressive than the story of Beth, but it is not in the least uncanny.

These explicit mothers can be characterized by their power over their sons, a power that sets the fabula in motion. Two of them trigger

the institutional struggle their sons get involved in. The other two entail transgression, the "going astray" of which the sons become guilty,
at their mothers' instigation.

Explicit Mothers: Sisera's and Israel's

Two different mother figures are evoked in Judges 5, in the Song of
Deborah. In Judges 5:28, right after the stunningly cruel evocation of
Sisera's death, we meet the latter's mother. She is represented in the
final stanza of the song, and her evocation there has been found hardly
appropriate after the impressive representation of the son's agony.[9] The
passage presents serious problems of translation, and there is no unambiguous rendering that would exclude other possibilities (see Globe
1975; Coogan 1978). Yet a more or less reliable reading runs as follows
(I start at verse 27, for the sake of the contrast):

> 27. Between her feet he knelt, he fell, he lay,
> between her feet he knelt, he fell,
> there where he sunk there he fell, devastated.

> 28. Through the window she looked forth, and peered,
> the mother of Sisera, through the lattice:
> Why so late his chariot in coming?
> Why tarry the wheels of his chariot?

> 29. The wisdom of her princesses answered her,
> Yea, she herself returned saying to herself:
> 30. Are not they finding, dividing spoil?
> A womb, two wombs for a hero's head,
> a spoil of colors for Sisera,
> a spoil of colors of embroidery,
> two colored embroideries for the neck of a spoiler?

The song is full of ambiguities, word plays, and ironic contrast, while
its rythmic composition makes it wonderfully euphonic. The question
we have to deal with is: how is this mother viewed as mother? The
contrast between her dreams of success and the evocation of her son's
death is evidently effective, as this contrast entails a view of her (lack
of) wisdom. The irony is further enhanced by the word "wisdom" in
the opening of verse 29. This mother fails to *know*, fails to predeter-
mine her son's fate. She has, as a consequence of that failure, no influence, no power. That powerlessness is enhanced in her situation, in
her position in the house. Twice the imprisonment of the mother be-

hind the bars of the window is mentioned.[10] We can imagine the situation better if we realize that the battle Deborah has just evoked was one between a superior but decadent civilization and the seminomadic tribes of Israel—the latter had no iron chariots while the former did; but it was precisely the iron chariots that, to use a biblical phrase, became a snare unto them. Sisera's army was defeated by a thunderstorm sent by Yahweh. Mentioning the chariot here shows, therefore, the mother's utter ignorance. At the same time, the position of the mother behind the lattice of the palace window displays, just as the battle itself, a contrast between the richness of the architecture and the powerlessness it entails. The enviable chariots of iron got stuck in the mud and made the occupants powerless; the rich palace makes its inhabitants powerless. The mother is worried about the return of her son, and the sound of the chariot is the only signal she is expecting to get of his return. This mother and her powerlessness are only there to stand in contrast to other forms of motherhood.

Her evocation of the reason for Sisera's delay consists of a twofold description of the spoil she assumes her son is busy dividing. There is no concern for the people in this battle she assumes that her son has won. The political consequences are ostensibly not discussed. The material advantages for the individual men are all she is concerned with. The specific items she evokes as part of the spoil are, however, even more revealing. The colored piece of embroidery must be read as symbolic and not, as one of the most outrageously ethnocentric and sexist commentaries has it, as evidence of female stupidity (Dhorme 1956, 73).[11] While her son has just been killed—as readers of or listeners to the poem, we have the evocation of his agony fresh in our mind—she evokes colorful cloths. The situation calls rather for a sackcloth of ashes, the symbol of mourning. The contrast between the sackcloth of ashes she should be calling for and the actual colorful cloth she does envision is a figure that we know from Genesis 37. When Jacob is shown the colorful garment of Joseph, stained with blood, he rends his clothes and puts on a sackcloth of ashes. This is, we are led to believe, proper mourning over a dead son. But Jacob was wrong, the son was not dead, hence, the mourning was uncalled for. The situation is reversed here. The overzealous father contrasts with the lighthearted mother.

If fatherhood and motherhood are opposed in this second part of the evocation of the spoil, we may assume that motherhood is being criticized in this stanza. But then motherhood is more directly criticized in its first part. "One womb, two wombs for a hero's head (*rosh geber*)" alludes to the custom of taking captive young women as slaves for private use (see Deut. 21:10–14). The vulgar term, here translated literally as womb, is used with contempt to refer to sexually useable women.[12] As the Americans have "slut," the French "nana," the Dutch "stuk" (piece), so the Hebrew has *raḥam*. The custom as well as the language was acceptable in the Hebrew culture as well as in the ambiant cultures.[13] If, then, the sharply ironic description of this "bad mother" criticizes the custom by the ironic use of the language, it does not represent the general Israelite ideology, but a more specific one. The mother of a *gibbor* who uses such words to celebrate the victory of her son is clearly a mother of a son, not of a daughter. Had she been the mother of a daughter, she would have realized that her daughter might eventually become part of a similar spoil—for example, in Judges 21:12. This indifference to the fate of daughters in the situation of war as opposed to her rejoicing in the son's *gibbor*-like power over daughters can be read as a pointed critique of the sort of mothers of sons who collaborate in the horrible fate of daughters. Failing to offer protection, this mother even positively supports the ideology that condemns daughters. It is this aspect that shows us how the book, at least in this woman's song, is concerned with the role of mothers.

In sharp contrast to Sisera's mother stands Deborah herself. Although no children of hers are mentioned, she is represented as the ideal mother. When the country was in a state of anarchy and oppression, she helped it out by her decisive intervention as prophetess, judge, and deliverer. In the song, the situation is described as hopeless until "you/I arose, Deborah / you/I arose, a mother in Israel" (5:7).[14] The verb form is ambiguous, and it is interesting to leave the ambiguity and let it make its statement about the communicative nature of poetry. Deborah is a mother in Israel, a social role the nuances of which can only be assessed if we evaluate the function she exercised, as it appears in both prose and lyric versions. The two versions are radically different, but regarding the presentation of Deborah's social role, they are more complementary than opposed. Each stresses different aspects of the same figure. Only in the lyric version is she called a "mother in Israel." Although translations of the first presentation of this figure in 4:4 have unanimously assigned a husband to Deborah, there is no reason whatsoever to do so. The verse does enhance her femininity: "Deborah, a woman prophetess, a woman of torches, she was judging Israel at that time." The complement "of torches" fits her character too well to allow for the unwarranted translation "wife of Lappidoth," a proper name unknown in Hebrew. There is no reason either to consider the torches as a synonimical description of Barak, thus turning Deborah into Barak's wife. Both solutions have been insistently proposed, and although few commentators fail to notice the various possibilities, no one that I know of refrains from translating "woman of torches" as "wife of Lappidoth." This insistence is even more revealing when we realize that being "of torches" is the essence of Deborah: an inflamed and inflaming woman whose prophecy is crucial for the story. Her status as wife of an unknown and obscure husband is clearly irrelevant, and hence, would not be mentioned. Again, it is the conflict between her narrative position and the role traditionally assigned to her that helps us understand the politics of gender underlying both the story and its reception. The heuristic key is once more the question of the subject.

The woman who, in chapter 4, is called a prophetess and a judge is a poet and a mother in the song. What do these features have to do with one another? The function of the judge in the book is an integrative leadership function on a local basis, which includes juridical, military, and political leadership. In combination with prophecy, which confers religious leadership as well, the function of Deborah is extremely powerful. In sharp contrast to Sisera's waiting and confined mother, she is the instigator and head of the battle. She is the only judge who is also a prophetess, and the combination is strikingly powerful.

Equally characteristic of Deborah's role is the ordering function of the judge. Where chaos reigns, a judge is raised to establish order. When chaos is caused by external threat—war or occupation—the first task of a judge is to liberate the people from its enemies. When no external enemy but internal chaos threatens, the actual work is different, but the idea remains the same: to create order in chaos. It is arguable that the title of judge was not fundamentally different from that of king (*melech*); both indicate the same type of integrative rulership. The major difference between the two offices is election by the spirit of Yahweh versus hereditary succession. If, toward the end of the book, the chaotic situation is commented upon with the phrase "In those days there was no king in Israel; every man did what was right in his eyes" (17:6), we have a description of the situation in which a judge used to be raised. Variants of the phrase occur in connection with religious and sexual promiscuity. It has been little noticed that in the same context a variant, "there was no deliverer" (18:28), also occurs. To deliver from chaos, to deliver from the enemy, to deliver from injustice: it all comes to an ordering leadership that was so blatantly lacking in Beth's story. It is perhaps not a coincidence that the only judge who combines all forms of leadership possible—religious, military, juridical, and poetical—is a woman and calls herself and/or is addressed as "a mother in Israel." Both "mother" and "in Israel" are significant aspects of the title.

Deborah's poetic gift is naturally associated with her prophecy. But it is more. We have seen that the young women called "daughters of Israel" commemorated Bath in the aftermath of her story. The verb used there, the same one as Deborah uses in 5:11, can be translated as "to recount," "to rehearse" by singing. It is the verb that refers to the act of commemoration by verbal art, the one that underlies the historiographic project in a different mode. It is not surprising, then, that the two subjects of this act are the "mother in Israel" and the "daughters of Israel." The connection between social roles and linguistic/narrative positions is important, especially within a narrative that represents social values and problems. If, in the Bible, fatherhood and sonhood are more often used in a social sense than motherhood and daughterhood, it is no less these latter roles that are, in the oldest parts of the Book of Judges,[15] related to language. As opposed to the cutting speech-act of which Jephthah is the uncontested master, the role of mothers and daughters is to perform speech-acts of memorialization.

In the Song of Deborah, poetry is related to judging in both the military-political sense and in the juridical sense. Deborah's song is full of judgments, of praise and curse. It is also an evocation of the victory prompted by her own activity. The prophecy, emphasized more in chapter 4 than in chapter 5, is implicitly present in the direct communication between Deborah and Yahweh. The combination of ordering qualities that the poetess displays allows for the description of her function as one who establishes order in chaos by means of the proper word. And the proper word is the commemorating word, the one that will not let daughters die in forgetfulness. A mother who deserves the title "a mother in Israel" stands for wholeness, completeness through order and memory. Caring for the people as a whole, she also cares for daughters.

It is this wisdom that is ironically set off against the pseudo-wisdom of Sisera's mother. Her word, the evocation of the distribution of "wombs," creates chaos, the sort of chaos that Beth's story exemplifies. Here as there, a woman is public property, can be taken by every man. But Deborah knows how to tell the difference between occasions for sackcloths of ashes and occasions for colorful cloths, or colorful language. She has the vision of reality, knowing what happened and what will happen. She has direct language for the representation of Sisera's agony, while his own mother only has thoughts of the spoil that accompanies, but does not constitute victory. Significantly enough, Deborah, this ideal judge, leader, and animator of the people, is not referred to as a *gibbor*. It is obvious that the concept of *gibbor* is exclusively male. It requires no wisdom, but only violence; no insight, only bodily strength; no poetry, only cutting words.

In this song which *performs* motherhood because it gives life in commemoration, we have encountered two explicit mothers, a good and a bad mother, and goodness and badness are related to the fate of daughters. It is also in the Song of Deborah that we meet the cruelest of the murderesses in the cruelest of the evocations of violence. Since Yael is so close, in linguistic contiguity, to the explicit mothers, we will look at her first in our search for traces of avenging mothers.

Displaced Mothers: Yael

Yael's murder of Sisera is represented twice, and the two accounts are radically different. We cannot ignore the gender difference between the two texts. The song of chapter 5 is clearly based on a female tradition, the prose text of chapter 4 on the more usual epic tradition, the male quality of which is widely accepted. The prose account is part of a heroic tale of war; the lyric one of a commemorative, triumphant song of war. As a first and striking difference, there is no hero in the song, not even an anti-hero (as Barak in the prose version may be called). This generic difference can be held at least partially responsible for the radical differences between the two figures, Yael-4 and Yael-5. I will first discuss Yael-4 and reserve the lyric version for the end of this chapter.

Yael-4 is, like Deborah-4, endowed with a suspect husband. The indication in verse 4:11, commonly translated as "Heber the Kenite," is, as many have argued (Gray 1986, 258), dubious as a proper noun and is more likely to refer to a clan. The Kenites were wandering smiths, and therefore, the introduction of the clan, in which Sisera later arrives, as the people-with-the-hammers seems more relevant than the introduction of a husband whose traces are nowhere else to be found. Later, when Yael herself is mentioned for the first time, the same ambiguity arises: "And Sisera fled on his feet to the tent of Yael a woman of Heber the Kenite, for peace there was between Jabin king of Hazor and the house of Heber the Kenite" (4:17). It is interesting to notice how one modern commentator gets into trouble when confronted with the simple mentioning of a woman's tent, without any man. It is worth quoting Gray's comment in full:

> 17. the tent of Jael: we should expect it to be termed the tent of *her husband* Heber. It may refer to the screened *harem* section of the long

Bedouin tent, which would be more secure. In this case Jael, true to the desert tradition, would be caught between the horns of a dilemma: *to grant the conventional sanctuary and hospitality* and at the same time *to vindicate her honour from suspicion,* which she did in the drastic way described. Alternatively, the specific mention of her tent may indicate that she was *an older, discarded wife of Heber.* (Gray 1986, 259; my emphasis)

The same critic who, apropos 4:11, pointed out the problems with the assumption of Heber being a proper name, has, one page later, forgotten his reservation concerning her marital status. The mention of a woman's tent is a problem that has to be explained. There are two options: the harem tent or the tent of the discarded wife. The option of women's tents, simply, as separated from men's tents, does not occur to the critic. In the case of a harem tent, the idea that a man would not be able to enter it without any guards preventing him, does not come up either—the problem clearly being to account for Yael's autonomy, not for other inconsistencies. The two options are interesting enough as such: the status of a woman can be either total dependence on, or total rejection by her "husband." In the former case, it is doubtful that Yael would have any choice between hospitality and prudishness; it was certainly not the harem women who offered hospitality to men. Even more interesting is the attempt, carried out by means of binary thinking, to exclude a third possibility, which would be Yael's wish to participate in political action. Being a member of a clan that lived in peace with Jabin, her action is politically subversive; but this is excluded, Yael being only either a harem-woman or an old hag.

When we take the counterpart of this piece of criticism, we may retain, as features of Yael's image, the fact that she lived by herself in a tent that was hers, that she lived in a tribe that was on the side of the enemy, and that she nevertheless chose the other side. Her name means "wild goat," and wild she seems to be. It is clear that the action described next, her initiative to go out and meet Sisera, does not at all fit the image of either harem-woman or discarded old wife. Yael comes out and invites Sisera to "turn in," thus offering hospitality, a warranty of safety. The next phrase, "fear not," however, comes from a quite different context; it belongs to the vocabulary of war. The contradiction between the invitation into the peaceful home and the encouragement to battle not only holds a warning for one who listens carefully, it is also a statement about the inseparability of the two domains. Yael lets us know that, although she lives inside the tent, she

will participate in the battle. Just like Deborah, she will not be confined to a private role.

Yael covers Sisera with a cloth. The noun used here, *semichah*, is
unclear. It is plausible that it refers to a curtain, and it would then
enhance the idea of the man transgressing by entering the woman's
space. But it can also just mean "rug," an object to cover him with. In
both cases, the gesture of covering is motherly. Yael takes a child into
her home and cares for him. The motherly care is depicted with insistence. Sisera asks for some water, and Yael gives him more: she gives
him milk. This detail is domesticated by commentators who affirm that
the request for water is just the minimal request for survival and that
milk is the least she could give (Gray 1986, 260). But milk is the drink
that mothers offer children. By giving milk, Yael, on the one hand,
reassures Sisera further; on the other hand, she prepares the scene as
an ironic one of anti-mothering. "She opened a skin of milk and gave
him drink" is the sentence that is framed by two "coverup" sentences:
she covered him—she gave him milk—she covered him. The sentence expressing the covering itself covers the nourishment. There is
yet another aspect to the gift of milk. It strongly reminds us of the gift
of bread in Beth's father-house. There, too, the hospitality turned out
to be a snare. Bread in the house of bread and milk in the tent of the
wild goat opposes nourishment in the father-house to nourishment in
the mother's space. The overdetermination of the milk motif provides
further support to the isotopy of the avenging mothers.

Sisera's attempt, in the next verse, to reestablish his former authority by giving her an order, falls through because of the interesting
pun it holds. He says: "Stand in the opening of the tent and it shall be
when a man comes and he asks you and says: is here a man? you shall
say: none" (4:20). The opening of the tent, the limit between inside
and outside, mirrors the threshold on which Beth falls down. Here, it
is the woman, not the man, who is to stand in the opening of the
home. She must stand there to secure safety, not to embody danger.
The request has an ironic double meaning. Not only does he ask her to
lie on his behalf; but, on a different level, he also anticipates that his
manliness may be questioned ("is here a man? none"). This level may
be called unconscious—a Freudian interpretation is quite plausible
here—but it can also be conceived of differently. The language comes
from a subject, not easily or unambiguously identified. It is Sisera who
speaks, and Yael who listens. But Yael, being the leading subject in the
episode, can also be considered the focalizer of the scene as a whole.
And the readers and listeners who witness the story participate in the

irony. Knowing the outcome, they rejoice in the unawareness of Sisera who thinks his speech-act functions only on one level. Ordering Yael—usurpation of power that is quite out of place in the situation—to say "none," that is, "no man," he orders her to lie. But she, in her autonomy, can decide not to lie and still fulfill the conditions required: to say "none" and yet to speak the truth. It can be done by killing the man who gives her the misplaced order, so that he will be truly none.

This pun also mirrors Beth's final gesture and the equally ambiguous situation there. Her husband failed to acknowledge her state and gave her an order, also totally out of place given the situation. When Beth's husband said "up," "none answered," because none could answer; Beth had been annihilated. Sisera asks Yael to say "none," ignorant of the power of motherly language. Seen in the light of an ambiguity that mirrors the one in chapter 19, what is at stake is Sisera's unmanning, symmetrical in this regard to Beth's undoing as a woman. Since Sisera is the enemy, his case gives the composers of this text more freedom to fantasize. He deserves death, but the specific kind of death that is prepared for him is related to other, more comprehensive issues.

We can also compare Sisera's destruction to Bath's. The battle scene suggests such a connection. Bath had to die in order to secure her anxious father the victory he felt unable to bring about alone. Jephthah is, therefore, in that stage of his career, a failed *gibbor*, one who abandons the challenge too early. Sisera did not resort to the solution of Jephthah; he simply fled. But his flight shares features with the rite of transition that Jephthah avoided. Sisera, the failed *gibbor* who fled away from his army in distress, came to Yael's tent on his way through a failed transition rite. Leaving behind his social position as a hero of might—his might consisting of iron chariots, not of any inherent quality of his own—he fled through the space in-between, suspended between the two armies, between the two worlds of war and peaceful civilization. It is no coincidence that this man happened to arrive at the tent of a woman, and of a woman who represented the other side, of his own, and of her own, world. The tent still has an opening, but Sisera orders her to stand in it, closing him off from the world, thus closing himself off from the possibility of becoming a *gibbor*. In this sense, too, his destruction is unmanning.

The most striking aspect of this murder is the manner chosen for Sisera's execution. He is killed while asleep, like a baby having been fed and covered by its mother. But he is at the same time killed with a specific instrument. "And Yael the woman of Heber took the peg and she took the hammer in her hand and she came softly unto him and she smote the peg into his temple and it went down into the ground and he was in a deep sleep and he was weary and he died" (4:21). The tent-peg and hammer are often explained with reference to the Kenites, who were smiths (Gray 1986, 260). Others (such as Slotki 1980, 192) assume that it was the women who, in nomadic society, drove the tent-pegs into the ground. But the violence of the murder suggests extreme anger. No one addresses this issue. Both traditional interpretations offer plausible, realistic explanations for the availability of the weapon in a woman's tent, but why do Sisera's brains have to be driven into the ground? In the epic version, it seems that the victim had to be fixed to the ground as a representation of a fall more radical, more absolute, than Beth's fall on the threshold. Where she was not able to obey the order "up," Sisera, having condemned himself to being no man, will not be allowed to get up either. His fall is expressed as drastically as possible.

The story of the murder of Sisera is often criticized as excessively cruel. Yael is blamed for transgressing the rules of hospitality, and indeed, hospitality does seem to be transgressed. But if this particular rule was chosen to be transgressed, this choice may also suggest a relationship between this story and Beth's story, between this scene and that other scene of the breaking of the rules of hospitality, not justifiable by military emergency, between this scene and a scene so infinitely more upsetting. In this view, Yael, who "mothers" Sisera, may do so because no one mothered Beth when her appeal to the same rule was not heard.

A final aspect of this murder establishes the relation with Beth's story more strongly. The man Sisera is turned into a non-man by means of the penetration of a hard object into his soft flesh. The murder takes the specific form and meaning of rape. Some critics have noticed this aspect (see Alter 1985), but no one has wondered why this form had been chosen. Not only does the weapon entail penetration; it also leads to the same result as the rape of Beth. Destroyed by the weapon, she, too, became "none" when fallen on the ground. Rape is, as I have argued, a specific way of destroying a subject from within and without at the same time, a specific way of destroying the victim as a woman. This reversed rape, indeed, also destroys the man as a man—his own words predicted it from without and within at the same time. It is for this reason, then, that the brains had to be so horribly described as penetrating into the ground (see Nicholson 1977).

We have now found so many elements that relate this murder story to the victim stories that a conclusion seems justified. The most striking elements—the hospitality and the nourishment, the opening of the home, the reversed rape—are all motifs that recur in Judges 19.

The motif that connects these is mothering: giving milk and protection, standing between the child and the threatening world, covering the sleeping child. If this fantasy is not, in the reception of the book, obviously related to chapter 19, it is not because the connections are lacking; it is because of the work of displacement. As we have seen, the mother is denied her place in the house where she belongs. She lives, here, in a tent.

The difference would be quite striking, if life in tents did not, by a return of the repressed, connect back to the house story in its own way. First, tents stand for nomadic life, and we remember that patrilocal marriage is often found in nomadic societies, where it is motivated by the wandering life of the younger men who herded the flocks. Second, tents stand for traveling, for the instability of the home that was also the outcome of Beth's story. Hence, the displacement of the mother from the house to the tent betrays its own repressive labor: dislocation is accompanied by distortion. Displacement is at work, too, in the reversal of rape. Beth was raped outside the house, Sisera within. Neither home is the home where the victim belongs. The differences between inside and outside are revealing for the problematic of gender that is at stake. A woman who went "after another man," other than her father that is, becomes public property. The gang-rape takes place, therefore, in the public space. A man who leaves his public place, his function, and enters the tent of a woman does exactly the opposite. Belonging to the people, he gives priority to his individual safety. It is appropriate, therefore, that his rape takes place within the private space.

The close connections between these two murder stories are so visible, in spite of the displacements, because Sisera is an enemy of the people. This is ultimately a displacement, too. The Levite, as we have seen, is redeemed in both the sequel and in the commentaries (see, however, Trible 1984). His guilt is written out of the book by the revenge expedition against the Benjaminites. Gray is one of many commentators who completely accepts this repression. He bluntly speaks of "the injured Levite" (1986, 18), thus, he represses the repetitive nature of the Levite's own actions. The Levite had to be redeemed because he is an Israelite, and the next chapters enhance the pan-Israelite theme explicitly. Sisera, however, is an enemy and, therefore, guilty of whatever has happened. Killing the Levite by the reversed rape would have been an appropriate way to avenge Beth. But this could not be done, so a displacement onto another victim was required.

At the same time, what this difference shows is the genderedness of the issue, the dissymmetry. Yael is a woman, just as the daughters are women. She is, therefore, confined to the limited space assigned to her. Killing a public man of might is radically different from killing a powerless daughter. The reversal of power displayed in the double meaning of Sisera's order to Yael is acceptable only because Sisera is an enemy, but barely so, since he is a man confronted by a woman. Interestingly, the blatant criticism of Yael's transgression of the hospitality rule contrasts sharply with the repression of the Levite's guilt. It is only because the victim is on the other side that Yael gets away with less— even if not so much less!—contempt than Delilah. Before we turn to this "classic" case of the treacherous woman, I will briefly discuss the second murderess who, thanks to displacement, also receives less accusation than Delilah. The woman-with-the-millstone relates to the murders of the daughters in a different, yet equally revealing way.

Displaced Mothers: The Woman-with-the-Millstone

In order to avoid the recurrence of this long description of the anonymous woman, we will give her the name *Pelah*, which means *millstone*. The noun thus indicates the instrument the woman used to assume her role in the tradition. But the noun is also similar to a verb, *palah*, which means to cleave, to slice. Through this connection, the name indicates also what she did: to cut, not with the mouth, but with the stone, the head of the leader Abimelech. Thirdly, the verb is used for giving birth, thus allowing for the resonance of the idea of motherhood.

Pelah comes into the story as "one woman." Some translations have "a certain woman," a translation rightly criticized by Janzen (forthcoming). The word "one" (*'ahath*) occurs so many times in the story, and in such pointed contexts, that we cannot translate the introduction of Pelah otherwise than as "one woman," "a single woman." She is thereby a symmetrical counterpart of Abimelech, who is, as one, single man, the alternative ruler over against his seventy half-brothers. She is also metonymically related to the "one stone" on which Abimelech killed his half-brothers. Having killed all those on a single stone, he is in his turn killed by a single stone, as one man killed by one woman.

Pelah comes to the exegetical tradition as the woman who brought shame to Abimelech. When he lies with his skull broken, Abimelech, defying any realism one might still cling to, calls his arm-bearer and orders him to kill him in order to avoid the shame of having been killed by a woman. The fallen head of the people has to be allowed to continue using his broken head to act as head in front of Pelah's and the reader's ironic gaze, to give the order, in order for the ideologeme

of shame and gender to be stated explicitly. The ideologeme occurs
once more in the book: in 4:9, Sisera's death by the hand of the
woman is foretold by Deborah to Barak's shame. And indeed, Barak
will consume his shame at the end of the story when he is, finally,
invited, like Sisera, into Yael's tent, only to find the object of his desire—the capture of the enemy leader which would bring him honor—
both within and outside of his reach. The shame that befalls Barak,
the Israelite leader, is a reflection of the shame that befell Sisera, to be
raped like a woman, by a woman.

And now Abimelech: his attempt to avoid the shame of his fate
can hardly be called successful, since a broken skull would be fatal
enough anyway. Therefore, the explicit narrativization of the ideologeme of shame must fulfill a different goal than to save Abimelech's
honor. Its purpose is, in my sense, simply to assert itself as a statement.
The ideologeme had to be asserted within the framework of the book;
we will have to clarify why.

Pelaḥ comes to my story, to the countercoherence of Judges, as
the visualization of the revenging mother. It was a visual image found
in Derchain (1970) that brought this aspect of the figure to my attention (see figure 7.1). The image represents an Egyptian relief, found on
Semitic territory and used by Derchain as evidence that child sacrifice
was common practice among the Western Semites. I will not use the
image for such a purpose; the story of Bath makes the argument superfluous, while the historical reality is less my concern than the imagina-
tive elaboration it produces and which cannot be disconnected from it.
The image serves here to make visual an otherwise complex thought.
On the image, we see a tower of defense, one like the "tower of
strength" of Judges 9:51. The tower is besieged, the enemy surrounds
its base, and the situation looks desparate for the occupants. How do
they respond to that situation? We see the men on the upper level
praying to some deity up in the air. The women sit, on the same level,
but since they do not stand, they seem to occupy a lower level as well
as a lower rank. On the outside platform of the tower, we see, at each
side, men throwing children down. The activity on the tower is clearly
a religious activity, as against the one down below which is military,
because the schematic composition of images of this genre would not
accommodate two different activities on the upper side of the image.

According to Derchain, the mothers of sacrificed children were
not allowed to lament over the deaths of their offspring. Neither were
they, in general, allowed to actively participate in the battle. That is
why the rank of the women is represented on a lower level than that of
the men. The women are sitting passively, without the freedom to pre-

Figure 7.1. Egyptian relief, found on Semitic territory. From P. Derchain, "Les plus anciens temoignages de sacrifices d'enfants chez les Semites occidentaux." Reproduced by permission from *Vetus Testamentum* 20 (no. 3):351–55. © 1977 by E. J. Brill.

vent or to lament the sacrifices. Would there have been a way to prevent them? One way to look at this image is to bring it to life. Imagine that one of the sitting women suddenly stands up. She pushes the men aside, with contempt for the inefficiency of a strategy that kills, not the enemy, but their own offspring, their *memory*. She looks down to the earth instead of up to an invisible god whose help can only be bought at the price of her child. Unlike Jephthah who, at a similarly crucial moment, used language, she needs no words; she acts militarily. She throws a millstone, the instrument of peaceful work, the only work she is allowed to perform, and kills the enemy. This is how the image visualized for me the act of Pelaḥ.

The image can help us imagine Pelaḥ as an avenging mother. The first indication that the murder is a murder of revenge comes from the dubious *gibbor* himself. Being an usurper who made himself king over his half-brothers' dead bodies—killed on a single stone—it is appropriate that he himself gets killed in a manner that is related to his crime. This relation is more complex than it seems at first sight.

The instrument of the murder, the millstone, is in the first place a reminiscence of Abimelech's evil deed, the killing off of the entire house of his father. His vested interest in destroying the virilocal father-house extends beyond just usurpation of power. Since the men of Shechem, of the patrilocal father-house, accepted his kingship—on the basis of his kinship—it seems obvious that the excessive violence against the virilocal father-house is meant, not only to extend Abimelech's power, but to do so through the destruction of that father-house itself. Indeed, such had been foretold in the prologue to the story. In 8:29 Gideon was said to have returned to his own house after his refusal of the kingship that was offered to him. This phrase has several meanings. While Gideon returned to his own house, Abimelech returned to his mother's father-house. The following mention of the seventy sons plus one turns the "house" as a dwelling into the "house" as an institution. The house that flourishes with so many wives and sons will soon be reduced to a single stone, a sacrificial altar on which the virilocal father-house will be exterminated by the hand of the single patrilocal son. The phrase may also refer to the refusal of the kingship. It suggests, then, that Gideon went back to his own private life after having served as a liberator of the people. Unfortunately, his refusal did not imply the refusal of other ambitions. His ambition prompted him to make an ephod, thus introducing the snare of idolatry. As an extension of the seemingly modest refusal of kingship, we may also connect it with the subsequent mention of the bad behavior of the Israelites toward Gideon and his house. One house becomes one stone; but Pelaḥ will turn the other house into one stone, too.

The millstone is a round stone, called the upper millstone or, more literally, the riding millstone, that women spun. The round stone with a hole in the middle has been connected with the chariots of war (Janzen, forthcoming). The overtones then bridge the gap that the stone also implies: as an instrument of peace, it contrasts with the weapons the assailants use, specifically, with the fire Abimelech seems to intend to destroy the tower with. Insofar as the "riding millstone" does indeed suggest warriors' chariots, it does so as a reminiscence of Sisera's useless chariots. This allusion to Sisera works in its turn as a reference to what Sisera's death alluded to, becoming part of the network that establishes the countercoherence and the spatial organization of the book.

Like Sisera, and like Samson who will be condemned to manipulate this female instrument, Abimelech is destroyed in a similar way: the stone falls on his head. It is, in other words, his position as head that is taken away from him by the very instrument he used to get a hold of it. Appropriately, it is after he has killed the civilian inhabitants of Shechem—not only the men, but the women too are mentioned—that he himself is killed by a civilian's hand and with a civilian instrument. But why is the final destruction of the usurper to take place in Thebez, a different city from Shechem, although also provided with a tower? Within the coherence that I am concerned with, it had to be a different city. For the ambition of Abimelech to become the head of both father-houses, the destructiveness of his ambition must first be demonstrated. He first exterminated the one father-house, then the other one. If he is killed by a mother figure, it is in the name of the destroyed father-house of the mother.

The figure on top of the tower is not only a motherly figure because of the mothers on the Egyptian image. She is also, as described, a metonymic extension of the tower of strength on which she stands; or rather, the tower represents her strength: while the whole population had not been able to deal with the tyrant in an efficient way, this single woman alone does so. While all the men of the tower of Shechem died, Pelaḥ triumphs because, rather than seeking refuge on a tower, she becomes one. The visual image of the usurper coming too close to the tower, losing his head figuratively, and thereby losing his head literally, resembles that of Samson's final revenge, when he stands between the pillars of the temple.[16] The connections between this brief story and the victim stories can be further elaborated. The door—opening, limit—is introduced in the first battle between Abimelech and his own kinsmen. "And Abimelech chased him [Gaal] and he fled before him, and many fell wounded, even on the entrance of the gate" (9:40). This man Gaal had challenged Abimelech's position with the words: "Is he not the son of Jerubbaal?" thus questioning his claim of rulership over Shechem, precisely because he belonged to a virilocal household. This is Abimelech's tragic flaw: he belongs nowhere. He remains a man of doors, of limits that he is unable to transgress. He stands again at the door in verse 9:44, but only to destroy the city of his mother, not to enter it.

Brotherhood is rejected on the one side, claimed on the other. When he comes to his maternal uncles, the two houses are systematically opposed, and what is more, the language used is the founding language of kinship. The mother's brothers are asked to remember that Abimelech is, as he says it, their bone and their flesh. In Genesis 2 the subject who is described by this phrase is the woman, she who later becomes "the mother of all living." As I suggested earlier, the expression in Genesis also implies patrilocy, for it is followed by the narratorial comment: "Therefore, a man leaves his father and his mother and cleaves to his woman" (Genesis 2:24).

Abimelech opposes the seventy virilocal brothers to his own single self, thus excluding the possibility of peaceful coexistence. The seventy, a figure that reminds us of seventy elders (Numbers) as a form of shared power, are claimed by some commentators to be after rulership just as Abimelech is. But there is no evidence whatsoever that this was the case. Clearly, it is the mother-son himself who cannot imagine any other political power than one-man tyranny.

The woman-with-the-millstone is not criticized as much as Yael is. True, this story is much less known, but then, why is this so? There are several reasons for this difference. The most compelling reason has to do with Pelaḥ's flawless status in relation to guilt. She did not cheat, seduce, or lure Abimelech into the home. Instead, she stands openly on top of the home, the tower of defense of the patrilocal city. Rather than praising her for killing a usurper, critics refrain from speaking too much about her, leaving the fame to Yael because she can be openly blamed. Pelaḥ's act is purely military; it contains no ambiguity. There are also several minor reasons imaginable. First, the story takes it upon itself to make explicit what a shame her action entails for Abimelech. Abimelech's swift response to his dishonor leaves its outcome ambiguous. His status in death is as ambiguous as his status in birth: born in a patrilocal house, he was raised in a virilocal one. But he was killed, not only by two different persons of two different genders, but also by two different sides—the woman belonging to the patrilocal party and his own servant belonging to another group, the "other" side. Abimelech's tragic misunderstanding, however, is that he himself and his army are attacking another patrilocal group; they are attacking their own side. The group itself has been divided, hence, destroyed. This vagueness around his death, its pointlessness, is therefore part of the shame. Instead of saving his honor, he further damages it:

he did not even fall for a cause. The explicit ideologeme of shame as related to gender saves modern critics the trouble of commenting on it.

The second reason why Pelaḥ is not so much subject to criticism could be, paradoxically, the reference to her in II Samuel 11:21. In fact, the story is much better known through this intertextual reference than by itself. In Samuel, the reference forms a strange dissonance that betrays the underlying preoccupations of the characters involved. The reference holds contradictions that make the story an uneasy fit in Samuel. There, it entails that the woman-victim is implicitly blamed for the murder that David commits in order to get her. The contradictions can be seen as a displacement of the tendency to criticize Pelaḥ. The implicit and unconscious argument runs as follows: since she kills an enemy, she deserves praise, like Yael; since she kills a man, she would deserve criticism, like Yael, but that has already been taken care of in the other text.

A third reason for the relative silence of the critics is, of course, her namelessness. Being anonymous, she only serves the purpose of the story by killing off the tyrant. But since the other two murderesses do have names, we need another reason. Such a reason can be assumed in her stance in the virilocal versus patrilocal rivalry. The oblivion represses her position as a subject: she defends the patrilocal father-house against the aggressor who initially belonged there and who was also accepted there. This is a strange position. She deserves more attention than she usually gets because of her implication in the institutional competition, as well as because of her image as an avenging mother; as I hope to have shown, the two issues are related. Abimelech, the excessive killer of brothers—he kills all brothers on both sides—is an easy victim for such revenge: his death is acclaimed as justified, and with it the competition he stands for is forgotten.

A fourth reason for her oblivion is the brevity of the story devoted to her act. She intervenes in a short episode within a long story. It is only when we realize that the moment of her intervention is the crucial, final moment of the destruction of patrilocy, a destruction that in its turn threatens patriliny so that the election of randomly chosen judges can be pursued, that her role becomes important for the book as a whole.

Pelaḥ's act is connected to the other murder stories through several details. The instrument reminds us both of the victim of the other murder story (Sisera) and of the place of death of Bath (a sacrificial stone) through the mediation of the single stone of the improper sacrifice of the Gideonites. More subtly, the peaceful provenance of the millstone shows that the murder is not so much a military act as it is an act of private revenge for murders committed against nonmilitary victims. Then the head, as the place of the body that is under attack, is related to the ambition to become the head of the two communities or of all Israel, the pan-Israelite ambition alluded to twice in the story in verses 9:22 and 9:55. But that ambition in its turn refers to Jephthah, who negotiated for his leadership and who stipulated that he would only deserve it through the conquest that he ends up performing at the price of Bath's life. Displaced from Shechem, the mother's place, to a different city, but still one belonging to the same side, Pelah is the figuration of the displaced mother whose mighty body is strong enough to cast shame upon the killer. When the rebellious son lies at her feet, at the feet of her tower, he is in complete submission to her. And his head is broken.

Displaced Mothers: Delilah

While the sexual aspects of the Sisera story are carefully, though not totally convincingly, censored away, and while Pelah's murder does not operate on the basis of sexual seduction at all, the story of Samson and Delilah is explicitly a love story. It is a story of love and betrayal that has become, in modern culture, the story of love as betrayal. I will not return to the love story aspects here, but will only select those features of the figure that relate her to the figure of the avenging mother.

We have already seen that, in a sense, Delilah takes over the mother's role in the decision about terms of the Nazirite. Samson's mother formulated the rule in the following words: "for the child shall be a Nazirite unto god from the womb to the day of his death" (13:7). Samson is enticed by Delilah, his lover, to betray the secret of his strength, and he does so in the words: "There has not come a razor upon my head, for I have been a Nazirite unto God from my mother's womb; if I be shaven, then my strength will go from me, and I shall become weak and be like any other man" (16:17). Samson does not repeat the addition "until the day of [my] death," but he does add "my mother's": he is a *gibbor* as his mother's son, consecrated as such at the moment she conceived him. He also adds that the Nazirite vow is the source of his strength—a fact which is nowhere else explicitly stated in the text—and that the end of his Nazirite will also be the end of the special quality that makes him a *gibbor*. The manner in which he makes this statement is revealing: "publication" of his secret will threaten not only his special competence in military matters, but, as the story of his first marriage has shown, also in sexual matters.

The confrontation here with Delilah is the outcome of a long competition among three parties: Samson, the Philistine princes who asked Delilah to discover her lover's secret, and Delilah. There is no doubt about the fact that there is a secret to be revealed, that Samson's strength has a special source that is open to annihilation by revelation. The secret had been posed by his mother: it was her amendment of the messenger's indictment that made the end of the Nazirite coincide with the end of Samson's life, or at least, with his life as a *gibbor*. Samson appreciates the link between the power of the mother and his life in replacing the expression of his death by that of his mother. By betraying the secret to Delilah, and in these very words, he appreciates also the similarity between her and his mother.

Delilah's function in the confrontation is to allow Samson to reveal himself, to her, to the Philistines, but most importantly to himself. Samson's hesitations in sexual matters, his eagerness to satisfy Delilah's requirement to abandon himself to her, his deep sorrow when she blames him for not doing so, all point to a desire to stop being the heroic performer and to let himself pursue his own inclinations. It is Samson who betrays his secret, we can almost say, voluntarily, compelled solely by the desire to "tell all his heart" to Delilah.

The formulation of the secret contains another striking addition: the razor, too, is absent from the mother's words. The messenger had mentioned it, the mother deletes it. What might be the motivation for that change in the message? The mother had insisted on the binding quality of the rule, but she omitted the razor from it. The son omits the fatal quality of the rule, but restores the razor, the instrument of his downfall. The cutting instrument represents the cutting of a bond, a bond that the mother had made more definitive than the messenger had foretold. Letting his hair be cut off is a way to let the bond with his mother be severed.

The visual image of the crucial scene is again revealing. Samson, we are told, goes to sleep on Delilah's knees. The expression in Hebrew allows also for the translation "between her knees," an expression used for giving birth. The image of Samson resting on/between Delilah's knees is that of a baby, confidently resting with his mother. Painters who depicted this scene eagerly in the seventeenth century enhanced the motherly aspect of this moment. Delilah often seems to attend the man at her feet with care, his head resting on her lap. Often an old woman is added, a procuress perhaps, but given the similarity between

Samson's mother and Delilah, the mother herself. In Rubens's drawing, the Philistine who actually cuts the hair seems to be tenderly devoted.[17] It is in this motherly quality that Delilah will bring about Samson's downfall.

Samson is not actually murdered by Delilah. She indirectly kills him by using his love and his need to undo his mother's power. The form of the violence against him, and which will lead to his death, is as interesting as the form he chooses for his suicidal last act. Haircutting, especially in this context, can hardly be denied some affinity with castration. The moment of the haircutting follows that of a sexual encounter—sleeping on his lover's knees cannot be seen otherwise—and it seems plausible to associate the relaxation after sex to the annihilation of the hero's strength. Thus, the underlying ideologeme has it that sexual discharge is damaging to physical strength. The haircutting becomes a way to make the temporary weakening after sex into a permanent one. It is also significant that Samson, like the other male victims, is assaulted on the head.

The next phase of the slow murder of Samson is his blinding. Reference to Freudian theory would evidently associate blinding with castration as well. Although Freud does allude to the Samson story itself in relation to castration, I prefer to refer the reader to his analysis of "The Sandman" in his essay "The Uncanny." There, the story has not only a few obvious symbols of castration, among them blinding and removal of arms and legs, it is also more focused on the literary, that is, the literal and visual aspects of the story. But even if we want to avoid the tricky question of the applicability of these fixed Freudian symbols to ancient texts, there is again, in the blinding, the penetration of the hero's soft flesh with a hard object. And this is where this episode shows relations with Yael's act. The sexual context, so much more obvious in the present case than in Yael's, makes a more direct allusion to rape unnecessary.

Samson's next phase is the sojourn in prison. Here, we encounter the millstone again. The millstone, which is not only Pelah's instrument of murder, but also, in the biblical culture in general, a female instrument of work, is now imposed on Samson. He does the labor of female slaves (Gray 1986, 22). This feminization seems a just revenge for the subjugation and murder of women for the sake of sexuality. The millstone connects the three murder stories together.

Samson's death is, again, a powerful visual scene. Standing between two gigantic pillars, which he undertakes to break with his bare hands, he is the object of public contempt. The scene of mockery by the feasting Philistines is not unlike the gang-rape of Beth by the men

of Gibeah. The penetration has taken place earlier, albeit equally col-
lectively, by the Philistines waiting in Delilah's bedroom. The second
part of this symbolic rape takes place now. Samson breaks the pillars,
thus breaking whatever ties still bind him, but this liberation kills him,
too. That is how he too tries, and quite successfully this time, to escape the shame that Abimelech escaped only halfway and that Sisera
could not escape at all.

Mothering, Murdering, Making Love: Yael

The Song of Deborah is, it is assumed, much older than the rest of the
book, at least its source. We will consider the evocation of Yael's murder in the song separately from the prose account because it is different
in content, form, symbolism—visual and otherwise. The visual character that we have seen in the other scenes is even stronger in the
Song of Deborah.

The first surprise we encounter in the song is the praise of Yael
that has disappeared in the prose version. I quote the scene in full:

> 24. Blessed be among the women Yael, a woman of Heber
> the Kenite, among the women in the tent blessed she be.
> 25. Water he asked,
> milk she gave,
> in a bowl for nobles she presented cream.
> 26. Her hand stretched out towards the peg
> and her right hand towards the worker's hammer
> and she hammered Sisera, crushed his head
> and she utterly destroyed his head
> and she pierced and annihilated his temple.
> 27. Between her feet he knelt, he fell, he lay,
> between her feet he knelt, he fell,
> there where he sunk he fell, devastated.

The scene of false hospitality that receives so much stress in the prose
version is almost totally absent here. As far as it is represented, it takes
the form of an honorable, respectful reception, solemn, almost priestly.
There is no entrance into the tent; the tent is simply there as the space
of Yael and of the women. While the prose version represented a dialogue, here there is no speech, only action visualized as in slow motion. The repetitive structure characteristic of early Hebrew poetry
allows us to follow slowly, in its full horror, the murder and the agony
of its victim, each action receiving one verse with a double tricolon.
The rhythm of the verses contributes to the acoustic representation of

the two major events, the hammering and the downfall. The hammering rhythm of the penetration enhances the isotopy of rape. Here, it is more brutally sexual.

But the murder is also more directly motherly. The victim falls between her feet, as an infant being born, but a dead infant, a stillborn baby. The expression "between her feet," repeated twice explicitly, and once more recalled in the indication of place, "there where he fell," connotes birth and submission: submission to the mother. When Sisera, as a result of Yael's solemnly executed act of penetration, slowly falls, as a dying *gibbor* and as a stillborn baby, the verb that expresses the first stage of his undoing is *karaʿ*, to kneel, which can imply spasmodic movement. The spasm of sex and the kneeling down in submission are expressed in one and the same word. It is only in the original language that the ambiguity of this passage can be fully appreciated, but even in the translation, the triple image comes across. We see the violent sexuality as a reversed rape. We appreciate the ironic anti-image of motherly care. This care is displaced from the daughter in front of whose fate the mother is powerless onto the man who took the daughter away from her. And ultimately, we see the murder, the extreme limit of power. The power denied to the mother in normal life is violently taken. It is significant that this representational orgy ends on the word "devastated."

This lyrical image of Yael expresses a strong pleasure in this representation of the event as triply meaningful. It is a celebration, a victory song. The victory is, in the rest of the song, the military, political victory over the enemy of the people. But in this particular fragment, we can read more. The victory is here also that of a strong woman over a man who used to be strong. The woman, here, takes over the power and enjoys it. The lyric form is appropriate to convey the enthusiasm that has since been severely criticized.[18] The concluding part of the song, the murder scene and the evocation of the victim's mother, are not so different from the previous sections; they are very well integrated into the whole song. The integration is based on the shift that the political issue of the main body allows. From the political issue the final part shifts to the "life" issue as a second isotopy. The ambiguities that are so predominant in the final section are not at all so in the political part. This points at a doubling, the integration of the second issue parallel to the first.

Again, we may wonder how this text has survived the later traditions. There, it has been incorporated as a doublet, following the later epic version in the canonical order. The most obvious motivation for its incorporation at all is, of course, the strong protection popularity guaranteed for oral traditions. The song could not simply be omitted, since it was too well known. But it also fulfills a catalytic function for emotions in other parts of the book. The other avenging mother figures receive a more solid background in this savage delight in the revenge. Protected by the status of the victim as the enemy of the people, the representation of the murder in its otherwise disturbing aspects has been acceptable enough to survive.

Clytemnestra's Absence

The three murders of men by women are connected to each other and are each connected to the murders of the daughters. The murderesses each display some motherly properties, and the symbolism of details adds, in a greater or lesser degree, to the impression that there is, somehow, or to put it spatially, somewhere, a relation between the two sets. The powerful mothers kill the *gibborim* in a most elaborate and meaningful manner. The most striking similarity between the three is the visual character of the murder scenes. In different ways there seems to be a remembrance of a fantasy that is represented in those scenes, as in a dream. Like the dream, the scenes do not explicitly tell what event is commemorated, but they do represent it in visual images that make the audience shudder. This dreamlike aspect can be accounted for with the help of the concept of displacement. In the dream, there is no way to put everything back in place, for there is no previous "original" scene. The dream builds the scene, in response to, not in imitation of, the experience that gives rise to it.

The fantasies of motherly revenge that are, in this reading, the displaced figuration of what the Greek tradition staged in Clytemnestra are solidly hidden under the interest in issues of political, religious, and military order. This fundamental displacement of the important issues of daily life—sexuality and marriage, violence, power within the home, the "building" of the house—onto "national" issues betrays a fundamental fear. That fear concerns the fragile foundation of fatherhood as the cornerstone of the social system. Deborah, as a "mother in Israel," a political, social mother, is the one figure who has neither father, husband, nor offspring. The competition for the establishment of virilocy is also a competition against her and the autonomy she stands for.

Deborah is also the poet who created the image that ignores the issue of shame as opposed to honor. The shame invoked, as we have seen, in two out of the three murder stories—and certainly supplied, for the third one, by later commentators—is a male shame that springs out of the realization of female power. That is not surprising, given what the men in the book have on their consciences, what they did to women, and hence, what anger they can expect. The uneasiness with the extreme violence done to the daughters out of insecurity about male power can be repressed, but it cannot be disposed of totally. It is for this reason that the redactors of the book had to leave the avenging mothers in it, albeit displaced and hardly recognizable.

It is even strange that the repression of the avenging mothers by displacement has been attempted in the first place. If we look again at the Greek tradition, it is obvious that there is no way the political could possibly not affect the private sphere. The conflict that almost any political act of consequence entails, there, in the family shows an awareness of the inextricable bond between the two worlds which motivate and produce each other. The attempt to repress that logic shows that some deep anxiety must have been the motor for this massive repression.

If this hypothesis makes sense, it implies that a poetics of displacement has the task of re(dis)placing what has been displaced in order to retrieve sight of how the men and the women lived in the era represented in Judges, how their space in the land was organized, and which subjects had power in which spaces. The life of the people on its way toward social stability can then be written back into history. The political and military conquest of the land and the slow and difficult implementation of monotheism will then be placed next to, and in interconnection with, the slow enforcement of virilocal fatherhood. The importance of the poetics of displacement for the history of gender relations stretches even further. It enhances the spatial dimension of the life of a people that is, from its beginnings, defined by the already inhabited land it was to conquer.

This spatial dimension of the history of Israel cannot be remembered without full awareness of other spatial issues. The establishment of the house, as a spatial metaphor for the chronological lineage, is exactly the intermediate figure that connects the two dimensions. If we want to understand the interconnections between the two dimensions, we have to account for the strategies of the spatial figure of displacement, including, however frightening it may be, the image of the avenging mother.

CONCLUSION

> Politics can be seen as that which makes it impossible to draw
> the line between "language" and "life."
>   Barbara Johnson

Reading the Book of Judges within the margins of the traditional readings has led us to realize how deeply violence is anchored in the domestic domain. I conclude with the suggestion that the political violence
of wars and conquests is secondary in relation to the institutional violence of the social order. This violence seems to be the inevitable consequence of a social structure that is inherently contradictory. Between
the two poles of the contradiction, x and y, the young woman, the
virgin daughter, has to pay with her life for the society's incapacity to
solve the conflicts.

If I have traveled through the book in an unorthodox way, jumping to and fro between the chosen core stories and integrating the
other stories only gradually, deliberately and partially focusing on the
positions, roles, and activities of women, that mode of reading was part
of a strategy. It was meant to enhance what usually passes unseen, to
relativize what is usually emphasized. Focusing on characters rather
than on storyline, on practices rather than on events, those motifs that
in traditional commentaries tend to be passed on as part of the bargain
became the central issue, *the* bargain. Literally speaking, it was, ultimately, the bargaining about daughters that was the first incentive
for the *gibborim*. The exemplary *gibbor* Othniel who, with his exploit
against the city of books, acquired the daughter of his elder brother set
the tone. His case was fraught with dangers kept under control by his
familial situation. This conciliatory familial situation was lacking in
the other stories of always-connected conquest and marriage. There-

231

fore, those stories showed the deep conflict in all its consequences in the astonishing way we have seen.

The connections between the domestic conflict and the political conflicts of conquest and war received their narrative symbolization in the repeated alternation between two types of stories. The book contains stories that are primarily domestic, yet fraught with political aspects; these are the stories readers read for. These stories give rise to military stories fraught with consequences for the domestic; the stories are considered historical. These historical stories, in turn, bring forth the next domestic story, keeping the reader's attention. The alternation between those two types of stories becomes a specific type of narrative discourse. The readers' attention shifts constantly between the two types, since in this narrative discourse the more appealing interest becomes the figure and the less appealing one the ground, according to what the reader can bear or what she or he finds disturbing.

The traditional exegeses of the book are the more remarkable since they seem inclined to reverse the sources of interest, pushing the domestic, individual stories into the background, on the basis of an a priori preference for political interests in the narrow sense. This act of repression, of displacement, can only be explained as a desire to forget the dangerous connections between the two, the awareness of the inevitability of the violence in both domains. The figuration of the intimate connections in the *house*, a socially sanctioned symbol of the domestic and yet a dominating figure for *and* issue in the conquest at large, allowed us to see how the conflicts that underlie the book also generated a type of narrative composition that leads to a discourse we may term *spatial narrative*, a type of discourse that requires different reading habits. With all its jumping from one story to the other, my reading was meant to show how such a "spatial" reading can illuminate new aspects of the book, while leading, in the end, to a view at least as comprehensive as that which others have presented before me. Reading ancient collections becomes then a journey through a land as yet unknown to us, but even to its most secret corners, one which we wish to discover. In those corners we discover much that was, after all, known to us.

This mode of reading rests on a view of language and of narrative that is not uncommon, yet has so far hardly been applied to biblical narrative. In this view, language is seen as action; as material, bodily, physical, historical, and social action.[1] As soon as such a view is adopted, we are almost overwhelmed by the penetrating importance of characters' speech as motors of the narrative. What I have called the cutting speech-act turned out to be a central narrative event. This is the speech-act that is unbalanced because the proportion between force and meaning tends to go wild, the excess or lack of meaning becoming the force. The force of the cutting speech-act does not affect the addressee so much as it kills—sacrifices, cuts—its object and that turned out to be a central narrative event. Indeed, we can call those acts generative events, since they produce the story and rush it to its end.[2] Actual sacrifice, that other founding event in the book, is in a *girard* sense but the insistently material realization of the cutting speech-act. It is called for when the *gibborim* begin to feel insecure about the material reality of their acts: their cutting speech-acts, as well as the sacrifice of their daughters, are nothing else than the obstinately material proof of what in their experience is not material enough: fatherhood,[3] the construction of a *house*, as a spatial, material possession *as well as* a historical, chronologically acknowledged position. Hence, the close bond between speech, language, and the conquest of the father-house. If this view is convincing, then "spatial" reading becomes an urgent task; it alone can truly account for the book on its own terms; it alone can bring out the book's obsessions and its stakes. Narrative becomes a warp onto which the stories are woven, not a thread that leads only through chronology.

Toward the end of our itinerary through the Book of Judges, we may well wonder where the journey has led us. We have witnessed the dangers of traveling in ancient Israel, especially for women caught between systems. But how dangerous has our own travel been? Moving between history and narrative, between anthropology and exegesis, the enterprise undertaken in this study has been a risky one in an academic context based on the division of disciplines. Far be it from me to compare the risks of an academic endeavor exercised in the comfort of, among other places, a Harvard office, to the real and deadly dangers incurred by the heroines in the book as soon as they left their houses. Yet, in one respect, these ventures have something in common: both are textual, anchored in the written word. If the status of the female characters as "wholly writ" has been, sometimes, forgotten, I have reached one of my goals.

In the preceding chapters, I have purposefully overwritten the textual status of my heroines. I have tried to make the reader forget about it, in order to let the heroines' awe-inspiring fate resound in the consciousness of the modern reader. I wished to let the experience of reading merge with the experience of suffering, to revive the characters into images of women in order for their female status to be acknowledged as fully as possible. The question of the status of my interpretation, of its background and goals, needs some assessment at this point.

The discussion of the status of my interpretation can be divided into a number of issues. First, the method of analysis, focused on the subject in narrative, cannot avoid the question whether the view of the subject inscribed in the text matches this model in some way. In other words, to what extent have I been pushing when talking about Jephthah and Bath, Beth and her "husband," Kallah and her father, as if about individuals we could meet in real life? Second, the gesture I have tried to accomplish, the replacement of the political coherence with a countercoherence, may well be accused of falling into the same trap I have been criticizing in the work of others. I need to address the status of my interpretation within the framework of my conception of semiosis in order to justify why I have not remained in the comfortably justifiable position of the deconstructionist of the discourse of others and risked entering into an endeavor that is in principle flawed. Third, the larger question of the position of the book as a historical book requires that I assess the historical meaning of my findings. The position of my own enterprise, as a response to the view of history underlying texts and commentaries, cannot escape critical analysis. Finally, the relevance of analyses such as this for today's culture relies on the place of textuality in that culture. In the following pages, I will address these issues briefly.

yes.

The I, the Eye, and Objectification

The structure of narrative, as I stated in the beginning of this study, can be seen as a network of subject-positions. Whenever there is story-telling, there is not only a story told, an object of narration, but there is first and foremost a subject, an I who tells it, hence, who makes it. Who, or rather, what, is such an I? In the case of stories that are the product of a collective imagination, this I can be seen as the spokesman of the community. But there the problems start. For the I is not a mere spokesman, an instrument that translates the collective images as a transparent medium. It is also a subject in its own right, although not necessarily an autonomous individual. One of the results of contemporary thought has been the assessment of the subject's anchoring in the social order of which she or he is a part. When I say that the subject of speech is a subject in its own right, I mean in the first place that the voice that tells the stories is that of a subject who is a member of more than the one group for whom she or he speaks. The biblical narrator in Judges can be assimilated to a person who is, for example, not just any member of the Israelite community, but also a member of its elite, probably a political and religious leader and, with the exception of the

Song of Deborah, most probably a man. Thus, this speaker has many stakes in the story he tells. One such stake, we can imagine, is to convey an idea of religious and military heroism through the concept of the hero whose semantic content is so central to the stories—the expression of this ideology may be, at least in part, the motivation for the act of storytelling.

The tension between collective imagination and individual wording of it is further complicated by the complexity of the narrative form. Not only is there a speaker, there is also a focalizer; the I is conflated with an Eye. The importance of this narrative agent is central in biblical narrative. We have seen how it is thematized in the use of the expression behold followed by an object whose status as object of vision I have enhanced throughout. It was first and foremost the women, the daughters, who were thus objectified and turned into the pleasurable or unpleasurable object of desire and murder. But the status of the daughters as objects, watched bodies, and public commodities is not the whole story. They did have access, sometimes, under clear conditions and within clearly defined limits, to the status of subject.

The view that underlies the stories as we have them is, in one sense, necessarily that of the speaker; this subject cannot but express its own view. We must assume, therefore, that the overall view of the stories is related to the status of the primary speaker and representative of the stake that subject has in a specific representation of the events, their social background, and their political motivation. On the other hand, the overall view of the narrator can at times encompass the views of others, of the characters that act in the story. We have seen this phenomenon at work most clearly in the double view of virginity, where the narrator expressed the male view of "exclusive possession" but also quoted the expression of the daughter, who held the female view of virginity as ripeness. We may wonder whether the subject of narration does always realize what meanings the expressions convey. Hence, the object of storytelling, the characters, do sometimes have access to the status of subject and are able to convey views alien to the speaker. In the case of this ancient book, I have termed these expressions "wandering rocks." Using that expression, I took some pleasure in the allusion to Joyce's allusion to that other significant ancient text. I also alluded to the implicit allusion I read in Joyce's chapter title and to the status of his own rewording of residual discourse from Homer. I have described those wandering rocks as residues of older discourse, of older views, perhaps no longer understood by the primary speaker and the audience, yet indestructible and—the word is appropriate—telling. Although today's readers of the book have even more trouble

[margin notes, handwritten:]
גׁׁׁ
גׁ
the phrase
objectifies
and turns
into
or
hypostatizes
and
turns into
in my basic
hebrew ?
does this both
in its role in
speech act
הׁׁׁ
are
in it's role as
the apodosis
of a conditional
sentence

reaching those very ancient subjects than the contemporary audience must have had already, the very antiquity of the text allows for the attempt to understand it on different levels at the same time and to work toward the "restoration" of the forgotten female views.

This possibility raises the problem of the tension between individual and collective cultural expression. I cannot disentangle here the entire complex of questions involved in this issue;[4] at most, I can risk a few tentative speculations.

If we consider the ancient book as a collection of cultural material, that material consisted of heterogeneous items: full stories, songs, mythical memories of older imaginations, residues of historical events, folkloristic formulas used at specific ritual occasions. All these elements were woven together and became the Book of Judges, not in one act of redaction, but in several stages that we cannot retrieve. But weaving needs a warp to support it. In this case, too, the weaving must have taken place against a political, social, and cultural background that made the elements understandable, against which they made sense as expressions of collective preoccupations. The political background has been overemphasized in preceding exegeses; therefore, I have chosen to ignore it as much as I could[5] in order to gain access to the other elements of the background, the social and cultural habits, institutions, and rituals that made the stories and songs meaningful. I did that not only to compensate for former neglect, but also because the political can in principle never be meaningfully seen without the background it arises from. Without the social domain, there is no politics.

The way the social and cultural background becomes meaningful has been demonstrated at several occasions. Some awareness of it is indispensable for a proper assessment of the effect of the stories *as* stories. For example, the horror story of Judges 19 fills us with terror, but at first sight we cannot make sense of it. Nor does it seem right to ignore both the horror and the lack of sense, to explain it away or too easily to subordinate it to major issues, for example, in an attempt to turn it into an etiological explanation of the war that the event causes. We are confronted with a difficult, disturbing, but instructive case. What can we do? Equally horrible stories circulate in our own culture, and the association with sadistic pornography is obvious. Yet this particular story, its motivations and its place in the culture, is not in itself meaningful to us. We can interpret the story as pornography, using the analyses of contemporary feminists like the article by Andrea Dworkin that I quoted at the beginning of this book and that in its turn draws upon biblical quotations, but although such an analysis makes sense for the awareness of the deep roots of pornography and violence in the religious traditions of our culture, it is not a sufficient account of the historical background against which this particular story made sense for the contemporary audience. As a matter of fact, this story has left commentators especially powerless because they saw in it a number of contradictions that I have tried to explain differently. One issue in that analysis was the position of Beth as the object of third-person narrative, the individual singled out to be objectified.[6] But why describe the effect of strangeness as contradictions in the first place, naturalizing them as redactional arbitrariness and copyist's mistakes? The reason earlier commentators have not succeeded in understanding the story on its own terms, while still acknowledging its character as a horror story, is simply that they have not had enough awareness of the socio-cultural background, especially the male-female relations therein, interested as they were in the religious-political background. It is my contention that they neither would nor could afford to pay attention to the possible anchoring of the story in the social background[7] because such an awareness would begin to make the story really horrible. The political coherence, as I call it, thus functions as closure; it allows critics to escape the painful experience of awareness of the deep-seated relationship between social institutions and violence against women that my analysis has brought to the fore.

It is the importance of this socio-cultural background that I have sought to enhance. For it is there that the "reality" of the characters lies; their substance lies over against the all-dominating narrator whose power is limited only by the wandering rocks, the structure of narrative, and the process of collective expression. The characters can come to life as representatives of real people, defending real stakes, and standing for real issues, but only if we take this background into account, turn it into a foreground, and let it speak, too. Paradoxically, then, the collectivity is better represented when we deny the single narrator as the spokesman of the collectivity and listen to other sources of meaning, other subjects.[8] Their reality makes their stories understandable, the ideologies underlying it analyzable, and the effect of their deaths on the further development of their society accountable. In order to *see* these women properly, we must see with them, be sensitive to their focalization, and try to grasp what happens to them and why.

In order to break the monopoly of the single I, the speaker whose status as spokesman of the entire culture is too readily acknowledged by commentators who share their stakes, we must develop insight into the whole network of subject-positions, not just the dominating one.

Modern narrative theory provides us with the tools to tell one subject from another and to acknowledge the views of even those individuals to whom speech is denied. The same narrative structure that allows the illusion of the single speaker to come through also allows us to understand its limits and to get access to alternative positions entailing alternative readings. At the end of our journey we are able to say: behold his daughter, rather than just seeing the *gibbor ḥayil*, the divine plan, and the conquest of Canaan.

The Incoherence of Coherence

Interpretation is necessarily a reader's response brought to a text; it is, at most, an interaction, at least, a purely subjective act. In the course of this study, I have frequently criticized biblical scholars for their pretentions to objectivity, their self-confidence and assertiveness, and their abuse of the constative mode. Yet I have not refrained from asserting my own interpretation, over against the current ones, but also asserting it in its own right. I have not shunned the constative mode either, although I have stated its false pretentions beforehand. How can I at this point justify the incoherence of my own coherence-seeking behavior?

I could not agree more than I do with those who, with Culler (1983), claim that any attempt to assess the status of interpretation as based on the text is contradictory and fallacious. Interpretation is never objective, never reliable, never free of biases and subjectivity. The epistemological status of interpretation is therefore extremely thin. Yet it is also indispensable as a mediation between subjects of cognition and objects of knowledge. Like speech-acts, interpretations have difficulty telling the force, the motivations of speech-acts from their meaning, their content; yet without force there can be no meaning. The force of my interpretations, for example, lies in a very strong motivation which is the desire to understand the relations between gender, violence, and politics in the texts that stand at the roots of our civilization. The meaning of my interpretations, the results, are strongly affected by that force. The questions I have tried to answer did not come from out of the blue; they came straight from that motivation. Yet, I contend that my interpretations do have a status that can be assessed negatively: they are no less reliable than the interpretations of others.

Here lies a primary motivation for my critique of the biases and fallacies of other commentators. Showing that, in spite of their claims, these scholars are motivated by unacknowledged biases, I have tried to assess the status of interpretation as biased in theory and in principle. By the same move, I have made room for my own overtly biased interpretations to have access to the equivalent status of scholarship. But this is not all.

The procedure of my analysis has been based on a method. Such methods do not protect us from the influence of our own private motivations. But they do allow us to formulate the findings in a discourse that is or can be made intersubjective. In order to promote its accessibility, I have put some effort into explaining it carefully and presenting it systematically (see Appendix 1). Using the method of narrative theory as a starting point from which my initial questions could be rationally derived, I have made it possible for readers to follow the steps I took, to ask the same questions and to formulate the answers that, albeit different, are rationally related to the same discourse. Third, I have shown on several occasions where one discipline reaches its limits and yields to another discipline. The limits between narratology and philology on the one hand, between narratology and anthropology on the other, are real, yet not solid. They can and should be transgressed in order to respond to the text as fully as possible. This principle of interdisciplinarity is crucial to my endeavor; without it, narratology would easily become sterile, as will any discipline when used to close off rather than to open up aspects of the object it cannot accommodate. I firmly believe no academic research can afford, today, to remain mono-disciplinary. In the best cases, what this amounts to is a lack of awareness of interdisciplinarity. In the worst case, it means being imprisoned in arbitrary or, worse, politically motivated boundaries set up against, rather than for, the enlargement of our knowledge and understanding. It is one of the major accomplishments of feminist research to have made a convincing case for the need for interdisciplinary openness in any academic endeavor. The difficulty of doing this in practice, the risks of eclectic, unsystematic borrowing, can be countered by a conscious reflection on the steps we take. I have tried to justify my transgressions each time I committed them.

There has been another limit that has been transgressed, a limit of an entirely different order. As the reader may have felt all through the last chapter, the tour de force practiced there was a transgression, inherent in interpretation, of the limits between reading and writing, of the boundary between subject of analysis and object analyzed. The argument I have tried to make in the chapter was to prove the presence of the absent, a procedure as fallacious as—but no more so than—the method of psychoanalysis itself. Yet, I claim it is as fruitful if exercised with caution, and as legitimate. The repressed can only return with the help of the other, the analyst who helps it return, and perhaps, creates it. The angry mothers I have written into the book are absent and present, and it is up to the reader to evaluate to what extent they are there or not. Absent they had to be, according to my argument, because they disturbed the consciousness of those who murdered the daughters; but present they also had to be for the very same reasons. I have given the textual evidence I could find; yet, the angry mother is my creation as much as the book's. So are all the other interpretations, however; those which claim philological support may even be more so. Soggin's attempt to write Yael out of the beginning of the Song of Deborah[9] is, in my sense, much less supported by the text than my interpretation of the murderesses.

Do I then claim that interpretation is text-based after all? Not at all, not *based*. The text is not an object upon which we can operate; it is another subject that speaks to us. We can listen, and just as in real life, we will hear our own voice reflected; yet we cannot attribute just anything to the other speaker. If we shout too loud, so that the other is reduced to silence, we will lack arguments to make our case. This is the point of rational argumentation, of the attempt to give evidence in the text while we do not believe interpretations can ever be truly based on it. It is not a matter of empirical proof; it is a matter of plausible interaction.

If my readers have not been able to hear the voice of the text resound in my interpretations, I have simply missed my goal and will not be believed. Hence, there is a third party in the dialogue, the witness who checks what happens and who will refuse to go along when the interpreter overwrites the text. The interpretations I have given are, in my sense, no less, and in many respects more, reliable as accounts of my understanding of what the text said than many of the respected scholarly endeavors discussed here. At least, I have not amended the text whenever it pleased me. That was one way to hold myself in check. Listening to what the text had to say by picking up the recalcitrant details that scholars had problems with was another way to keep track of what I thought I was hearing. But I have also tried to hear what the text tried to conceal, what in real life would be the speaker's body language. Psychoanalysis has taught us how important that language is, yet how easy to misunderstand. It can in no way be ignored. In order to hear and see more, I have used tools, the lenses of narratology that allowed me to see the microscopic details that other tools would have left out of sight; but lenses distort, too, and keep other details out of sight. This has to be acknowledged, but it should not make us powerless. Interpretation is interesting precisely to the extent that it allows us to see, not what the text has to say—the assumption of humble, neutral listening is in fact arrogant and positivistic—but how it speaks to us. It is a dialogue, a speech-act that includes, in its meaning, the discourse of the other. This view of interpretation as a speech-act, hence, as an inextricable mixture of force and meaning and of sender and addressee, allows us, finally, to approach the problem of history in a tentative way.

Once Upon a Time

Judges, it has been said, is one of the Bible's historical books. The notion of history inscribed in it is far removed from today's conception of history and of historical truth. In one sense, however, they are close. If we read Judges superficially, we recognize its historiographic project in the emphasis on political history and military exploits. This aspect, common to both the book and today's commonplace view of history, even allows some to force a chronology upon the recalcitrant events. But what we tend to forget is the graphic part of the idea of historiography. Writing history is not just noting the facts. It is selecting what the writer finds relevant for his own purpose.

The Song of Deborah is a good example, or rather, a good counterexample. Thanks to its respectable antiquity, the song is generally considered "closer" to the events it recalls than the epic version of the preceding chapter. The song is a commemoration of the battle against Sisera, including the murder by Yael. As such, it is not an attempt to describe it selectively, but to turn it, again and again, into an experience that has been lived. Deborah's poetic work consists of making the assembled people experience the triumph again, *feel* the pleasure and pride of victory, *experience* the shame of cowardice for those who did not participate, *participate* in the speech-act of blessing Yael for her act. The situation of communication, the poetic interaction, is here part of the historical work of the commemoration. The gap between this form of history-making and the epic version that *explains* the event rather than sharing it, that chooses to enhance the rational interpretation over the emotional revival, cannot be overestimated. When we compare those two texts, we get a sense of the differences between possible forms of history-making. A trace of this distinction can be seen in the traditional Jewish name for the genre to which Judges belongs: the prophetic books. Prophetic history is one form of historiography, in which the speech-act of *graphein*, of writing, is primarily considered as *force*.

I have systematically emphasized the individual events over the collective, political ones, and I have tried to present them as lived experience rather than as retold facts. The question whether Bath has been really sacrificed or not (see Trible 1984) I have not found relevant; instead, I have emphasized throughout the question of how she was sacrificed, in reality or in imagination, by which weapons, by which speech-act, in which drama. The difference is one between "facts" as the major content of historiography and experience as the major content of historical commemoration. The project of selectively writing the history of the people as a military-political history of the *sons* of Israel has not been ignored, but is only part of the object of study. In other words, the way the political coherence has repressed and subordinated the domestic violence, an endeavor already inscribed in the book and further pursued by the critics, is what I have tried to bring to the fore through the enhancement of its counterpart, the emancipation of the other side, the accentuation of the domestic events and experiences.

Just as interpretation in general is a dialogue involving at least two and frequently more subjects, so is historical work a dialogue—not the objective description of some distant object but a conversation between subjects and their vestiges from the past, and subjects in the present. The questions I have addressed to the text come clearly from my own position. As a woman living in the era of modern patriarchy, at a moment where its institutions are challenged yet still strongly anchored in the past, the questions I address to the ancient book cannot but be focused on women who are in some sense in a symmetrical position to mine. The very institutions that today protect the late monuments of patriarchy were on their way to establishing themselves with difficulty in the era represented in Judges. It is from today's perspective that I see the need to distract the exclusive attention from political preoccupations and to look at the social basis they come from and work upon. To give one obvious example: if we want to understand the motivations of modern monogamy as Freud expressed them, we must look at the excessive ways in which the *gibborim* of Judges act upon those motivations within different yet comparable institutions.

Once More: Body Language

Finally, we may ask ourselves, what is the relevance of this sort of analysis for today's society? Claiming that a better understanding of ancient texts, especially of those founding texts upon which much of our culture has been based, is useful is only a partial answer. This answer raises new questions. For why are texts relevant at all compared to "real" things like weapons, hunger and violence, power and oppression? It is not sufficient to claim that much of that "real" life is justified by an appeal to these texts either, although that is undeniably the case and needs serious examination. I think, however, that there is a deeper relation between textuality and violence, especially sexual violence, that comes from the material status of speech-acts. The power to speak is directly related to the power to act; so far, this is commonplace. The linguistic powerlessness of some categories of subjects is congruent to their physical objectification. In the Book of Judges, the exemplary speech-act that objectifies the "third person," the subject excluded from the speech-event yet thoroughly affected by it, was the riddle-vow. In general, we can say that the speech-act par excellence, the one that signifies the materiality as well as the implication of the subject in the act itself, is *judging*. Judging is absolute referentiality brought about by absolute textuality. It is like marriage: one word is enough. But it is also different. It does not bind, but separates; it does not change lives, but cuts lives off. As Barbara Johnson brilliantly exposes in her analysis of *Billy Budd*, "What every act of judgment manifests, is not the value of the object but the position of the judge within a structure of exchange" (1980, 107). Judging is mainly different from marriage, then, in that it excludes the subject it affects, hence, objectifying it. We have seen how decisive, how *cutting*, the speech-acts of the heroes of the Book of Judges could be and how much more those acts and their consequences bore judgment upon the subject that pronounced them rather than on their object. Disturbingly, however, the object is the one who suffers the consequences. The exchange is not that of marriage, but that of murder. The subject of speech, of the cutting speech-act, used his power to exchange positions with the object, making her assume the consequences of his misjudgment. This is what the slip about Jephthah did not manage to completely repress. It did not completely repress the displacement, wherein Jephthah returned to the place—the place of the victim—which he had exchanged in the vow for the better place of the *gibbor*.

The all-encompassing materiality of speech-acts of judgment is not equally strong in any speech-act. The tension between the materiality of language and its fugitive quality, its restlessness, its propensity to escape, has been a problem for those who wished to establish their power. It is through attempts to fix the fluidity of language that a new form of speech-act has been invented—the written word. Writing is a revolutionary materialization of speech, one that can cut and kill at a distance. Writing has, from its early days on, worked to support, to become, *law*. The law is the crucial text in literate societies, the one that enables judgments to be predictable and to be determined by the centralized power of the state. Textuality, therefore, has its roots in the objectification of justice that literacy helped to generate. As Johnson put it: "Judgment . . . would seem to ground itself in a suspension of the opposition between textuality and referentiality, just as politics can be seen as that which makes it impossible to draw the line between 'language' and 'life'" (1980:104–5). Whoever became the object of writing, the textual *thing,* to whom access to writing was denied, lost all power over her own life. The heroes of Judges attempt to objectify the objects of their power by turning them into textual things; in the cases I have studied, the daughters were those objects.

The strange thing about Judges, at first sight, is the absence of any act of judgment in the modern sense, in spite of the title of the book.[10] Scholars have broken their teeth over this problem and set up impressive theories to argue that the actual heroes of the book, the so-called "deliverers," were not the real judges, while the so-called "minor judges" who appear only in a list in the middle of the book were judges in the juridical sense. There is not the slightest evidence in support of this theory. There is no indication whatsoever that the "minor judges" did actually judge or that the deliverers did not. If we consider judging as the exemplary speech-act, as the most material manifestation of speech-acts, the term helps us better understand the effect of the *gibborim*'s central speech-acts of riddle and vow. In fact, then, the main characters of Judges do judge, in the sense that Johnson describes. Only their acts are so opposed to what we assume to be jus-tice, their fatal speech-acts are uttered so bluntly out of sheer power, that critics forget that this *is* judging; they prefer to call it military bravery rather than acknowledge the bare judgment on judging that the stories demonstrate. It is the assumption that judging is based on justice, expressed in a language that uses the same root for both, that is our unjustified bias.

There is, however, a single figure who escapes the division be-tween "deliverers" and "minor judges," and who is even, in my sense, the motivation for the theory having been designed at all.[11] That is, not surprisingly, Deborah. She is both a heroine, albeit not a *gibbor,*[12] and a judge, according to the description in 4:4. That description is the most comprehensive account of the office that we have; hence, the character represented therein is the judge par excellence. If we want to get an idea of what judgment could also be, in the ancient context, the song of this exemplary judge gives ample information. Judging, there, is proposing to the audience a view of the subjects involved: the un-willing and the heroic tribes, the bad mother at the window, and the good mother in the tent. Cursing and blessing replaces riddle and vow.

Not only do they replace them, they also comment on them. As Johnson says, "Judgment is an act, not only because it kills, but because it is in turn open to judgment" (1980, 102). If we now reverse the argument, we can say that the speech-acts of the deliverer/judges, of the *gibborim*, are judgments, not only because they kill, but also because they are in their turn open to judgment. Denying that the acts of the *gibborim* are acts of judgment, then, is a way to escape the need to judge them in their turn. Deborah gives the example for such a form of metajudgment, and the present study has attempted to continue that endeavor. By this reversed argument it attempts to prove that Samson, Jephthah, Beth's husband and father do behave like judges. We must judge such "judgment" and justice and expose its being anchored in power.

APPENDICES

APPENDIX 1: A MODEL FOR NARRATOLOGICAL ANALYSIS

	Role: Delimitation of subjects Basic question: Who?	Position: Hierarchy of subject/object Basic question: From who/around who?	Action: organization, distribution, result Basic question: What, why, how?

language	identity of speaker:
	 implicit vs. explicit
	  (authority vs. responsibility)
	linguistic model used:
	 dialogue vs. narration
	 role-exchanging vs. elimination of
	  object
	 dialogue vs. pseudo-dialogue
	linguistic modes used:
	 affirmative vs. mystifying
	 imperative vs. lack of authority
	 legitimate orders vs. illegitimate
	 interrogative vs. imperative
	 question vs. request
	who never speaks?
		causal vs. grammatical subject: who is
		  the semantic subject of both?
		agent-process-effect
		causality vs. classification
		nominalization of verbs
		unique vs. general; concrete vs.
		  abstract
		negation in verb
		 grammatical subject vs. reactive
		  subject
		 causal subject vs. secondary subject
		 who is responsible?
			distribution of speech:
			 number of utterances for each
			  speaker
			 length of utterances
			 effect of utterances:
			  is speech adequate to the function
			   of the linguistic model used? are
			   utterances successful?
			 transition formulas

vision	identity of focalizer:
	  is focalizer identical with speaker?
	  reflective vs. nonreflective focalization
	mode of focalization:
	  verb of perception vs. mental acts
	  direct vs. indirect focalization
	  who never focalizes?
		two alternative versions of one event
		first vs. last focalizer
		attribution of focalization:
		  explicit vs. implicit evaluation
		  privileged focalizer vs. lack of visibility
		distribution of focalization
		spatial position of focalizer
			distribution of focalization:
			  number of focalizations for each subject
			  distribution related to place in text
			  distribution related to place of event in fabula
			kind of focalization:
			  checkable vs. inaccessible to others
			  object internal vs. external to subject
			  relation to focalization-speech:
			    who focalizes more than he/she speaks?

action	identity of actor:
	  actor-character vs. actor-object
	  relation to action-focalization:
	    does actor focalize his/her action?
	  relation to actor-*destinateur*:
	    free vs. delegated actor
	  who never acts?
		direction of action:
		  who takes initiatives?
		  who accomplishes central action?
		  relation to actor-narrative program
		  are there transformations in the fabula similar to linguistic transformations (e.g., mystification of causal subject)?
			distribution of actors on actional chain:
			  number of actions for each actor
			  importance of their actions
			  place of actions in fabula
			effect of action:
			  successful with respect to intention
			  successful with respect to program
			  relation to action-focalization-speech:
			    are actions effective?
			    are they carried out as a result of evaluation by focalization or by speech?

APPENDIX 2: NOTES ON LANGUAGE

This study addresses a general audience; no specialized knowledge of the language of biblical literature is necessary for reading it. A few notes on the way I have treated the language are, however, in place here.

Translations of fragments are my own, unless otherwise indicated. Whenever I have contrasted my translation with other ones, I have translated as literally as possible, sacrificing, where necessary, the fluency of the language for closeness to the Hebrew text.

Sentences that have no verb in Hebrew have been translated as such whenever the meaning of that structure was relevant. This was the case when the sentence thematized the subject on which the sentence gave information, rather than actions or events.

The general Hebrew conjunction *ve* has been translated as *and*. In principle, the very fact that it is so general allows different translations. Replacing a conjunction of juxtaposition by, for example, causal conjunctions is already modifying the character of a text that originated in oral traditions and adapting it to literacy. Moreover, any choice for a particular conjunction other than *and* implies an act of interpretation, and on several occasions, such interpretations are strongly distorting. I have preferred to enhance the typical structure of the ancient language.

The following idiomatic expressions have been translated in a polemical way, opposing traditional and in my view distorting translations:

ʿishah: the word for "woman," often translated as "wife," has been rendered as *woman*. The modern concept of marriage is so different from the types of relationships that underlie the Book of Judges that the translation "wife" did not seem acceptable to me. Moreover, in several cases, there is no evidence that anything like marriage is at stake, as in the case of Deborah and Yael. It would be consistent to translate the masculine form of this noun, ʿish, as *man* rather than as *husband*. The one time I have used the word *husband* I did so with polemical intent. In the case of chapter 19, scholars have too easily assumed that the "concubine" had no status as a married wife; in order to enhance the relationship between the woman sacrificed and the man who owed her protection, I have rendered the status of the latter as *husband*.

gibbor: The noun has almost never been translated. Although *hero* is the most obvious rendering, I have mostly used the Hebrew noun. This was done in order to emphasize the particular semantics of heroism that underlay the book. The status of the *gibbor* is constructed through murder, the usurpation of power, and the cult of masculinity. The positive word *hero* is too vague and too obscuring to be of use in these cases.

messenger of Yahweh: I have used this expression rather than *angel*. The concept of "angel" seemed to me too much determined by the Christian use of it. Moreover, the messenger so frequently replaces a husband whose status as father is doubtful that the gender of the messenger has to be signified. Angels are, in Christian culture, too gender-neutral for this use.

hinne: I have systematically kept this word as *behold*, since I believe the thematization of focalization in the frequent use of the word is a meaningful aspect of Hebrew narrative structure.

The following idiomatic expressions are literal, and clearly awkward, translations of Hebrew expressions. I have chosen to use them nevertheless because I believe they stem from a concrete view of what is at stake in their meaning. I list them here with the traditional English translations as well as with a short explanation of my motivation for literal translation.

girls, uterus: damsels. The Hebrew word expresses contempt.

the nose of Yahweh burnt: Yahweh became angry, the anger of the Lord was kindled. The bodily aspects of the image of the deity are too often repressed.

the mouth of the sword: the edge of the sword. The metaphor *mouth* relates killing to language, while the bodily metaphor is also otherwise meaningful.

woman of torches: wife of Lappidoth. There is no evidence that a proper name is meant. The idea that Deborah was married therefore springs from nowhere.

a woman of "unfaithfulness": harlot. It is doubtful that harlotry in the modern sense was at stake. The idea of unfaithfulness can refer to entirely different issues than sexual promiscuity.

patrilocal wife, "concubine": concubine. I use the word in quotation marks until I interpret it as patrilocal wife.

The dictionary used is the slightly outdated Koehler and Baumgartner (1958); I have justified this choice where it is was relevant for the first time.

NOTES

Introduction

1. The murder of Eglon by the left-handed Ehud, one of the male tricksters who contribute to the liberation of the people from oppression by "foreign" (or should we call them native?) forces. This story, told in the third chapter of the book, resembles the woman-man murders in several aspects. Ehud's behavior as *trickster* relates him to the female murderers. See the special issue of *Semeia* (1988) for the relation between trickster-stories and the divine project.

2. The theoretical background of that study is more fully developed in a French version of *Lethal Love*, entitled *Femmes imaginaires*.

3. This is how Zola saw his own enterprise of realistic writing. Many a modern scholar implicitly still adheres to this mode of reading, even though it is not only anachronistic in relation to ancient texts, but also ideologically biased. Ignoring language, language is used to impose the critic's own view of reality, thus obscuring the reality he claims to display.

4. In spite of the opposition between this position and the realistic one, these two attitudes toward texts have much in common. Each in its own way obscures reality, runs away from it, albeit in opposite directions. The overestheticizing approaches to the Bible that have developed as the 'literary' approaches serve their ideological purposes as much as do the realistic ones. We will encounter a few significant cases in the course of this study.

5. I mean here by commentary the systematic study, chapter by chapter, of the book that presents itself as a guide for readers. Of the commentaries I will refer to throughout this study some are scholarly, some popular. As is often the case with biblical commentaries, the scholarly commentaries are also meant for a larger audience, sometimes religious. It is a commonly practiced

genre, so much so that it is hard to find a study of the book as a whole that does not adopt that form of following the text line by line.

Chapter One

1. The concept of intertextuality and the method of analysis derived from it, on which more will follow later, entail a set of specific terms that I find useful to define from the outset. I use the term *post-text* for any rewriting of a previous text which is always a reading, be it a commentary or a different version of the text. In the present case, both popular and scholarly commentaries, children's Bibles, even paintings representing the stories are post-texts. The term *ante-text* refers to a prior text which resonates in the text under scrutiny. For Ben Sira's text, Judges is an ante-text; for Judges, a hypothetical prior version or its oral variants are ante-texts. *Pre-text* is used, following van Alphen (1988), to refer to the sociohistorical reality on which a given text plays. The pre-text for Judges is, as I will argue in this study, the transition between two types of marriage in early Israelite society. With Genette (1979) I use the term *architexte* for the generic type underlying a given text. Judges' architext is mythical or, in the Jewish tradition, prophetic historiography. The term *intertext* is the general term which encompasses the others. The term has little specific meaning; its derivative *intertextuality* is used for any type of relations between a text and any of its post-, ante-, pre-, or archi-texts.

2. *Coherence* is a concept that is both "experience-near" and "experience-distant" (Geertz 1983). In everyday language, it refers to the presupposition of unity; in linguistics, this presupposition is technically elaborated. The major point I wish to make in this study is that coherence is a readerly act, rather than a textual feature, but that the impulse to project coherence on a semiotic object is unavoidable. It is therefore not relevant to denounce coherent readings, but to specify the *kind* of coherence projected, and to analyze the interests that motivate those choices. In this respect, coherence is structurally similar to the concept of ideology (van Alphen 1987).

3. This view goes against the received view of "open" versus "closed" texts, where the open work would be the more literary, modern, sophisticated work, and the closed one, the simpler, realistic, ideological ones. See for example Eco (1962 and 1976) versus various interpretations of Barthes' *S/Z*. A brief but convincing argument is given by Alphen (1985).

4. The issue is dated 21 January 1986. It is interesting to look at the other subjects presented in the same issue. The cover article was about "Boy, 9, has twins with teacher, 43." The theme of a young child seduced by an older woman is extremely frequent in this journal.

5. As I argue in *Lethal Love*, Delilah is outspoken and open about her project from the start. The first time she asks Samson to reveal his secret, she says that she wants to know how he can be "dominated," and Samson, responding in the third person plural (. . . they can dominate me) shows that he got the message. Each time, Delilah warns him that the Philistines are in the room. Modern readers who claim she lied to him need the lie in order to fulfill

other requirements, such as Samson's heroism, which is threatened by his alleged stupidity.

6. I use five commentaries, all globally of the same genre, but of different ideological backgrounds. In alphabetical order, the books are: Boling (1975), Gray (1986), Martin (1975), Slotki in Cohen (1980 [1950]) and Soggin (1981). Slotki is explicitly Jewish and meant for a general audience; Soggin is ostensibly Catholic; Boling presents his book as coming from an "interfaith" project; the other two are less outspoken. Why do I use no commentary written by a woman? Because there is none.

7. The genre of the biblical commentary seems more conservative in this respect. Current scholarship (Childs 1986; Smith 1971) insists on the particular and in some sense ahistorical view of history that prevails in Judges and the other Deuteronomistic texts. Thus Childs states, "Any attempt to exercise a value judgment on the sources [of Judges] in relation to an extrinsic norm of historicity makes neither literary nor theological sense in the context of the canon" (1986, 262). Although the commentators are clearly aware of this relativistic view, the point I wish to make is that this awareness does not preclude anachronistic relapses into historical realism. Moreover, if the best we can get at is historical relativism, other chances are being missed. I will argue for a different view of historicity which avoids the traps of factual and chronological history while allowing strong claims on the historical pre-text of Judges.

8. This alternative composition, which, for reasons to be specified, I call the architectural coherence of the book, will be developed in the course of this study and explicitly defined in chapter 6. "Architectural" points both at the difference if not opposition from chronology and at the importance of the double concept of the "house" as the site of the construction of history.

9. Where chronology is ostensibly failing, it seems simply unthinkable that any attempt to start from any other than a chronological perspective be congenial to the book. However, the chronological concern seems alien both to its composition and to its thematics as I will try to propose it. It is just because of this lack of imagination that my counterproposal appears to be radical while it is in fact so simple.

10. E.g., Sternberg, where Deborah's obviously important political role is thus described: "At the sequential position reserved for the deliverer, she springs at us from nowhere, complete with husband, national role, foreign antagonist, seat of judgment bearing her name: all expositional features calculated to bring her sex into marked dissonance with her office past and to come" (1985, 272). And further: "To flaunt his omnipotence, after all, God has already picked his instruments in contempt of human norms of seemliness and efficacy" (p. 273). Introduced in this way, with irony and hardly concealed irritation, Deborah cannot really become a historically relevant figure; she is God's creation to challenge history. I side with this challenging god, then, and I would like to see what happens to Sternberg's view of history.

11. See the interesting and convincing discussion of this problem by Pomata (1983), whose article places women's history between anthropology and biology. The relation to anthropology is based on the continuity-change

opposition, the relation to biology, on universalistic fallacies about the "nature" of women. My attitude toward both these connections is more dialectic. Although I fully agree with Pomata's rejection of the underlying fallacies, I want to show them at work, and effectively so, in both texts and interpretations of texts; that is, I reject them but will not ignore them. Part of changing "history" is to include historiography in it.

12. If she has a home at all—that is, if her "husband" is not a qualifying description of herself, as many have suggested but not really proposed. In a hermeneutics of suspicion, the fact that most commentators signal the "problem" that the "name" of the alleged husband is strange, while they still keep him alive, is a symptom of repression and a motivation to try out the other alternative, as I will do in chapter 7.

13. I exclude from this generalization the scholars of the literary approach. They have an opposite, equally suspect attitude toward history: they ignore it or deny its relevance for the study of the Bible. I will discuss this esthetic attitude as yet another escape from social reality. There is still another possible attitude: *to consider the historiographic project as such as a literary endeavor.* This approach is perhaps the most tricky one; it turns the literary structure that is first extrapolated on the basis of purely subjective projection into the voice of God, which coincides with the voice of history. This is what Sternberg does (1985) and I need to make explicit that it is for that reason that I want to distance myself from his use of "literature," in spite of his many interesting insights.

14. Why, some have asked, if we have to assume a redactor, does he have to be stupid? This pointed question was asked by Robert Alter at the Colorado conference on the Bible and Critical Theory, 3–5 April 1986, organized by Regina Schwartz. The figure of the redactor, whose indication in the singular has quickly turned "him" into a *purely fictional* character, a hero of the superimposed history of the text, serves to justify the projection of anachronistic, mostly romantic conceptions of literature and textual coherence on the book. A disturbing example is Richter (1963; 1964). See *Murder and Difference,* chapter 2, for a critique.

15. Boling's amusingly elaborate attempt—which included visual material—to make a case for Jephthah's innocence is consistent with his initial quotation. The quote prepares the reader for the subsequent apology. The attempt is more interesting than the answer which, given the motivation for the question, cannot lead to a satisfying solution anyway.

16. See *La violence et le sacré* (*Violence and the Sacred*), which develops a theory that all sacrifices in the whole world stem from the same source: scapegoating and mitigation of primary violence onto another object. Girard (1972) does not hesitate to affirm that women are never sacrificed. This is how the politics of coherence works for Judges.

17. See Nancy Jay, 1985. Jay's theory is more fully developed in a book that is unfortunately not yet available, but that I have had the privilege to see in part. The relation she establishes between patrilineage and sacrifice is most convincing, but does not pay enough attention to violence as an underlying

motivation that *also* plays a part. Her rigorously social framework forbids the symbolic interpretation those motivations need. I feel here is a case for inter-disciplinarity. Jay's analysis of the patriarchal stories in Genesis confirms my intuition that, especially as far as the focus on lineage is concerned, Genesis represents a form of patriarchy that is radically different from that in Judges. If measured in terms of development, Genesis represents a good step ahead in the establishment of 'patriarchal' patriarchy.

18. The allusion to *Oedipus the King* in this word "crossroad" is meant to draw attention to the fact that many of the stories from Judges reverse the oedipal scheme. Not only is the son replaced by the daughter, but also, the father becomes the holder of the master-position in the triangle; his becomes the perspective. The men who, for a short while, occupy a son's position do not kill their father but their brothers, in order to become the father.

19. Three is a magical number in many folktales. In the Samson story, Samson lies three times to Delilah. Often, it connotes the exhaustion of all possibilities and, hence, stands for completeness. I would like to retain that possible meaning for the case at hand: three murdered young women in one book, and then, three men killed by women.

20. That does not mean that this "justice" is the only motivation for their centrality. In fact, this study is, as a whole, an argument for the idea that the composers of the book were to some extent sensitive to the issues I will be raising. It is my contention that the awareness of social history as the back-ground—or foreground—of political history made the composers include the women's stories, as did the presence of these stories in the primarily oral culture.

21. I use this dictionary (Koehler and Baumgartner 1958; K&B here-after) throughout my study. Some prefer Brown, Drivers, and Briggs (1962; hereafter as BDB), which I use comparatively. As we will see, K&B included sometimes strange associations which have disappeared from BDB. I have used K&B in an unorthodox, often provocative manner, now adopting their asso-ciations, now rejecting them, each time for nonphilological reasons. I will ac-count for each use in due place.

22. But it is less questionable, although more problematic, than the traditional translation of "prostitute" regarding the suggested status of his mother. I will return to this. Even apart from this specific problem which Jephthah has, the idea of some feudal nobility is in no way justified if we place the text in its context.

23. Rather than opting for any of the extant translations, I will use the Hebrew word *gibbor*, sometimes for stylistic reasons, replacing it with "hero." The use of the Hebrew word is meant to recall regularly that the status, the social role, of these men is not yet defined but is being defined throughout this study—in relation to their behavior, not only military and political, but pri-marily toward women.

24. It is power, then, more than any individual quality, that defines the *gibbor*. Power has to be specified, however. As we will see, the political power is not self-evident, it has to be conquered. The idea of the conquest as the topic of the book can be expanded; it is not only the conquest of the land that

is at stake, but also the conquest of power. The power over young women is clearly easier to get than the power over land. We will see that the two forms of power are not unrelated.

25. Delilah's action cannot be qualified as betrayal, since she explicitly tells Samson, both before and after each attempt at discovery of his secret, for what purpose she intends to use the desired knowledge. See *Lethal Love*, chapter 2.

26. Maybe it is because of the indirectness of the killing that this story has become the most used ideo-story. It is so then because it allows readers to project onto it more convincingly the unreliability of women and the danger of love. If that is the case, then it is all the more important to see the symmetry, in this respect, with the indirect murder of Samson's first wife. Note that the bride was killed first. This becomes relevant in chapter 7.

27. In *Lethal Love*, I analyzed a few samples of popular rewritings of the story, including a number of children's Bibles and a popular commentary. See also the bibliography in *Lethal Love*.

28. A very traditional interpretation of the Samson saga is given by Crenshaw (1978); more interesting are Exum's articles (1980; 1983). On Yael's act and the scholarship struggling with it, see Bal (1988a).

29. I keep the word order of the Hebrew, in spite of the odd English syntax that results, because of the particular rhythm produced by the order of verbs and nouns, which enhances the exchange between the characters much more than would be the case with the English word order.

30. This notion will be elaborated later. The quotation marks indicate that this traditional conception of his status does not do full justice to the tensions at stake. At this point, his problematic status is relevant in relation to the concept of *gibbor*, but should not be taken too much in the modern sense of "bastard," for that is not the case.

31. It is important to understand this relation between a mythical gender-bias and a concrete social problem; it will be discussed in the next chapter. See Korsten (1986) for an analysis of the same ideologeme in the *Niebelungen Lied*. It is one of the clearest cases of the relation between ideology of gender on the one hand, and social history on the other, that I hope to point out in this study. See for the ideologeme of honor-shame/gender, *Murder and Difference* and the bibliography there. I will return to this briefly in chapter 7. On Abimelech's status, Morgenstern (1929; 1931) comes closest to my view. His suggestions have not been taken up, which I see as evidence of their radical implications.

32. No mention is made of either husband or father. About the claim that "Heber the Kenite" indicates Yael's husband, see chapter 7. It suffices here to say that commentaries generally agree that it is unlikely that Heber is a proper name. More likely, the indication of a tribe or clan should be supposed. Delilah clearly lives by herself, handles her own finances, and receives in her house whomever she wishes. She is referred to as "a woman" (*'ishah*), not as a prostitute (*zonah*).

33. This is especially true for the motifs that suggest care: the gift of

milk and the covering with a cloth in chapter 4. In chapter 5, it is the fall "between her feet" that connotes a mother-child relationship, although not by care but by the bodily imagery.

34. For the term *isotopy*, which indicates a semantic field, see Greimas (1965). I will return to the visual quality of the image in chapter 7. The woman with the millstone can be visually compared to the Yael of the Song of Deborah.

35. Only of a sexually ripe young woman would one bother to say whether or not she had sexual experience. The dichotomy between "to have known man" and "to have not known man" is in itself evidence of the relation between ripeness and sexual possession that underlies the expression. See further discussion of this in chapter 3.

36. The difference is one of language use, of speech-acts, in the first place. Interestingly, seduction is the central example of Shoshana Felman's book *Le scandale du corps parlant*, a book that I wish to honor in the title of my chapter 5, wherein I will discuss the speech-act of power that replaces seduction in the victim stories.

37. Again, the etiological function must not be overrated because that would isolate the story from the longer sequence of which it is part. Indeed, the murder of the concubine causes the subsequent war; it is the war's first episode, and it shows in exemplary fashion the deep relations between the private and the public domain. It is a good case for the priority of the murder stories over the political coherence; the latter would be futile without the former.

38. I use the word labor in the Freudian sense of "Arbeit" in order to stress that repression in a collective endeavor has to a certain extent the same status as the individual "dreamwork" (better translated as "dreamlabor") to which Freud applied his term. Not only is the story a "dream," but the readings are a recurrent, yet changing nightmare.

39. The commentator immediately adds that we should not take this as a sign that the Canaanites were literate. This defensiveness is typical, but it has a more interesting aspect. There are other, stronger signals in the book of a superiority in the development of the Canaanite civilization, the strongest one being the "chariots of iron" in chapters 4 and 5. This should be kept in mind whenever we encounter ideologemes that try to place the Israelite religion above the local ones as not simply different, but of a superior stage of development. See the analysis in *Murder and Difference* of commentaries that use words like "primitive" to describe the Canaanite religions. Given the results of the present analysis of the institutions of marriage that were in conflicting competition, it is not surprising that an ideologeme of dichotomistic evaluation of civilizations in terms of "higher" and "lower" would tend to be inscribed.

40. I translate this expression for rising anger literally because of its relation to fire and to the body. A more "normal," conventional translation is "and Yahweh became angry with Israel." See Appendix 2 at the end of this book.

41. This is striking in the reception of the Song of Deborah. This is a clear link between the political coherence and the countercoherence. The daughters, whenever the word is used in the plural, are the collective representation of the "daughter" as the victim in the "private" stories. They are the shifter between the two isotopies, the political and the private.

42. Of course, the question whether they really are independent or not is irrelevant. They are not real persons but textual figurations and can be interpreted as such. Since no dependency other than of Israel is mentioned, we must consider them as independent. As for action, they behave autonomously, as my proposal for a different translation of the verse implies.

43. An example of an excessive aestheticizing approach is Fokkelman's otherwise interesting book on David (1982). As I have tried to show in *Lethal Love*, Fokkelman cannot avoid taking ideological positions, and indeed, his book is at times bluntly moralistic. The literary approach in this narrow sense does not prevent those choices but, rather, provides them with an exculpatory alibi. Pretending to "describe" the text and to avoid moralism, the critic is not held accountable for judgments that are, and cannot avoid being, his own.

44. For an introduction to narratology as I conceive it, see Bal (1985). There are many other publications, and they all present different views of the field, different theories, different goals. An American introduction that I find flawed is Chatman (1978). Labov (1972) developed an interesting linguistic theory of narrative; see also Polanyi (1986). Prince (1983) is useful, but limited and focused on issues less applicable to ancient texts. Genette's most important contributions (1980) have been incorporated in my introduction (1985). Cohn's distinction between fiction and historical novel as presented in the 1986 Gauss lectures at Princeton is based on her earlier narratological work (1978). *Poetics Today, Style,* and *Poetics* have published special issues on narratology recently and regularly publish work in that field. For more information, see bibliographies in the works mentioned above.

45. In *Murder and Difference,* I discuss the relation between literacy and ideology and the relations between the narrative and the lyric genre and orality. I consider epic, even oral, as a first step of the narrative project that leads to writing and specifically historiography, a project that set in with early patriarchy. The placing of the Song of Deborah in a second position partakes of that project. Theories of ancient genres which claim priority for epic over lyric participate in it, too. See also Ria Lemaire (1987).

46. This is the technical term for the series of events that are presented in a story. See my *Narratology* for an explanation of the term and its theoretical background. The term is often used as a synonym of "story" or of "plot"; as some theories use the terms story and plot to distinguish between two levels while I work with three, I find them both confusing.

47. I use the term "subjectivity" in this technical sense, in spite of, or rather, because of, its ambiguity. I wish to enhance the deep relation between the linguistic possibility of saying "I," to speak one's history, to narrate, and the experience of subjectivity as a psychological dimension of life. The degree to which female characters in a culture are represented as speaking, as express-

ing their views, and as acting reflects the degree of subjectivity a society is ready to grant its women. See Bal (1986) for a discussion of this relation between narrative categories and social position.

48. Needless to say, such enterprises can be tremendously useful for other purposes. Trible's work (1978) is doubtless helpful for Christian women who wish to remain church-bound while revolting against their ecclesial status. Fuch's work (e.g., 1985) will be very satisfying for women who see expressed in it their anger toward their oppression. I do not question these and other uses of these works. It is within the clearly delimited purpose of the present study that I must reject their approaches.

49. See Ton Lemaire (1984) and the bibliography there. For a critique of the more specific gender aspects of the enterprise, see Ria Lemaire (1987).

50. The term focalizer is meant to replace the highly ambiguous term of "point of view." It refers to the subject from whose perspective the fabula is presented. This subject can, but need not, coincide with the identity of the narrator or speaker. See Bal (1985) for an exposition of the term; (1986) for a discussion and background.

51. If Samson identifies with the view expressed by the women, he is in fact willing to abandon himself to the Philistines. These come to stand in a different light, then. See *Lethal Love* (Bal 1987), chapter 2.

52. The few references to the Hebrew will always be carefully presented, so that noninitiated readers can easily follow and evaluate the argument. Moreover, Appendix 2 explains the choices I have made in translations.

Chapter Two

1. Sypherd (1948) documents the later rewritings in Western culture. Some of the rabbis insisted on her wisdom. See Slotki (1980, 258) for a quote to which he subscribes with enthusiasm: "The pathos of the situation and the readiness of her submission must elicit admiration."

2. The very fact that the speech-act is, first, superfluous for the action of the fabula as such; second, repeated in other instances; and, third, breathtakingly consequential, spoken solemnly, and religious, allows for the hypothesis that it is a ritual act.

3. I would not even go into this argument if it were not so popular. Scholars and Midrashic writers alike frequently interpret Yahweh's silence as a punishment. Jephthah took the risk that an unclean animal would be appointed for sacrifice. In this view, Yahweh's personal satisfaction is more important than the daughter's life. Moreover, there is hardly a clean animal that could be expected at all. For Pseudo-Philo's interesting Midrash on this point, see Baker (forthcoming).

4. This is not a decisive argument in either direction, since both this construction and the prepositional construction are possible. But it is because both are possible, and the one has always been chosen rather than the other, that I make it my point to try out the other. My countercoherence takes the form, on the microlevel, of a counterphilology.

5. Of the four cases where ʿalmah is used in the singular, only three

have possible relevance for this hypothesis. In Genesis 24:43, Eliezer recounts the story of his identification of Rebecca as the appropriate bride for Isaac. The interpretation of the word ʿalmah as already given is not very compulsive here, but not altogether impossible. It was Yahweh who had, in his prediction (another vow), already given her to the husband. The case of Exodus 2:8 is not relevant. Proverbs 30:19 supports my interpretation. Isaiah 7:14 uses the noun to refer to the mother of the king. Needless to say that this occurrence is most interesting. In light of the discussions where it is claimed that Mary's virginity came as a late mistranslation of *parthenos,* this case strongly supports both my interpretation and Mary's status as comparable to the other mothers of heroes who, when the birth of the hero becomes an issue, have not yet conceived: Sarah, Rachel, Samson's mother, Hannah . . . I am grateful to William Scott Green for pointing these cases out to me.

6. The sexual meaning of the "tree of knowledge," which is called at other times "the tree of life," is widely accepted. See the concluding chapter of *Lethal Love* for an analysis; see also Trible (1978) and Nyquist (1987). It is the woman who, in paradise, initiates the acquisition of sexual knowledge. The resulting misery is therefore blamed on her. Any man who requires virginity, then, can be seen as a new Adam who tries to keep the initiative to himself.

7. It is well known that these shifts are often due to the strict gender rules in the German grammar. It is not my purpose to criticize Freud for his own sake, but to criticize the general ideological background that his work exemplifies. The development of his language into one that makes this sort of shift so easy, or rather, so hard to avoid, is part of the development of ideology that we are concerned with here. Let it be clear that I am not just "picking on Freud" but reading an exemplary text—a contemporary Bible, as far as gender relations are concerned.

8. The term refers to an ideological unit. Often, those units take the form of some "logical" semantic structure, a dichotomy being the most obvious example. Greimas's semiotic square (1965) can be put to use to map out the implications of ideologemes. The logical appearance of ideologemes makes them very effective in our overtly rationalistic culture.

9. The term *collocation,* borrowed from linguistic pragmatism, refers here to the use of two or more expressions in an automatic combination. The one expression seems to entail the other, seems to be incomplete without the other, even though there is no semantic need for the two expressions. By extension, the term is used to show how two ideas, issues, concepts, etc. can be twinned, thus entailing a seemingly logical "consequence" that is not at all necessary.

10. This difference between the act—in the present—and the promise of future fulfillment will be discussed in chapter 6, where it will be used to differentiate the speech-act of marriage from the vow to kill.

11. To the question "why bother?" so often addressed to feminist literary critics of Freud by social scientists and historians, I answer: first, because in

spite of his exceptional genius and his eccentric ideas, his work is so representative of modern man; and second, because he provided us with the tools to undermine his biases and to expose his ideology and his interests. It is crucial for a profound understanding of culture that we do not ignore the tools the culture itself gives us, nor the leading structures of thought that founded the status quo to be criticized.

12. I cannot help reminding the reader of the painful connotation this possession of daughters by fathers has recently received.

13. Mary Jacobus's fascinating analysis (1986) of this same essay of Freud focuses on the part devoted to Hebbel's *Judith*; a significant sentence from Hebbel's text, quoted by Freud and then by Jacobus, has been quoted at the beginning of the present chapter. In the biblical book of Judith, the heroine's "virginity," her undefiled status that is, is explicitly mentioned, while of her counterpart Yael (Judges 4 and 5) it is alleged that she had intercourse with her victim (Zakovitch 1981). Van Dijk Hemmes (in preparation) extensively studies the changes in the concept which have taken place between Judges and Judith. I contend that Judith's place in Freud's essay is a core element in the rhetoric of the idea we are discussing, so much so that it can be seen as a *mise en abyme* of our ideology of femaleness as a whole. This term refers to a figure, popular in French theory and in modernist and postmodernist fiction, which represents a figurative summary of the overall story of which it is itself a detail. See Dällenbach (1977) and Bal (1986).

14. The essay on the uncanny will be a second subtext used to read the architecture of the book's "unhomeliness." Freud's use of the concept of uncanny here does not seem to fit entirely his own definition in the essay "The Uncanny." The confusion between the fear of defloration and the actual feeling of uncanniness, however, seems highly significant.

15. A most subtle understanding of the myth of Tobias can be found in the many drawings Rembrandt made of this myth. There, too, the story is about father and son, and the woman, first dreaded, is carefully isolated. See also Held (1969).

16. At least, in the view that predominates in Genesis. We will return to this issue later. It is helpful to realize how much the establishment of "proper" lineage is the major concern of Genesis, so much so, that we must assume it was not self-evident. There are many indications, indeed, that straight patriliny was not a firmly established custom but rather one in the process of establishing itself polemically against other systems. See Morgenstern (1929; 1931) and, for a suggestive analysis, Jay (1985). Ishmael's position as the son of the "Egyptian" woman and the forefather of the Arabic people turns the issue into a political one.

17. Strangely enough, my prejudice in favor of the Masoretic Text can be easily mistaken for fundamentalism, and therefore, I must insist on my motivations to leave the text alone. It may well be that other scholars come up— and indeed, have come up, in publications other than those I chose to work from—with convincing arguments for the emendations proposed by the com-

mentators. It is not for their decisions but for their motivations that I wish to explore the possibilities that emerge once we refrain from adopting the ideological tenets that underlie the emendations.

18. What Seidenberg calls renunciation can also be seen as repression. Chapter 7 will show why this repression of the mother is vital for Judges and how the repressed return in the book.

19. The distinction between narration and description can be considered from a linguistic (Banfield 1982), a pictural (Alpers 1983) or a literary (Bal 1982; Hamon 1982) perspective. I refer here to the narratological distinction: a representation of a *state* is a description; a representation of an *event* is a narration. The term description is meant to stress the visual aspect of the scene, the still-life character of the view Jephthah is confronted with. That view, which may be a repetition of an ancient, prehistorical view (Seidenberg 1966) of the mother's body, is the medusa-head that paralyzes Jephthah and submerses him in dread, anger, and mourning at the same time.

20. Here we can see, also, an intertextual allusion to the final strophe of the Song of Deborah, where Sisera's mother mistakenly celebrates the beautiful pieces of embroidery when rending her clothes would have been more appropriate. See chapter 7.

21. For an analysis of Joseph's story from a perspective different from but compatible with mine, see Regina Schwartz's wonderful article "The Bones of Joseph and the Resurrection of the Text" (1988).

22. See Turner (1969) for an analysis of the relation between the rites of transition in Turner's version and the experience of time. See also Bynum (1984) for a critique of Turner's concept of liminality. According to Bynum, liminality is gender-bound. The loss of status, status reversal, and status elevation are only relevant for those who have status in the first place and who will have access to status after the transition. This cannot be the case for women in those societies where women have no status or no possibility to change their status. The liminality of women, then, exists only in the view of them that men hold. See an application of this idea to Bath's story by Gerstein (forthcoming).

23. I would have called this the *patriarchal line*, if it were not for the crucial difference, in precisely this respect, between Genesis and Judges. The patriarchal line that is the central motivation of the patriarchal narratives in Genesis is either absent, or highly problematic, in the book we are studying. I said before that only sons provide offspring to their father; this remark must now be qualified. Only sons provide it within a patrilineal system; daughters are much more important for the father in a system where lineage is regulated differently. We will see shortly that this is, indeed, what I suppose to be at stake in Judges.

24. Usually, the plural "sons" is translated generically as "children," in the sense of "descendants." Such a translation is obviously correct. Within the framework of this study, however, it makes sense to translate it literally as "sons," because the activities ascribed to the "children of Israel" are invariably fighting and going astray, activities generally presented as male. Moreover, the

occurrence of "daughters" in the passage under scrutiny, as well as that of "mother in Israel" for Deborah, suggest we take these nouns as referring to gender-specific social roles. The very fact that the noun "sons" is, on the one hand, related to male activities, and on the other, traditionally interpreted as "children," implies a relevant conception of social roles and the domination of the male perspective there.

Chapter Three

1. It is obvious that the text only uses *zachar* in the sense of male; I chose to enhance the connection to memory because of the present discussion of virginity, as an intertextual reference to Freud's scientific opening paragraph. I insist, however, that the word for maleness does not allow us to "forget" the root of memory it holds.

2. See Blok (1982). The total insensitivity to what is happening is what I do not manage to understand. Of the authors of this collective book, fifty percent are women. The case I want to make here is for a feminist perspective as being more fruitful for even the purely scholarly endeavor. The evaluation "merry ending" obviously does not account for the issues involved and is based on anachronistic judgment.

3. Assuming too easily a relation would be thoroughly anachronistic. On the other hand, erasing any relation between the obviously central fact that to see, for a *gibbor*, is to catch a woman, and the excuse so often alleged by and for rapists, that the *sight* of the short-skirted girl made restraint impossible for them, would be missing a chance to understand how deeply rooted the relationship between sight and power must be. This relationship is foregrounded even in the oldest sources of the Lucretia legend, for example, in Livy and Ovid (Bal 1988b). See also Brownmiller (1975).

4. The irresistible association here is with the well-known visual pun in the rebus of the eye and the saw, meaning "I saw," the saw being as cutting an instrument of separation as the sword whose mouth kills as it kills "mouths" when seen . . . and to add the position of the reader, the visual pun fits the one Cynthia Chase uses (1986): "first I read, then eye saw."

5. Mary Douglas's pathbreaking work is relevant background literature here. Her work is so well known that I need not enter into its details here. I do not claim that Levitical law is the background of the events in Judges. It is not clear that the laws were already in place at the times of the conquests described in Judges; I take it that Leviticus is a representative symbolic expression of implicit taboos with a much more general tenacity.

6. If the opposition between not-really-married and properly married suggested here is valid, we have already mapped out the issue of marriage in its problematic aspects. Consider that Samson's failed bride is the second victim of the book, and, like Bath, she died by fire.

7. The casual use of the noun "concubine," equally latinate, equally sexual, and equally negative, justifies this strategic and temporary move.

8. Those critics who painstakingly argue that *'ednah* here means something other than sexual pleasure are in good company; the divine speaker of

the next sentence also tries hard to forget this particular challenge of the man's potency. This view can only be held if one also reconsiders the idea that the garden of Eden, whose name is derived from the same root, is not a pleasurable place.

9. Of course, strictly speaking, announcing a conception is not the same thing as fertilizing. But word and deed are the same in Hebrew, and, beginning with the creation, the biblical poetics emphasize the power of words on which its own status is based.

10. It is commonly assumed that in the Bible barrenness is always blamed on the woman and that men are presupposed to be both potent and fertile. I question this assumption; the quoted subversive doubts of Sarah is one case that leaves room for the marginal but persistent acknowledgment of the opposite view. Here, like elsewhere, I contend that the insistence on the one view—that barrenness is the woman's fault—addresses, and is an attempt to repress, the opposite possibility—that the men are impotent. The famous wife-sister stories in Genesis, where the "plagues" that strike the foreign ruler who takes the ʿalmah for wife are either not specified (in chapter 12) or related to impotence (chapter 20), are another case in point.

11. Samson does not die on the day the Nazirite vow is broken. The mother's power is restricted by Delilah's; see chapter 7 of this volume on this issue.

12. Staatliche Kunstsammlungen, Dresden. Rembrandt's biblical representations deserve a study that I am planning to undertake shortly. Needless to say, I am obviously not using the Rembrandt material as evidence but, just like Freud's essay, as an illuminating subtext through whose interaction with the Judges text we can understand which issues are addressed in the book's reception.

13. Stockholm National Museum.

14. The death of Sisera in turn alludes to giving birth. The women in biblical times appear to have given birth kneeling on two stones, the baby falling between their feet. The expression is commonly used in this sense. Samson sleeps between Delilah's feet when he is caught. I see in the expression—or its visual representation—a figuration of the close relation between mothering and lovemaking and, in Judges, murder of men by women. See chapter 7 of this study, and Lethal Love, chapter 2.

15. It is not necessary to agree with my interpretation, which admittedly leans toward one possibility rather than mapping out all possibilities, in order to pursue the question this chapter is addressing. It is only when all the figures have been discussed that the similarities between them make my case.

16. Strictly speaking, then, Samson breaks the Nazirite rule long before his death. It is only the sexual transgression, however, which Yahweh appears to resent, the haircutting being the direct consequence of his sexual "going astray" with Delilah.

17. This is further elaborated in Lethal Love, chapter 2, and in chapter 5 of the present study.

18. Verse 15:6 repeats and "publicizes" this motivation for the revenge.

19. Staatliche Kunstsammlungen, Dresden. Rembrandt's interpretation of this episode makes an unusually protofeminist use of the Christian tradition of typological interpretation.

20. Underlying these choices we see, of course, the split between the Jewish and the Christian traditions. On the one hand, such traditions are cultural facts that cannot be denied or ignored. On the other hand, the disastrous consequences of unreflected adherence to either one of these traditions are too well known to linger upon here. Yet, in the perspective of the present study, the most interesting notion that emerges from these divergent interpretations is the convergence of the two otherwise divergent and even hostile traditions when it comes to adopting commonplace, unsubstantiated, and persistent views of women. My adherence to the MT text is not adherence to the Jewish tradition, but a starting point that allows us to measure what has been done to this text and why.

21. Soggin (1981, 281) discusses a few suggestions to amend the text and to separate its sources, none of them serious and all of them uncalled for.

22. The vocabulary of all commentators is partial to this presupposition, which is more congenial to the nineteenth-century adultery novel than to the Book of Judges, where the concept of marriage itself is hardly understood. Boling has "run home," Soggin has "matrimonial crisis," and Trible has "desertion." As soon as we leave that assumption behind, the problems disappear.

23. This term, which puts the tendency to argue from the central position of the present, in parallel with androcentrism and ethnocentrism, was suggested to me by Margaretha Alexiou.

24. The reference of personal pronouns is not always clear. In the same story, the reference of "his" in verse 25 is not necessarily the same as that of "the man."

25. Again, only for those who adopt a specific ideology of sexual relations does the combination of "marriage" and "unfaithfulness" immediately suggest sexual promiscuity or adultery. There are many other possible connections, which may include solidarity or the lack thereof, much closer to other types of faithfulness; on the other hand, sexual intercourse with a person other than the spouse does not automatically entail a lack of solidarity.

26. It is in order to systematically compare the archaic form of patriarchy with the newer virilocal one that I keep the set of terms patrilocal versus virilocal marriage. Note that these terms refer to the spatial figuration of the institution, the *house*, which of course affects, but does not coincide with, the lineage. It is precisely the tension between "local" power and "temporal" power, between house as space and house as lineage, that informs this impressively violent book.

27. The expression "between men" is an allusion to the title of Eve Kosofsky Sedgwick's book (1985), entitled *Between Men*, on homosocial desire in the English novel.

28. We should not overestimate—nor, for that matter, underrate automatically—the freedom of movement the daughter might have had. There is

no indication in the text either that she went willingly to her husband because she felt like seeing him or that she was abducted, like the nubile women of Shiloh. Whatever the answer to this question, she is, *narratively*, the subject of the action, and instead of taking that as a clear sign of her "guilt" for the "matrimonial crisis," I suggest taking that as a signal of the ethnographic issue at stake: her autonomy *from the father* is signified in this act, whether or not she gained any autonomy in the absolute sense.

29. As Fokkelien van Dijk rightly remarked in a private conversation, this evaluation of patrilocal marriage as more drastically patriarchal may well be precisely what the rhetoric of the book tries to convey. The very fact that this woman apparently had the option to leave her father's house suggests that under the patrilocal regime, daughters had more autonomy than under the virilocal tradition.

Chapter Four

1. A proofreader's response made me aware that the ironic allusion to Freud's title "Contribution to the Psychology of Love," seemingly unpretentious, yet extremely pretentious in its generality, intended in the title of this chapter, might pass unnoticed. This would be the more regrettable as the irony goes together with a limitation of my title's meaning. Just as Freud could not possibly cover the entire field of psychology with the exclusively male content of his essays, just so, the present chapter does not really deal with ethnography *strictu sensu*, but rather with elements of the representation of fatherhood in a given culture which, if I were to adopt the same generalistic fallacy as Freud, I would have no less reasons than the latter to take as an ethnography.

2. The word "decomposed" is meant to draw attention to the "rotting" effect of taking apart what was whole, as in the case of Bath, her wholeness as a nubile woman; but also, the destructive effect of those philological gestures that take the text apart in a defensive decomposition. The term is borrowed from Cynthia Chase's book *Decomposing Figures* (1986) where the opposite, that is, the constructive effect of subtle analysis, is demonstrated; that is also one of my aims here.

3. To take the deaths of the three young women as sacrifices is, of course, an option among other possible interpretations. I chose to treat them as sacrifices because of sacrifice's relation to fatherhood and the anxieties about it. Thus the interpretation of the deaths as sacrifice helps to understand better the importance of the complex notion of fatherhood as their underlying motivation.

4. Cannibalism is a more relevant option in ancient mythology than is generally assumed. The story of the "fall" in paradise makes much more sense if it is related to cannibalism. According to Reed (1975), the primary goal of the test of the tree was to teach the humans to distinguish. Eating your own kind and mating with your own kin ultimately reflects a similar inability to distinguish.

5. And his act would be overtly incestuous. Sacrificing one's children is, then, also a repression of the desire of incest, closely related to cannibalism of an "incestuous" kind.

6. The Catholic practice of a real trade in sacrifice, the purchase of masses for the benefit of somebody's soul, which counts among the motivations for Protestant reform, is a clear case.

7. As we will see later, the two burnt victims are sacrificed for the sake of the father's possession of her, while the victim who is not burnt is killed for the sake of the husband's possession of her.

8. The textual genre of *problematic* sacrifice stories in this particular book, that is to say. I am not trying to establish a sociological typology of sacrifice; that has been done by others (Jay 1985). I am interested in the problematization of sacrifice, that, in this book, comes with a problematization of fatherhood and with the establishment of *gibbor*ship based on a different structure than in Genesis.

9. Naomi Schor (1984) analyzes a fascinating case of a sacrifice of a female victim, which undercuts Girard's theory in a similar way.

10. It is interesting to notice, then, that the narrative structure of the story is reversed compared to our expectations as readers of realist fiction. His sacrifice was *first* rejected, and *then* he makes the mistake of killing the wrong victim. This reversal is also at stake in the Eden story: the humans transgress *before* they possess the knowledge that is indispensable for transgression. This order of events is typical for mythical discourse; it is by no means exceptional in the Bible. The Book of Judges will be shown to have this structure at several crucial moments in the text.

11. There is much of the better-known matrilinear system in patrilocal marriage as I have defined it. Yet, as I pointed out earlier, the differences concern precisely the power of the father. Since matriliny is too often confused with matriarchy, I prefer the term patrilocy in order to avoid the illusion that mothers had more power than the book shows.

12. "Weak" *as* signification: they require existential grounds; symbolism is not enough. In a different sense they are, of course, "strong" precisely because they possess that existential basis. The competition between these two classes of signs, the existentially grounded ones and the arbitrary, purely symbolic ones, reflects the competition between motherhood and fatherhood, where, also, the "strong" existential relation (motherhood) is devaluated in favor of the "weak" symbolic relation, which becomes *thereby* the "strong" one.

13. This provides a more systematic basis to Marmesh's interpretation of certain Genesis stories as 'anti-covenant' (forthcoming).

14. See Marmesh (forthcoming) for a fine analysis of Sarah's subversive behavior. It is all the more interesting to underscore the subversive potential in Sarah's story because this figure has so often been taken as the model of the obedient wife, patiently waiting for her life's fulfillment to come in her old age, obediently remaining in her tent when the messengers come, and feeding

them properly. To take it strongly, Sarah's laughing in her tent recalls Deborah's enthusiastic celebration of Yael the tent-dweller and her subversive act. See *Murder and Difference*.

15. This difference between direct and rhetorical discourse is analyzed by Baker (forthcoming) in a study of Pseudo-Philo's rewriting of the story of Bath (he calls her Seila).

16. Although the deity has not asked for her, there is no indication that he does not accept her as sacrifice. Jephthah's military successes are pursued as before, and there is no sign whatsoever of the deity's disapproval.

17. Assuming an intertextual relation is not presupposing a chronological priority in either direction. Generally, we can suppose that both these and other similar but now unknown stories circulated in the basically oral culture.

18. Patai (1959, 147) reverses this problem by attributing either euphemism or lack of historical knowledge to the text: "ancient Hebrews who called Jephthah 'son of another woman' when in fact he was the son of a whore." The implication is that the modern scholar knows better what "really" happened than the text which is his sole source of information.

19. The status of Jephthah as a *head*, a permanent position, which he claims over against the temporary position of deliverer, is analyzed in more detail in *Murder and Difference*. The eagerness of this character to establish himself beyond temporary action is also a revolt against the divine ideology of election as it is represented in this book. He does not want to be elected by Yahweh in the arbitrary procedure that turns the hero into a blind instrument of divine predestination; he wants to negotiate, to fulfill his ambition and obtain, through speech-acts, a more permanent status based on more individual merit. This revolt against the divine plan and the instrumentalist view of the individual it entails is typical for this character.

20. Of course, this improperness only holds within the perspective of the Israelites, which, as I have argued, can easily be reversed in this story. Moreover, the perspective is limited to the party which, long after the events, edited the stories: the minority called by Smith the "Yahweh-alone movement" (1971).

21. This statement implies that there is a logical connection between treating a subject as an object and the readiness to sacrifice her. This connection is equally valid for modern situations of man-woman relations, with rape as one extreme, the "golden cage" at the other. It needs to be recalled that the idea of sacrifice subsists even where all elements of sacredness have disappeared. Sacrificing has become a well-rooted cultural element even in entirely desacrilized societies. The continuity between sacred, ritual sacrifice and worldly, but perhaps equally ritual because institutional sacrifice is spelled out in this chapter precisely because of its survival in modern society.

22. It is remarkable that this ideologeme has been so little noticed in its structural function. The other gender-related ideologeme that the book thematizes, the relation of the opposition honor-shame to male-female, is closely related to this one. It becomes prominent in the stories of the murderesses.

23. Although the rapists initially want him, not her, and actually never

ask for her, it is hopefully clear by now that I still consider her to be the object of a contest, the one between virilocy, represented by the Levite, and patrilocy, represented by the rapists who defend the rights of Beth's father. The host, standing in-between, since he lives in the patrilocal community but comes from the virilocal country like the Levite, here takes the side of the patrilocals, motivated perhaps by fear, perhaps by his position as father of a nubile daughter.

24. "Durative" is a term from narratology. It refers to events that take place over a longer stretch of time, as opposed to "punctual" events that take little time. "Writing a letter" is durative, "ringing the doorbell" is punctual. I could also have qualified the event "repetitive," another term of the series, but that would imply a different view of rape. In my sense, rape is an event that takes as long as the victim is in the rapist's power, not just the actual, physical rape.

25. This male bonding in violence against the other, female or otherwise different, is the underlying motivation of the violence of David against Uriah, in my interpretation of II Samuel 11. See *Lethal Love*, chapter 1. It is an important, frighteningly frequent phenomenon that has to be acknowledged more systematically.

26. This is, again, a "logic" that is recurrent, even today. The woman who announces her separation from the man she has been living with experiences it; suddenly, she is considered generally available. This is one of the motivations underlying this event, as the "logical" consequence of the "unfaithfulness" of the woman toward ("against") her "natural" owner, the father.

27. To use the term "durative" here may be illuminating. Death is generally conceived of as a punctual event; Beth's death has been turned into a durative one.

28. I have argued earlier that the pronoun-suffix in verse 2 is ambiguous and can refer to both father and husband. The verse means, then, both "she was unfaithful to her father [by going to live with her husband]" and "she was unfaithful to her husband [by returning to her father]," the two meanings being perfectly compatible if taken in sequence. I am here referring to the first meaning, in other words, the first episode of the sequence.

29. In chapter 6, which will deal with the *place* and the *house*, I will return to this moving scene. It is the matrix-scene of the spatial, architectural structure of the book. Although the place where this obviously symbolic event happens is extremely significant, the focus of the present discussion will be on the actions and nonactions of the characters involved.

30. If there is a way to redeem the story, it would be by its acknowledgment of its own horror. Any attempt to unwrite the compulsory narration of the durative destruction of Beth is an attempt to unwrite this horror. In my sense, every commentary I know of tries hard to accomplish this: leaving out narrative aspects that produce duration, conflating subject positions, overwriting the coherence of gender by the political coherence—all these strategies are evidence of the discomfort the story produces.

31. This is my argument in an analysis of rape, which juxtaposes Beth

with Lucretia, on the one hand, and with the rape victims in a few texts by women authors on the other. See Bal (1988b).

32. In the philosophy of Habermas, this kind of mastery falls under the "technical" knowledge of the natural sciences, while the interrelation between human beings would impose at least a form of "hermeneutical" knowledge. See Habermas 1972.

33. The intimate connection between the relation of mastery over nature and over women has been convincingly argued by Keller (1985) in her masterful *Reflections on Gender and Science*.

34. This connection between the events of chapter 19 and the bride-capture scenes has been suggested to me by Terasa Cooley, a student in my seminar on ideo-stories at the Harvard Divinity School, spring 1986.

Chapter Five

1. The term *constative illusion* or *constative fallacy* is derived from Austin's category of constative speech-acts, so often challenged (e.g., Derrida 1972) and from the metacritical slogans in New Criticism with which this book is implicitly polemic. For an excellent account of the discussion between Searle and Derrida on this subject, see Culler (1983, 110–25). I use the terms "illusion" or "fallacy" with the Austinian adjective "constative" to form a set with other fallacies of reading that we encounter in this study, like the *realist fallacy*, in its turn coined on the model of the well-known New Critical concept of the *intentional fallacy*, still quite lively among biblical scholars. My term refers to the illusion that there are constative speech-acts, pure of any performative aspect. This illusion allows claims about the "true" or "only" meaning of a text. It is also frequently used in everyday speech, where it functions as an exercise of power, such as when the claim that a statement is "just descriptive" prevents the challenge of its manipulatively selected content, or when an authoritative person gives to his subordinates the "right" interpretation of an expression at issue.

2. The power to misunderstand is not only crucial because it entails a position of participation in the communication process. Misunderstanding is, as Culler argues (1983), a central aspect of semiosis. Where Eco defined signs as everything that can be used in order to lie (1976), Culler stresses the other side of the same definition: a sign is everything that can be misunderstood. The Bible, with all the constative fallacies it gives rise to, makes a good case.

3. At the end of the play, Don Juan is killed by the statue that suddenly comes alive. Metonymically speaking, he is *touched* by stone and thus turned into stone, petrified: he is swallowed by the earth.

4. It seems discouraging that Don Juan becomes material when he ceases to speak. His materialization replaces speech, although the contiguity between the two does make a case for materiality. Symmetrically, Beth speaks when she is become sheer materiality: dead flesh.

5. For a discussion of the term *scandal* in relation to its material concretization in literature, see Schor 1984.

6. The terms "repetitive" and "singular" form a set with "iterative" and

have to be placed in the same framework, which I explained earlier, as "durative" and "punctual." Repetitive is an event that occurs several times while it is presented several times; iterative means that the oft-occurring event is presented once, and singular means that the event happens once and is presented once (see Bal 1985).

7. It is in the interaction between commentators and text that we see Gallop's (1984) point, that the relation of transference between text and reader must be in constant exchange. If the commentator is the analyst who points out the slips in the text—traditionally called copyist errors—the text is the commentator's analyst as well, in that the confrontation between the two displays the commentator's transference onto the text which irritates, worries, frightens or seduces him.

8. For this reason I have insisted, in the previous chapter, that the translation of the execution of Bath be translated literally: he *did* unto her the vow that he had vowed=done. From speech-act, the vow is turned into real murder, but the speech-act already held in itself the death of the victim.

9. This "touchy" relation between speech-act and the real is precisely where its importance lies for the establishment of fatherhood.

10. As I have suggested earlier, the distinction between asymmetry and dissymmetry is crucial for this study. The word asymmetry refers to an absence of symmetry, while dissymmetry refers to a relevant relation wherein the expected and "logical" symmetry is replaced by a distortion of it, a distortion that allows power to take its place between the two related subjects.

11. Bettelheim (1976) suggests that riddles in fairy tales represent the secret of femininity, not only in their answer, but that the very act of posing riddles is a gesture of curiosity about that secret. The Samson saga is generally considered a mythical folktale of a genre quite similar to fairy tales.

12. I use the term *vow* for all conditional promises of a gift. A vow is verbalized with its condition and is a narratively central speech-act. Narratively, the crucial feature of the vow is the inexorable fulfillment once the condition is fulfilled; thus, it promotes the narrative. For the purpose of this study, the distinction between secular gifts and sacred vows—gifts to Yahweh—otherwise important, must be considered irrelevant; it only blurs the structural similarity between the different vows whose objects are invariably women.

13. To know and to possess, both expressions for the sexual encounter from the male perspective, are thus intimately related. One cannot possess what one does not know, for how can one know whether or not one possesses it? And one cannot give what one does not possess, hence, giving the unknown is a priori an act of abuse.

14. We have here an obvious case where neither ethnocentrism nor cultural relativism can respond adequately; the event is clearly in accordance with social traditions and can only be criticized when distanced from the context. I do not want to argue that it should not be criticized; it should be, but on a different level than the other events that I call "improper." It is only when a distinction such as this is carefully made that we can establish the

system of values that is inscribed in the book, which is a preliminary condition to critique.

15. Here is again the question of evaluating a different cultural practice. The first of the two abduction scenes implies so much violence, however, that the negative value judgment, if implicit, is not impossible. For the problem of evaluation in critique as opposed to ethnocentrism, see Ton Lemaire 1982 and Fabian 1982.

16. I use the term body language in the simple sense of meaningful semiosis acted out, not by linguistic behavior but by semiotic behavior of any part of the body. In order for any act to be body language, it has to be primarily nonverbal, bodily, and it has to allow for interpretation as sign, as standing for something else, that is.

17. This is a strong argument, both for my interpretation of the crucial issue in the book, and for the so-called prologue to be considered an important element of the book as a whole. The structure of the book is then generated by this ideal, but impossible, first case, which shows, precisely in its "proper" details, where and why future exchanges will have to go awry. As will become apparent shortly, the symmetry between Achsah's and Beth's stories, hence, between the beginning and the end of the book, makes a case for a reading of the book with a strong, and ideologically self-imposing, (counter-)coherence.

18. This view of the book's composition, as based on a core scene that contains both the ideals and the virtual conflicts further elaborated in the other stories, corresponds to what I try to establish as an alternative composition called "architectural"; see chapter 6. Gooding's analysis (1982) is the extant one that comes closest to mine, although its symmetrical basis is different, and the relations between the political and the domestic spheres are not worked out in detail in his article. His is the most convincing structural analysis of the book I have come across.

19. The first one of these two verbs reoccurs in the Samson story and receives from that context a typically female meaning. The other one occurs also in chapter 4, describing, there, either Yael striking Sisera's brain into the ground, or Sisera's brains oozing out into the ground. Aside from the precise meaning, these other occurrences seem interesting.

20. Here, too, I do not mean to take the reader into the specialized discussion for its own sake; I take philology as a business, as a socially anchored enterprise. Hence, I am again more interested in the speech-acts of the critics—in their turn considered not for their own sake but as representatives of a group—than in the intrinsic scholarly value of their results.

21. The repetition between the two passages is verbal, but will not concern us here.

22. Metathesis is a reversal of consonants, assumed to be due to a copyist error.

23. It is striking that these "wandering rocks" deal with some form of both self-confidence and self-assertion. It is equally striking that modern commentators so often tend to explain them away or ignore them.

24. Reversing the perspective and taking Achsah's story as an integrative part of the countercoherence is easier than keeping it within the political coherence. The gift of Achsah is just another shifter from the one unto the other; the claim she makes in this mini-story, however, has no obvious relation with the political coherence. This is no reason to confine the story to the private domain, since Achsah's claim concerns the possessions of her descendance. Hence, this is one of many examples where the opposition between private and public is untenable.

25. This can be seen in relation to Bath's first appearance; the comerforth out of the doors of the house is here, the comer toward the house.

26. The verb is an imperfect *hiph'il*. The Masoretic manuscript (MT) has the feminine with a masculine object, while the Septuagint and the Vulgate have reversed it, supposedly because of the illogical sequel, where Achsah is again the subject. The question of the subject is again a revealing one. In isolation, the case would, of course, be less troubling than it is in combination with the numerous other subject questions that turn out to be gender questions. This is a structural cause for philology's trouble to deal with gender, since philology shuns macrostructural considerations.

27. The entire footnote runs as follows: "The verb usually denotes 'persuasion to do evil, enticement.' Here it might be rendered 'coaxed him to give her permission.' It was her suggestion, and the execution of the plan devolved upon her." Needless to say, first, the verb does not necessarily denote enticement to evil; second, the question of permission is not denoted anywhere in the text; and third, the word "plan" introduces the idea of plotting that is uncalled for. We must conclude that the footnote is another typical instance of the use of philology for ideological purposes.

28. It is a particular ideologeme that critics have traditionally written into the book—Yael and Delilah exemplifying it—but that, in my sense, is not at all so often at stake as is generally claimed.

29. Many commentators, and Soggin (1981) is the most extreme case, go back and forth between the Hebrew text and the Greek Septuagint, as it suits their interpretation. Soggin quite often just amends the text, without saying where the correction comes from, and often enough, it comes from himself alone. Of all my sample commentators, he is both the most authoritative and scholarly in tone and the least verifiable in argumentation. For example, the traditional meaning of the verb is in the quoted statement called "manifestly absurd," while the argument, the impossibility of attributing a negative verb to the ideal judge, is not mentioned. A less informed reader will easily assume that there is a linguistic argument at stake, which is then assumed to be too obvious to be mentioned. Thus, the nonspecialized reader will both buy the statement and feel more insecure, hence, will be more vulnerable to the next manipulations.

30. The fact that it is so obviously disturbing indicates a resistance against otherness, which comes close to ethnocentrism. The resistance is so strong that imposing this translation would close the text off; readers would simply refuse to accept it. I would not exclude the possibility, however, that in

the cultural context the act of breaking wind was used as a speech-act to express contempt.

31. Again, the visual aspect of the scene helps us in understanding it. Visual imagination is obviously crucial for a meaningful reading of the stories and an important tool for the interpretation of difficult—because foreign, ancient, or otherwise "other"—texts.

32. The term *shifter* comes from linguistic theory, where it denotes words or aspects that cannot be interpreted without reference to the speech-situation. More generally, it points at elements that allow for transitions between units, like isotopies, narrative situations, coherences.

33. In other words, a sign is always part of a "text," a syntactically and semantically related set of signs that is perceived as a whole by the interpreter.

34. The term *phatic function* is one of six that Jakobson (1960) introduced in his model of communication. The phatic function is that aspect of a speech-act that refers to the speech-situation itself; usually, expressions are meant which check the success of the communication itself. In the case of Achsah's gesture, it *opens* the communication.

35. It is this phatic expression that is totally lacking in Jephthah's communication with Bath at his return. Therefore, we can assume that his self-indulgent accusation of her is in fact an inner speech, or functions as one; it is not addressed to her as a standard communicational act would be.

36. Patrick D. Miller, Jr. drew my attention to this verb, whose significance for the construction of the countercoherence is considerable. His thoughtful and sympathetic response to a previous version of this analysis has been an important encouragement to me.

37. Explaining the story of Beth as etiological, as an explanation *a posteriori* of the intertribal war, is an act of imposing the political coherence into a position of dominance.

38. In *La volonté de savoir* (1976), Foucault convincingly argues the inseparability of language and sexual experience, indeed, the formative effect of the former on the latter. It is obvious that Alter misses this relation. As a result, he comes close to the absurd and homophobic assumption that the entire population of the town of Sodom was driven by homosexual desire. The repression of the linguistic presence of homosexual rape in Judges 19, on the other hand, is also evidence of the realistic fallacy.

39. Rape being motivated by hatred, not by lust, men who hate and fear women and their attraction to women will rape women, while men who hate and fear other men and their attraction to other men will rape men. Homophobia and heterocentrism parallel gynophobia and androcentrism.

40. This interpretation rests on two grounds, which would both be dubious if isolated: the assumption that the Levite's deviation was known to the rapists, and the "empirical content" of the interpretation—the number of otherwise incomprehensible details it helps us to understand. The first ground is historical and runs the risk of the realist fallacy; the second is literary and comes close to the convention of unity. To the first charge, I respond by refer-

ring to the genre of mythical narrative that, although fictional, emerges out of real, social concerns. I do not attribute knowledge to the rapists as characters, but to the audience which would make such an assumption. To the second charge I respond that unlike my sample commentators, I have consistently respected "problematic" details and based my interpretation on their very problematic nature; but to leave things at that would be missing a chance to understand a culture other than our own precisely in regard to the status of women. This is exactly what vulgar deconstruction is usually blamed for.

41. In a psychoanalytic framework, the rejection of her can also be seen as abjection, not just abjection of her as a woman but more specifically, as the crucial figure in the line, the mother-to-be. Beth's ʿalmah-hood, which makes her hover between positions, allows for this rejection-abjection. See Kristeva 1982.

42. This happens three times, in Genesis 12:12–16; 20:2; 26:7. In each case, the wife is given as the husband's sister, which arguably she is. The recurrence of this wife-sister motif is a sign that the motif needs further explanation. In the framework of my interpretation of Judges, these wife-sister stories can also be related to the transition between types of marriage. I would not too easily criticize the patriarchs' behavior without assessing the social habits underlying it, but defending Beth's husband's behavior on this basis seems pushing cultural relativism too far. Brenner's interpretation of the wife-sister stories, which includes the view that the second and the third are explanatory Midrashim addressing the gaps in the first, is the most appealing one I know (Brenner 1987).

43. Passwords are paradoxical with respect to meaning. On the one hand, it is their meaninglessness that makes them appropriate as passwords, since it guarantees that they cannot be inferred or guessed by others. On the other hand, some—secret, or seemingly irrelevant—meaning gives the password often an encouraging connotation, as a secret language that strengthens the group.

44. Abimelech's name will be discussed in chapter 6, for it is intimately connected to the problematic of the father-house.

45. The noun "heart" reminds of the expression "to speak to her heart" in verse 3. There, it referred to the site of reason, and the expression meant "to persuade her" rather than "to speak kindly to her." If we take it that the heart has a similar function here, the father's words might suggest that the husband be more reasonable, that he accept the house of bread as a better place to be and the father-house as the appropriate place for the daughter to be.

Chapter Six

1. The "reality" referred to is, of course, the semifictional reality of the mythical fabula. I am not concerned with the factual reality status of that fabula, but only with its content as collective fantasy, which, as I argued in chapter 1, does respond to a real-life background. If reality is part of what I am looking for, it is that historical-anthropological reality only. For the sake of

readability, I will simply refer to this background as reality, omitting, in subsequent uses of the term, the quotation marks.

2. There is some risk of anachronism in imposing the political-domestic opposition in terms close to public-private (Rosaldo 1980). Yet, the possibility that the house is a function of this opposition, and of its breakdown, is relevant for the overall conception of the book that I am working out.

3. See Franco (1985); see also Scarry (1985) for an in-depth analysis of the importance of the house in the production of pain as a support of power.

4. Franco studied the invasion of the domestic sphere by the political domain. Father-daughter rape is another instance where safety within the home is an illusion that is used against the victims, first to preclude their understanding of the situation, then, to blackmail them into hiding it. This case shows clearly that the oppositions themselves are constructions produced in order to preserve maximal inequality.

5. The upper room or the cool room where the murder takes place is considered to be the bathroom. If Eglon's guards did not suspect the murder, it was because they assumed the king was relieving himself. This story, of which little is said in this study, fits into the countercoherence in many respects. The riddle and trick, the danger within the house, and the subsequent discrimination, at the shore of the river, between enemies and partisans are only a few examples. The most remarkable aspects are perhaps the concrete bodily details of the murder. The penetration of the two-sided sword in the fat belly of the king is not without connections to the sexual representations of murder that will be discussed in chapter 7.

6. The better-known opposition between polytheism and monotheism is of course also a site of this self-definition. In light of the hypothesis worked out in this study, it might be plausible that this religious opposition is basically an aspect of the anthropological opposition, and perhaps one of its consequences. The structure of the monotheistic ideology is so clearly isomorphic with the virilocal-patrilineal system that it might well be its symbolic exteriorization.

7. This is one reason to agree with van Dijk's (personal communication) earlier mentioned suggestion that, in spite of the pressure in the book in favor of the virilocal ideology, the position of women may have been relatively freer in the patrilocal system. When still fully patrilocal, Beth was free to move around, to visit her husband, while her life is threatened only when she is recuperated by the virilocal husband.

8. As in my two previous studies, I use the Greimasian design to show problems, not to solve them; to illuminate the deceptive "logic" of ideologemes, not to establish some reliable, semiotic logic. See Greimas 1965, 1970.

9. Laban's protest against Jacob's departure, in Genesis, is a clear indication that there is a real struggle at stake. Laban is Jacob's mother's brother, hence, a matrilineal housekeeper, but the focus of the story is on the competition between the two men that ensues from the difference between the two systems. It is only because Jacob outwits his shrewd father-in-law that he manages to get away with his "theft" of the father's property, his children, and that

he can become a hero of (virilocal-patrilineal) Israel, in spite of his deceptions. This is another case that shows us how out-of-place our moral judgments can be in a context so different from our own.

10. Genesis 34 shows the limits of this situation. The story of the rape of Dinah is also the story of the sons taking over the power of the father. Jacob, the son who has been patrilocal for a long time, is also the weak virilocal father who cannot handle his sons' ambitions to replace him in sexual and in familial matters. His sons, in this episode, act as patrilocal sons, whose duty it is to protect their sister (although their way of protecting her can be more than questioned). Thus the sons show that the house has been contaminated by patrilocal tendencies.

11. Metaphor is reassuring because it works as a mirror. The subject recognizes the sameness of the same-sex child, while the subject's relation to the other-sex child is more problematic, less obviously visual, hence, more dependent on enforced contiguity.

12. Genesis represents the idealized view of how things *should* be, while Judges represents a more real background, the struggle for that ideal state. Of course, this difference is relative; Judges is also, to a large extent, imagined. Yet, the imaginary character of the book does adopt the contradictions more openly in order to act the conflict out and master it subsequently. Judges is not only probably an older text than Genesis (although scholars are less certain about this than they used to be), but also it represents an older phase in the construction of the people. In other words, even if the text as it stands turns out to be younger than has been assumed, the traditions it is built upon deal with the traumatic experiences that precede those of the patriarchal stories of Genesis.

13. For Slotki, "it is obvious that hereditary kingship was intended" (1980, 229). The attempt, which underlies this unwarranted statement, to match the negation of kingship in the final chapters and its establishment in the Books of Samuel partakes of exactly the same ideology of historiography as legitimation that we are concerned with here. Both "obvious" and "intended" are questionable scholarly notions.

14. Patrilocal marriage implies matrilineal descent. As I have suggested earlier, I chose to use the residence terms rather than those referring to descent because the latter tend to overrate the power of the woman and, hence, to obscure the issue of competition between the two systems, which is a competition between men.

15. The expression "from his body begotten" refers clearly to a social, not a physical, specificity. The son of the "other woman" is also physically "from his body begotten," but the contiguity signified in the *house* as a social construct makes for the status of sons as "bodies" of their father.

16. This sentence contains two significant expressions. We know now how heavy the implications of "to remember" are, especially in relation to descent. The reference to Genesis 2 also makes the sentence crucial. There, too, the identity of one's bone and one's flesh was the token of kinship. And if we take the Genesis verse at the letter, the marriage form alluded to is pa-

trilocy: the son leaves his parents to cleave to his woman('s house). If we add the case of Ruth who "clave to her mother-in-law," patrilocy becomes even more predominant and may be the first meaning of the verb "to cleave," which would then simply mean "to go and live in the woman's house."

17. The ways that exclusion takes place vary. Sometimes, stories are called etiological, as in the case of Bath's sacrifice. Apparently etiology threatens chronology; hence those stories are not taken seriously into account. In other cases, they are called legendary, hence, not "real" enough to be counted. This is alleged of the Samson cycle. The most interesting exclusion is that of the three final chapters, excluded because they have no "judge" or "deliverer" to speak of. Here, the mythical unity of the book receives historical status and is turned against everything that does not "fit." Needless to say, all the exclusions concern stories of women.

18. For an extensive analysis, see *Murder and Difference*. In the Song of Deborah, the antichronological composition is the most obvious; the poetics of that text require a semiotic attitude that we are not used to, so that we might appreciate its movement, its accents, and its meaning. I will briefly return to this problem in chapter 7.

19. This is the poetic reason why the question of whether or not Jephthah "knew" is irrelevant; the episode must be read in the opposite direction, from the later climax to its earlier preparation.

20. For a view of Bath's request as a rite of transition, see Keukens (1982) and the excellent interpretation by Gerstein (forthcoming). Gerstein makes much more of the idea of transition. She interprets the spatial details of the text and criticizes the exclusively male perspective in Turner's account (1967) of the rites. See also Bynum (1984) for such a critique.

21. In the traditional translations, "the woman his concubine," the same effect is present. Moreover, if the idea of concubine does have any sense in this story, it would be here: spatially taken, the woman does *lie* (cubine) in contiguity (con) with the man, the door closed between them being the function of the "concubinage." With some imagination, then, we can see in this particular moment the figuration of the transition from the relatively respectable status of patrilocal wife to the lowly status of concubine. If the scene is moving and seems to enhance the woman's impossible position in one perspective, in the other perspective it is an ideological imposition of a new view of this type of now "abnormal" woman.

22. This fallen state requires that a *gibbor* fall to avenge her; see chapter 7 on Sisera's fall. The symmetry is striking: both falls are represented in highly poetic imagery and are widely read as symbolic.

23. This translation does not keep the ambiguity in the German word, which was already lost in "uncanny." The advantage over the latter is simply the reference to the house, which lies at the basis of the German word, and the relevance of which this chapter means to show.

24. It is this detail in the plot, and the moment when the arrival of the lover is *not* the end of her ordeal, that makes this movie, *Voice in the Mist*, more uncanny than its classic model, *Gaslight*.

25. These forms of uncanniness occur frequently in houses of father-daughter rape (see Ward [1985]), as well as in titillating movies that come close to pornography.

26. See Elizabeth Wright's (1984) introduction to psychoanalytic criticism for a discussion of Lyotard's view. Freud's analysis of "The Sandman" is also discussed there.

27. Although the comparison is absurd in many ways, in just this respect we may think of the opening scene of the movie *E. T.*, where the vulnerable, because exiled, and little E.T. is watching, from below, the impressive legs and the noisy keys of the policeman. The success of that scene lies precisely in this focalization by the victim of the legs of his persecutor.

28. The term house-daughter was suggested to me by Mercy Oduyoye. She used it to refer to the position of the eldest daughter in her own matrilinial—and clearly patrilocal, in my sense—Akhan society in Ghana. The term implies the parallel with house-wife, and rightly so, since like house-wives, house-daughters are fully responsible for the house-hold. They are also house-daughters in the kinship sense, so acutely problematic in Judges, since the children they may produce belong to their fathers; they are also house-held.

29. This is one way in which the women murderers can be seen as reversing and subverting the power relations: they speak, take initiative to speak, and speak more, and better, than the men they deal with.

Chapter Seven

1. Although I am aware that this word is slightly awkward, it expresses so adequately the idea at stake that I persist in using it. Murder is not simply gender-related; it is almost identical with gender. Gender is defined through murder; hence, murder is gendered.

2. Brooks's conception of narrative as pushed forward by the ambition of its heroes is problematic as a generalization, especially as it tends to repress female roles. It is, however, illuminating for the ambition-narratives in Judges.

3. This seems an appropriate place to remind the reader of Elisabeth Schüssler Fiorenza's book *In Memory of Her* (1982). Although her method, object-text, and philosophical and ideological positions are different from mine, Schüssler Fiorenza pursues a similar goal: to reinscribe women's past back into cultural history.

4. This statement has to be qualified in two senses. First, the notion that the book has an overall ideology simply means that we can argue a dominance of one ideology over the other(s). There is no monolithic ideology in any text, let alone in a collection coming from disparate sources. Second, it is part of this dominating ideology to also show, in order to "conquer" them, the other sides, the problems inherent to its own stance. In that respect, the very term of "dominant ideology" is misleading.

5. We have seen earlier that there is no religious unity in the Hebrew Bible, and even not within the limits of the Book of Judges. We must remember that the book emerged from extremely varied traditions. Even if the editors who put the book together in roughly its present form explicitly defend

the Yahweh-alone line, and if that line by then may be assumed to support the now-established virilocal tradition, they have not been able to wipe out traces of different deities and different stands, perhaps simply because the struggle I am trying to bring to the fore had lost its relevance.

6. Manoah is located in Zorah, Danite territory (13:2). His wife lives with him, in his tribe. The fact that she conceives (receives the message of the conception of) her son outside the house is a slight trace of conflict at the one end of Samson's life; the transportation of his body to his father's house at the other end confirms that his adult (*gibbor*) life was spent elsewhere: in patrilocal houses.

7. This woman reminds us of the *zonah* Rahab, the heroic woman who saves the Israelite spies in Joshua 2. It is not clear whether Rahab lives with her father, but she is apparently on good terms with him, as she wins the safety of the father-house as a whole.

8. Scarry (1985) provides an excellent analysis of the relation between the body and its limits in Judaism, and the way the image of God is influenced by that relation. The curse befalls him whose name—a symbolic sign—recalls the icon instated by the deity himself in Genesis 1:27 but later tabooed.

9. I will not repeat the extensive analysis of this murder scene. See *Murder and Difference* and its bibliography for evidence of the extremely strong emotional response this passage of the song has triggered. Especially in comparison with the rationalizations on chapter 19, this different treatment is revealing.

10. A more thematic interpretation of the woman-at-the-window places this passage in a wider tradition which includes Homeric epic.

11. "Ce sont des femmes, d'où l'insistence sur les étoffes coloriées et brodées" (They are women, hence the insistence on colored, embroidered cloth).

12. This word, then, stands on a line with *bethulah*, as the latter's contemptuous variant. As we have seen, sexual ripeness means, in the eyes of the *gibbor* and his representatives, sexually abusable.

13. There is no reason to exonerate the Hebrew culture from this behavior; nor does it make sense to accuse the Israelites specifically. It is the male perspective, rather than any specific national party, that is criticized here.

14. It is not clear at which stage of the transmission of the text this title of honor has been incorporated. But as elsewhere, we are not concerned here with the philological, text-historical debate, but with an interpretation and, to a certain extent, explanation of the collection of Judges as it has been put together and as it has reached us through the Masoretic Text.

15. The Song of Deborah is generally acknowledged to be one of the oldest texts of the Bible, while the end of Judges 11, the passage on Bath's ritual commemoration, is seen as the insertion of an older tradition (see Richter 1964).

16. In *Lethal Love* I have argued that the perspective of the final scene

can be reversed when we assign focalization to Samson, not to the spectator who overviews the entire scene. From the perspective of the man standing there, the pillars can be related to the thighs of the mother, which the child pushes aside at birth. This psychoanalytic interpretation, not compelling but interesting, can be applied to the scene of Abimelech's death as well. This perspective establishes yet another link between the three male victims: they all die as failed babies under the spell of a mother figure.

17. This image is represented in *Femmes imaginaires* (Bal 1986). The gesture makes an impression of tenderness mainly because the fingers of the man are crossed, as if to do a subtle haircut. As a consequence, the man bends over the sleeping Samson.

18. I can only refer to *Murder and Difference* for a long list of distressingly biased critical statements. To give only one example, Yael is referred to by one critic as a "bloodthirsty lady."

Conclusion

1. An encouraging exception is the experimental journal *Semeia*, which does pay attention to speech-act theory, to the sociohistorical background, and to the orality-literacy debate which is related to the view advocated in this study.

2. This is an allusion to Peter Brooks's book *Reading for the Plot* (1983), wherein the author develops what he calls a dynamic model of narrative which is based on the push toward the end, desired yet delayed. This model applies particularly well to Judges.

3. I wish to insist once more on the valuable contribution to a feminist anthropology by Nancy Jay, whose forthcoming book gives such convincing evidence for the bond between sacrifice and fatherhood, for the latter as motivating the former, that no other theory of sacrifice can stand without integrating this view.

4. For the views of the individual in societies other than our own, see Foucault (1984) and Vernant (1987). The socially oriented classification proposed by Foucault in *Le souci de soi* distinguishes (1) the place of the private individual as autonomous from the rest of the group she or he belongs to; (2) the valorization of private life as distinguished from the public domain; (3) the "souci de soi" proper: the practice by which the individual takes the self as an object of preoccupation. Vernant proposes a more psychological reformulation of these categories, and distinguishes (1) the individual, his role and place within the group; (2) the subject of speech, the "first person"; (3) the "ego" or self-reflexive individual. Translated into narratological categories, this becomes (1) the individual as object of narration, the "third person"; (2) the individual as subject of narration or focalization, the "first person"; (3) the metasubjective subject: the I reflecting on itself.

5. I have not really ignored the political background, but underscored the other elements of the background. I consider the political domain a derivative of the social, rather than the other way around.

6. This is the first category of the narratological classification of individuals. This category contains all three daughter-victims, although they each succeed in outgrowing that position at times.

7. Some commentators do pay attention to the background, like Niditch (1982) for example, but they treat it as alien, distant, and incidental. There is no awareness of the inevitability of the event as produced by that background. In fact, we should no longer call it background; the social stratification and the institutions become actants in the story, powerful agents that generate the events.

8. The clearest case of a third-category individual is Deborah, who reflects on her status as a subject when she refers to herself as "I, Deborah, a mother in Israel." In contrast with this self-consciousness and self-confidence, we can see Jephthah's outcry when he sees his daughter. He immediately turns himself into an object—you have brought me to kneel—rather than reflecting on his own self as subject of the feelings he himself generated.

9. He claims that the expression "at the days of Yael," although unambiguous in the Hebrew text, has to be amended into "in the days of the yoke," just because he, Alberto Soggin, does not find use for the expression as it stands.

10. Titles of biblical books are later additions. It would be an easy way out to claim that the book has received its title on the basis of a misinterpretation. This assumption, found also in judgments about the redactors, rests on an evolutionist and parontocentric bias. There is no justification to assume that everybody who dealt with the Bible before our era was stupid. Rather, it would be useful to reconsider the concept of justice and judging on the basis of what the book has to say.

11. I devoted a chapter to this problem of the function of the judge and the theory of the two types, those in the list and those whose activities have engendered the title "deliverers," in *Murder and Difference*. Today I would even more strongly argue that the theory that is still taken seriously by major biblical scholars has been invented to get rid of the "problem" of Deborah, the only female judge. The results of the present study strongly confirm that earlier intuition.

12. She cannot be a *gibbor* since that concept is fraught with masculine values and stakes. Basically, the reason why Deborah is a problem as a judge is precisely, I think, because she escapes the notion of *gibbor*. She is not, however, beyond violence and does actively participate in the war. Prejudices about the "nature of the feminine" do not stand against this character.

BIBLIOGRAPHY

Albrektson, B. 1967. *History and the Gods.* Lind: Gleerup.

Albright, William F. 1922. "The Earliest Forms of Hebrew Verse." *Journal of the Palestine Oriental Society* 2:69–86.

———. 1968. *Yahweh and the Gods of Canaan.* Garden City, NY: Doubleday.

Alexiou, Margaret, and Peter Dronke. 1971. "The Lament of Jephthah's Daughter: Themes, Traditions, Originality." *Studi Medievali,* 3d series, 12 (no. 2): 819–63.

Alonso-Schökel, L. 1961. "Erzählkunst im Buche der Richter." *Biblica* 42: 143–72.

Alpers, Svetlana. 1983. *The Art of Describing: Dutch Art in the Seventeenth Century.* Chicago: The University of Chicago Press.

Alphen, Ernst van. 1985. Review of Thomas Docherty, *Reading (Absent) Character: Towards a Theory of Characterization in Fiction* (New York, Oxford University Press, 1985). *Poetics Today* 6 (no. 4): 777–80.

———. 1987. *Bang voor schennis? Inleiding in de ideologiekritiek.* Utrecht: Hes Publishers.

———. 1988. *Bij wijze van lezen. Verleiding en verzet van Willem Brakmans lezer.* Muiderberg: Coutinho.

Alter, Robert. 1981. *The Art of Biblical Narrative.* New York: Basic Books.

———. 1984. *Motives for Fiction.* Cambridge, MA: Harvard University Press.

———. 1985. *The Art of Biblical Poetry.* New York: Basic Books.

Auerbach, Erich. 1930. "Untersuchungen zum Richterbuch I." *Zeitschrift für die Alttestamentliche Wissenschaft* 48:286–95.

———. 1933. "Untersuchungen zum Richterbuch II. Ehud." *Zeitschrift für die Alttestamentliche Wissenschaft* 51:47–51.

———. 1957. "Odysseus' Scar." In *Mimesis,* 1–20. New York: Doubleday & Co.

285

Auld, A. G. 1975. "Judges I and History: A Reconsideration." *Vetus Testamentum* 25:261–85.

Austin, J. L. 1975. *How To Do Things with Words.* Cambridge, MA: Harvard University Press.

Auzou, G. 1966. *La force de l'Esprit. Etude du livre des Juges.* Paris: Cerf.

Baab, O. J. 1962a. "Virgin." In *The Interpreter's Dictionary of the Bible,* edited by George Arthur Buttrick et al., vol. 4, 787–88. Nashville, TN: Abingdon Press.

———. 1962b. "Concubine." In *The Interpreter's Dictionary of the Bible,* edited by George Arthur Buttrick et al., vol. 4, 666. Nashville, TN: Abingdon Press.

Bachelard, Gaston. 1949. *La psychanalyse du feu.* Paris: Gallimard.

———. 1964. *The Poetics of Space.* Translation by Maria Jolas, with a foreword by Etienne Gilson. New York: Orion Press.

Baker, Cynthia. Forthcoming. "Pseudo-Philo and the Transformation of Jephthah's Daughter." In *Anti-Covenant: Counter-Reading Women's Lives in the Hebrew Bible,* edited by Mieke Bal. Sheffield, UK: Almond Press.

Bal, Mieke. 1982. "Mimesis and Genre Theory in Aristotle's *Poetics.*" *Poetics Today* 3 (no. 1):171–80.

———. 1985. *Narratology: Introduction to the Theory of Narrative.* Translated by Christine van Boheemen. Toronto: The University of Toronto Press.

———. 1986. *Femmes imaginaires: L'ancien Testament au risque d'une narratologie critique.* Utrecht: HES; Montréal: HMH; Paris: Nizet.

———. 1987. *Lethal Love: Literary Feminist Interpretations of Biblical Love-Stories.* Bloomington: Indiana University Press.

———. 1988a. *Murder and Difference: Genre, Gender and Scholarship on Sisera's Death.* Bloomington: Indiana University Press.

———. 1988b. *Verkrachting verbeeld: Seksueel geweld in cultuur gebracht.* Utrecht: HES.

Baley, Lloyd R., Sr. 1979. *Biblical Perspectives on Death.* Philadelphia: Fortress Press.

Banfield, Ann. 1982. *Unspeakable Sentences.* London: Routledge and Kegan Paul.

Barr, James, 1959. "The Meaning of 'Mythology' in Relation to the Old Testament." *Vetus Testamentum* 9:1–10.

———. 1962. *Biblical Words for Time.* London: SCM.

———. 1974. "After Five Years: A Retrospect on Two Major Translations of the Bible." *The Heythrop Journal* 15:381–405.

Barthel, P. 1967. *Interprétation du langage mythique et théologie biblique.* Leiden: Brill.

Barthes, Roland. 1970. *S/Z.* Paris: Editions du Seuil.

Beecher, W. J. 1984. "The Literary Form of the Biblical History of the Judges." *Journal of Biblical Literature* 103:3–28.

Berlin, Adele. 1985. *The Dynamics of Biblical Parallelism.* Bloomington: Indiana University Press.

Bettelheim, Bruno. 1976. *The Uses of Enchantment.* New York: Knopf.

Blenkinsopp, J. 1963. "Structure and Style in Judges 13–16." *Journal of Biblical Literature* 82:65–76.

Blok, Hanna et al. 1982. *Geen koning in die dagen. Over het boek Richteren als profetische geschiedschrijving.* Baarn: Ten Have.

Boling, Robert G. 1975. *Judges: A New Translation with Introduction and Commentary.* Garden City, NY: Doubleday & Co. (The Anchor Bible).

Bourgignon, Erika. 1979. *Psychological Anthropology.* New York: Holt, Rinehart and Winston.

Brams, Steven J. 1980. *Biblical Games: A Strategic Analysis of Stories in the Old Testament.* Cambridge, MA: M.I.T. Press.

Bremond, Claude. 1972. *Logique du récit.* Paris: Editions du Seuil.

Brenner, Athalya. 1987. Public lecture given at the University of Utrecht. University of Haifa, Israel.

Brooks, Peter. 1983. *Reading for the Plot: Design and Intention in Narrative.* New York: Alfred A. Knopf.

Brown, Francis, S. R. Drivers, and Charles A. Briggs. 1962. *A Hebrew and English Lexicon of the Old Testament.* Oxford: Clarendon Press.

Brownmiller, Susan. 1975. *Against Our Will: Men, Women and Rape.* New York: Simon and Schuster.

Brueggemans, W. 1972. "Weariness, Exile and Chaos: A Motif in Royal Theology." *Catholic Bible Quarterly* 34:19–38.

Bruns, J. E. 1954. "Judith or Jael?" *Catholic Bible Quarterly* 16:12–14.

Buss, Martin J. 1978. "The Idea of Sitz in Leben. History and Critique." *Zeitschrift für die Alttestamentliche Wissenschaft* 90 (no. 2):157–70.

———. 1981. "An Anthropological Perspective upon Prophetic Call Narratives." *Semeia* 21:9–30.

Bynum, Caroline Walker. 1984. "Women's Stories, Women's Symbols: A Critique of Victor Turner's Theory of Liminality." In *Anthropology and the Study of Religion,* edited by Robert L. Moore and Frank E. Reynolds. Chicago: Center for the Scientific Study of Religion.

Carroll, Robert P. 1979. *When Prophecy Failed: Dissonance in the Prophetic Traditions of the Old Testament.* New York: Seabury.

Chase, Cynthia. 1986. *Decomposing Figures: Rhetorical Readings in the Romantic Tradition.* Baltimore: Johns Hopkins University Press.

Chatman, Seymour. 1978. *Story and Discourse: Narrative Structure in Fiction and Film.* Ithaca, NY: Cornell University Press.

Childs, Breward S. 1986. *Introduction to the Old Testament as Scripture.* Philadelphia: Fortress Press.

Clark, Kenneth. 1978. *An Introduction to Rembrandt.* Newton Abbot, Devon: Readers Union.

Cohen, A., ed. 1980 (1950). *Joshua & Judges.* The Soncino Books of the Bible. Translation of Hebrew text by Jewish Publication Society of America. London, Jerusalem, New York: The Soncino Press.

Cohn, Dorrit. 1978. *Transparent Minds: Narrative Modes for Presenting Consciousness in Fiction.* Princeton: Princeton University Press.

———. 1986. "Fictional versus Historical Lives." Gauss Lectures, Princeton University (unpublished).

Coogan, M. D. 1978. "A Structural Analysis of the Song of Deborah." *The Catholic Bible Quarterly* 40:132–66.

Crenshaw, J. L. 1974. "The Samson Saga: Filial Devotion or Erotic Attachment?" *Zeitschrift für die Alttestamentliche Wissenschaft* 86:470–504.

———. 1978. *Samson: A Secret Betrayed, a Vow Ignored.* Atlanta, GA: John Knox Press.

Crim, Keith. 1976. "Virgin." In *The Interpreter's Dictionary of the Bible*, edited by George Arthur Buttrick et al., vol. 9, 939–40. Nashville, TN: Abingdon Press.

Cross, F. M. 1973. *Canaanite Myth and Hebrew Epic.* Cambridge, MA: Harvard University Press.

Crown, A. D. 1961–62. "A Reinterpretation of Judges 9 in the Light of Its Humor." *Abi-Nahrain* 3:90–98.

Culler, Jonathan. 1983. *On Deconstruction: Theory and Criticism After Structuralism.* London: Routledge and Kegan Paul.

Culley, Robert C. 1976a. *Studies in the Structure of Hebrew Narrative.* Philadelphia, PA: Fortress Press.

———. 1976b. "Oral Tradition and the OT: Some Recent Discussions." *Semeia* 5:1–33.

Dalen, Aleida G. van. 1966. *Simson.* Assen: van Gorcum.

Dällenbach, Lucien. 1977. *Le récit spéculaire. Essay sur la mise en abyme.* Paris: Editions du Seuil.

Davies, Douglas. 1985. "An Interpretation of Sacrifice in Leviticus." In *Anthropological Approaches to the Old Testament*, edited by Bernard Lang, 151–61. Philadelphia, PA: Fortress Press.

Davies, G. Henton. 1962. "Vows." In *The Interpreter's Dictionary of the Bible*, edited by George Arthur Buttrick et al., vol. 4, 792–93. Nashville, TN: Abingdon Press.

Delay, Jean. 1973–74. *La jeunesse d'André Gide*, 2 vols. Paris: Corti.

Derchain, P. 1970. "Les plus anciens témoignages de sacrifices d'enfants chez les Semites occidentaux." *Vetus Testamentum* 20:351–55.

Derrida, Jacques. 1972. *Marges de la philosophie.* Paris: Minuit.

———. 1976. *Of Grammatology.* Translated by Gayatri Chakravorti Spivak. Baltimore: John Hopkins University Press.

———. 1978. *Writing and Difference.* Translated by Alan Bass. Chicago: The University of Chicago Press.

———. 1986. "Shibboleth." In *Midrash and Literature*, edited by Jeffrey Hartman and Sanford Budick, 307–47. New Haven: Yale University Press.

Dexinger, Ferdinand. 1977. "Ein Plädoyer für die Linkshänder im Richterbuch." *Zeitschrift für die Alttestamentliche Wissenschaft* 89 (no. 2): 268–69.

Dhorme, Edouard. 1956. *La Sainte Bible. L'Ancien Testament.* Paris: Editions de la Pléiade.

Dijk-Hemmes, Fokkelien van. 1983. "Een moeder in Israel." *Wending* 9: 688–95.

————. In preparation. "Blessed among the Women: An Intertextual Study of a Label." University of Utrecht, Netherlands.

Dillenberger, Jane. 1985. "George Segal's *Abraham and Isaac*: Some Iconographic Reflections." In *Art, Creativity and the Sacred*, edited by Diane Apostolos-Cappadona, 105–24. New York: Crossroad.

Dougherty, Molly C. 1978. "Southern Lay Midwives as Ritual Specialists." In *Women in Ritual and Symbolic Roles*, edited by J. Hoch-Smith and A. Spring, 22–34. New York: Plenum.

Douglas, Mary. 1966. *Purity and Danger*. New York: Praeger.

Driver, G. R. 1957. "Problems of Interpretation in the Pentateuch." *Mélanges bibliques rédigés en l'honneur d' André Robert*. Paris: Travaux de l'Institut Catholique de Paris IV.

Dupont-Roc, Rosalind, and Jean Lallot. 1980. *Aristote. La poétique*. Paris: Editions du Seuil.

Eco, Umberto. 1962. *L'Opera aperta*. Milan: Bompiani.

————. 1976. *A Theory of Semiotics*. Bloomington: Indiana University Press.

Eissfeldt, O. 1910. "Die Rätsel in Jud 14." *Zeitschrift für die Alttestamentliche Wissenschaft* 30:132–34.

————. 1963. "Der Geschichtliche Hintergrund der Erzählung von Gibeas Schadtat (Richter 19–21)." In *Kleine Schriften* II, 64–80. Tübingen: Mohr.

Exum, J. Cheryl. 1980. "Promise and Fulfillment: Narrative Art in Judges 13." *Journal of Biblical Literature* 99:43–59.

————. 1983. "The Theological Dimension of the Samson Saga." *Vetus Testamentum* 33:30–45.

Fabian, Johannes. 1982. *Time and the Other: How Anthropology Makes Its Object*. New York: Columbia University Press.

Felman, Shoshana. 1980. *Le scandale du corps parlant*. Paris: Editions du Seuil.

————. 1981. "Rereading Femininity." *Yale French Studies* 62:19–44.

Fensham, F. C. 1980. "A Few Observations on the Polarization Between Yahweh and Baal in I Kings 17–19." *Zeitschrift für die Alttestamentliche Wissenschaft* 92:227–36.

Finnegan, Ruth. 1974. "How Oral Is Oral Literature?" *Bulletin of the School for Oriental and African Studies* 37:52–64.

Fokkelman, J. 1982. *King David*. Assen: van Gorcum.

Foucault, Michel. 1976. *La volonté de savoir*. Paris: Gallimard.

————. 1984. *Le souci de soi*. Paris: Gallimard.

Fox, Michael V. 1981. "Job 38 and God's Rhetoric." *Semeia* 19:53–61.

Franco, Jean. 1985. "Killing Priests, Nuns, Women, Children." In *On Signs*, edited by Marshall Blonsky, 414–20. Baltimore: Johns Hopkins University Press.

Freud, Sigmund. 1973 (1900). *The Interpretation of Dreams*. In vol. 5 of *The Standard Edition of the Complete Psychological Works of Sigmund Freud*, edited and translated by James Strachey. London: The Hogarth Press Ltd.

———. 1957 (1918). "The Taboo of Virginity." In vol. 11 of *The Standard Edition*, 191–208.

———. 1981 (1919). "The Uncanny." In vol. 17 of *The Standard Edition*, 219–56.

Fuchs, Esther. 1985. "The Literary Characterization of Mothers and Sexual Politics in the Hebrew Bible." In *Feminist Perspectives on Biblical Scholarship*, edited by Adela Yarbro Collins, 117–36. Decatur, GA: Scholars Press.

———. 1988. "For I Have the Way of Women: Deception, Gender, and Teleology in Biblical Narrative." *Semeia* 42:68–83.

Gallop, Jane. 1984. "Lacan and Literature: A Case for Transference." *Poetics* 13 (4/5):301–8.

Geertz, Clifford. 1973. "Ethos, World-View, and the Analysis of Sacred Symbols." In *The Interpretation of Cultures*, 126–41. New York: Basic Books.

———. 1983. "From the Native's Point of View: On the Nature of Anthropological Understanding." In *Local Knowledge*, 55–71. New York: Basic Books.

Genette, Gérard. 1979. *Introduction à l'architexte*. Paris: Editions du Seuil.

———. 1980. *Narrative Discourse: An Essay in Method*. Translated by Jane E. Lewin. Ithaca, NY: Cornell University Press.

Gennep, Arnold van. 1960. *The Rites of Passage*. Chicago: The University of Chicago Press.

Gerstein, Beth. Forthcoming. "A Ritual Processed: A Look at Judges 11:40." In *Anti-Covenant: Counter-Reading Women's Lives in the Hebrew Bible*, edited by Mieke Bal. Sheffield, UK: Almond Press.

Geus, C. H. J. de 1965–66. "De richteren van Israel." *Nederlands Theologisch Tijdschrift* 20:81–100.

Gibson, Arthur. 1976. "SNH in Judges 1:14: NEB and AV Translations." *Vetus Testamentum* 26:275–83.

Girard, René. 1972. *La violence et le sacré*. Paris: Grasset.

Globe, Alexander. 1975. "Judges V 27." *Vetus Testamentum* 25:362–67.

Gooding, D. W. 1982. "The Composition of the Book of Judges." *Eretz-Israel* 16:70–79.

Gray, John. 1986. *Joshua, Judges, Ruth*. New Century Bible Commentary. Basingstoke: Marshall, Morgan & Scott Publishers, Ltd.

Green, Alberto Ravinell Whitney. 1975. *The Role of Human Sacrifice in the Ancient Near East*. Decatur, GA: Scholars Press.

Greimas, Algirdas Julien. 1965. *Sémantique Structurale*. Paris: Larousse.

———. 1970. *Du sens*. Paris: Editions du Seuil.

Gruber, Mayer I. 1980. *Aspects of Nonverbal Communication in the Ancient Near East*. Rome: Biblical Institute Press.

Gunn, David M. 1974. "Narrative Pattern and Oral Tradition in Judges and Samuel." *Vetus Testamentum* 24:286–317.

Habel, Norman C. 1964. *Yahweh versus Baal.* New York: Twayne.

――――. 1976. "Appeal to Ancient Traditions as a Literary Form." *Zeitschrift für die Alttestamentliche Wissenschaft* 88 (no. 2):253–74.

Habermas, Jürgen. 1972. *Knowledge and Human Interests.* London: Heinemann.

Hamon, Philippe. 1977. "Pour un status sémiologique du personnage." In *Poétique du récit,* edited by R. Barthes et al., 115–80. Paris: Editions du Seuil.

――――. 1982. *Analyse du discours descriptif.* Paris: Hachette.

Held, Julius. 1969. *Rembrandt's Aristotle and Other Rembrandt Studies.* Princeton: Princeton University Press.

Hempel, J. 1953. "Glaube, Mythos und Geschichte im Alten Testament." *Zeitschrift für die Alttestamentliche Wissenschaft* 65:109–67.

Hirsch, Marianne. Forthcoming. "Clytemnesta's Children." Dartmouth College.

Hubert, H., and M. Mauss. 1968. "Essai sur la nature et fonction du sacrifice." In *Oeuvres,* edited by M. Mauss. Paris.

Hyde, Lewis. 1983. *The Gift: Imagination and the Erotic Life of Property.* New York: Vintage Books.

Jacobson, Richard. 1981. "Satanic Semiotics, Jobian Jurisprudence." *Semeia* 19:63–71.

Jacobus, Mary. 1986. *Reading Woman.* New York: Columbia University Press.

Jakobson, Roman. 1960. "Linguistics and Poetics." In *Style in Language,* edited by Thomas A. Sebeok. Cambridge, MA: MIT Press.

Jameson, Fredrick. 1981. *The Political Unconscious: Narrative as a Socially Symbolic Act.* London: Methuen.

Janzen, J. Gerald. Forthcoming. "A Certain Woman in the Rhetoric of Judges 9." Indiana University, at Indianapolis.

Janzen, W. 1972. *Mourning Cry and Woe Oracle.* Berlin: De Gruyter.

Jay, Nancy. 1985. "Sacrifice as Remedy for Being Born of Woman." In *Immaculate and Powerful: The Female in Sacred Image and Social Reality,* edited by Clarissa W. Atkinson, Constance H. Buchanan and Margaret R. Miles, 283–309. Boston: Beacon Press.

――――. Forthcoming. "Throughout your generations forever." Ph.D. diss., Harvard Divinity School.

Johnson, Barbara. 1980. *The Critical Difference: Essays in the Contemporary Rhetoric of Reading.* Baltimore: The Johns Hopkins University Press.

Katzenstein, H. J. 1981. "Some Remarks Concerning the Succession to the Rulership in Ancient Israel (The Period Until the Davidic Dynasty)." *Proceedings of the 7th World Congress of Jewish Studies,* 29–39. New York: Studies of the Bible and the Ancient Near East.

Keller, Evelyn Fox. 1985. *Reflections on Gender and Science.* New Haven: Yale University Press.

Keukens, K. H. 1982. "Richter 11.37f: Rite de passage und Übersetzungsprobleme." *Biblische Notizen* 19:41–42.

Koehler, L., and W. Baumgartner. 1958. *Lexicon in Veteris Testamenti Libros.* Leiden: Brill.

Korsten, Frans Willem. 1986. "Brunhilde's voorbeeld." In *Ik zing mijn lied voor al wie met mij gaat: Vrouwen in de volksliteratuur,* edited by Ria Lemaire, 183–98. Utrecht: Hes Publishers.

Kristeva, Julia. 1982. *Powers of Horror: An Essay on Abjection.* New York: Columbia University Press.

Kugel, James. 1981. *The Idea of Biblical Poetry: Parallelism and Its History.* New Haven: Yale University Press.

Labov, William. 1972. *Explorations in Semantic Theory.* The Hague: Mouton.

Leach, Edmund. 1985. "The Logic of Sacrifice." In *Anthropological Approaches to the Old Testament,* edited by Bernard Lang, 136–50. Philadelphia: Fortress Press.

Lemaire, Ria. 1987. *Passions et positions: Contribution à une sémiotique du sujet dans la poésie lyrique médiévale en langues romanes.* Amsterdam: Rodopi.

Lemaire, Ton. 1982. *Over de waarde van culturen: Een inleiding in de kultuurfilosofie.* Baarn: Ambo.

———. 1984. "Antropologie en schrift. Aanzetten tot een ideologiekritiek van het schrift." In *Antropologie en ideologie,* edited by Ton Lemaire. Groningen: Konstapel.

Lévi-Strauss, Claude. 1964. *Le cru et le cuit (Mythologiques I).* Paris: Plon.

———. 1967. *Les structures élémentaires de la parenté.* The Hague: Mouton.

Licht, Jacob. 1978. *Storytelling in the Bible.* Jerusalem: Magnes Press.

Lindars, B. 1971. "Some Septuagint Readings in Judges." *Journal of Theological Studies* 22:1–14.

———. 1983. "Deborah's Song: Women in the Old Testament." *Bulletin of the J. Ryl University Library,* 65 (no. 2):158–75.

Lindblom, J. 1963. "Die Vorstellung vom Sprechen Jahwes zu dem Menschen im Alten Testament." *Zeitschrift für die Alttestamentliche Wissenschaft* 75:263–88.

Lipinski, Ed. 1967. "Juges 5, 4–5 et Psaume 68, 8–11." *Biblica* 48:185–206.

Long, Burke O. 1976a. "Recent Field Studies in Oral Literature and Their Bearing on Old Testament Criticism." *Vetus Testamentum* 26:187–98.

———. 1976b. "Recent Field Studies in Oral Literature and the Question of *Sitz im Leben.*" *Semeia* 5:35–49.

———. 1981. "Social Dimensions of Prophetic Conflict." *Semeia* 21:31–53.

Lyotard, Jean-François. 1983. "Appendix: Answering the Question: What Is Postmodernism?" In *The Postmodern Condition: A Report on Knowledge.* Minneapolis: University of Minnesota Press.

McCarthy, D. J. 1969. "The Symbolism of Blood and Sacrifice." *Journal of Biblical Literature* 88:166–76.

———. 1973. "Further Notes on the Symbolism of Blood and Sacrifice." *Journal of Biblical Literature* 92:205–10.

McCurley, F. R., Jr. 1968. "A Semantic Study of Anatomical Terms in Akkadian, Ugaritic and Biblical Literature." Ph.D. diss., Dropsie College.

McKane, W. 1958. "The Gibbor Hayil in the Israelite Community." *Transactions of the Glasgow University Oriental Society* 17:28–35.

McKenzie, J. L. 1963. "The Hebrew Attitude toward Mythological Polytheism." In *Myths and Realities: Studies in Biblical Theology*, 133–45. London: Chapman.

———. 1966. *The World of the Judges*. Englewood Cliffs, NJ: Prentice Hall.

Malamat, A. 1955. "Doctrines of Causality in Hittite and Biblical Historiography: A Parallel." *Vetus Testamentum* 5:1–12.

———. 1976. "Charismatic Leadership in the Book of Judges." In *Magnalia Dei—The Mighty Acts of God: Essays in Memory of G. Ernst Wright*, 152–68. Garden City, NY: Doubleday & Co.

Margulies, H. 1974. "Das Rätsel der Biene im Alten Testament." *Vetus Testamentum* 24:56–76.

Margulis, B. 1965. "An Exegesis of Judges V 8 a." *Vetus Testamentum* 15: 66–69.

Marmesh, Ann. Forthcoming. "Anti-covenant." In *Anti-Covenant: Counter-Reading Women's Lives in the Hebrew Bible*, edited by Mieke Bal. Sheffield, UK: Almond Press.

Martin, James D. 1975. *The Book of Judges*. Cambridge: Cambridge University Press.

Mauss, Marcel. 1968. *Oeuvres*. Paris: Minuit.

Mayes, A. D. H. 1969. "The Historical Context of the Battle against Sisera." *Vetus Testamentum* 19:353–60.

Mendelsohn, I. 1954. "The Disinheritance of Jephthah in the Light of Paragraph 27 of the Lipit-Ishtar Code." *Israel Exploration Journal* 4:116–19.

Milgrom, J. 1976. "Sacrifice and Offerings, Old Testament." *The Interpreter's Dictionary of the Bible*, edited by George Arthur Buttrick et al., vol. 9, 763–71. Nashville: Abingdon Press.

Miller, Patrick D. 1965. "God the Warrior: A Problem in Biblical Interpretation and Apologetics." *Interpretation* 19:39–46.

———. 1973. *The Divine Warrior in Early Israel*. Cambridge, MA: Harvard University Press.

Money-Kyrle, R. E. 1965. *The Meaning of Sacrifice*. London: L. and V. Woolf and the Institute of Psycho-analysis; New York: Johnson Reprint Corporation.

Morgenstern, Julius. 1929. "*Beena* Marriage (Matriarchat) in Ancient Israel and Its Historical Implications." *Zeitschrift für die Alttestamentliche Wissenschaft* 47:91–110.

———. 1931. "Additional Notes on '*Beena* Marriage (Matriarchat) in Ancient Israel.'" *Zeitschrift für die Alttestamentliche Wissenschaft* 49:46–58.

Muller, H.-P. 1970. "Der Begriff 'Rätsel' in Altem Testament." *Vetus Testamentum* 20:465–89.

Naastenpad, Th. I. M. n.d. (1975). *Simson*. Kampen: Kok.

Nicholson, E. W. 1977. "The Problem of *shinah*." *Zeitschrift für die Alttestamentliche Wissenschaft* 89 (no. 2):259–65.

Niditch, Susan. 1982. "The 'Sodomite' Theme in Judges 19–20: Family, Community and Social Disintegration." *Catholic Bible Quarterly* 44: 365–78.

Nielson, Ed. 1961. "La guerre considerée comme une religion et religion

comme une guerre. Du Chant de Déborah au Rouleau de la Guerre."
Studia Theologica 15:93–112.

Nohrberg, James. 1988. "Ideology of Election." In *The Bible and Critical Theory*, edited by Regina Schwartz. Oxford: Basil Blackwell's.

Nyquist, Mary. 1987. "Gynesis, Gensis, Exegesis, and the Formation of Milton's Eve." In *Cannibals, Witches, and Divorce: Estranging the Renaissance*, edited by Marjorie Garber, 147–56. Baltimore: Johns Hopkins University Press.

Orlinsky, Harry M. 1942. "Critical Notes on Gen 39.14–17, Jud 11.37." *Journal of Biblical Literature* 61:87–97.

Overholt, Thomas W. 1981. "Prophecy: The Problem of Cross-Cultural Comparison." *Semeia* 21:56–78.

Patai, Raphael. 1959. *Sex and Family in the Bible and the Middle East*. Garden City, NY: Doubleday & Co.

Penna, A. 1961. "The Vow of Jephthah in the Interpretation of Saint Jerome."·*Studia Patristica* 4. Texte und Untersuchungen 79, Ost Berlin, 162–70.

Perdue, Leo G. 1981. "Liminality as a Social Setting for Wisdom Instructions." *Zeitschrift für die Alttestamentliche Wissenschaft* 93 (no 1): 114–26.

Polanyi, Livia. 1986. *Telling the American Story: A Cultural and Structural Analysis*. Norwood, NJ: Ablex.

Polzin, Robert M. 1977. *Biblical Structuralism: Method and Subjectivity in the Study of Ancient Texts*. Philadelphia: Fortress Press.

———. 1980. *Moses and the Deuteronomist*. New York: Seabury Press.

Pomata, Gianna. 1983. "Die Geschichte der Frauen zwischen Anthropologie und Biologie." *Feministische Studien* 2 (no. 2): 113–28.

Porter, J. R. 1963. "Samson's Riddle: Judges 14.14–18." *Journal for Theological Studies*, n.s., 13:106–9.

Power, E. 1928. "He Asked for Water, Milk She Gave (Iud. 5,25)." *Biblica* 47:6–8.

Prince, Gerald. 1983. *Narratology: The Form and Function of Narrative*. Berlin, New York, Amsterdam: Mouton Publishers.

Rabin, C. 1955. "Judges V,2 and the 'Ideology' of Deborah's War." *Journal for Jewish Studies* 8:125–34.

Radday, Y. T. (in collaboration with G. M. Leb and L. Nazitz). 1977. "An Analytical Linguistic Key-Word-in-Context Concordance to the Book of Judges." *The Computer Bible*, vol. 11. Wooster, England: Biblical Research Associates (285 p.)

Reed, Evelyn. 1975. *Women's Evolution: From Matriarchal Clan to Patriarchal Family*. New York: Pathfinders Press.

Richter, Wolfgang. 1963. *Traditionsgeschichtliche Untersuchungen zum Richterbuch*. Bonn: Peter Hanstein Verlag GmbH, Bonner Biblische Beiträge 18.

———. 1964. *Die Bearbeitung des 'Retterbuches' in der deuteronomistische Epoche*. Bonn: Peter Hanstein Verlag GmbH, Bonner Biblische Beiträge 21.

———. 1965. "Zu den 'Richter Israels.'" *Zeitschrift für die Alttestamentliche Wissenschaft* 77:40–71.

―――. 1966. "Die Uberlieferungen um Jephtah. Ri 10.17–12.6." *Biblica* 47:485–556.

Ricoeur, Paul. 1967. *The Symbolism of Evil.* Boston: Beacon Press.

―――. 1975. "Biblical Hermeneutics." *Semeia* 4:27–148.

―――. 1976. "Psychoanalysis and the Work of Art." In *Psychiatry and the Humanities,* edited by Joseph H. Smith, 33–56. New Haven: Yale University Press.

―――. 1978. "The Narrative Function." *Semeia* 13:177–202.

Rogerson, J. W. 1978. *Anthropology of the Old Testament.* Oxford: Basil Blackwell's.

Rosaldo, Michelle Z. 1980. "The Use and Abuse of Anthropology: Reflections on Feminism and Cross-Cultural Understanding." *Signs* 5 (no. 3): 389–417.

Rösel, Hartmut N. 1977. "Zur Ehud-Erzählung." *Zeitschrift für die Alttestamentliche Wissenschaft* 89 (no. 2):270–72.

―――. 1980. "Jephtah und das Problem der Richter." *Biblica* 61:251–55.

Scarry, Elaine. 1985. *The Body in Pain: The Making and Unmaking of the World.* New York: Oxford University Press.

Schor, Naomi. 1984. *Breaking the Chain: Women, Theory and French Realist Fiction.* New York: Columbia University Press.

Schulte, H. 1972. "Das Richterbuch." In *Die Entstehung der Geschichtschreibung im Alten Israel,* 77–105. Berlin: de Gruyter.

Schüssler Fiorenza, Elisabeth. 1982. *In Memory of Her.* New York: Crossroad.

Schwartz, Gary. 1985. *Rembrandt: His Life, His Paintings.* New York: Viking Penguin Inc.

Schwartz, Regina. 1988. "Joseph's Bones and the Resurrection of the Text: Remembering in the Bible." *PMLA* 103 (no. 2): 114–24.

Scullion, John J. 1984. "Märchen, Sage, Legende: Towards a Clarification of Some Literary Terms Used by Old Testament Scholars." *Vetus Testamentum* 34 (no. 3):321–36.

Sedgwick, Eve Kosofsky. 1985. *Between Men: English Literature and Homosocial Desire.* New York: Columbia University Press.

Segert, Stanislaw. 1984. "Paranomasia in the Samson Narrative in Judges XII–XVI." *Vetus Testamentum* 34 (no. 4):454–61.

Seidenberg, Robert. 1966. "Sacrificing the First You See." *The Psychoanalytic Review* 53:49–62.

Semeia. 1988. Special Issue edited by J. Cheryl Exum. "Reasoning with the Foxes: Female Wit in a World of Male Power," 42.

Simon, Bennett. 1978. *Mind and Madness in Ancient Greece.* Ithaca, NY: Cornell University Press.

―――. 1987. "Tragic Drama and the Family: The Killing of Children and the Killing of Story-Telling." In *Discourse in Psychoanalyis and Literature,* edited by Shlomith Rimmon-Kenan, 152–75. New York: Methuen.

Simpson, Cuthbert Aikman. 1958. *Composition of the Book of Judges.* Oxford: Oxford University Press.

Slotki, Judah J. 1980. "Judges: Introduction and Commentary." In *Joshua & Judges*, edited by A. Cohen. Translation of Hebrew text by Jewish Publications Society of America. London, Jerusalem, New York: The Soncino Press.

Smith, Morton. 1971. *Palestinian Parties and Politics that Shaped the Old Testament.* New York: Columbia University Press.

Snaith, N. H. 1957. "Sacrifices in the Old Testament." *Vetus Testamentum* 7:308–17.

Soggin, J. Alberto. 1981. *Judges.* London: SCM Press.

Spiegel, Y., ed. 1972. *Psychoanalytische Interpretation biblischer Texte.* München: Kaiser.

Sternberg, Meir. 1985. *The Poetics of Biblical Narrative: Ideological Literature and the Drama of Reading.* Bloomington: Indiana University Press.

Sypherd, Wilbur Owen. 1948. *Jephthah and His Daughter.* Newark: University of Delaware Press.

Talmon, S. 1975. "In Those Days There Was No King in Israel." *Immanuel* 5:27–36.

Thompson, E. P. 1980. "Volkskunde, Anthropologie und Sozialgeschichte." In *Plebeische Kultur und Moralische Oekonomie.* Frankfurt/Berlin: Ullstein.

Thompson, R. J. 1963. *Penitence and Sacrifice in Early Israel Outside of the Levitical Law.* Leiden: Brill.

Thomson, H. C. 1968. "Shophet and Sishpat in the Book of Judges." *Transactions of the Glasgow University Oriental Society* 19:74–85.

Trible, Phyllis. 1978. *God and the Rhetoric of Sexuality.* Philadelphia: Fortress Press.

———. 1984. *Texts of Terror: Literary-Feminist Readings of Biblical Narratives.* Philadelphia: Fortress Press.

Turner, Victor. 1967. *The Forest of Symbols: Aspects of Ndembu Ritual.* Ithaca, NY: Cornell University Press.

———. 1969. *The Ritual Process: Structure and Anti-Structure.* Ithaca, NY: Cornell University Press.

———. 1977. "Sacrifice as Quintessential Process: Prophylaxis or Abandonment?" *History of Religions* 16:189–215.

Van Selms, A. 1950. "The Best Man and the Bride." *Journal of Near Eastern Studies* 9:65–75.

———. 1964. "Judge Shamgar." *Vetus Testamentum* 14:294–309.

Vaux, Roland de. 1958. *Les institutions de l'Ancien Testament,* vol. 1. Paris: Editions du Cerf.

———. 1972. *The Bible and the Ancient Near East.* London: Longman Todd.

Vernant, Jean-Pierre. 1987. "The Private Man Inside the City-State." Public Lecture, Harvard University, Center for Theory and Criticism.

Vorwahl, Heinrich. 1932. *Die Gebärdesprache im Alten Testament.* Berlin: Dr. Emil Ebering.

Vos, C. J. 1968. *Women in Old Testament Worship.* Delft: Judels & Brinkman.

Ward, Elisabeth. 1985. *Father-Daughter Rape.* New York: Grove Press, Inc.

Warner, Sean M. 1978. "The Dating of the Period of the Judges." *Vetus Testamentum* 28 (no. 4):455–63.

Weber, Samuel. 1982. *The Legend of Freud.* Minneapolis: The University of Minnesota Press.

Weinberg, Werner. 1980. "Language Consciousness in the Old Testament." *Zeitschrift für die Alttestamentliche Wissenschaft* 92:185–203.

Weinfeld, M. 1977. "Judge and Officer in Ancient Israel and the Ancient Near East." *Israel Oriental Studies* 7:65–88.

Weisman, Ze'eb. 1977. "Charismatic Leadership in the Era of the Judges." *Zeitschrift für die Alttestamentliche Wissenschaft* 89 (no. 3):399–411.

———. 1981. "The Personal Spirit as Imparting Authority." *Zeitschrift für die Alttestamentliche Wissenschaft* 93 (no. 2):225–34.

Wenham, G. J. 1983. "Why Does Sexual Intercourse Defile (Lev. 15 18)?" *Zeitschrift für die Alttestamentliche Wissenschaft* 95 (no. 3):432–34.

Wenning, R., and E. Zenger. 1982. "Der siebenlockige Held Simson. Literarische und ikonographische Beobachtungen zu Ri 13–16." *Biblische Notizen* 17:43–55.

Wharton, J. A. 1973. "The Secret of Yahweh: Story and Affirmation in Judges 13–16." *Interpretation* 27:48–66.

Widengren, G. 1958. "Early Hebrew Myths and Their Interpretation." In *Myth, Ritual and Kinship,* edited by S. H. Hooke, 149–203. Oxford: Clarendon Press.

Wifall, W. R. 1983. "The Tribes of Yahweh: A Synchronic Study with a Diachronic Title." *Zeitschrift für die Alttestamentliche Wissenschaft* 95 (no. 2):197–209.

Wilson, Robert R. 1977. *Genealogy and History in the Biblical World.* New Haven: Yale University Press.

———. 1980. *Prophecy and Society in Ancient Israel.* Philadelphia: Fortress Press.

Wolff, Hans Walter. 1963. "The Understanding of History in the Prophets." In *Essays on Old Testament Hermeneutics,* edited by C. Westermann. Atlanta, GA: John Knox Press.

Worden, T. 1953. "The Literary Influence of the Ugaritic Fertility Myth in the Old Testament." *Vetus Testamentum* 3:273–97.

Wright, Elizabeth. 1984. *Psychoanalytic Criticism: Theory and Practice.* London: Methuen.

Zakovitch, Yair. 1981. "Sisseras Tod." *Zeitschrift für die Alttestamentliche Wissenschaft* 93:364–74.

Zuchschewerdt, Ernst. 1976. "Zur literarischen Vorgeschichte des priestlichen Nazir-Gesetzes." *Zeitschrift für die Alttestamentliche Wissenschaft* 88 (no. 2):191–205.

INDEX

299